Better One Day
As A Lion

> *'Better one day a lion than a hundred years as a lamb'*
> *Jack (Treetop) Straus*
> *World Hold 'Em Poker Champion, 1982.*

Cover Pictures

FRONT COVER: Caroline Norris captures the moment as Conor O'Dwyer returns to the winner's enclosure to a tremendous reception on Imperial Call after his memorable win in the Gold Cup at the 1996 Cheltenham Festival meeting. And (below) Conor in happy mood as he receives his trophy from the Queen Mother, who also joined in congratulating winning trainer, Fergie Sutherland.

BACK COVER: Graphically caught for posterity by Tom Honan of INPHO photographic agency is the unfurling of the banner with the words IMPERIAL CALL on it as the crowd sang the Cork anthem, *The Banks Of My Own Lovely Lee* in moments of overflowing emotion and enthusiasm. And (inset top) Imperial Call clearing the last in style and (bottom left) Tom Foley, trainer of Danoli and (bottom right) Fergie Sutherland.

Other books by Raymond Smith include:

Under the Blue Flag (1980)
The Poker Kings of Las Vegas (1982)
Charles J. Haughey: The Survivor (1983)
Garret: The Enigma (1985)
Haughey and O'Malley: The Quest for Power (1986)
Vincent O'Brien: The Master of Ballydoyle (1991)
The High Rollers of the Turf (1992)
Tigers of the Turf (1994)
Urbi Et Orbi And All That (1995)

Better One Day As A Lion

By
RAYMOND SMITH

Sporting Books Publishers
Dublin
1996

Better One Day
As A Lion

First Published 1996
Copyright @ Raymond Smith 1996

Published by Sporting Books Publishers, Dublin
Design by Madison Design Management
Origination by Image Centre
Picture Sections by Impress Communications Group Ltd.,
14 Fitzwilliam Place, Dublin 2.
Printed by Colour Books

Contents

PART TWO

MEN OF THE FLAT WHO RIDE THE HIGH SIERRAS

PART THREE

THE HIGH ROLLERS WHO NEVER LIVED LIKE LAMBS

Author's Note

I was inspired to write this book principally by the romantic story of Imperial Call's triumph in the 1996 Gold Cup.

There was romance also in the return of Danoli, 'the people's champion', to challenge for the 1996 Smurfit Champion Hurdle after it had seemed that his career was ended when he suffered a cruel injury in the 1995 Martell Aintree Hurdle. His comeback races at Leopardstown and Gowran Park were unforgettable occasions and showed the place he had won in the hearts of all lovers of the jumping game. While he failed in his bid to lift the Smurfit Champion Hurdle, the very fact that he was back and that he had come unscathed through his races gave immense satisfaction to a lot of people both in Ireland and Britain.

This book is the natural successor to *The High Rollers Of The Turf* and *Tigers Of The Turf*, both of which are now out of print.

The emphasis in the main is on National Hunt racing with fifteen chapters devoted to the moments, the races and the men immortalised now in the history of the Sport. We make no apologies for that as it is the jumping game that really turns the Irish on, especially when they sense that the Cheltenham Festival meeting is just around the corner. However, the "Big Four" of the Irish racing scene on the Flat – Dermot Weld, John Oxx, Jim Bolger and Aidan O'Brien – merit a section to themselves.

The book concludes by putting the spotlight on fearless punters who blazed a trail, legendary figures like 'Mincemeat Joe' Griffin, Tommy O'Brien and Tim O'Toole. More recently J.P. 'The Sundance Kid' McManus, Barney Curley and Noel Furlong have achieved immortality with spectacular gambles that are now part of the lore of racing. And we record the passing in '96 of 'The Flyer' Begley who loved nothing better in life than a tilt at the ring and who before his untimely death told friends to have a punt for him on Barney Curley's 'good thing' All Talk And No Action. It duly obliged. And somewhere up there in the Great Beyond an action guy was drinking a toast to the intrepid Barney.

Many people contributed to ensuring that this book has met its launching date.

First of all, my special thanks and appreciation to Tony Lyster and Peter Nicholson for the professionalism they displayed in preparing the copy for the printers. I must pay tribute also to Peter for producing with Stephen Pepper such a fine cover that captures the unforgettable atmosphere at Cheltenham on Gold Cup Day '96.

My thanks also to Michael Daly and the staff of Independent Newspapers Library for providing essential cuttings and to Aengus Fanning, Editor of the *Sunday Independent* for permission to reproduce data. My appreciation also to the Editors of other newspapers and magazines for permission to quote from articles and features relevant to this book; in particular the Editors of the *Racing Post* and *Sporting Life*.

My appreciation of the hospitality of Sean and Mai O'Mahony during my research in the Carrigadrohid area for the chapters on Fergie Sutherland and Imperial Call and Seans, valuable assistance too in relation to the chapter on the O'Sullivans of Lombardstown.

I must pay tribute to the racing photographers who supplied the prints for the photographic sections. Again I put on record my thanks to Tony Sweeney, the acknowledged expert on statistical matters, who was readily available to answer my queries.

The pressure of the final intensive sessions of writing was made easier by finding the right conditions and atmosphere. In this respect, I am extremely grateful to my friends Terence and Annette Sweeney and Aidan and Mary Moriarty.

I wish to put on record too my thanks and appreciation to Bill Kelly and all the staff of Kelly's Hotel in Rosslare, who were so courteous and co-operative in every way, also to my friends Austin Skerrit and Padraig Conway in Rosslare Golf Club and to Phil Meagher of O'Ryans of Rosslare, who when the writing day was finished engaged me in memorable conversations on football going back to his own days with St. Vincent's and the emergence of the great Dublin team of the Fifties.

I put on record my deep appreciation to my wife Sheila for her editorial assistance. I would like to think that the finished work is all the better for her untiring efforts.

I dedicate this book to the memory of young Justin Butler, who had his last holiday in Kelly's Hotel in Rosslare a few weeks before he died of a terminal illness in the summer of '96; I shall remember the days I spent with him and his parents, Padraig and racing lover Anne Marie of Kilkenny, whose courage was an inspiration to all.

I dedicate it also to a young sportsman Brendan O'Mahony, who, having just completed his final exams in Cork University, was tragically drowned in a swimming accident in the River Lee in the summer of '96. Again Des and Anne bore it with inspiring courage and fortitude.

Raymond Smith

Dublin, September, 1996.

PART ONE

DAYS OF A LION
FOR JUMP TRAINERS
AND JOCKEYS

Those Epic Gold Cup Triumphs

TEN YEARS ON....Conor O'Dwyer is acclaimed in the winner's enclosure at Cheltenham '96 after Imperial Call had brought Ireland its first Gold Cup triumph in a decade and (below left) Dawn Run (Jonjo O'Neill) being led in the parade by John Clarke before going out to contest the 1986 Gold Cup and (right) Jonjo is chaired by ecstatic Irish racing fans after his epic triumph on the gallant mare. (Pictures: Peter Mooney and Caroline Norris).

1

The Making Of The Cheltenham Tradition

It all goes back to Arkle. Indeed, the making of the Cheltenham tradition goes back even further for the Irish – to the days when Vincent O'Brien made his post-World War Two assault on the meeting, winning the Gold Cup three years running with Cottage Rake (1948-'50) and again in 1953 with Knock Hard and three successive Champion Hurdles with Hatton's Grace (1949-'51). But his fabulous record did not end there. In the period 1952-'59 he turned out ten winners of the Gloucestershire Hurdle, counting the two Divisions and also won the Spa Hurdle (1954), the Birdlip Hurdle (1955), the National Hunt Chase twice (1949 and '54) and the National Handicap Chase (1952).

The photo in my book, *Vincent O'Brien – the Master Of Ballydoyle* of Mrs Moya Keogh leading in Hatton's Grace (Aubrey Brabazon) with Vincent and his brother, Dermot directly behind shows a winner's enclosure much smaller than the present amphitheatre, with its tiered viewing rows, accommodating hundreds of onlookers that is the Cheltenham inner sanctum today.

Vincent O'Brien's exploits, his fearless tilts at the ring in an era when, as he admitted to me himself, "we had to gamble to survive" quickly caught the imagination of the public. People wanted to be there as he threw down the gauntlet to the English bookmakers, watching them visibly squirm in face of a succession of spectacular coups, especially on the Gloucestershire Hurdle.

T.P. Burns, who was associated with five of Vincent's triumphs in the Gloucestershire Hurdle told me that all five – Illyric, Saffron Tartan, Admiral Stuart, Prudent King and York Fair – were gambled on without exception. "The stable had to gamble. The money in jumping in those days was peanuts compared with the prize money today for the major events. You knew the money was down. When there is gambling, there is always pressure. And, believe me, the pressure was far greater then, far more intense than when Vincent was turning out Derby winners for wealthy patrons", said T.P.

Of the Cheltenham bets which I saw recorded in Vincent's ledger from that era, the biggest of all was that on Ahaburn to win the County Handicap Hurdle in 1952. The amount invested was £1,452 equivalent to £20,114 by the values of 1989. Ahaburn, with Aubrey Brabazon in the saddle, was only cantering at the second last when he burst a blood vessel. In a moment like that Vincent would show no emotion but would say simply "it's lost, we'll get it back". And the money lost on Ahaburn was got back with interest, as he was laid out to win the Irish Cesarewitch later that year and then in 1955 he won the Birdlip Hurdle at Cheltenham.

Yes, the money that went on in the big gambles was REAL money in the financial terms of those days and I recall Dermot O'Brien telling me that he stepped in one day to have £1,000 at evens "for openers" with William Hill. And that at a time when I was earning £104-a-year as a cub reporter on *The Tipperary Star*.

The late Nat McNabb, who did the commissions for Vincent with Bob Mulrooney, told me that the period immediately after the Second World War was the boom period for betting. It was one marked by fearless gamblers and by bookmakers prepared to take them on.

"Our big bets in England were credit bets – on the nod. We had accounts with Hill, Ladbrokes and McLeans", he said.

He recalled going over to the Liverpool Grand National meeting just after the War. "I had my eyes opened to the scale of betting and how much you could take out of the ring if you brought off a successful coup".

He explained that there was "a phenomenal amount of black market money around in England and the only way it could be laundered was to get a cheque from a bookmaker".

He remembered standing beside William Hill's perch before one particular race. "This guy came in and said '£9,000 to £3,000' as William Hill was shouting '3/1 the field'. William Hill never batted an eyelid but continued to shout '3/1 the field'. Another chap came in and took '£9,000 to £3,000'. And a third. It was only then that Hill dropped the price to 11/4.

"I had seen nothing like it and I knew in my heart that we had a market once Vincent decided to tilt at the main prizes in England. Before the English bookmakers woke up to how good Vincent really was at preparing a horse to win the race he had it earmarked to win, we took them to the cleaners more than once. Yes, we stung them very badly with Hatton's Grace the first year he won the Champion Hurdle in 1949. I know the starting price was 100/7 but we backed him ante-post at 33/1, 25/1 and 20/1 and continued to back him right down the line."

Reflecting on the day – November 19, 1952 – that Knock Hard, with Tim Molony up, ran in the Nuneaton Hurdle at Birmingham, Nat said: "He must have been the greatest certainty of all time when you consider that he had won the Irish Lincolnshire with 8st 12lbs. I had £10,000 to put on him".

Yes, T.P. Burns was right. You couldn't afford to lose a race like the Gloucestershire Hurdle because of an unforced error. There was a world riding on your skill in the saddle when Vincent went to the well – so

2

different from being on a super colt like Ballymoss when he won the English St. Ledger in 1957. When Vincent turned his attentions completely to the Flat, success for Classic colts meant turning them into stallions that were syndicated for mind-boggling sums. Now the gambling was on his judgement of horseflesh in the sales ring. He picked out Nijinsky even before he went into the sales ring and saw what he told me was "the look of eagles" in his eye. The rest is history.

Charter flights were as yet unknown when Vincent O'Brien launched his assault on Cheltenham in 1948. The invasion of the Cotswolds that the Eighties would bring was still a long way off. No one could have visualised then a day when the attendance of Gold Cup Day would reach 50,000. There was no question of selling Club badges in advance of all three days. It would have been unthinkable for the Manager of Cheltenham racecourse to go to Ireland, as Edward Gillespie did before the 1988 Festival meeting, to explain why they were compelled to go all-ticket.

"We didn't fly initially", Moya Keogh recalled. "We went over by boat and took the train on to Cheltenham. Later we would take over the car in the ferry to Liverpool and drive the rest of the journey. The Queen's Hotel and The Plough (now no more) were the centre of much of the action for the Irish. We always stayed outside the town, the first year in an old manor house that had a big blazing fire. Dan and Joan Moore stayed there that year also. Someone said it was haunted. I got a funny feeling myself. We didn't stay there again.

"I remember the gatherings, the O'Briens and their friends and we and our friends. Nat McNabb was there, of course. I remember Aubrey at dinner. Nothing but race talk.

Vincent and Aubrey and Nat McNabb talking about the opposition, talking tactics, and you had to be impressed with the knowledge they showed. You got the feeling of people being keyed up, an air of expectancy about the morrow".

＊　　＊　　＊

The post-War "invasion" of Cheltenham got under way when Tom Dreaper sent over the great Prince Regent to win the 1946 Gold Cup in the hands of Tim Hyde, who would ride him into third place in the Aintree Grand National behind the 25/1 shot Lovely Cottage. They were the days when Irish racing enthusiasts travelled to England armed with steaks and bacon and eggs, sausages and black pudding and all of these were virtual currency in a country where no one talked then of the danger of cholesterol.

Even though the Second World War had ended and Britain was on the "winning" side, the food shortages of earlier grim days – days of the Blitz, the black-outs and V.2 raids – continued right up to 1950. It may seem impossible to imagine it now but the traditional full English breakfast, taken for granted by those who comprise the annual exodus to Cheltenham nowadays – and to Aintree as well – was a luxury in the 1946-'50 period.

3

The innovative Irish brought the 'makings' to their regular "digs" and friendly landladies viewed like gold dust the rashers and sausages, eggs and black puddings and, of course, there was no more acceptable gift to a friend.

Incidentally, as Tony Power, former *Irish Press* racing correspondent pointed out in an article in the 1991-'92 edition of the *Irish Racing Annual*, the front-line troops in the invasion force brought liberal quantities of Irish whiskey to fortify themselves for the boat journey and for the convivial gatherings after racing that went on into the early hours, as they sang and played cards and talked horses and form. Thus were the traditions born that live on into the Nineties and gather force as the new Millennium approaches.

Martin Molony and Aubrey Brabazon, two of the greatest Cheltenham riders, both agreed that the intervention of the Second World War killed Prince Regent's hopes of gaining immortality like Golden Miller and Arkle.

He was actually eleven when Tim Hyde rode him to victory by five lengths and four lengths respectively over Poor Flame and Red April. Supposing he had arrived in 1942, the year he won the Irish Grand National under 12st 7lbs – what then? Might we not have been talking of five-in-a-row to equal Golden Miller's record five-timer?

The views of Martin Molony command deep respect as do those of Aubrey Brabazon. They figured in some tremendous Gold Cup duels that in the racing sense were on a plane with the legendary *mano a mano* between Luis Miguel Dominguin (died May, 1996 at the age of 69) and his brother-in-law, Antonio Ordonez in the summer of 1958 that inspired Hemingway to write *The Dangerous Summer* because of the way both matadors were repeatedly gored as they tried to outdo each other in the bullring.

Vincent O'Brien was standing down at the last fence on Gold Cup Day 1948 as Happy Home, with Martin Molony in the saddle and Cottage Rake, the mount of Aubrey Brabazon rose to it together. Men who were there that day and who know what horsemanship is all about, have talked to me in awe of the way Martin Molony drove Happy Home into the last, knowing that his only hope of beating Cottage Rake was to come out of it in front. He did – gaining a length to a length-and-a -half with one of the most fearless jumps he had ever essayed. "But Cottage Rake beat my one for speed in the run to the finish", said Martin factually. The verdict was one-and-a-half lengths.

Martin Molony considered the 1948 Gold Cup the best race he had ever ridden over jumps, though defeat was his lot. "God gave me great courage", he said simply and Aubrey Brabazon in a very generous and sporting tribute commented: "I don't think anyone could have ridden into that last fence with such sheer guts and gusto as Martin did on Happy Home".

The mystique surrounding Martin Molony and his genius both on the Flat and over jumps could not be dimmed, even by his premature retirement at the age of 26, brought about by a cruel fall on the 4/6 favourite Bursary in the Munster Chase at Thurles on September 18, 1951.

Phonsie O'Brien, who rode in the same race, went to see him every day in hospital. "The waiting was awful, as we wondered would he pull through. Our two families were so close, you know. We were so glad when he did".

And Phonsie summed up: "Martin was good, very, very good. No doubt in the world about that. He never gave up. Going into the last you might have half-a-length to spare over him and he would gain half-a-length. It was a pity to see his career cut short in an ordinary race in Thurles when he had come through so much. But that's what National Hunt jockys live with, that's what makes them".

✳   ✳   ✳

The day that Arkle lowered the colours of Mill House in the 1964 Gold Cup and went on to become in my book the greatest chaser in National Hunt history was unquestionably the occasion that built a new totality of tradition around the Festival meeting and enhanced still further the special aura surrounding the Gold Cup itself. For now it spanned the years from Golden Miller (with his five wins in 1932-'36) to Cottage Rake...on to Mill House and Arkle...and to come were the epic moments that would be created in turn by Dawn Run and Imperial Call.

Arkle's legend was the legend of unsurpassed greatness. Dawn Run's legend was that of sheer courage and the unspoken way she conveyed to us all on March 13, 1986 that nothing can be deemed lost in racing or in life until the last crunching uphill battle to a mythical winning post is lost. And Dawn Run's heart didn't allow her to lose her final battle at Cheltenham. How we remember still Peter O'Sullevan telling the world in his memorable commentary: "The mare is beginning to get up."

She may have died later in action in France but she left that outsize spirit of hers under the shadow of Cleeve Hill.

"The greatest chase I have ever seen" was how John Francome described the 1986 Gold Cup as Dawn Run made history by becoming the first horse to complete the Champion Hurdle/Gold Cup double.

The factual recording of such a feat can give no indication of the scenes that marked the moment when Jonjo O'Neill rallied Dawn Run up the hill, after she had looked beaten at the last, and gave that triumphant arm-aloft gesture to the heavens as he passed the winning post to an "Irish roar" that we knew could never be surpassed.

At a moment like that it would be churlish to categorise people into nationalities. It was for the aficionados of the jumping game. And its overwhelming impact would live deep inside all who were there. Again it was the very essence of the challenge of Cheltenham for man and horse and it explains why we shall always return.

Already the balladeers were singing to the tune "He's Got The Whole World In His Hands" their own happy version, "Dawn' Run Got The Gold Cup In Her Hands". It echoed out towards Cleeve Hill from every bar on the course and I heard it later that evening in the Golden Valley Hotel as the celebrations continued into the early hours of Friday morning. Cheltenham was drunk dry of champagne as we saw the dawn come up over the town and its environs.

"I did not know emotion like this even when our own horse, For Auction won the Champion Hurdle", said Danno Heaslip, who was among the first to congratulate Paddy Mullins.

Picture the scene if you missed out on being there on Gold Cup Day '86. Already every vantage point on the tiered terraces overlooking the unsaddling enclosure itself had been occupied. Paddy Mullins, the Quiet Man from Goresbridge, County Kilkenny standing there awaiting the moment when Jonjo O'Neill would bring Dawn Run back in. For years Paddy had avoided the spotlight, now neither he nor his wife, Maureen could avoid it. Everyone seemed to want to shake their hands in congratulations.

There had been so much in the count-down to the day itself that added to the heightened drama and made for an occasion when the whole Irish nation – and Britain too – seemed to be caught up with the mare's bid for glory. The jocking off of Dawn Run's regular rider, Tony Mullins in favour of Jonjo O'Neill, who knew the task before him...he knew, as he put it to me himself, he had the best horse in the field, that she had the ability to triumph in the Blue Riband of chasing – if she jumped the course. It was for him to deliver her at the last in the position to win. No words can express the pressure on the Cork-born jockey.

"She was only a baby in terms of jumping fences and even though she won, she was still not a natural jumper", said Jonjo. "But, thankfully, everything came right on the day and she came out on top. She could have fallen at the first and that would have been that. Then at the end she looked beaten. She was a brave mare to win like she did, a very brave mare".

But Jonjo in saying that was playing down his own brilliance on the day – the way he went for everything at the second last with thrilling courage and superb horsemanship.

His eyes lit up with the glint of battle as he recalled for me how "I asked for everything again at the last and got it".

It was won ultimately with those two jumps.

Because the weather had affected racing in Britain, the phone lines to Goresbridge were humming in the weeks before the BIG DAY. Maureen Mullins will never forget the demands of those days and how the build-up of publicity made it more than an actual race. Defeat was not contemplated. The only climax that the Irish people would accept – indeed, what they demanded – was that they would have the opportunity of acclaiming a famous victory.

*　　*　　*

I remember the way it rose up from the tiered terraces, up from the milling crowd who had swarmed in past the security men, the most sustained, deep-throated roar that I had heard greeting a winner in my time going to Cheltenham. You felt it tingling in your spine right down to the toes of your feet. It was the final release of all the pent-up emotion when Dawn Run looked beaten at the last. Jonjo, the smile of victory spreading across his countenance and obviously enjoying every minute of the adulation sweeping over him, was the unquestioned hero of the hour.

It could not die for him, it would never die for him. Ten years on in the count-down to Cheltenham '96 he told Jon Freeman of *The Sporting Life* that "nothing will ever match the feeling of that day".

"That was different. That was a day in a lifetime. You can't compare anything with that. I suppose really that it wasn't just that she did it. It was also the way that she did it.

"Everything was against us and it looked as if we were beat going to the last. But I knew Wayward Lad and I knew Forgive 'N' Forget (both in front of Dawn Run at the time) and I knew that if I could keep her going we had a chance up that hill.

"I knew we had won before the line and it was then that it started. It was unbelievable. All those years I had been riding, but this was the first time I could actually feel the *weight* of the crowd, if you can appreciate what I'm saying. I remember thinking that if all these lot mob me, I'm gone, and they almost did!".

The unforgettable moments surpassed in sporting spontaneity the awkwardness and tension of Jonjo's getting through the "invasion forces" in the winner's enclosure, of Paddy Mullins' justifiable concern that someone would get hurt if Dawn Run were to kick out. Nothing will erase the memory of Jonjo hoisting Tony Mullins on to his shoulders and carrying him over to the presentation stand, where the Queen Mother was waiting to present the Gold Cup to winning owner, Mrs Charmian Hill...a gesture that brought a tremendous response from Irish and English alike.

Jonjo O'Neill did not get away from the racecourse until around 10 p.m. He was swept into a hospitality tent on a tidal wave of rejoicing. It was wild in there, as if a dam had burst and everything was out of control. "Some of the boys took some of the sheeting at the side of the marquee off and used it to start bouncing me up and down in the air. I was going really high and I was as sober as a judge. They were all stone mad with the joy of victory. I think I was more frightened of hitting the ground doing that than in the race".

This was hero worship if ever there was hero worship – an overwhelming spontaneous tribute that only the Irish could give to one in the National Hunt sphere of racing that they knew had delivered a masterly victory out of the jaws of defeat.

Jonjo could understand them going over the top.

Nothing lives on from that unforgettable day of the party by the winning connections to end all parties – nothing to compare with the legacy the Heaslips left of a long day's journey into dawn in the Golden Valley Hotel. The Hills held their celebration in the Cotswold Grange, a small hotel where they had always stayed. "Boisterous parties went on elsewhere but not at the

Cotswold Grange", wrote Denis Walsh in the *Sunday Tribune* on the eve of Cheltenham '96, looking back on the mood created by Dawn Run's Gold Cup triumph. "A salamanzar of champagne was popped. It would take ten ordinary bottles of champagne to fill a salamanzar. Nothing else was over the top.

"The celebrations livened up at one point when a video of the race was re-run in the bar. While all around her cheered, Mrs Hill sat in front of the screen, transfixed".

Denis Walsh noted that Tony Mullins went to the Rising Sun Hotel and partied until day break. Dawn Run's lad, John Clarke and the Travelling Head Lad, Jim Murphy went home with the mare. They had a draught of champagne in the lad's canteen at the course and they had a bottle of beer on the plane. But they hadn't been drinking. For them, it had been a working day as usual.

"Charmian Hill was not noted for her generosity to lads", concluded Denis Walsh. "Very fair, very correct, but short on gifts. On a stable lad's meagre income, gifts add up".

The legends of her prudence remain part of the lore of Irish racing.

A year after that day, Jonjo O'Neill having recovered from cancer, was possessed with a new passion for life...the kind of passion that only those who have come so close to losing it can fully appreciate and comprehend. He had experienced personal difficulties too. There was about him now a certain calmness, a certain acceptance that added extra dimension to the qualities that had always made him one of the most popular and likeable personalities that I have had the privilege of meeting in my time covering the racing scene.

"Gentleman Jonjo" he has always been – and always will be.

*   *   *

A decade later, Jonjo was there in the winner's enclosure waiting for Imperial Call and Conor O'Dwyer to come back in after that momentous triumph in the 1996 Gold Cup. "Smashing" was the word he used when asked how he felt about it. It didn't matter really what he gave us as a quick, ready quote for our report. You knew that he was overwhelmed by the moment, delighted that a new Irish chasing star had arrived on the scene to add to the traditions created by Prince Regent, Arkle, L'Escargot, Tied Cottage, Dawn Run and the others. And through his own Cork connections he felt a special affinity with Fergie Sutherland and with the area from which Imperial Call had come to challenge for immortality.

The bronzes of Arkle and Dawn Run overlooking the parade ring were reminders of what was demanded to achieve a place with those who had created something way beyond the ordinary.

Fergie Sutherland with his seven-horse stable at Killinardrish in County Cork. The colourful character who had his left leg blown off in the Korean War. Now an adopted Irishman. Making his own Field of Dreams as they sang *The Banks Of My Own Lovely Lee* in the winner's enclosure after unfurling a banner with the words on it: IMPERIAL CALL. A day that we shall not easily forget.

And then *The Danoli Story*. Now an integral part of the lore of the Festival meeting. Danoli the first horse owned by Dan O'Neill, the bonesetter from Myshall in County Carlow and trained by his friend and neighbour, Tom Foley – "the smallest of the small men". It was Tom's first time out of Ireland and his first trip on a plane when he hit Cheltenham in 1994, preferring to stay with "the lads" at the racecourse rather than in a hotel. Making headlines when there was a doubt as to whether or not he would have a tie on when he met the Queen Mother – that is after, as we all assumed, Danoli had done the business in winning the Sun Alliance Novices Hurdle in the hands of Charlie Swan.

What a roar greeted that success. What a welcome of epic proportions for horse and trainer and jockey in the winner's enclosure.

We had thought that Danoli would return in '95 and win the Champion hurdle. But he could finish only third to Alderbrook. There followed the injury at Aintree that looked like ending his career. But he made an amazing recovery and his comeback races at Leopardstown and Gowran Park were occasions that proved beyond any shadow of doubt what a unique place he and his trainer had won in the hearts of the Irish people.

It was his journey to Cheltenham '96 to contest the Champion Hurdle again that added to the romance of *The Danoli Story*, irrespective of the fact that this time he again failed to come out on top but had to be content with fourth place.

Over the span of twenty years that I have now been making my annual pilgrimage to Cheltenham each March, three days stand out above all others – namely, Dawn Run's Gold Cup win in 1986, Danoli's success in '94 and Imperial Call breaking the Gold Cup hoodoo at last in '96 and taking the Blue Riband of chasing for Ireland for the first time in a decade.

These were the special times...these the victories that convinced one that if you decided to be cremated and hadn't made up your mind where to have the ashes placed, no better idea than to have them scattered at the point approaching the winning post where Jonjo raised his arm to the heavens...or at the last flight where Danoli went clear for victory in '94 or at the last jump which Conor O'Dwyer took in such magnificent style on Imperial Call in '96.

In the scattering of the ashes would be your benediction – your last farewell gesture – to the course where you had derived more pleasure, more thrills, more adrenalin-pumping moments than at other racecourse. People watching the ashes being spread, who had savoured similar moments, would not exactly cross themselves. There would be no need for that. They would smile an understanding smile.

For they too perhaps had taken the road in from Birmingham and from the hill have seen the wonderful sward of Cheltenham racecourse under the shadow of Cleeve Hill, sometimes snow-capped in March. Then the heart beats in anticipation of the days ahead. All else is going to be secondary now to Anglo-Irish rivalry in a theatre where there can be no excuses – a course that invariably finds the horse for the day and the jockey for the hour. We revel in the banter, the craic and the intensity of debate. In enjoying an atmosphere that can be discovered nowhere else in the racing world.

✳   ✳   ✳

I remember the Monksfield years, especially the High Noon duel between Dessie Hughes and Jonjo O'Neill in '79...a memory of the sheer majesty that could never be captured on television of the climactic moments of the race as Hughes and O'Neill went into the last and then got down to it, locked in something that was optic and beautiful in the rhythmic movement of horse and rider towards the finishing post, the perfect balance maintained by two of the finest National Hunt jockeys of that era and yet the power they produced as they drove for victory was truly electrifying. Hughes prevailed on Monksfield over Sea Pigeon. Personally, I write it down as the greatest hurdle race finish I have seen.

I remember the victory parties that Galway-born owner, Dr Michael Managan threw in the Queen's Hotel...and the 300 bottles of champagne being demolished when For Auction won the Champion Hurdle for the Heaslip brothers, Danno and Mick from Galway in 1982...the singing around the piano in the Golden Valley Hotel as sportsman and raconteur, John Mulholland, son of noted Galway footballer, Ned Mulholland tinkled the keyboards...Golden Cygnet wearing the colours of Ray Rooney, also from Galway, pulverising the opposition in the Supreme Novices Hurdle in 1978 and just when it seemed that a champion of champions had hit the scene, he was fatally injured at Ayr shortly afterwards and trainer, Edward O'Grady was left to ponder if one as potentially great would ever come through his hands again.

Out of the West too came the Boys from Bohola, the Durkan brothers, who had their hour at Cheltenham when the brilliant mare Anaglog's Daughter turned in an exhilarating display of jumping when winning the 1980 Arkle Chase with ears pricked by twenty lengths, beating in the process the pride of England, Beacon Light, winner of seven chases in succession. To Bill Durkan, third eldest of seven brothers, fell the honour of training Anaglog's Daughter but he was quick to acknowledge the debt he owed to Ferdie Murphy, who played a vital role in the success of Anaglog's Daughter and, indeed, in all the other successes enjoyed by the Glencullen stable and who in '96 was back at Cheltenham, now as a trainer in his own right, bringing off a memorable double with Stop The Waller in the Kim Muir on the Tuesday and Paddy's Return in the Triumph Hurdle on the Thursday.

Etched in the mind is the memory of Tied Cottage slipping up on landing after the last in the 1979 Gold Cup, giving a bloodless victory to ill-fated

10

Alverton and Jonjo O'Neill and then under an inspired ride from master horseman Tommy Carberry delighting Irish punters by making ample amends the following year, only to be disqualified subsequently on technical grounds (the punters, however, had got their money).

I remember most of all the tremendous races for the Queen Mother Champion Chase...the way Adrian Maguire went so fearlessly Martin Molony-like into the penultimate and ultimate jumps on Viking Flagship and then Charlie Swan, taking over from Adrian when his mother died on the eve of the '95 Festival meeting, revealing horsemanship of a standard that won the spontaneous acclaim of trainer David 'The Duke' Nicholson and put him up there on a pedestal forged by a true champion.

When Kribensis won the 1990 Champion Hurdle in the colours of Sheikh Mohammed, there were prophets of doom who predicted that Arab oil money would dominate the jumping scene and that the Willie Lomans of the game could pack up their tents in the night and move on quietly. But the same year Sirrel Griffiths came out of Wales with Norton's Coin and won the Gold Cup with this 100/1 outsider. Bonfires blazed in an area made famous by legendary stand-off half Barry John and flying winger Gerald Davis not for rugby heroes now but for a steeplechaser who had been brought to the track in Griffith's cattle-truck (he did not have a horse-box) and home again the same evening and, instead of breaking champagne, he sent his sons out for ten bottles of Scotch and nothing was left of them when the party finished.

*   *   *

During Cheltenham '96 Joe Duffy from the Gay Byrne RTE Radio Morning Show took over the lounge of the Queen's Hotel and put out a special programme centred around Danoli and the enchanting appeal of the Festival meeting. Tom Foley came along and Tom Treacy and his father, Jim and there was even a man with a guitar who sang a ballad he had composed about "the people's champion".

Sporting Swords owner and Cheltenham regular, J.C. Savage regaled the audience with some good racing yarns and Fr Sean Breen – known as "The Breener" to the regulars who patronised Irish racecourses – was in excellent form. Of course, he had become Parish Priest of the townland of Eadestown (between Naas and Blessington) since Cheltenham '95 and, as the Hinge of Fate would have it, his parish was right in the heart of a racing area. "The Lord looks after his own", was how he put it to me one day at the races.

Now we remembered St. Patrick's Day '94 in the Golden Valley Hotel – Gold Cup Day to be exact – when he lifted his hands to heaven and thanked the Lord for giving Ireland a horse like Danoli.

He didn't have to interject at that moment of prayer that this one had rescued many an Irish punter who was facing extinction after the whitewash of the opening day.

After collecting our winnings on Danoli from a bookmaker who had given us 2/1 a few nights previously, I had a brandy and port (for the sake of a delicate stomach!) as I chatted with my good friend and great Cheltenham enthusiast, Liam Dillon in the very bar that would shortly be transformed into a temporary "chapel" while Fr Breen was saying Mass. They left on the spot behind his head the price-list for the drinks, including the champagne. He wore the shamrock over his priestly clothes. We all wore our shamrocks proudly.

I found myself part of a congregation that included three trainers – Arthur Moore, Michael Hourigan and Homer Scott – and one of the leading "rails" bookies on Irish racecourses, David Power, also well-known Dublin owner and hotelier, Paddy Fitzpatrick and familiar hard-bitten faces from the betting ring, veterans who would be back in the trenches that same afternoon in hand-to-hand combat with the "enemy" (bookies to the uninitiated) and, after Charlie Swan's treble on the Wednesday, especially Danoli's unforgettable triumph in the Sun Alliance Hurdle, they now had the fire-power to really go over the top with a vengeance.

Fr Breen had done a head-count beforehand of the number of people likely to partake of Holy Communion. He did another quick head-count during Mass itself. But he under-estimated the last-minute rash, like the rush of the previous day to get on Danoli despite the restricted odds of 7/4. He actually ran out of consecrated hosts, having already split half of his supply.

We understood fully his sentiments as he said in the audible silence of the bar-turned-chapel "Thank you Lord for giving us a horse like Danoli" and we appreciated his gesture when he prayed that the Irish punters would be guided from on high in their battle with the bookies – and that they would hit more good winners.

Standing at the back of the congregation, I could not but smile at the incongruity of the champagne prices over-shadowing the bowed head of the priest sporting his shamrock at Mass, of the prayerful appeals to the good Lord to lend us wisdom on this day and the truly cosmopolitan nature of the congregation itself. But nothing surprises us anymore where Cheltenham is concerned.

I chronicled that episode in my book *Tigers Of The Turf* and English racing writers, who are good friends of mine, asked me at Cheltenham '95 would it be diplomatically correct for a man who was not a Catholic to drop into Fr Breen's Mass in the Queen's. "No trouble whatsoever...all are welcome", I told them, adding: "Of course, don't miss out when the hat comes around for the collection!".

They piled into a taxi and were gone in the direction of the Golden Valley Hotel.

Sadly, St. Patrick's Day did not fall during Cheltenham '96. It fell on the following Sunday. If it had coincided with Gold Cup Day, there would unquestionably have been an overflow congregation as Fr Breen prayed to the Lord to be with Imperial Call and Conor O'Dwyer on this day.

✳　　✳　　✳

The Friday of the '96 Festival meeting became yet another long day of "craic" and it convinced me that to rush home on the Thursday night if you have no pressing engagements the next day is akin to leaving undrunk a bottle of rare vintage wine. The Friday fun can cap the week.

Jimmy (The Buck) Ryan from Fethard, from the county that harbours the world-renowned Coolmore Stud complex and the stables of Edward O'Grady and "Mouse" Morris, was telling us how he had run into a spot of bother at his "local", McCarthy's pub, where Annette Murphy maintains the traditions set by four generations of her family. It is the most unique hostelry of its kind you will find anywhere in the world and was aptly described by Clive Gammon in an American magazine as "the horsiest pub in Ireland". Incidentally, I know of one Englishman of the Old Etonian type who happened to visit it in the era when the Republic of Ireland soccer team was engaged in the World Cup just to absorb the atmosphere and enjoy the "craic". Legend has it that he'd gone to "the gents" when a golden goal was scored by the men in Green...

Jimmy Ryan was out in the wilderness, so to speak, for a period and decided to ask Noel Davern, member of Parliament or rather of Dail Eireann, to intercede on his behalf. Noel, a former member of the European Parliament and a man not want to miss the fun in a given situation, duly wrote a letter on headed paper to Annette Murphy pleading for his constituent. He finished with the promise that Jimmy Ryan would be a good customer right to the grave!

As Annette happens to be the local undertaker as well as being a publican. Jimmy Ryan had his "suspension" duly lifted...and was back with characters right out of Jimmy The Priest's in Eugene O'Neill's classic *The Iceman Cometh* that he described to me as "half drunk and half sober".

Once he was "bad news", as we say in Ireland, when he got back from Cheltenham. The only one to give him a welcoming and knowing nod was "the ould gander" – "as he knew what it was like to be in trouble domestically!".

Between Cheltenham '95 and Cheltenham '96 Jimmy made it to the local paper in South Tipperary, *The Nationalist* under the heading "Believe It Or Not!".

"It could only happen in Fethard", wrote the Fethard correspondent. "A duck, the property of Jimmy Ryan, Watergate, was drowned!

"Jimmy erected a sunken bathtub in his poultry yard. The unfortunate duck got in and could not get out. Jimmy says the fact that the duck was housed for the winter deprived it of its natural feather oil and it became waterlogged, with fatal results".

Jimmy Ryan's own house, down near the river, is called The White House.He is insistent that his own funeral procession will not take the route that Cromwell took when he passed through Fethard. Cromwell was actually allowed through without any effort to stop him after the Governor of the town, intent on averting a massacre, surrendered to him on very favourable terms. Clonmel surrendered also but after a siege that lasted a number of days. It's anathema in Jimmy's eyes that when he dies his coffin should be borne along any street that was sullied by the presence of Cromwell passing through.

"They'll shove it out the window into the waiting boat and my mortal remains will go down the river of no return like those of a Holy Man in India", was how he graphically described his departure from this life. "They won't place me on a pyre and make a bonfire. They'll find a spot for me in the graveyard beside Fr Phil Noonan, who asked that he be buried with the poorest of the poor. I accompanied Fr Phil on his last journey home from Dublin, where he had died in hospital, and we stopped the hearse opposite the Curragh racecourse where he had so much fun and enjoyment so that he could say farewell. I know he'll like the idea of me being buried beside him".

✳   ✳   ✳

The addendum comes from the moment when the producer of Joe Duffy's Show from the Queen's Hotel asked me to tell a yarn or two for listeners back home in Ireland.

I said that the best one going the rounds at Cheltenham '96 was about the guy who went to see his doctor before Christmas and was told that the news was bad – he had just three days to live.

"Could you ever make it the three days of the Cheltenham Festival meeting", was the patient's last request.

Even if it couldn't be granted, he was what my good friend, Johnny Chan, one of the greatest poker players of the modern era and twice world champion, would term "an action guy".

A French billionaire who was dying of cancer wanted one last blow-out at the poker table. He invited "The Orient Express", that is Johnny Chan and Doyle (Texas Dolly) Brunson and other top American pros to Paris for a two-week session. Chan returned home richer by a cool million dollars. The billionaire – "a very nice man, plus being an action guy", was Johnny's tribute to him – died a month later.

Chan summed up his philosophy on life and living thus: "The government takes a bit of you, the mortgage takes a bit. Life is too short, you have to enjoy it".

2

From Agony In Korea to Gold Cup Glory

The day the lower part of his left leg was blown off by a land-mine in the Korean War, Fergie Sutherland could never have entertained the dream that thirty-five years later he would be the Lion King of Cheltenham on Gold Cup Day.

The walking stick he sported in the winner's enclosure on Thursday, March 14, 1996, as he was mobbed by well-wishers and almost swamped by delirious Irish racing enthusiasts, stood now as a reminder of the day when he was so lucky not to be killed outright. He became a soldier from the war returning when he might so easily have been returned as dead meat in a body-bag. He would remember always the moment after one of his comrades tripped the wire of the land-mine and set off the blast and that comrade said: "You're okay, Mr Fergie, it's only your leg".

"I knew that already because I had looked down and checked", he remarked to me with a whimsical gleam in his hour of greatest triumph as a trainer.

He had come from a wealthy background in Scotland and took the classic route from Eton and Sandhurst into the British Army but his military career as a Lieutenant with the Fifth Dragoon Guards of the Commonwealth Division ended in that one fateful incident in the Korean War.

The stints he had as assistant to Geoffrey Brooke and Joe Lawson led in time to his becoming a trainer on his own and he got his big break when his father bought Carlburg stables, Newmarket where Clive Brittain now trains.

Sutherland quickly established himself. In his first year at Carlburg – 1958 – he turned out A.20 to take the Queen Mary Stakes at Royal Ascot and that year also his great friend and sporting rival, W.R. (Dick) Hern sent out his first Royal Ascot winner, None Nicer in the Ribblesdale Stakes.

His friendship with the man who would become renowned throughout the world of racing has stemmed from the period when Fergie's father sent him as a teenager to Porlock in Somerset to learn to ride. Dick Hern was actually his instructor. The close ties that were established between them have stood the test of time. They took a yard in Leicestershire during the hunting season and rode virtually every day.

They went on to start training on the same day. Hern went right to the top. In 1962 when private trainer to Major L.B Holliday he won the St. Leger with Hethersett. He then set up on his own at West Isley in Berkshire the following year, putting some of the greatest horses of modern times through his hands, none more so than Brigadier Gerard, winner of seventeen out of eighteen races and he also handled St. Leger and Coronation Cup winner, Bustino, who was narrowly beaten by Grundy in an epic battle for the 1975 "King George"; Derby winners, Troy (1979), Henbit (1980) and Nashwan (1989); Oaks winners, Bireme (1980) and Sun Princess (1983) and 1981 St. Leger Winner, Cut Above. Dunfermline won the Oaks for the Queen in her Silver Jubilee Year in 1977 and the same filly was successful in the St. Leger that season. Hern won the "King George" a record five times in all with Brigadier Gerard (1972), Troy (1979), Ela-Mana-Mou (1980), Petoski (1985)and Nashwan (1989).

The 75-years-old trainer no doubt smiled his own private smile when Fergie Sutherland confounded those who thought One Man was unbeatable in the 1996 Gold Cup and no one could have been happier at the smashing success of Imperial Call.

Now they were both Blue Riband winners. The circle was complete. In 1958 Sutherland won the King Coal Handicap with Fox King and in 1960 scored in the Union Jack Stakes with Armour Star. His total of winners on the Flat in 1961 reached 22.

That was the year that he won the Dockers Derby at the now-defunct Manchester track with Erinite, ridden by Stan Smith to a 1 1/2 lengths victory. Indeed, Manchester became something of a happy hunting ground for him and his strike rate there was outstanding over a five-year period. Little wonder that the legend grew up around his name at this time that he once swam the Irwell river in Manchester – for a bet! Ask him about it and he will neither confirm nor deny it. "I had a lot of vitality when I was younger. I did swim a few rivers in Korea and Egypt, but which ones I've long since forgotten", is how he rides the punch – or rather the question!

He brought off some nice "touches" from Newmarket to Manchester and Brighton to Redcar. He confessed that most of the owners with horses in his stable liked to gamble. One of his best patrons was Jack Woulfe, a leading rails bookmaker of the time.

"You've got to remember that many owners wouldn't have been able to indulge their hobby of having horses running in their colours if they didn't gamble", he explained. "And small stables certainly couldn't have survived very long if they weren't able to say to a potential owner – 'we can organise one for a touch if that is what you want'".

"The prize-money was buttons – £207 for a winner and the equivalent of a sack of spuds for the runner-up!', he said with a great belly-laugh.

"The whole Sport was entirely different then", he went on. "An owner expected – even demanded it as a right – that he should get on at the right odds first time out before an animal became exposed and graduated maybe to the category of being a 'public horse', if you know what I mean. Secrecy then was regarded as vital. Owners were paranoid about it. If it was suspected that someone in the stable leaked information about a would-be winner or moved in to take the price ahead of the owner, there could be serious repercussions. Woe betide the guilty one if the finger was pointed at him."

Fergie Sutherland had about 20 horses in his Newmarket establishment and, indeed, at one point he was accommodating 40.

But he wasn't really happy with big numbers. "I couldn't know each of them as well as I wanted and neither could I devote the kind of attention I like to give to a horse". Already he was hinting at the life he would relish as a trainer when he settled in West Cork – handling a stable of horses you could count on the fingers of two hands.

Even though training was his life in the Fifties and early Sixties in Newmarket, he had a great passion for hunting and not even the loss of his left leg could dim that passion. "You might say that I was keener on hunting than racing", he confessed to me in his home in Killinardrish. In fact, it was nothing to him to go hunting five days a week and there was remembrance of times past in the air as he recited for me:

I would barter ten years of a peaceable life
For a day when I rode with The Quorn.

He was – and still is – a passionate lover of game shooting and will even shoot clay pigeons in summer, out of season, to keep his eye in. And it's a deadly eye, believe me.

He worked hard and played hard. Men marvelled at the manner in which he could answer the call of the hounds, despite his disability. They marvelled too at the way he could swing his gun and bring down a snipe in gusty conditions when the odds were against him.

They responded to a born character who created the legend that when he arrived to stay with friends, he would carry with him three spare legs – one for riding, one for shooting and one for dancing.

Today at 65 he has lost the appetite for tilting at the ring and anyway it's not necessary to gamble to keep the wolf from the door.

✳   ✳   ✳

It was inevitable that in time the Irish would accept him as "one of our own". There is something deliciously distinctive, I have always felt, in that saying – reaching out beyond nationality, class and education to the down-to-earth facets of a man with which those in the rural heartlands can readily identify. The human qualities which allow one to walk with kings and keep the common touch. An ability that sees men at ease in your company in your "local", in Fergie's case The Angler's Rest pub in Carrigadrohid.

It's a romantic story in itself how Fergus Carr Sutherland made the move from Newmarket to Killinardrish in West Cork culminating in the classic shot that appeared in *The Corkman* of the trainer of Imperial Call being acclaimed by the thousands lining the streets of Macroom as he led the 1996 St. Patrick's Day parade. Fergie was like royalty sitting there in the passenger seat of an open-topped Mercedes convertible, basking in the hero's welcome he received. The covers that had been draped over Imperial Call in the winner's enclosure at Cheltenham were now draped over the bonnet and back of the car. And right there among his own people was Fergie, who fully merited the final accolade – "more Irish than the Irish themselves".

His mother, Lady Carton De Wiart had a place in Cork and was thinking of selling it at the time Fergie was still in Newmarket. He asked her to keep it, pointing out that he might come there to train and hunt. Nothing planned about it – but the philosopher in him knew that the turning points in a man's life may happen out side of the realm of personal planning.

Fergie was no stranger to the country at that point in time. He revealed to me that he had been coming over to buy hunters since 1950. "I would buy them and break them and sometimes even sell a few on when I didn't require them for my own use".

In fact, when he was training in Newmarket he had made quite a number of friends in this country and it wasn't surprising either that he looked to Ireland when recruiting staff for his stables. "Sometimes a letter would be sent to me with the address 'Newmarket-on-Fergus' on it and it would arrive at my home, marked on the front of the envelope:'Try Newmarket'. The person in the Post Office in Newmarket-on-Fergus was obviously a racing follower!"

It was 29 years back from Gold Cup Day '96 that Fergie Sutherland made the vital move. But he was never to regret the day he left Newmarket and became an adopted Irishman.

Lady Carton De Wiart would move to Ireland and live permanently in County Cork and today she has her own place beside Sutherland and his wife, Ann.

When Fergie turned out his first winner in Ireland in 1968 – a year after his move to this country – it was fitting that Primrose Posy should carry the colours of his mother in taking a ten-furlong event at Limerick, ridden by the top apprentice of the time, Christy Roche.

Lady Carton De Wiart was able at 93 to savour on television the ecstatic scenes that greeted her son's unforgettable Gold Cup victory. Sutherland himself refers to her fondly. "She's very keen on racing, still drives a car, she's a masterpiece", he will tell you.

Fergie Sutherland recalls with a sense of nostalgia childhood days in Peebles, about twenty miles from Edinburgh. "The family were originally from Caithness, right at the most northern tip of Scotland but I think of Peebles as home when I reflect on my young days", he said.

He has nothing but very happy memories also of school days in famous Wellesley House on Loch Rannoch.

His father, Lieut. Col. Arthur Sutherland fought with the Black Watch on the Somme, fought with such bravery that he was awarded the D.S. O and M.C. He lost a leg but returned and was promoted to Colonel. He survived where so many others fell in battles where the cost in human terms was simply appalling. Each day *The Times* listed the names of those who had been killed or were missing. The list seemed endless.

I mentioned to Fergie that it was coincidental that his father should lose a leg in the First World War and he should lose a leg in the Korean War. "We were regular soldiers and it was expected of us that we would be willing to die if necessary", he said simply.

The War took its toll too in another sense, a heavy toll. Fergie's parents were divorced. His mother, Joan married again - this time to a famous general, General Carton De Wiart, who had also fought on the Somme, being awarded the V.C., the highest honour of all, for bravery in battle. Earlier he had fought in the Boer War. "He was a born soldier", said Fergie of his step-father.

Not surprising then that Fergie Sutherland should find himself graduating also into the British Army. Service to King and country. And all that it signifies to your typical sporting Englishman. But, as he put it to Marcus Armytage of the *Daily Telegraph* in the count-down to Gold Cup Day '96, history had no relevance to Imperial Call's chance in the Blue Riband of chasing. He saw it as "old hat, cold potatoes".

"All I know is that my 'oss is lepping out of its skin. What counts is the good record I have this year. Nine winners, all over fences, a strike-rate around the 50 per cent mark".

Ironically, up to the time that Imperial Call landed the Hennessy Cognac Gold Cup at Leopardstown on Sunday, February 11,'96, beating the 1995 Gold Cup winner, Master Oats in the process, few outside of the regular coterie of seasoned enthusiasts who 'do' the circuit knew or cared about Fergie's strike-rate or his pride in it. He was dwarfed, indeed completely overshadowed by the strike-rate of the new "wonder boy" of the Irish scene, Aidan O'Brien, who at the end of 1995-96 National Hunt season had amassed 155 wins with 85 horses and his nearest rival in the National Hunt trainers table, Arthur Moore had 45 wins with 25 horses while Willie Mullins had 44 wins with 28 horses.

But the regulars of the Irish racing scene knew he had talent and could not be rated just another small run-of-the-mill trainer – one of that intrepid band who eke out a living mainly through buying and selling on, staying ahead of the posse not by the number of winners they turn out in a given season but by what they bank as a result of their adeptness at picking out talent and disposing of it before it reaches its sell-by date or ends up in the knacker's yard. Some know no other life or are capable of no other life, slipping maybe imperceptibly into it from the time when they were toothless wonders in the saddle, happy to pick up a bread-and-butter fee for riding any old nag, be he a half-crock of a hurdler or a novice chaser that a top-notch rider would avoid like the plague.

Then perhaps relying heavily on doing the rounds of the point-to-points when it was a nightmare to get a winner under Rules. Reduced maybe to the final ignominy of seeking a winner in the anonymous world of the flapper tracks where no questions are asked and you arrive with a wink and a nod and depart in the same vein. The Dingle Derby could eventually become the ultimate dream when all other dreams were shattered. An old actor walking the boards or a sad comedian squeezing laughs from a cynical audience like the last drops from a lemon. Going on until one dropped. Meriting no obituary in *The Times* (the London *Times* that is). Maybe a few lines in one of the national dailies in Ireland and something more generous in *The Irish Field*.

The distance between the top trainers and those at the very bottom of the heap – outside the handicap proper, you might say – is so cruel that it's not worth dwelling upon. A top trainer ponders the percentage he may get out of a potential Classic winner on top of a minimum annual training fee of £10,000. The other may be afraid to complain at the annual gathering of the Trainers' Association about the cut-price merchants in case some "cowboy" will step in and take what he has and train them for proverbial buttons. Happy not to look beyond Listowel as Mecca. You land what we writers term an "inspired coup" with one that has got to the right mark in the handicap after maybe two years having "easy" outings and you acquire the doubtful tag of being "shrewd". But it's akin to dropping a pebble in the wide expanse of Lough Derg when it comes to the headlines that matter. The Cheltenham Festival meeting delivers those headlines as nothing else can in the National Hunt sphere, especially when you have an animal in your stable that has become a "talking horse" for the Irish nation and caused the English media to sit up and take note, keeping the phone humming and beating a path to your door.

By the time Gold Cup Day '96 arrived, everyone in Ireland knew – as a result of the sheer weight of column inches in the papers – about the Korean War veteran who was training the chaser carrying the hopes of a nation. Colm Murray and the RTE team found their way to Killinardrish for a spot in the main evening news bulletin and that alerted a wider public to the prospects of a horse called Imperial Call.

Granted, Imperial Call and Fergie Sutherland hadn't as yet captured the imagination of the public to the same all-embracing extent as "the people's champion", Danoli and Tom Foley. But here too was romance with a capital "R". Here was a trainer with a seven-horse stable far from the Curragh and the madding crowds reaching for the stars and well might we echo the immortal words of Sean O'Casey in *Juno and The Paycock:* "What is the stars, what is the stars".

If Imperial Call had not come along, Fergie Sutherland would have remained in the eyes of the masses a Willie Loman of the Irish racing world. When a horse delivers as Imperial Call did on Gold Cup Day '96, all is changed, changed utterly overnight.

✳   ✳   ✳

He wears his cap nonchalantly in that typical Irish way, so befitting the National Hunt scene. The features are ruddy and weather-beaten and speak of a rejection of the ascetic in favour of going with the roll of life, the timeless moments with friends and acquaintances of similar outlook that no money can ever buy.

A world removed from the tails and top hats, the lobster and platters of prawns and smoked salmon, the strawberries and cream and champers of Royal Ascot and the insufferable snobbery and false values that the members of "The Set" bring to it, who are not there for the best that Flat racing can offer – yes, racing of a standard and competitiveness matching what Cheltenham provides over the jumps – but without the snobbery. Fergie Sutherland's Queen Mary Stakes winner of close on thirty years back meant nothing now to the Irish aficionados of the chasing game who wanted only that Imperial Call would win an O.K. Coral-style shoot-out with One Man, England's pride. A.20 could have been a road somewhere in dear old England. A Royal Ascot winner lost in the mists of time.

The stuff of legends that stirs the imaginations of the writers of ballads emanate from the heat of battle at Cheltenham. So too the Peter O'Sullevan-style commentaries as they took it up from the top of the hill. They loved nothing better than "doing" the Arkle v Mill House commentary and O'Sullevan's memorable calling of the horses as Dawn Run got up in the '86 Gold Cup. Now in the hostelries around Carrigadrohid, Macroom and beyond, they would take it up from the moment One Man ranged up to Imperial Call and just when the English cheers began to rise in anticipation of an imperious sweep down the hill, the grey cracked and was gone. We knew this would be a day that would be etched in the mind like the day Dawn Run won the 1986 Gold Cup and Danoli stormed to victory in the 1994 Sun Alliance Novices Hurdle.

A great deep-throated "Irish roar" echoed from the stands and enclosures as Imperial Call came down the hill under an inspired ride from Conor O'Dwyer and turned for home looking set for victory. We realised that it was all over bar a fall. The cheers gathered momentum, becoming a veritable wall of sound, awesome in its intensity, as O'Dwyer attacked the last fence and Imperial Call made no heart-stopping error now as had been the case at Leopardstown. He took that ultimate jump in magnificent style and swept up the hill to win by four lengths from Rough Quest with Couldn't Be Better coming late to take third place.

At the fourth last Richard Dunwoody on One Man had come up to Imperial Call and just before the third last, he turned to Conor O'Dwyer and said "it looks between the two of us now". It was then that the English were convinced that here was the moment when they would be acclaiming another "grey wonder" to match Desert Orchid. In fact, those who had the temerity to back One Man to win by a set number of lengths (money from America for the big English ante-post layers!) were even counting their chickens prematurely. Those chickens would never be hatched.

Dunwoody confessed that One Man's collapse was so sudden and the favourite got so tired in the last two furlongs that "if he hadn't been in third place at that point, I probably would have pulled him up at the last". As it was One Man barely scrambled over the last and was officially sixth of the ten runners.

One Man's trainer, Gordon Richards was completely baffled by the performance of the grey, especially by the manner in which he "had fallen away to nothing" at the top of the hill. He asked for the horse to be dope tested.

Thirty-one years a trainer and with more than 2,000 winners to his credit, he was left still searching for a winner of the Gold Cup. His first Gold Cup challenger, Playlord in 1969, finished third. He had not come close since. In fact, nine years had elapsed since he had enjoyed success at the Festival meeting. The statisticians were quick to inform us that One Man was his 38th consecutive loser and represented the hardest pill of all to swallow as some had given him the tag 'unbeatable' beforehand.

Dessie's mantle was still secure as the grey who had won his way into English hearts.

*   *   *

The connections of Imperial Call and the hundreds who travelled from West Cork swept into the inner enclosure in the parade ring. Tricolours were waving triumphantly everywhere around me. One had been placed in Conor O'Dwyer's hand as he came back in on the gelding who had ended the famine years for Ireland in such convincing style.

A timeless moment caught by the cameras as Conor bent down to kiss his partner Audrey Cross, her countenance showing the ecstacy of her feelings.

And then the Cork hordes began singing "Here We Go, Here We Go, Here We Go". This was no morons' chant as one English writer mistakenly assumed. It was a throw-back to the golden Jack Charlton era in soccer when famous victories were won from Italy to the States and the Irish followers won the name of being the best-behaved to be found anywhere in the world. Defeat could not kill Irish enthusiasm, camaraderie and bonhomie.

The Corkonians followed with "He's A Jolly Good Fellow" – for horse and trainer and jockey.

With the unfurling of the banner came the singing of *The Banks Of My Own Lovely Lee* – the Cork anthem that I have heard sung from Pairc Ui Chaoimh to Killarney, from Limerick to Thurles, the birthplace of the Gaelic Athletic Association, and on to Croke Park on All-Ireland Final Days. A song that has its own deep significance for those of us who are aficionados of hurling and gaelic football, for it is bound up with great occasions when the men in Red and White jerseys were locked in pulsating battles, maybe against the Green and White of Limerick, the Blue and Gold of Tipperary or the Black and Amber of Kilkenny in hurling or the Green and Gold of Kerry or the Blue of Dublin in gaelic football. Yes, it was part of the Gaelic scene just the same as other county anthems, *Slievenamon* (Tipperary), *The Rose of Mooncoin* (Kilkenny), *Boolavogue* (Wexford), *The Rose Of Tralee* (Kerry) *and Cockles and Mussels* (Dublin).

I had heard "The Banks" sung at the Curragh on the day that Tirol, owned by the Horgan brothers of Cork won the 1990 Irish 2,000 Guineas, beating Royal Academy by a neck and it had been sung also at Newmarket when Tirol took the English 2,000 Guineas by two lengths from Machiavellian (Freddie Head), who was only fourth in the Irish equivalent.

But these were occasions on the Flat and, while they were memorable for their spontaneity and for the celebrations that followed afterwards in The Briar Rose, the Horgans' "local" in the Douglas area of Cork, they could never generate the same fierce tidal wave as was generated on this March day at Cheltenham '96.

I found myself joining in the chorus as if I were in Semple Stadium, Thurles on Munster Final Day with Cork and Tipperary in contention or in Croke Park with Cork and Kilkenny renewing ancient rivalry.

Where I sported and played, 'neath each green leafy shade,
On the banks of my own lovely Lee
Where I sported and played, 'neath each green leafy shade,
On the banks of my own lovely Lee

Under the heading "Celebrating the Irish Way", Brough Scott wrote in the *Racing Post* that "there had been breaches in the unsaddling enclosures security wall after the other Irish victories but this time the dam burst completely".

"Rough Quest came in first", he went on. "There was warm and well-deserved applause for the pride of Beare Green in Surrey. But a look at his trainer and jockey reminded you that even here we were deeply in debt to the Irish. Terry Casey seemed shell-shocked with the great performance, Mick Fitzgerald in the saddle had a smile of rare fulfilment.

"They brought just a few supporters with them, and across at the main gates to the enclosure the dam still held. Then the gates opened and in a great rush the one horse and thousand-person crowd swept in. It was like being at the wrong end of a friendly avalanche."

He concluded: "This witness was privileged to bob around on a sea of happiness possibly unequalled in Cheltenham history. He had to content himself with Ted Walsh's triumphant summary – 'Yes, you need us a lot more than we need you. Why this place would be a morgue without us'.

There was this terrific picture by Tom Honan of INPHO photographic agency (carried over six columns in the *Sunday Tribune* of March 17) of a young chap, his right arm held aloft to the heavens in a victory salute, the banner with the word IMPERIAL CALL spread out at his feet, as if in a way it was supporting him – and it was all against a background of waving hats and tricolours and a sky with a strange glow to it – the glow that you associate with the battle for the last hill on some foreign field.

Only Cheltenham on an epoch-making day could have produced a classic picture like this – and we are proud to have the opportunity to reproduce it for posterity on the back cover of this book.

✳   ✳   ✳

In the middle of the sea of humanity and waving Tricolours we managed to get to Fergie Sutherland, who was soon surrounded by a media scrum. "I was confident we would win a mile from home. The race went just as we planned and from the top of the hill there was a feeling of inevitability," he said.

"I knew Imperial Call had the race sewn up. He jumped the last fence like he did all the rest – like a buck".

"Conor gave him a brilliant ride", said Fergie. "He did just what we planned, get him jumping, keep to the outside and kick on when he wanted.

"It worked, didn't it? That's easy to say when it does work, it looks good. The horse did it very stylishly – he put them in their place and imposed his superiority, didn't he?".

Will he come back again next year, asked one scribe? He hesitated for what seemed an eternity before replying with laconic wit:"What do you think?".

Sutherland revealed that he watched the drama unfold with his son, in the owners' stand. "I haven't been to Cheltenham for thirty years and this is the only way to come back".

Imperial Call was the first Gold Cup winner to be trained in Cork since Vincent O'Brien sent out Cottage Rake to win the coveted crown for the third successive year in 1950.

Not alone was it an unforgettable afternoon for Fergie Sutherland but for Billy O'Connell and Denis Daly who had handled the gelding with the kind of care befitting equine royalty.

There was a special affinity between the Gold Cup winner and 20-year-old Denis 'Dinny' Daly, who had his proudest day as he watched his horse pass the winning post.

"It hasn't really sunk in yet that I look after a Gold Cup winner", he said in the immediate aftermath of victory. Daly had been with Sutherland for two years, having joined him from Andrew McNamara's County Limerick yard.

"I had ponies at home in Co. Limerick but I didn't win anything big with them, and I had a few rides when I was with Andrew McNamara but didn't have a winner".

From the moment he moved to Fergie Sutherland's stable his luck changed in more ways than one. Even on the winner front. By Gold Cup Day '96 he had ridden seven winners, all but one for the Cork stable.

Imperial Call is one of two horses he looks after at the Sutherland stable.

Fergie Sutherland brought a halt to the questions from the racing scribes when he said:"Excuse me, I've got to go and see the Queen Mother".

Being presented to her would be the proudest moment of his life, he acknowledged.

Seldom have I seen so many people looking up at the Royal Box as at the moment when Fergie Sutherland and Conor O'Dwyer could be seen with their trophies in hand chatting amiably with the Queen Mother, who is, of course, a great favourite with Irish racing fans. And this brings to mind the time when a man from the West of Ireland stepped forward during one presentation in the winner's enclosure and planted a kiss on the Queen Mother's cheek, sending shock waves through the security men around her. He wrote subsequently to the Palace to apologise for his impetuosity and got a lovely note back indicating that the Queen Mother hadn't been in the least perturbed and actually wished him and all his family well.

＊　　＊　　＊

Back in Carrigadrohid the mother of all parties began in The Angler's Rest from the moment that Imperial Call passed the winning post. Grown men were seen to wipe away tears of joy as they downed their pints. Many of them had backed him at 33/1 and now, as they watched re-run after re-run of the video, the cheers seemed to gain in intensity as the brilliance of that victory was borne home.

There was a further reason for celebration in that Imperial Call's success was a throw-back to 1974 when Captain Christy, trained by Pat Taaffe and ridden by Bobby Beasley, scored at 7/1. 'The Captain' was bred by George Williams of Inniscarra, a couple of miles down the road from Carrigadrohid.

They were singing in the rain at Cork Airport on Friday evening, March 15 (as Peter Leonard reported on Page 1 of *The Examiner*) when Sarah Lane of Lisselan Farms arrived home with the Gold Cup. Euphoric racing enthusiasts braved the elements to raise the roof as Sarah (Lane), appropriately in green, stepped down on to the tarmac and the first leg had begun of the victory journey.

The Lord Mayor of Cork, Cllr. Joe O'Callaghan was there and so also Dail Deputes Joe Walsh, a former Cabinet Minster, and Jim O'Keeffe.

The Cup was filled with champagne and did the rounds in the Airport lounge and Sarah Lane described the welcome home as "absolutely fantastic".

"It's like meeting the Queen Mother again. Winning the race has been one of my happiest moments. Since Imperial Call passed the winning post all I can remember is people singing and congratulating me", she said.

Amidst the excitement, the Lord Mayor announced that a civic reception would be hosted in Cork in honour of Imperial Call.

"This is the first time a horse has been honoured in such a fashion", he noted. "Indeed, all day long we've been trying to figure out how to get Imperial Call up the steps (twenty marble steps at that!) of City Hall. We've been assured there is no problem on that front".

Back in Carrigadrohid it seemed that the party would never end. All through St. Patrick's Day week-end they sang and they danced and drank the health of Imperial Call.

On the eve of St. Patrick's Day – that is the Saturday night – Fergie Sutherland arrived at The Angler's Rest to a deafening roar. It seemed that everyone wanted to shake his hand and be photographed with him.

The air was filled with the sound of his beloved traditional Irish music.

The Corkman filled a half-page with its report of the victory party and with accompanying pictures.

Tony O'Callaghan, proprietor of The Angler's Rest, said: "It's been really hectic. A packed house all the time. We've had no sleep or anything but the 'craic' has been mighty.

"Saturday night was simply incredible from the moment that Fergie Sutherland arrived. He had stopped by briefly the previous night but was too tired then after the journey to really start the partying. We all knew that Saturday night was going to be the night. It was one almighty bash".

Bonfires had blazed throughout all the area around Carrigadrohid and beyond from the Thursday night. Publicans from Bandon to Ballinascarthy, home of Lisselan Farms, flew banners in honour of a famous victory.

"WELCOME HOME" read the banner that Tony O'Callaghan put up in Carrigadrohid.

Those two words said it all – but a week elapsed, indeed longer, before the celebrations began to wind down somewhat.

Already they were looking forward to Cheltenham '97 and its aftermath. "This is everybody's horse and everybody's success", said Sarah Lane of Lisselan Farms.

That was the way they felt about it in Carrigadrohid and Ballinascarthy and throughout all the towns and villages of that area of County Cork.

Imperial Call had been trained by Fergie Sutherland – "one of our own". You could ask for nothing better.

3

How 'Imperial' Became
The King Of Killinardrish

Imperial Call was a seven-year-old the day he won the 1996 Gold Cup. But from the time he was five, Fergie Sutherland was convinced that he was a potential winner of the Blue Riband of chasing.

It all evolved from the day when Sutherland bought Imperial Call as a just-broken three-year-old from Tom Costello, the Man from Clare who needs no introduction to those on either side of the Irish Sea looking for champions in the making. You would never expect him to be an automatic choice on the list of guests for a Turf Club dinner. But that wouldn't worry Tom or cause him sleepless nights.

Costello and Sutherland go right back thirty years. "We got on immediately. We were kindred spirits", said Fergie.

You might say that their association and developing friendship stemmed from horse dentistry. "I had learned horse dentistry and I used to do all Tom's horses' teeth", Sutherland revealed. "We're both basically horse-dealers. I've even bought cattle and sheep from Tom in addition to horses".

Fergie's problem was like that of many other small trainers in Ireland. When you got one that was good and it looked like hitting the high spots or even attained some meaningful targets on the domestic front, you sold on at the behest of the owner or owners if you felt that it was in their best interests to grasp the initiative while it was there. That was how you "got by".

The best horse that Sutherland had before Imperial Call was Ebony Jane but she was switched to Francis Flood's Grangecon, County Wicklow stable in Paddy Sleator country before Fergie could enjoy the fruits of all the hard work he had put into developing her chasing ability. "Perhaps her owner wanted a more fashionable stable", he said with total frankness as he shrugged his shoulders philosophically.

How must he have felt then when, as an eight-year-old, Ebony Jane won the Jameson Irish Grand National in 1993 for Flood with Charlie Swan in the saddle.

However, Sutherland was never one to sit down and weep at a mythical Grand Central Station over the might-have-beens. He soldiered on with the courage that saw him soldier on in life itself after losing his left leg in the Korean War.

"I was having a good run in point-to-points when Lisselan Farms approached me four or five years ago to buy a couple of horses to go into training. The limit on each was set at Ir £5,000 and between them they managed to win six races – Commanche Nell won four and Fair Lisselan two.

"That was a good start to our relationship and when I was told I had about Ir£20,000 to spend on a good horse, I immediately rang Tom Costello".

It was to be one of the most important phone calls he ever made in his life. Costello invited him to his Fenlow House establishment in Newmarket-on-Fergus to look at a three-year-old he had just broken and a few others as well. "I happened to be in the right place at the right time on the right day with the money needed to make a purchase", was how Fergie summed up that fateful moment for me.

Sutherland watched the three-year-old jump one fence at an indoor arena. After the second fence he put his money on the table, confident that he had found something special. It wasn't exactly the "look of eagles" that Vincent O'Brien saw in Nijinsky's eye but all the years of horse-dealing came together at that one moment. No doubt if asked to rationalise what it was, to explain in exact detail the factors that made him reach such a quick and spontaneous decision, he would not have satisfied the uninitiated. It was sureness of touch. But he did notice the good limbs and in an uncanny way too he saw evidence of a good outlook, no rogue look in the eye.

Tom Costello must have known also what he was presenting to Fergie and out of a thirty-years friendship the two gave Irish chasing the horse that would see the Gold Cup hoodoo that had lasted ten years broken at last.

In addition to Imperial Call, Fergie Sutherland bought Coming On Strong. And on November 9, 1993 at Clonmel when Imperial Call caught the eye of more than one professional judge by winning the Morris Oil Chase (Grade 3) by four-and-a-half lengths - being not extended in doing so - Coming On Strong took the Kilsheelan Handicap Chase on the same afternoon. Of course, both were wearing the Lisselan Farms colours.

*　　*　　*

Imperial Call was bred by retired chemist, Tom O'Donnell, the well-known breeder from Taghmon in County Wexford.

Horses have been very much part of the family background, with Tom's uncles and cousins who live outside Gowran, County Kilkenny familiar names on the racing circuit.

Tom developed an interest in horses from an early age and came to love the racing scene.

He sold Imperial Call as a foal, for £3,500 – "and that was a very good price at the time". Tom Costello says he acquired him as a yearling for 6,000 guineas.

It was at The Cools Stables in Taghmon that Imperial Call, by Callernish out of Princess Menelek, first saw the light of day. Princess Menelek was by Menelek, who in turn was the progeny of a mare by the great jumping sire Arctic Slave.

Tom O'Donnell had purchased the dam (now 19 years old) some ten years back from Pat Hughes, who trains at Fennistown, Bagenalstown. Tom is not slow to praise the contribution of Michael Hickey of Garryrichard Stud, the man he credits as his capable adviser over many years.

He can never forget the day that Fergie Sutherland told him that he had bred a potential Gold Cup winner. That was in 1994.

On another day at Gowran Park, Fergie proclaimed: "I will make you rich, Tom".

Tom had long ago been afflicted by the "Cheltenham bug" and was a regular at the Festival meeting. But 1996 was something else again, for he was stirred by the thought that the horse he bred would put his name and that of the village of Taghmon on the racing map.

His wife, Billie, who had created her own niche on the drama circuit, was visiting a daughter in Hong Kong but flew home to join her husband at Cheltenham. "I thought for a moment that I was at Wexford races, there were so many familiar faces from County Wexford to be seen", said Tom.

Viewing the race with his wife from the Bank of Ireland hospitality marquee, Tom could see that once One Man cracked, that Fergie Sutherland's prediction of two years previously was going to be justified. "Imperial Call ran the race of his life. His jumping was immaculate with Conor O'Dwyer riding a superb tactical race".

The Wexford celebrations took place in the Golden Valley Hotel and Tom O'Donnell was pressed into singing *When Irish Eyes Are Smiling*.

It didn't end there for the breeder of the Gold Cup winner. The O'Donnells were met at Rosslare Port when they arrived home on the Friday evening and whisked off to a family celebration and Tom's three-week old grandson, named after him, was allowed to stay up for the occasion.

Then a victory party in Paddy Roche's pub in the village and it seemed that every die-hard enthusiast in the county had found his way there for the occasion.

Yes, a night to remember.

* * *

The greatest pleasure in Fergie Sutherland's life was, as he put it himself, "knocking a young jumper into shape".

The challenge was in the making and the greatest challenge of all was in the making of the King of Killinardrish.

Sutherland took a completely individualistic approach to training. His methods were his own.

Not for him putting Imperial Call up on a horse-walker – "I'd imagine he'd go mad".

Not for him either playing operatic music to soothe Imperial Call's nerves in the count-down to Cheltenham '96.

He loved the idea of being "virtually isolated here in Killinardrish". And he was quick to stress that the fact that the place "isn't crawling with horses certainly helps a horse's attitude to life".

"I can't imagine what it would do to Imperial Call, and to me, if we were in a rushing split-arse environment", was his immortal comment to Tony O'Hehir of the *Racing Post*.

Coincidentally then, his preference for isolation in a place like Killinardrish was a throw-back to Vincent O'Brien being happy at the outset of his training career to plan his Cheltenham onslaughts and his spectacular coups from Churchtown in County Cork. The big Curragh trainers would have seen Vincent as "a country boy" when first his name began to enter the winners' list – a morning glory who would have a brief hour in the limelight and then vanish like many others before him. They didn't realise that this was a species of a different kind. In time they were forced to acknowledge his genius by what he achieved not alone on the domestic plane but at Cheltenham and Aintree.

Later when Vincent decided to turn his attention completely to the Flat, he decided to keep away from the Curragh. He wanted his own "patch" and once he spotted the rolling acres that would eventually become the famous Ballydoyle gallops, he was content.

In his Churchtown days he ensured that he replicated the uphill pull from the last fence and the last flight at Cheltenham, so that no challenger of his would be found wanting in a battle from the last. And at Ballydoyle he built a gallop that was a replica of the downhill sweep to Tattenham Corner at Epsom. The Master left nothing to chance.

And Fergie Sutherland had it so at Killinardrish that there could be no question in the world of Imperial Call being caught out by the hill at Cheltenham once he cleared the last and no question whatsoever that he would fail for want of stamina.

Consider what Pat Keane of *The Examiner* and Tony O'Hehir of the *Racing Post* found when they called to Killinardrish for a pre-Gold Cup briefing. Fergie brought them in his Land Rover to show them his uphill gallop. Tony O'Hehir had seen Aidan O'Brien's famous uphill gallop at Piltown, County Kilkenny and couldn't believe his eyes when he saw the severity of Fergie's in comparison. Pat Keane suggested to Sutherland that he christen it "Kilimanjaro Hill". And Fergie was quick to see the humour in that.

Like Tony O'Hehir I had marvelled at Aidan O'Brien's uphill gallop when I first visited the Piltown operation, realising immediately how his bumper horses could win with cool panache first time out. But when I saw Fergie Sutherland's in June of '96 I concluded that it was something else again. The surface was of cinders to avoid the horses slipping as they worked uphill and Fergie concluded too that it would lessen the possibility of back problems.

I made the point to him that if I "worked" up that steep incline once I would either be brought down on a stretcher or in an ambulance. He replied:"Mine go up it three times – not at a hectic gallop but nice and steadily and, believe me, it gets them fit, very fit. Yes, my horses are *always* fit".

And he laughed that great belly laugh as he reflected on those who had doubted whether Imperial Call might come up the hill in a driving battle from the last in the Gold Cup.

Sutherland himself guessed that his uphill gallop rises by some 800 feet from the start of the five-and-a-half furlongs stretch to the top.

But before his charges ever reach the point where their ultimate fitness for a race is sharpened to perfection on "The Hill" – if you might call it so – they learn to acquire the art of jumping by "being long-reined over banks and drains", as Fergie describes it. Then they progress to tree-trunks before being sent down "The Tunnel".

"What?", you might ask incredulously. Training horses to be chasers by sending them down a tunnel!

"The Tunnel" is a narrow overgrown boreen with a cinder base on which three sets of tyres – joined together – are embedded.

Ditches surround "The Tunnel" on both sides and the horses have no choice but to keep going straight. Sutherland believes it teaches them good habits. "They go up and down and they can do nothing but jump", he explained. "They can't run out. When they've got used to it, we put them over normal fences. Before they run, I like to give them a school on a racecourse or a point-to-point course.

"One of the reasons also why my horses are so fit is that Jack Maurice Mulcahy allows me to use the local point-to-point course at Aghabullogue", he said.

He had no need to add that the reason you never saw a Sutherland-trained horse run out during a race was because of the experience gained in "The Tunnel".

During their visit to Killinardrish Pat Keane and Tony O'Hehir went and viewed Imperial Call, looking fit and ready for the task ahead. And then it was back to Aginagh House where Sutherland's wife, Ann had soup, tea and a mountain and sandwiches on the table and there was plenty of brandy, whiskey and wine available also.

Fergie revealed something about his approach to the media on that occasion when he remarked: "I feel quite happy talking to you fellows. I know you will quote me properly".

Obviously he drew a distinction between the "Racing Press" and the news hounds of the tabloids in particular and from his Newmarket days, he was careful to be on his guard. He knew only too well how a story could be twisted or angled. In fact, I noticed in the winner's enclosure on Gold Cup Day, as the questions were coming in at him from all angles, how he would not be drawn into downgrading One Man, even though Imperial Call had left him for dead in the end.

He admitted too in the count-down to the Gold Cup that the huge media pressure was getting to him, but he knew he would have to learn to live with it. He had suddenly been catapulted from the day Imperial Call won the Hennessy Cognac Gold Cup into a public figure – and one for whom there was going to be no escape. "I find it very intrusive", he said. "I have to train the horse as well".

"When I first came to Killinardrish, I could never have visualised this happening to me some day. I don't like crowds. I prefer to let my horses do the talking!"

✳   ✳   ✳

That November day at Clonmel in '93 – Thursday, the 9th to be exact – when Imperial Call really burst on the scene as a six-year-old in taking the Morris Oil Chase, you did not find the same gathering of racing writers as would have been the case if it was a chase at Leopardstown or one of the other venues in the Metropolitan area on a Saturday or Sunday. But Ray Glennon of the *Sunday Independent* recalls the total confidence exuded by Fergie Sutherland as he proclaimed that he had a potential Gold Cup winner on his hands.

The race was over 2m 4f and Imperial Call had left no doubt about his superiority over King of The Gales, Jassu, Bishops Hall and Nuaffe. Jassu in his previous race had won under 12st at the Galway October meeting while in February of that year Nuaffe, carrying 11st, had won the Greenalls Gold Cup Handicap Chase (Class B) at Haydock Park over 3m 4f.

But Sutherland was still an unknown is the eyes of a majority of Irish racing followers – so that Clonmel victory, for all its merit, did not make the impact that in retrospect you feel now it might have made. The writers listening to Fergie could be forgiven for being sceptical about his hard-and-fast prediction that Imperial Call was booked for Gold Cup glory. Perhaps it was a rush of blood to the head.

But Sutherland had approached the task of the making of Imperial Call into a chaser with military-style precision and planning, in keeping with his Army background. No praise is high enough for the manner in which he eschewed tilting at one of the big Cheltenham hurdle prizes, when there was immense pressure on him to do so, in order to keep rigidly to his original goal – delivering Imperial Call at the opportune moment to win the Gold Cup.

Consider then how Imperial Call looked in January '94 to be tailor-made for the job of becoming one of the prime Irish challengers for the Sun Alliance Novices' Hurdle (2m 5f) at the Festival meeting. Giving 10lbs to Dorans Pride in the Celbridge Handicap Hurdle at Naas, he was beaten a short head, having been hampered somewhat two out. It's hardly necessary to recall that Dorans Pride went on to contest the 'Sun Alliance' and was challenging Danoli when he came down at the last flight. The following year the Michael Hourigan-trained hurdler had five lengths to spare over

Cyborgo when winning the Bonusprint Stayers Hurdle in smashing style and at Cheltenham '96, with Dorans Pride unable to defend his crown because of injury, Cyborgo took this race for the Martin Pipe stable in an epic finish with Mysilv who earlier in the week had finished sixth behind Collier Bay in the Smurfit Champion Hurdle.

So the Naas race between Dorans Pride and Imperial Call of January 29th, '94 represented form with a capital "F".

Imperial Call had appeared at Thurles on February 11th, '93, finishing seventh behind Direct Lady in the Vista Therm 4-Y-O Hurdle. Next time out he won the Shannon 4-Y-O Maiden Hurdle at Limerick on April 1st by fifteen lengths in the hands of Gerry O'Neill, having started 100/30 favourite. Put by for the summer, he graduated to handicap class at the Listowel Festival meeting in September but in this Listed Race (Grade 2)he was never seen with a chance behind the Noel Meade-trained Life Saver, who was completing a hat-trick.

However, he revelled in the heavy conditions at the Limerick Christmas meeting on Monday, December 27th, taking the Bank of Ireland Handicap Hurdle by a length from the favourite, Parliament Hall. He started 100/30 that day.

It is an indication of the strength of the field in the Celbridge Handicap Hurdle that Dorans Pride started at 13/2 and Imperial Call at 8/1. Derrymoyle, who had finished fourth behind Atone, Arctic Weather and Judicial Field in the Ladbroke Hurdle earlier in the month, went off at 9/4 favourite with Cock Cockburn, seventh in the 'Ladbroke' at 11/2 and Ground War, beaten half-a-length in the Sandymount Handicap Hurdle at Leopardstown on his previous outing, at 6/1.

On St. Patrick's Day Imperial Call, when he might have been on his way home from Cheltenham, won the Castrol GTA Hurdle (2m. 4f)at Leopardstown from the 9/4 favourite Idiots Venture by fifteen lengths with Heist a further five lengths away third.

✳   ✳   ✳

There were those who impressed upon Fergie Sutherland in the euphoria of that scintillating victory that he had a potential Champion Hurdle winner on his hands – that the target now should be to gear everything towards winning that race in '95.

But Fergie said to himself, as he patted Imperial Call on the neck in the winner's enclosure: 'That's it, my boy. Your hurdling days are over. Now for the Gold Cup in '96'.

Remember, it was exactly two years before he would go for gold – before he would make his bid for the most prestigious prize of all at the Olympics of the chasing world.

"I was not tempted in the least to contemplate the Champion Hurdle of '95", he told me later in his home in Killinardrish. "I had made up my mind not to take the route so many others would have taken in the circumstances.

33

I was convinced that there was a point at which to say 'Stop'. If I had kept Imperial Call at hurdling, even with any eye to winning a Champion Hurdle, I could have killed stone-dead his prospects of landing the Gold Cup in '96".

So Imperial Call went out to grass. Not for him a tilt at one of the big Fairyhouse prizes in the hurdling sphere. Not for him either an appearance at the Punchestown Festival meeting when there was a lot to play for and he looked to have the form to be very much in the reckoning for one of the big sponsored events.

He didn't reappear until October 10th at Roscommon and in his very first run over fences in public he took on Sound Man in the Kilbegnet Novice Chase (2m) on good going and was staying on at the finish as he finished third behind Edward O'Grady's charge and the Michael O'Brien-trained Shawiya, beaten a total of twelve-and-a-half lengths. But while in a way it might be described as a schooling run, Sutherland had already been testing him over the bigger obstacles at home and knew he was a 'natural'.

He put his faith to the test in the Dunstown Wood Chase (2m 2f) at Punchestown on Thursday October 22nd, '94. Mubadir, who had finished third in the Digital Galway Plate behind Feathered Gale and Minister For Fun, beaten a head and a head and who had won on his previous outing at Thurles, was a warm order at 4/5, even though carrying 11-11 to Imperial Call's 11st.

Imperial Call led from start to finish and, despite a slight error at the last, still had three lengths to spare over Tug Of Peace with Mubadir a neck away third. Now we were talking about a "serious horse" in Imperial Call, even though it was only the autumn of '94 and if you had been prepared to approach a bookmaker friend of yours at that point and ask for a quote about the Gold Cup of '96, you would have got very, very generous odds about Fergie Sutherland's charge.

Indeed, the ante-post docket you would have held would have opened the way for a round-the-world holiday with no worry about spending money, come March '96.

Next time out he started 11/8 favourite to win the Irish Field Chase at Punchestown on November 6th but, ironically, finished third to the Victor Bowens-trained Buck Rogers, which had been owned and trained by Tom Costello when scoring in a bumper at Clonmel in April. Runner-up that day at Punchestown was Strong Platinum. But it had to be noted that Imperial Call was giving 4lbs to the winner and 2lbs to Strong Platinum.

The year ended on a winning note for Imperial Call as he easily disposed of the 5/4 favourite Monalee River in the Murphys Irish Stout Novice Chase at Limerick on St. Stephen's Day. Monalee River had strolled home by twelve lengths on his previous outing at Tipperary.

✳　　✳　　✳

Imperial Call followed up that success by starting the year 1995 with a four-lengths triumph in the Ras Na Ri E.B.F. Chase in heavy going at Naas in March. Again Fergie Sutherland had given Cheltenham a miss in favour of his long-term goal.

But he was now moving Imperial Call on to a higher plane, not in the least perturbed as to how the professionals judged his charge at that point, whether they simply saw him as another novice of promise who would graduate to handicap company, win bread-and-butter races maybe for his small trainer but never command the kind of headlines that would fall to a Tied Cottage or a Dawn Run.

So Imperial Call took on the two big guns, Strong Platinum (Conor O'Dwyer) and Sound Man (Charlie Swan) in the Power Gold Cup (Grade I) at the 1995 Fairyhouse Easter Jameson Irish Grand National meeting. With Gerry O'Neill in the saddle, he was only beaten three lengths and one-and-a-half lengths and was staying on at the finish as Strong Platinum triumphed over Sound Man. The going was good to firm officially that day.

It was clear that eventually when he raced at distances of three miles and further, the class he had revealed that day at Fairyhouse would be shown in new light.

Again he was put out to grass for the summer, delighting in the space and the freedom which he enjoyed at Killinardrish.

On his reappearance, as we have seen at Clonmel on November 9th '95, he scored with real authority in the Morris Oil Chase (Grade 3)over 2m 4f.

In his next race the same month at Punchestown, Imperial Call was pitted in a Grade I event against Merry Gale and Klairon Davis over 2m 4f. Even though set to carry 12st, Merry Gale, viewed very much at that point as Ireland's brightest Gold Cup prospect for years, started favourite at 6/4 with Klairon Davis next at 9/4 and Imperial Call on 9/2 (from 7/2).

Fergie Sutherland was not in the least overawed by Merry Gale's reputation or by the spotlight trained on the classy Jim Dreaper-trained chaser. In fact, he was quietly confident of victory and was convinced that Imperial Call not alone had the ability to stay with Merry Gale but beat him for speed at the finish.

Before the field went to the start, Sutherland publicly expressed his worry about the low sun and feared that it might cause a problem to his charge, who was still only a novice at that stage. Imperial Call came a cropper at the first and, in retrospect, it might well be attributed to the sun getting in his eyes as he rose to the fence. In light of subsequent events, it was a very uncharacteristic error. And you can search the *Form Book* from that eventful afternoon to Gold Cup Day '96 and you won't find that Imperial Call came down in any of the races he contested.

Klairon Davis went at the 5th in the Punchestown race when lying in fourth place. Merry Gale strolled home a very easy winner of a bloodless contest by ten lengths from King of The Gales.

So in the year 1995 there was only one blemish really in Imperial Call's record – that one fall in the race won by Merry Gale at Punchestown.

Strong Platinum was being touted as a likely Irish winner of the Queen

Mother Champion Chase at Cheltenham '96, so there was tremendous interest in his showing in the McCain Handicap Chase (2m 2f) at Leopardstown on Saturday, January 13, '96. On his previous outing at Punchestown in December, he didn't have to be asked a question when disposing of Monalee River.

The heavy going was all against Strong Platinum at Leopardstown, but even though he was carrying 12st to Imperial Call's 11st 7lbs, he started joint-favourite on the strength of his achievements to date. Charlie Swan was on Imperial Call and Conor O'Dwyer on Strong Platinum.

Strong Platinum put in a very strong challenge from the last but Imperial Call rallied well under pressure and had one-and-a-half lengths to spare at the line. Even allowing for the fact that the ground conditions did not favour Strong Platinum that day, it had to be acknowledged that Imperial Call had now arrived as a serious horse and the opinions of his trainer were going to be taken far more seriously.

* * *

The Hennessy Cognac Gold Cup Chase (Grade I) was set as the next target and Fergie Sutherland made it crystal clear to the racing world that his charge would be seen in a completely different light once he stepped up in distance.

The fact that Leopardstown was put back a week from Sunday, February 3rd to Sunday, February 11th because of frost proved a blessing in disguise for Imperial Call and Fergie Sutherland.

The connections of Flashing Steel, which John Mulhern had trained to win the 1995 Jameson Irish Grand National under 12st in the hands of Jamie Osborne for his father-in-law, former Taoiseach (Irish Prime Minister) Charles J. Haughey, were very confident of victory had the meeting gone ahead on February 3rd. Flashing Steel would have got the good ground that had suited him so well in his 'National triumph. As it was, when the announcement of the postponement came around midday, they had ample time to discuss the might-have-beens over lunch in the Berkeley Court Hotel.

Fergie Sutherland had been looking to the skies all the week. The rains came just in time in the lead-up to the rescheduled meeting to bring the answer to his prayers. When I rang him for my "Stable Whispers" column in the *Sunday Independent*, I was so taken by his confidence that I plumped for Imperial Call to repel the challenges of the 1995 Gold Cup winner, Master Oats and the other English contender, Monsieur Le Cure. Anyway, Kim Bailey indicated to me on the phone from Upper Lambourn that everything in the preparation of Master Oats was being geared to a Gold Cup repeat victory. If he won the Leopardstown race it would be seen as a bonus but defeat wouldn't be regarded as the end of the world. Still Master Oats started 5/4 favourite with Imperial Call at 4/1.

Under an attacking ride from Conor O'Dwyer, Imperial Call, who led from the outset, produced a brilliant display of jumping until the last fence when he made a mistake that brought a gasp from the big crowd. However, O'Dwyer ensured that he recovered well from the error and he was cheered to the echo as he beat Master Oats by six lengths with Monsieur Le Cure a further one-and-a-half lengths back in third place.

It was only the second success for an Irish-trained chaser in the ten-year history of the race (inaugurated originally as the Vincent O'Brien Gold Cup Chase), Carvill's Hill having won for Jim Dreaper in 1989.

Imperial Call was always going too well for Master Oats and Kim Bailey admitted that "we will need a real mudbath to turn the tables on imperial Call at Cheltenham".

Richard Dunwoody had declined when offered the ride on Imperial Call at Leopardstown, preferring to stay with Flashing Steel, who faded completely from the tenth and was tailed off after a bad blunder four out.

Jamie Osborne, who deputised for the injured Norman Williamson on Master Oats, was immensely impressed by Imperial Call's performance. "Imperial Call was always going that bit better and only if it came up much softer at Cheltenham could I see Master Oats turning the tables", he said.

"My fellow jumped well, but Imperial Call looked a real star – Conor (O'Dwyer) even took a pull two out. I knew I needed a miracle at the last and I thought I got it when he made that mistake", added Osborne.

"Imperial Majesty" was the heading on Monday morning over Geoff Lester's report in the *Sporting life*, as he revealed that Ireland's new chasing star was down to 5/1 with Ladbrokes for the Gold Cup while Hills were going 6/1 and Corals 8/1.

He reported also that Imperial Call was reputedly on the market at about IR£300,000 but it was obvious that, with victory in the Gold Cup now beckoning, he had become – like Danoli – a horse that money couldn't buy. Irish National Hunt enthusiasts just wouldn't countenance a sale at that point.

Fergie Sutherland in the aftermath of victory said: "He is definitely a bit special, he has so many gears, so much class. Until he won the Hennessy today, he was only playing at racing".

There would be no playing against One Man at Cheltenham. Sutherland's moment of destiny had arrived.

4

The Day Finds The Man In Conor O'Dwyer

G old Cup Day '96 found the man in Conor O'Dwyer – as a decade previously Jonjo O'Neill was expected by the entire Irish nation to deliver on Dawn Run and duly obliged.

The 29-years-old jockey had never ridden a winner previously at the Festival meeting. He had experienced seven barren and frustrating years. But in ending the famine period, he fully vindicated Fergie Sutherland's faith in him as he gave Imperial Call what the trainer described to me as "a copybook ride".

O'Dwyer had proved before Cheltenham '96 that he was a horseman through and through. And, furthermore, he had the experience not to get ruffled or overwhelmed by the big occasion. He had won the Ladbroke Hurdle in 1990 on the 20/1 shot Redundant Pal for the Paddy Mullins stable, was runner-up in the Jameson Irish Grand National in 1988 on Captain Batnac and third in the Aintree Grand National in 1992 on Laura's Beau.

However, like a true professional O'Dwyer knew deep down that what mattered in the final analysis were the championship races. He viewed the Aintree Grand National as "a lottery race" compared with the Gold Cup. As the poker "Kings" of Las Vegas might put it, you needed "the nuts" to win the Gold Cup. You might be waiting the duration of your career in the saddle for the right horse to come along. There had to be an element of fate in it.

O'Dwyer realised before he became associated with Imperial Call how a good horse could change one's career – by grabbing the headlines and putting your name right up there along with its own.

The horse that initially had a major influence in changing matters for Conor O'Dwyer was Strong Platinum. And you might say that he would never have got the ride on Imperial Call had he not put his name on a new plane through the exploits of Strong Platinum, especially the Strong Gale gelding's two wins during the three days of the 1995 Punchestown Festival meeting.

"It's very important that a jockey keeps himself known and big race winners on television keep you there", he said. "Strong Platinum did that for me during '95. He put me on the map. Everybody was watching him and, as a result, me too.

"I'd a very good year anyway but he really boosted it", he went on. "Suddenly I was finding myself on better horses. There was King Wah Glory who won three races when I was riding him in '95 and, apart from those successes over the jumps, he had won two on the Flat as well".

O'Dwyer finished the 1994-'95 National Hunt season with 43 winners. With four months still to go in the 1995-'96 season, he had surpassed that total and by the season's end in May, he had reached a tally of 75, second in the Irish Jockeys' Championship table to Charlie Swan, who because of his association with Aidan O'Brien could not be beaten. In fact, Swan finished with a total of 150.

It was when he joined Francis Flood in 1985 that Conor O'Dwyer took the first vital step up the ladder that would lead to that crowning moment on Gold Cup Day '96. He was a claiming professional then, riding as second jockey, with Frank Berry No. 1 to the stable. Berry, of course, had won the Gold Cup in 1972 on Glencarrig Lady for Francis Flood and had other memorable moments at the Festival meeting on Drumgora (Queen Mother Champion Chase, 1981), Doubluagain (Mildmay of Flete Challenge Cup, 1982), Bobsline (Arkle Chase, 1984) and Antarctic Bay (Sun Alliance Chase, 1985).

Instead of envy and tension, a close friendship was built up between the two. Conor O'Dwyer is the first to acknowledge how much he owes to Frank. "I learned a lot from him as he was the consummate professional. But, more than that, he was very generous in the way he set out specially to try and get me rides. For example, if a trainer contacted him to ride a horse and he couldn't do so because of another commitment, he would put in a word for me".

It resulted in Conor O'Dwyer winning the claiming professionals' title in 1986 with sixteen winners.

Ultimately, Frank Berry presented O'Dwyer with his own personal accolade when he asked him to ride Laura's Beau in the Aintree Grand National in '92 and owner J. P. McManus admitted to getting a special thrill as he watched his horse getting into the frame behind Party Politics and Romany King.

O'Dwyer had his ups-and-downs, as any jockey seeking to make it to the top must be prepared to suffer.

He had his most embarrassing moment in a 2m 6f chase at Tramore in 1988. Riding Lucius for the Francis Flood stable, he came to the second last with a double handful, cleared the fence in style and went on to "score" impressively, patting Lucius on the neck at the thought of another winner.

Then to his horror he saw the rest of the field setting off on another circuit. "Yes, I don't mind saying now that I still squirm at the thought of that moment, and making it worse, I chased the rest of them and was actually second coming to the last – the final jump bar none! – when Lucius unseated me. When I contrast the reception I got that day with being carried shoulder high in the winner's enclosure on Gold Cup Day '96, I laugh to myself. But then I wasn't the first jockey to make that mistake and I will have the greatest sympathy for any rider who suffers that embarrassment in the future".

*   *   *

Charlie Swan at one point had been No. 1 to the "Mouse" Morris stable but decided to go freelance to widen his opportunities. And Conor O'Dwyer, after a spell as stable jockey to Morris, took the same route. It was an amicable break. O'Dwyer continued to ride for the Everardsgrange establishment outside Fethard in South Tipperary, coming up with a nice tally of winners and taking third place behind Cyborgo and Mysilv on 33/1 shot What A Question in the Bonusprint Stayers Hurdle at the Cheltenham '96 Festival meeting.

O'Dwyer knew that going freelance could be a two-edged sword. You were setting aside a retainer in the hope that you would have more opportunities and a wider choice in the long term. Granted you could have certain "arrangements" with individual stables that saw the trainers using your services on a regular basis but it wasn't demanded of you to ride a particular horse for one of them if you saw a better opportunity of a winner elsewhere. It was, however, a finely-balanced situation.

The man going freelance was trusting his talent and skill and his belief that he could continue to ride at the top of his form. If he hit a bad run, if a spate of injuries affected his nerve, owners and trainers wouldn't want to know. That was the chasm that no jockey wanted to contemplate.

But if the winners were flowing, if you were commanding favourable notices in the media, if the professionals were impressed, then the freelance of real ability instead of having to make the calls or wait for his agent to ensure that he had a good book of rides, would find that it was the other way round. If he hadn't an agent, he could rest assured that the phone would ring constantly at home as also his car phone as he headed for a meeting – or on his return.

Strong Platinum first left no doubt that O'Dwyer had taken the right decision in going freelance and Imperial Call clinched matters.

Now Fergie Sutherland is on the line from Killinardrish to Conor O'Dwyer. At another time it would have meant little – a small trainer from the deep South, this one isolated in County Cork, inquiring if he would be in a position to take the ride on Tempo for him in the first race at Gowran Park the following day. That was before the meeting at the Kilkenny venue on Thursday, January 25th (Tempo was to finish fifth in the Toyota Starlet Maiden Hurdle).

But Sutherland, in offering him his first-ever ride for the stable, was inquiring also: "Would you be available to ride Imperial Call in the Hennessy if Richard Dunwoody opts to ride something else?"

This was the moment when the Hinge of Fate brought all the pieces together on the jig-saw for Conor O'Dwyer, when all the experience he had acquired in the saddle, all the horsemanship that was his forte would be summoned to answering that call for his country. Like Ronnie Delaney carrying Ireland's hopes on the track in the Melbourne Olympics.

When he said "Yes" to Fergie Sutherland, he was effectively saying "Yes" to the Irish nation. That might seem to be painting too extravagant a picture – but Jonjo O'Neill will know what I mean. Ask Jonjo. When he got the fateful call that led to him riding Dawn Run, he knew it would be the greatest challenge of his riding career but, he has confessed to me since, even he could not have visualised the build-up to that day at Cheltenham in '86 or the flood-gates of emotion that would be opened when he triumphed on the gallant mare.

Richard Dunwoody, as might be expected, decided to ride Flashing Steel in the Hennessy Cognac Gold Cup. He had an "understanding" with the flamboyant and colourful John Mulhern and it was not easy for him to ride something else in the race. Anyway, granted he got the going to favour him, Flashing Steel looked to be in with a big chance and had far more experience for a race like this than Imperial Call.

After the way he won the Hennessy on Imperial Call, there was no way that Conor O'Dwyer was going to be replaced for the Gold Cup. What he now had to do was deliver – as Jonjo O'Neill had delivered in '86.

✳   ✳   ✳

Conor O'Dwyer came from Ard Carman in Wexford town and his people had no involvement with horses. But, as his mother, Kay recalls, he was "stone mad from the outset with the obsession that he wanted to be a jockey".

Indeed, so great was his obsession with horses that from the time he was six years old, he would go straight from school to John Berry's place to ride his pony. John was then his greatest pal in school and, of course, he would later become a top amateur rider and is now a trainer, with stables in Ballyroe, near the beautiful little village of Blackwater. The long summer holidays were glorious times for young Conor as he indulged the fashioning of his art.

He has a vivid memory to this day of Tommy Carberry – his idol – coming to the last in the 1979 Gold Cup and looking all over a winner, only to slip up on landing, leaving Alverton and Jonjo O'Neill to go on to a bloodless triumph. Those images would be imprinted in the mind of an aspiring young jockey, as would that of Tommy Carberry gaining compensation twelve months later as he rode Tied Cottage to a scintillating victory in the Gold Cup. Conor was too young to understand the subsequent disqualification on technical grounds.

When he was nine it was decided to purchase his own pony for him and hardly a Sunday went by but he was off to a gymkhana in some part of his native county.

His mother would spend much of Saturday getting ready for the particular gymkhana at which he would participate next day. Often, after early Mass, the O'Dwyers would set off as a family with a picnic basket, returning home the same evening proud at the fact that Conor had won yet another red rosette in his category.

Kay O'Dwyer and her husband, Senan, remember those Sundays with nostalgia as "great and happy times".

But ambition was now stirring – the ambition to move on to bigger things. Just before his 15th birthday he announced to a shocked close family circle that he wanted to leave for R.A.C.E., the Jockey Apprentices School at the Curragh. "We couldn't believe it. We thought he'd be better off at anything else", his Mother recalled.

In fact, she was so worried about letting him off on his own that she was loath to say "Yes" initially. But Conor had made up his mind and nothing was going to deter him from his purpose. Eventually his parents relented and he joined R.A.C.E.. He was allowed home every second week-end. On the week-ends he remained on the Curragh, one of his parents would travel up from Wexford to be with him.

That seemed a long time ago to Kay O'Dwyer on Gold Cup Day '96 – the day she received a congratulatory call and the person at the other end of the line said simply: "You bred a champion".

It was one of numerous calls but it was the call that meant most of all to her.

In the count-down to the moment when she knew that the commentary would be on television, she busied herself in the kitchen of her Ard Carman home. "I made plenty of noise, because I just couldn't bear to watch or hear", she admitted later to the reporter from the *Wexford People.*

Then her son, Richard, put his head around the door and said: "Mum, if you want to see Conor winning the Gold Cup, you better come in quickly".

"I knew then that it must be nearly over. I went into the sitting-room and roared him home. They nearly had to scrape me off the ceiling I jumped so high with joy as he passed the winning post".

It was then that the phone started to ring. It rang non-stop all that evening and between the calls and the well-wishers coming to the front door, Kay O'Dwyer was overwhelmed. But she was walking on air. Nothing mattered only her immense and justifiable pride in her son's achievement.

Conor is a grandson of a former Mayor of Wexford, James Gaul. And now a special message of congratulations arrived at the O'Dwyer home from the man who was Mayor in March '96, Alderman Ted Howlin who was promising a full civic reception for the successful Gold Cup jockey.

Conor had to ride Three Brownies for the "Mouse" Morris stable in the Midlands Grand National at Uttoxeter on the Saturday (the 33/1 shot was pulled up before the 19th after leading to the 15th fence), so it was that night before there could be a family reunion. It took place in the Montrose Hotel in Dublin just over an hour before Conor's appearance on the Kenny

Live TV Show on RTE.

The O'Dwyers had to thank Conor's sponsor, J.J. Byrne for ensuring that they made it to Dublin for the Show. "We were having trouble with our own car, but J.J. really came up trumps and had a car delivered to our door from his garage", noted Kay O'Dwyer.

"I never thought I'd see the day when Conor would win a Gold Cup", she added. "When I saw him walking through the doors of the hotel, I just looked and said to myself: 'He has really made it'.

It was fitting that John Berry and his wife, Anna should be pictured smiling happily with Conor O'Dwyer and his partner, Audrey Cross at the Montrose Hotel get-together.

Yes, the wheel had come full circle from the time John Berry had played a crucial role in putting his school-pal on the road that would lead to Cheltenham glory in '96.

*　　*　　*

The long haul after apprentice academy days to full-fledged professional jockey really began when Conor O'Dwyer got his first job with Frank Oakes back in 1982.

O'Dwyer remembers that spell with the Newcastle, County Dublin trainer with pleasure – and a sense of gratitude for the opportunities provided and he acknowledged: "I probably didn't deserve them".

He started off as an apprentice, riding solely on the Flat. But it quickly dawned on him that he wasn't light enough really to make a successful Flat jockey – that his future lay over the jumps. "It was all National Hunt from then on".

From Frank Oakes he went to Francis Flood and, as we have seen already, that was the move that led to his becoming champion claimer in '86 and the curve was upwards from then on.

He got a big break early in 1990 when Maureen Mullins rang him and told him that they had three runners in the Ladbroke Hurdle and to stand by to ride one of them – she didn't indicate at that moment which one he would be riding. As it turned out, he got the mount on Redundant Pal (11-5)and beat Dis Train from the Jenny Pitman stable by half-a-length with Fragrant Dawn from the Jimmy Fitzgerald stable a further three lengths back third.

But it is hard to believe now that he had to wait ten years to know the glory in what he has aptly described as the "Olympics of National Hunt racing". To win one of the championship races at the Cheltenham Festival meeting was akin to taking gold and for seven years he had been thwarted in the realisation of that goal. He hadn't even known the joy of winning a handicap race in the shadow of Cleeve Hill.

When it did happen at last, it happened in a way that wiped away in one unforgettable afternoon all the disappointments and frustrations that he had experienced in all his previous visits to Cheltenham.

*　　*　　*

43

It is the 'done thing' nowadays to sing the praises of writers who dare face mortality in the face. In a very perceptive piece under the heading "Hello darkness, my old friend" in *The Observer* in early June '96, Nicci Gerrard touched on the writers who are trying to stare death in the face, referring specifically to Dennis Potter's rapturous embrace of life as cancer killed him; the meticulous lyricism of the philosopher Gillian Rose's dying love song to life in *Love's Work* and William Styron's poignant description of grappling with death in *Darkness Visible* ...recalling too that when Tallyerand died, it was, – Duff-Cooper wrote, – as a diplomat who "had set forth on his last mission with his credentials in order, his passport signed".

And novelist Robert McCrum echoed those words after surviving a stroke: "It sounds a cliché, but I've crossed an invisible line, to a country where I have no passport, no maps. And one of the things that has happened since I have returned from there is that I don't care so much any more. Things that once worried me don't worry me any longer. I'm going to be myself now".

The jump jockeys know that they stare death or serious injury every time they go out in a race. They don't dare to look mortality in the face each time they leave the Weighroom. They don't reflect on it because that way, they know, you could end up seeking to avoid the perils and lose the badge of courage that is the most glorious facet of any great National Hurt rider's appeal, especially as you watch him going for broke as he attacks the penultimate and ultimate fences.

Jump jockeys in a way then live on the edge. You could end up in a box or a wheel-chair or you could be like a punch-drunk boxer with your friends affectionately calling you "The Champ" but it would be a sad legacy of the golden times, of days when you had all your faculties.

Perhaps you can forgive them for living it hard, for taking the fast lane. A guy's got to make the best of it while he can. Tomorrow is another day but then the world may never bloom for you again after a cruel fall. As Elisa Seagrave, survivor of cancer, put it: "I now live life for today, for itself".

But the irony of it is that owners and trainers and the racing public, who put their money down on the nose, want the riders at the same time to be disciplined. In a word, they admire professionalism – and demand it.

And that professionalism can impose strict observance of the regime of the sauna and watching one's diet and being careful with the alcohol and maybe even cutting it out altogether in the count-down to major races. The irony is that a jockey who is noted for his power in a finish can't afford to take off too much in the sauna, for, as Conor O'Dwyer pointed out to me, you must be certain that you have the strength to be fully in control of your mount at the end of a three-mile chase, maybe in exhausting conditions.

Conor O'Dwyer knew what it was to live in the fast lane. He loved to drive fast cars. He drove too fast at times to his own cost and more than one car was written off. Fortunately for himself he survived.

But he still carries two steel plates in his left arm from a car accident nine years ago.

He actually broke both arms in that accident – compound fractures and the surgeons battled to try and ensure that his riding career would not be prematurely ended. "I was lucky to escape being killed", he said factually as he showed me the scars.

He's wiser, more mature now and with Audrey he has found an anchor in a secure relationship that has made all the difference.

∗   ∗   ∗

On Friday, March 1st, 1996 Fergie Sutherland brought Imperial Call to Clonmel for a final schooling session. Conor O'Dwyer was in the saddle.

Describing it afterwards, Sutherland said: "Conor schooled him over eight fences. The horse jumped brilliantly. He was electric and I believe he's better than ever".

"Some believe he must have the ground really soft, but I don't share that view. Only very fast ground would be a worry", added the trainer.

Conor O'Dwyer for his part rejected also the theory that Imperial Call could only perform at his best on really soft going. "I remember back to Fairyhouse '95 when he finished third to Strong Platinum and Sound Man in the Power Gold Cup and that was on very, very fast ground. One thing is sure – the ground won't stop him".

Later at Cheltenham, as the ground dried out in the lead-up to the Gold Cup, O'Dwyer said: "I know the feelings is that the going might be just a bit quick for him but I don't think it will worry him too much. Both the hurdles and chases will be on a new track and it is ground that is good but not fast and the fact that our race is the first on the chase course will also be an advantage".

In the space of four races in the lead-up to Gold Cup '96 Imperial Call had made the Great Leap from second season novice to a contender for the Blue Riband of chasing. What's more, his official rate of improvement from the start of the 1995-'96 season was 26lbs. His progress was simply phenomenal.

Conor O'Dwyer, by the manner in which he excelled on Imperial Call in the Hennessy Cognac Gold Cup Chase and in the Gold Cup itself, contributed handsomely to making 'The King of Killinardrish' into a true champion of the chasing world.

Jamie Osborne, who produced a fabulous five-timer at the '92 Festival meeting, went on record to note that "every aspect of a jockey's craft is minutely examined at Cheltenham". One of the reasons for this, he stressed, is that the races are faster, fields are bigger and jockeys have a fraction less time to react. And the racing is more cut-throat since so much is at stake.

"Mortgages can be paid, reputations won and lost and no one wants to be responsible for failure", he said in the course of a very revealing piece in *The Times* done in collaboration with Andrew Longmore.

He made the important point that at Cheltenham "it is difficult to find a rhythm in the way you can around more straightforward and oval tracks, such as Newbury. There are hills, dips, no real straights, some tight bends. It always throws up some uncertainty".

He went on: "This can be the best week of the year – and the worst. Drive out to the course on Thursday with a few winners under your belt and there is no better feeling in the world. Drive out with doubts and they will haunt you for the rest of the year. I have experienced both emotions.

"In 1992 I rode five winners. In 1995 I had five seconds, including Large Action in the Champion Hurdle. On the way home, I ran through each race in my mind to check whether I could have done anything differently. Large Action had a dream run. I was exactly where I wanted to be throughout the race. I even thought for a split second after the last that I had won. In a way, that was even harder. Knowing we had done everything right and yet still being beaten".

Conor O'Dwyer didn't arrive at the third day of the '96 Festival meeting with a winner under his belt. But that wasn't going to affect his outlook or his confidence in any way.

Achieving third place on 9/1 shot New Co from the "Mouse" Morris stable in the Coral Cup Handicap Hurdle on the Wednesday (beaten a head and one-and-a-quarter lengths by Trainglot and Treasure Again) was a bonus, as was the third on What A Question on Gold Cup Day itself.

Jamie Osborne had come up to him after the Hennessy and said he could not believe how well Imperial Call had gone away from Master Oats. O'Dwyer knew that Imperial Call had come on a lot since the Leopardstown race and had grown in confidence. He had come on even more – much, much more – from the time that he rode him before the Hennessy. "We only jumped six fences to get a feel of him. I thought he was a bit novicy for a race like the Hennessy but his performance that day was really brilliant," he recalled.

Conor O'Dwyer confessed to me that he was surprised how calm he was on Gold Cup Day. "I surprised myself really. I thought I would be much more nervous. I even expected to be rattling".

"Quite a deal of the credit must go to Fergie Sutherland, who is a very easy man to get on with", he said.

It was a help also that he had the mount on What A Question in the Stayers' Hurdle, the race preceding the Gold Cup. It meant that he was active instead of sitting around waiting.

✳   ✳   ✳

The day dawned like any other race day for Conor O'Dwyer and yet he knew it was different. And by 3.40p.m. when it was all over and the tumult and the cheering was echoing out from the winner's enclosure to Cleeve Hill and beyond, he realised that he might never know a day like this again. There could be a repeat, yes, but the first Golf Cup win was special. And in the case of this one he had become part of something unique, something beyond words. Indeed, the only word that came to his lips as he recalled the incredible reception accorded Imperial Call and himself and also Fergie Sutherland was: "Unbelievable".

He was up early to ride out at the course. Then it was back to the hotel for a sauna before heading back to the course well before the first race.

Describing the tactical plan devised with Fergie Sutherland and the race itself, Conor O'Dwyer told me: "The one clear instruction Fergie gave me was to stay on the outside and, after that, he said I must go out and enjoy it – and be positive and ride him as confidently as I had ridden him at Leopardstown.

"I agreed fully with his instructions about taking an outside route, even though it meant giving away ground to the others. The fact of the matter was that Imperial Call was still a comparative novice for a race like this and it was essential that he should see all of each fence.

"Indeed, Fergie Sutherland's attitude was that it would be better that he finish second or third in his first attempt at the Gold Cup as a seven-year-old than that he end up on the floor.

"As the race evolved, we did not have to go that awfully wide to get the clear run I wanted to get. He put in a great jump four out and it carried him into the lead. I decided to let him stride out and once we were in front to stay there.

"Every time Graham (McCourt) tried to wrest the advantage from us on Couldnt Be Better, Imperial Call had responded in fitting style.

"The one real moment of worry I had was when Richard (Dunwoody)came upsides three from home. He remarked:'Are we stepping on the gas too soon?'. It was a clever ploy on his part as he obviously knew that it would make me ponder whether I was ahead too early.

"I knew, though, that I had plenty of horse under me, but I didn't know how much Richard had left, as he didn't actually head me. Then he sits so quietly on a horse and is such an excellent judge of pace that it's very difficult to assess how much he has in hand, if anything.

"Imperial Call was moving very smoothly at the top of the hill and I got another magnificent leap out of him at the second last. Coming to the last I was still expecting Richard on One Man to challenge. In retrospect, it's amazing how he cracked so completely when the pressure was really on.

"When I took a peak over my shoulder, it was One Man I was on the look out for, but I could see Rough Quest behind me. I reckoned that if Mick Fitzgerald was coming with a double handful, he would seek to take me on the outside. Another quick glance told me he was on the inside and, while to television viewers it might have seemed a closer battle than it was, I knew I had his measure at that point. My one was idling a bit and I am sure I could have pulled out more if it was needed."

"It's from the second last jump that you hear the roar of the crowd. It's something deep, sustained – in fact, huge. You feel you are being carried along on that surge of cheering and in my case, I knew that it was now a great Irish roar, once the Irish realised that the challenge of One Man had been repelled.

"I tried not to think of the wall of sound that was almost engulfing us. I was concentrating totally on ensuring that I would bring Imperial Call perfectly into the last fence. Naturally, Leopardstown and the last was on my mind. But this time when I asked him for one, he popped over it and I realised then it was all over, as there was no way he was going to be beaten up the hill from the final jump.

"Mick Fitzgerald reached across and shook my hand warmly in congratulations after we had passed the post. Charlie Swan, who had ridden King of the Gales, gave me a bear-hug. That's the spirit you always find among the jump jockeys. There can be fierce rivalry but they rejoice in a fellow-jockey hitting the target and Mick and Charlie, I knew were delighted at my Gold Cup success after so many fruitless trips to the Festival meeting.

"Imperial Call's jumping was really good for a relative novice, so he should be even better in '97".

"I have never seen anything like the reception that greeted us as we came back into the winner's enclosure", he said. "It was truly unforgettable. It outstripped anything I myself have experienced and anything I have seen in my riding career.

"I always hoped and dreamed that I would ride a winner at the Festival meeting some day. I never thought that when I did get that winner it would be Imperial Call winning the Gold Cup".

Limerick on the Sunday, and on a miserable March day at that, was a far cry from the golden moments at Cheltenham and the immediate aftermath.

But for a top jockey the mundane can go hand-in-hand with the heady heights and the glory. A man's got to go where he has to go.

It was the following Wednesday night, very nearly a week after Gold Cup Day, that he was feted at a big welcome-home celebration party in the Talbot Hotel in his native Wexford.

Quite a number of his fellow-professional jockeys and amateur riders were there to acclaim him.

The lad who once rode his pony at gymkhana all around the South East and for whom a red rosette represented a pinnacle of achievement in his particular category had joined the select band like Martin Molony, Aubrey Brabazon, Fred Winter, Bobby Beasley, G. W. Robinson, Pat Taaffe, Tommy Carberry, Dessie Hughes, John Francome, Mark Dwyer, Jonjo O'Neill, Adrian Maguire and Norman Williamson and, of course, Frank Berry who had conquered in the Gold Cup at Cheltenham.

Some of them on great horses that live in the annals of the Festival meeting – from Cottage Rake to Arkle. Others simply creating legends.

Now bridging the decade from the romantic chapter written by Jonjo O'Neill and Dawn Run was Conor O'Dwyer on Imperial call.

The young lad astride the banner with the words "IMPERIAL CALL" on it in the winner's enclosure will stand like an epic masterpiece to Gold Cup Day '96 and to the arrival of a new champion of the chasing world.

5

The Fear That Haunted Fergie And Ann

It was summer over all of Killinardrish, over the mountains in the distance, each one of which Fergie Sutherland has climbed in his time, over the picturesque stretch of the River Lee, to which English coarse fishing enthusiasts flock and over the broad expanse of the seven-acre field where Imperial Call was besporting himself with his pony-pal, Trigger.

I had come on from Cork through Dripsey, Coachford and Carrigadrohid to talk to Fergie on his own ground, to get further insights into his training methods and take a journey back in time to the days of the Korean War when he played poker in a tough "school", not caring about losing – "as we had nothing else to do with our money" – but the experience gained would be turned to the fullest possible advantage when later he found himself facing lesser opponents.

I caught him in expansive mood. The initial formal interview over a Paddy led on to an invitation to join Ann and himself for an impromptu dinner, which she prepared with the same masterful ease as he had shown in presenting Imperial Call for his Gold Cup challenge at Cheltenham '96. The more relaxed we became over the Cabernet Sauvignon, the more I marvelled at the *joie de vivre* that had been central to his journey through life to the attainment of his 65th birthday.

He confessed to being a passionate field sportsman – extending from a love of hunting to game shooting in season and out of season he would keep his eye in by making the clay pigeons his target in summer. I could have painted a picture in colours of Fergie out after the snipe and laughingly he remarked:'You wouldn't slam too many doors as you took up position and waited for them to rise'. He educated me on the intricacies of 'the drive' and acquiring the know-how to assess where they were likely to go. They always fly into the wind. If the wind was strong and gusty, then it becomes a real test to "bag" a pair or more.

And then I was back in Korea with him over 45 years ago as he faced up to North Korean troops on the battle-field and to the Canadians in poker sessions where no pity was shown for the uninitiated. British troops had gone into action on September 6th, 1950. Fergie was with the Fifth Dragoon Guards as part of the Commonwealth Division, that included also Canadian and Australian contingents. The Americans had landed in Korea on July 2nd and General MacArthur was designated Commander-in-Chief of the United Nations forces.

In the evenings Fergie learned when to hold and when to fold. And again that deep, hearty laugh erupted as he recalled being "skint" by the "vicious Patricias" – Canadian officers, who would have been eminently at home at the tables in Binion's Casino in Downtown Las Vegas. Fergie was a young Lieutenant of 25 then. He would rise to the rank of Captain.

He expressed no regret whatsoever at going in at the deep end into the shark-infested waters that the Canadians created. He found himself in shark-infested waters again, in the poker-sense, when he came back as an invalid to London after his left leg had been blown off; he had seen service for just six months in the killing fields. "Going up hill, one of the four soldiers I was with tripped the wire of a landmine and set off the blast. I was the only one badly injured" he recalled. He never did get to cross the 38th parallel.

He spent six months playing poker at Crockfords Club as he was waiting first for a new leg and then having it fitted. The "sharks" at Crockfords comprised ladies of ample girth and even more ample means, who passed away the afternoons ready to pounce on any innocent abroad who was willing to part easily with his or her money.

"You had a £5 game, a £25 game and a £100 game", he told me. "I didn't even contemplate the £100 game as I knew I would be devoured. I was able to hold my own in the £25 'school' after the way I had been toughened by the Canadians. But, I'm afraid I was still not tough enough for some of those bejewelled ladies who could eat you without salt".

He emerged from Crockfords leaner of purse but a still more hardened poker player and like 'The Kid' he was ready now to face 'The Man' – wherever 'The Man' was willing to throw down the gauntlet to him.

He had seen many of his comrades die in Korea."A lot of Irish serving with the British units gave their lives in that War as they had done in the First World War and in the Second World War and, indeed, right back two hundred years to the Crimean War.

"I was lucky myself not to be blown to bits. I counted myself very, very fortunate to come back home, even though it was minus one leg".

Fergie Sutherland returned to his Regiment and found himself in the thick of things again during the Suez crisis. But a bout of malaria ended his involvement and he was then assigned to Catterick, training recruits there. By now he had risen to the rank of Captain. He has a lot of memories of those times but here we are concerned with the graph of Fate that led him eventually to training in Killinardrish.

He had been coming to Ireland long before he decided to settle in Cork in the Sixties. In some ways it was a home-from-home for him. He had been coming over from the early Fifties, in fact.

"I came over to hunt. I must have hunted with every leading Hunt in Ireland. I was buying horses on these trips and, while some were for my own use back in England, where I was hunting five days a week, I was also selling on. "I got to know many Irish people in the hunting and racing spheres and made many friends.

Nowadays he doesn't hunt anymore. He had still hunted after returning from the Korean War. Amazingly, the loss of his left leg didn't lessen his horsemanship all that much. "I was lucky I knew how to ride before I went to Korea. All I had to do when I came home was to adapt to the fact that I had now just one leg. I got along fine".

The area in County Cork where he decided to settle was great hunting country. He could hunt with the Duhallows, with the Muskerry and the Aghabullogues, and as each had a different day, he had ample opportunities to indulge the great passion of his life.

In fact, it was while they were both hunting that he met his future wife, Ann Dorgan, who was employed with noted breeder George Williams in Inniscarra. Ann herself, they will tell you locally, could ride very well to hounds.

Fergie had passed his 59th birthday when he was finally forced to call it a day. "The knee in my good leg began to give me a lot of trouble and it was too much to go out anymore".

He said it with a sense of regret but I could not but reflect on the wonderful times he must have enjoyed.

*　　*　　*

Quality meant everything to Fergie Sutherland. Quality when it came to buying a hunter. Quality when it came later to 'making a chaser'. And quality when it came to deciding the kind of training life he wanted.

Really, he had no time for handling a big string of horses, especially when one's livelihood and one's very future depended on the landing of gambles in an era when, as he put it to me across the dinner-table, "we were racing for £300 and a sack of spuds".

"I have always been rather choosy", he said. "I am still a bit choosy".

It would lead him inevitably, as we have seen, to rejecting the life of a Flat trainer in Newmarket to become a trainer of point-to-pointers and National Hunt horses from his base in Killinardrish. It would see him saying goodbye to Royal Ascot and all that. Ask him today if he is ever tempted to attend the Royal Ascot meeting and he replies simply: "I've been there in my time. I've turned out a winner there. I know the scene. There's no need to return".

He had, amazingly enough, only been to Cheltenham twice before he returned in 1996. He was there in 1953 when Tim Molony rode the Vincent O'Brien-trained Knock Hard to victory in the Gold Cup and he was there in 1967 when Terry Biddlecombe won the race on Woodland Venture for the

Fred Rimell stable.

And, almost thirty years on from that second visit, when he found he had to go to supervise Imperial Call's bid for the Gold Cup, he did not attend the races on any day but the Thursday. He looked at the racing on television on the other two days. "I'm a horseman, not a racegoer", is how he puts it. In fact, going racing as such doesn't attract him at all, neither does gambling on horses as a recreation – or a business.

One of his memories of Gold Cup Day '96 will be the battle he had to get up on the Owners and Trainers Stand to view the race. "It was bloody awful. I nearly had to get a bit physical to fight my way up to get a perch," he confessed. "I managed to see most of it on the big screen and when Conor (O'Dwyer)took it up and was in command coming down the hill, I knew it was all over bar a fall. It was a wonderful moment, especially as everything had gone exactly according to plan".

Arthur Moore, thinking back no doubt to when his own father, the late Dan Moore, turned out L'Escargot to win a second successive Gold Cup exactly twenty-five years beforehand in the hands of Tommy Carberry, was one of the first to congratulate Fergie Sutherland as Imperial Call passed the winning post. Fergie was literally mobbed by other well-wishers before he made his way down to the winner's enclosure.

✻   ✻   ✻

Hardly any of those who surrounded him now to slap his back or shake his hand in congratulation knew of the fear that had haunted him – and Ann also – in the count-down to the Big Day. And it could never have crossed the minds of the hordes of Irish enthusiasts who invaded the inner enclosure to give Imperial Call and Conor O'Dwyer the kind of welcome that was a throw-back to that accorded Dawn Run and Jonjo O'Neill a decade earlier.

The nightmare began for Fergie and Ann when a message was received from the Turf Club that Lisselan Prince had tested positive after winning the Red Mills Trial Chase at Gowran Park on February 17th, '96 – the meeting at which Danoli had thrilled a record crowd in winning the Red Mills Trial Hurdle by eight lengths from Tiananmen Square.

Fergie's mind immediately went back to 1980 when Tied Cottage, after winning the Gold Cup in brilliant style for the Dan Moore-Tommy Carberry combination, was disqualified on technical grounds and the same year the Mick O'Toole-trained Chinrullah, who had pulverised the opposition when winning the Queen Mother Champion Chase in the hands of Dessie Hughes, was also disqualified on technical grounds. In both instances the prohibited substance had been unwittingly administered in the horse's feed – and it was established that none of the connections was responsible. Furthermore, analysis revealed that in each case the quantity of the forbidden substance found was so minute that it could not possibly have affected the running of either horse.

The prohibited substance had somehow got into a container carrying the

52

feed but that was little consolation to the owners, trainers and jockeys who had put so much into winning prestigious races for Ireland and won them on merit. Now the record books would show them as having finished first past the post – but to have had the prizes taken from them subsequently. The photographs, recording for posterity the moment of the presentation of the winning trophies, would attain a hollow ring and there was the galling experience of sending back the Cups after they had been brought home in triumph.

No blame whatsoever was apportioned to Fergie Sutherland when eventually *The Calendar* reported the findings of the Turf Club's I.N.H.S. Committee enquiry into the Analysts' Report. No fine was imposed either on the trainer. The Committee found that a "prohibited substance" was present in the samples contrary to Rule 21 (iii). Consequently, they disqualified Lisselan Prince from first place and ordered the records to be amended accordingly.

But well in advance of the Committee taking that decision and, indeed, once he got word that the sample taken from Lisselan Prince had tested positive, Fergie Sutherland set about checking everything that Imperial Call was getting to ensure that the same disaster would not befall him that had befallen Tied Cottage and Chinrullah sixteen years earlier – and now Lisselan Prince as well.

Would he change the horse's feed now that the count-down had already begun to Gold Cup Day?

He knew the responsibility rested squarely on his shoulders. "The Irish people – indeed, the entire nation – will come after me if Imperial Call finishes first past the post and is then disqualified", was the thought racing through his mind again and again.

It was too awful to contemplate a scenario of the Cup crossing the Irish Sea for the first time in ten years and then having to be sent back.

"You cannot imagine what it was like for both of us", said Ann. "Already we had all the pressure from the phone ringing constantly with calls from the media. Everyone had to be facilitated because Imperial Call had somehow caught the imagination of the people in this country and, of course, people in Britain wanted to know everything also about the horse that was seen as the main obstacle in the path of One Man winning the Gold Cup.

"We had to put on a brave face and pretend nothing. We had to keep to ourselves our deep concern that we might not get things right in time to make it one hundred per cent certain that Imperial Call would not be disqualified. I would never want to go through a time like that again".

Fergie Sutherland was carrying an imaginary gun like Clint Eastwood in *The Unforgiven* – and he let it be known in no uncertain terms that he was carrying that gun on behalf of every Irish racing follower. He insisted that the men in the white coats in the laboratories had to work around the clock if necessary to produce the feed that would be shown to be entirely free of anything that might bring disqualification. Every container too would have to be thoroughly checked and cleaned so that there could be no risk whatsoever of any foreign body contaminating the feed.

He knew the buck would stop at his desk should Imperial Call be disqualified – so he was leaving no stone unturned as he rode shot gun into town, so to speak, to get the response that he was now demanding.

The wires hummed. Everyone got the signal he was sending out. It was clear and unequivocal.

Back came the reply that he was awaiting. Back came the guarantee he wanted. He was told that exhaustive tests had shown that he need not worry anymore.

He got similar assurances from every concern that he was dealing with in the case of Imperial Call.

The nightmare days and nights were over. He put away his imaginary gun.

✳   ✳   ✳

The period before Imperial Call set out for Cheltenham was a whirlwind time for Fergie Sutherland. He could never have imagined how great the pressure would be as he sought to satisfy all the needs of the print media and the radio and television networks. It didn't happen suddenly overnight. It built up inexorably from the afternoon that Imperial Call won the Hennessy Cognac Gold Cup at Leopardstown. Literally hundreds of letters of congratulations. Never a day without the postman bringing a batch of them. Some with English postmarks addressed simply to:"Imperial Call, Ireland".

Someone even sent a smoked salmon. And, as Fergie observed to me, he was obviously a man of wit with an artistic turn, for accompanying the salmon was this very clever drawing executed behind a man who was walking along a road past a signpost that had "Cheltenham" written on it and under his arm he carried a Cup.

It was unmistakably Fergie himself and the trophy was clearly the Hennessy Cognac Gold Cup. But what made Fergie laugh heartily now as we got to the cheese-board and the cognacs was that the drawing wasn't a very flattering one of his rear quarters but the guy had obviously studied him at close range.

He turned it over again and again in my presence like Sherlock Holmes – with no Watson to turn to – and expressed himself baffled as to the identity of the sender. "Bloody clever, I've got to admit", he mused aloud. And again that hearty belly-laugh.

Fergie's style had always been to do his own thing away from 'the madding crowd'. Now he found himself pitched right out centre-stage under a glaring spotlight and there seemed to be no end to it.

"We had to get on with putting the finishing touches to Imperial Call's preparation. "But at times there were so many television cameras about the place that I thought I was a bloody entertainer rather than a trainer".

Fortunately, he had built up an outstanding relationship with the two key

THE JOY AND THE GLORY . . . The exultation of victory spills over in The Angler's Rest in Carrigadrohid as Imperial Call passes the winning post in the 1996 Gold Cup and (below) the overwhelming scenes of enthusiasm in the winner's enclosure as the banner with the words 'Imperial Call' is unfurled. (Pictures: *Cork Examiner* and Bernard Parkin.)

Fergie Sutherland is congratulated by fellow Irish trainers, Michael Hourigan and Willie Mullins and (below left) Imperial Call cracks the grey, One Man and (right) clears the last in style ahead of Rough Quest.

Ms Sarah Lane of Lisselan Farms proudly holds the Gold Cup Trophy aloft after Fergie Sutherland, Conor O'Dwyer (both with trophies) and herself had been received by the Queen Mother (left) and (below) Conor O'Dwyer and Imperial Call are acclaimed by joyous Irish racing enthusiasts, many of them waving mini-Tricolours.

SHARING A PRIVATE MOMENT . . . Conor O'Dwyer and partner, Audrey on Gold Cup Day '96 and (below) the Hennessy Cognac Gold Cup victory at Leopardstown that proved that Imperial Call had the class to win the Blue Riband of chasing. (Pictures: Peter Mooney and Caroline Norris.)

The return of 'The People's Champion'

In the shadow of the Blackstairs Mountains Tom Foley is pictured with Danoli in the countdown to Cheltenham '96 and (below) horse and trainer at Dublin Airport before departure for the Festival meeting. (Pictures: Tom Honan and Caroline Norris.)

Tom Foley greets Danoli and Tom Treacy after 'the people's champion' had finished third in the AIG Europe Champion Hurdle on his reappearance at Leopardstown and (below) thousands acclaim Danoli after his triumph in the Red Mills Trial Hurdle at Gowran Park.

Charlie Swan gives an Olympic-style victory leap from Life Of A Lord after winning the 1996 Digital Galway Plate. Below Anne Marie and Aidan O'Brien have reason to rejoice after the gelding's brilliant victory the previous year and (inset top) Aidan O'Brien with Charlie Swan following Urubande's success in the 1996 Sun Alliance Novices' Hurdle. (Pictures: Caroline Norris.)

Richard Hughes (son of Dessie Hughes) with a delighted Mike Channon (above) after another big stable success and (right top) being led in after winning the Jersey Stakes on Sergeyev at Royal Ascot '95 and (left) Paul Carberry (son of Tommy Carberry), now one of the most gifted National Hunt riders in Britain, pictured after winning the 1996 Tote Gold Trophy Handicap Hurdle at Newbury on Squire Silk for owner Robert Ogden, who brought him to England on a three-year contract. (Pictures: Ed Byrne and Bernard Parkin.)

men associated with the stable, Billy O'Connell and Denis ('Dinny')Daly. Billy O'Connell worked part-time and could be described as the Travelling Head Man. He carried the responsibility of ensuring that Imperial Call got safely to Cheltenham and back again and that there was no question of his being 'got at' while quartered there. Fergie trusted him completely.

Dinny Daly was the work-rider who put Imperial Call through his paces on the gallops and who established a rapport with the gelding that was uncanny.

Again the trainer had immense faith in him.

*   *   *

Billy and Dinny were both proud men at Cheltenham on Gold Cup Day '96. They saw the fulfillment of a dream. And they had reason to be satisfied that their total dedication and commitment had paid off in a historic triumph in the Blue Riband of chasing.

Now after dinner Fergie Sutherland brings me out in his Land Rover up the uphill gallop on which Imperial Call's stamina had been developed to the point that there was no fear whatsoever that he would fail to get the Gold Cup distance. I realised now why, after Imperial Call had won the McCain Handicap Chase over 2m 2f at Leopardstown in mid-January, Fergie immediately proclaimed to the world that the gelding would be seen to far greater effect when he raced at three miles and further.

He stands there at the top of the hill like an Army commander, indicating with his arm to me the mountains all around. Over beyond Mushera Mor and Mushera Beag and Nad mountain and Mullaghanish with the TV mast. We are looking north to Mallow and south to Bandon and Skibbereen and to the left is Derrynasaggart and in the glow of the setting sun, he points to the county bounds between Cork and Kerry.

He has climbed all those mountains he tells me with a a sense of pride; and also the Macgillycuddy's Reeks and has stood at the top of Carrauntoohil.

Such a man, I felt, was capable of conquering any peak in racing that he set his mind on conquering.

Now he heads the Land Rover down towards the field in which I can see Imperial Call with his pony pal, Trigger, known affectionately as "The White Fellow". The King of Killinardrish is out on grass for a well-earned summer holiday.

He stops the Land Rover and we both get out. Leaning against the fence, I look across the wide expanse of the field to where the Gold Cup winner of '96 can be seen over in a corner. Suddenly his ears prick and Trigger and himself come galloping across towards us. I only wished I had a camera and had the ability to capture and freeze the moment with the skill of an experienced professional.

Imperial Call offers his head to Fergie Sutherland who takes it in his hands and talks softly to him about having no "goodies" now but he will have them in the morning. Fergie pats him on the forehead, remarking: 'That's my boy'. There's no mistaking his pride in the horse that had become the idol of a nation.

Now the setting sun has given way to a sickle new moon. Fergie instructs me that if I have a pound coin (Irish) in my pocket to take it out, place it in the palm of my hand and turn it towards the moon. I comply.

He is back momentarily in Peebles in Scotland, learning as a child of an ancient Scottish belief that if you turn a coin towards the new moon, it will bring you luck and prosperity in the period immediately ahead.

Somehow, as I looked at the sickle moon and Imperial Call galloping back to his favoured corner, I found myself making a silent wish that Gold Cup Day '97 would give us another day to remember like that which we had experienced in '96. I put the coin back in my pocket.

Now Fergie Sutherland heads the Land Rover down another hill towards the stretch of the River Lee which attracts English coarse fisherman like a magnet and they find here in the long days something that keeps calling them back. Fergie breaks into a verse of *The Banks of My Own Lovely Lee* and I am happy to join him in the chorus.

I knew I would not have been enjoying the experience of this evening but for Imperial Call. He would always now hold a special place in my heart as Danoli did after my visits to Tom Foley's stables in Aughabeg. You touch the very pulse of what National Hunt racing means in a country like Ireland when you get close to the men who have taken on the challenge of conquering Cheltenham come Festival time – as they might face up the sheer rock face of an intimidating mountain – and succeed in that challenge.

I say farewell to Aghinagh House and to Fergie and Ann's pet dogs. Now Fergie obliges by bringing me in to Carrigadrohid where he joins me over a relaxed drink and I will relive with the locals the memorable parties that followed the Hennessy Cognac Gold Cup triumph and the Gold Cup victory itself. Fergie isn't staying late this evening as Ann and himself are off to Wexford early next morning.

First there had been a great exodus from all the area around Carrigadrohid, from Clonakility and Ballinascarthy, indeed from every town, village and hamlet in the county to Cheltenham. They had stepped in to back Imperial Call at 33/1 with the bookmakers in Macroom and Ballincollig before the general body of punters woke up to the fact that the seven-year-old was a real live prospect to win the Gold Cup. These ante-post dockets were like gilt-edged shares once Imperial Call had repelled the challenges of Master Oats and Monsieur Le Cure in the "Hennessy".

Diarmuid O'Flynn of *The Examiner* accompanied a group that made their base at the Marriott in the Bristol. The Hotel management provided a warm-up act – The Boat band, a local folk group from Bristol with a strong Irish influence in their music – on the eve of the start of Festival meeting. By the time they left the stage at 1 a.m. they had set the scene and the mood for the memorable sing-song that followed.

It was inevitable, of course, that there would be a rendering of the song beloved by Corkonians on sporting occasions which I had heard sung in a pub in Liberty Square in Thurles on the day in 1984 when Cork won the Centenary All-Ireland Hurling Final:

And when the war is over
what will the slackers do?
They'll be all around the soldiers
for the loan of a bob or two

And when the war is over
what will the soldiers do?
They'll be walking around with a leg and a half
and the slackers will have two.

In that party in Bristol that saw night give way to dawn, they sang another evocative Cork number about Kildorrery Town which Diarmuid O'Flynn noted was written by a Ballyhea man by the name of Sheedy.

The Bristol sing-song was replicated in other gatherings and already it was building up for the 'the mother of all parties' that would explode back in Carrigadrohid in The Angler's Rest when Imperial Call passed the winning post.

Their stamina had already been tested to the limit in the celebrations that followed the victory at Leopardstown on Sunday, February 11th. "The Hennessy nearly killed us with excitement. I don't know what this one will do to us. It'll be a week of festivities at least", said Georgia O'Sullivan to Ailin Quinlan of *The Examiner* when she arrived in The Angler's Rest to report on the aftermath of the Cheltenham Gold Cup victory.

Tony and Claire O'Callaghan, the owners of The Angler's Rest hardly had time to recover from the 'Hennessy' celebrations when they were almost overwhelmed by what followed the Gold Cup success.

Pat Barry Murphy, Joe O'Sullivan, Johnny Healy and Paddy Ring recalled the bonfires outside the pub as people awaited the return of Fergie Sutherland and Imperial Call.

The Saturday night was the big night when Fergie and Ann and the stable lads were feted and the Gold Cup was filled and passed around...and a man with a guitar played Country and Western...and Fergie stepped out for an impromptu dance...and then he took the microphone and sang first *The Derry Air* and brought the house down with his rendering of the number made so popular by Harry Lauder, *Roamin' In The Gloamin'*.

They played the video of the Gold cup. The rafters rang with the cheering as Conor O'Dwyer came down the hill and turned for home and after passing the post, raised a clenched fist to the heavens in the joy of victory.

It was good to be alive and in Carrigadrohid on this night, if you had the good fortune to be part of the victory celebrations.

The cheering crowds lining the parade route in Macroom for the 1996 St. Patricks Day parade were at one in echoing their acclaim for Fergie Sutherland..

It was Fergie's day...and he took it all with the same aplomb as he did when entering the Royal Box at Cheltenham to be greeted, and congratulated, by the Queen Mother.

He had come a long way from Peebles in Scotland...from the blast of landmine in Korea to the acceptance he now enjoyed among his own community in Cork.

57

6

The Amazing Comeback of 'The People's Champion'

The romance was in the return. What matter in the end if he failed to win the Smurfit Champion Hurdle. The very fact that he was there at Cheltenham '96 being cheered all the way into the parade ring and cheered again as he finished a creditable fourth on going that was all against him was something of a miracle in itself. You had only to consider that when he suffered that cruel fracture in winning the Martell Aintree Hurdle for the second successive year on Grand National Day '95 – April 8 to be exact – he could so easily have been put down.

It did not seem possible then that he would be back racing inside a year. We could never have visualised the hero's welcome he would receive on the day of his initial comeback race at Leopardstown on Sunday, January 21, 1996 when he very nearly made it a fairy-tale return as he came within a head and half-a-length of Collier Bay in finishing third in the AIG Europe Champion hurdle.

One could have been forgiven for thinking he had won instead of being placed, the way the massive attendance cheered him all the way back into the enclosure.

"I must admit I couldn't hold back the tears of joy at that moment. It was overwhelming, something I will cherish for the rest of my life", said Tom Foley.

Normally the media representatives would head for the winning trainer. But on this day Jim Old found himself completely ignored as the Irish and English racing writers crowded around Tom Foley, who had the spotlight totally on him.

"I know the connections of Collier Bay couldn't understand the way they were ignored. But I know that Irish racing enthusiasts are among the best sportsmen in the world. It wasn't a question of sour grapes because Danoli had been beaten by an English challenger", explained Tom Foley.

"Far from it. It was simply that everyone at Leopardstown that afternoon – man, woman and child – could not hold back a great sense of relief that Danoli had emerged from his comeback race unscathed and, not alone that, but had come quite close to lifting the prize".

✳   ✳   ✳

Leopardstown was special. But it was dwarfed by what followed at Gowran Park on Saturday, February 17 – the day of the Red Mills Trial Hurdle.

A record crowd of 10,000 and more – with spectators literally hanging out of the trees – turned out to give another hero's welcome to Danoli. Cars abandoned all along the road as I arrived at the track. People not prepared to risk missing out on a moment they knew they would be recalling for their grand-children in years to come.

The sense of anticipation reserved for great champions of the boxing world – like Muhammad Ali as he entered the ring at 'The Garden' in New York for that epic bruising world title fight against Joe Frazier – was accorded Danoli as he was led into the parade ring. The applause from those standing ten-deep around the perimeter of the ring was spontaneous and prolonged.

As Danoli trounced Tiananmen Square by eight lengths, turning the race into a mere formality, the cheers echoed out beyond this lovely racecourse to Cleeve Hill and the Cotswolds – sending a message to the connections of the reigning champion, Alderbrook that Danoli, the pride of Ireland, was ready to throw down the gauntlet at the Festival meeting less than a month away. Foley led him back into the winner's enclosure to an overwhelming emotional roar. Again the trainer, unspoilt by fame and adulation, was mobbed by back-slapping well-wishers. Again he was the centre of attraction for the media, being interviewed first by the Man from BBC Radio. He had come to take it all in his stride.

Another day, another time the chief racing writer of the *Sunday Times* would not have been found at Gowran Park on a Saturday afternoon. He might well have opted for Newcastle where the Eider Chase was being run. But John Karter was there and reported that Danoli received "the kind of reception not heard since the days of Arkle", adding rather colourfully (for the *Sunday Times!*) that if "the people's champion" had been beaten, "they might have declared a day of national mourning".

What the Red Mills Trial Stake proved to us was Danoli's well-being, that such had been his recovery that we did not have to fear now that the doubtful leg would give way under race pressure.

His two comeback races had gripped the imagination of the racing public in Ireland and Britain in an amazing way. Every small punter in Ireland was aware that Danoli was returning to the scene of his memorable '94 triumph. He would carry their modest bets on the day.

The professionals, however, who do not deal in sentiment but must live and survive by their judgement, doubted if after all he was a true two-mile hurdler able to win a Champion hurdle. The bookies were willing to lay him. Alderbrook was the horse that the big English bookies prayed would be beaten, not Danoli. Money speaks all languages in the end.

An Alderbrook-Danoli double, if it had come off, would have meant a massive pay-out day. Had Danoli obliged along with Imperial Call, it would not have sent shivers down the collective spines of Ladbrokes, Corals and Hills. That was the reality.

Young Tom Treacy did everything required of him in winning on Danoli at Gowran Park, as was the case at Leopardstown. Granted, there were those who wondered why Tom Foley had now decided that he would have the mount at Cheltenham instead of engaging a big-name jockey.

"The way I approached it", Foley told me, "was that if I had given the ride to one of the top Irish or English riders at Leopardstown, he would have to stay with Danoli for his remaining races – including the Champion Hurdle. I couldn't get that commitment before Danoli ran at Leopardstown. So once Tom Treacy got the ride, I decided to keep faith with him".

Tom Treacy was recognised by National Hunt followers in Ireland as one of the better of the younger brigade, a rising star who in the count-down to Cheltenham '96 was lying fifth in the Jump Jockeys' Championship table. His partnership with Danoli was made possible by Charlie Swan's decision to stick with Hotel Minella, who in the AIG Europe Champion Hurdle had been beaten only a head by Collier Bay. But he had been associated with Danoli in the gelding's novice season.

It seemed natural that Tom Treacy should become linked with the Paddy Mullins stable. His father, Jim worked for the Goresbridge, County Kilkenny trainer for ten years and travelled to Cheltenham with Counsel Cottage, winner of the 1977 Sun Alliance Hurdle. Counsel Cottage was ridden to victory by Jim's brother, Sean, who is today quite a successful trainer.

Jim Treacy had graduated from the bar and grocery trade, in which he was employed, to becoming Head Man in time to Paddy Mullins. The Hinge of Fate led to his partnership with Tom Foley and Danoli. Tom Foley was ill in hospital at one stage and Jim and his brother Martin and young Tom would go to the Aughabeg yard from Borris in County Carlow to ride out the horses. That led inevitably to Foley asking Jim Treacy if he would call on all the experience he had gained at Paddy Mullins' to accompany Danoli to Cheltenham for the 1994 Sun Alliance Hurdle. He was no easy horse to handle. And Treacy admitted in an interview with Tony O'Hehir of the *Racing Post* that his biggest task was "to keep Danoli calm".

After Cheltenham '94 Jim Treacy went everywhere with Danoli. He was proud that Tom Foley had the confidence in his son to keep faith with him for the Champion Hurdle after his successes at Leopardstown and Gowran Park.

His mind went back to the time when young Tom wanted nothing else in life only to be with horses. He started to go hunting with the late Dinny Cordell when he was training. "Horses were like a drug to Tom and he was hooked on them", said his father.

"When Dinny closed down and went back to the music business, he arranged for Tom to go to Paddy Mullins. They hit if off immediately and Tom has blossomed ever since".

He rode Notcomplainingbut in the 1995 Daily Express Triumph Hurdle (it finished 14th) and on Champion Hurdle Day '96 had the rather galling experience of being unseated at the first on Beakstown when he blundered his chance away in the Supreme Novices Hurdle.

*   *   *

The build-up to the '96 Smurfit Champion Hurdle was phenomenal. Columns were devoted in Irish and English papers to Danoli and the trade papers, the *Racing Post* and *Sporting Life* led the field in overlooking nothing right down to the fact that Fr Ned Dowling would be blessing Danoli before he departed for the Festival meeting.

Tom Foley's phone never stopped ringing. His face had become one of the most familiar of all as he stood for photographs with Danoli to supplement a plethora of feature articles.

There was one magnificent black-and-white print by Tom Honan of Tom leading Danoli in the shadow of the Blackstairs Mountain to back up an outstanding article by Graham Rock of *The Observer*.

And there was a smiling Tom Foley, holding Danoli, looking out at readers of the *Sunday Telegraph* in full colour over a six-column article by Brough Scott. Connie Clinton, Sports Editor of the Irish edition of *The Star* asked me over lunch to write *The Danoli Story* and I produced it in three parts before I took the plane to Birmingham on the Sunday. It was a labour of love.

Yes, the romance was in the return. In every little nuance of the story including the fact that Danoli would wear a St. Benedict's medal on his bridle as he went into battle in the Champion Hurdle.

"I see it as my lucky omen as he wore it when storming to victory in the Red Mills Trial Hurdle", said Tom Foley, who recounted to me how the medal was sent to him by a lady in Cork.

"She originally intended to bring it herself to the stables in Aughabeg and pin it on Danoli's bridle. But she got sick and then posted it on. In fact, she sent me two medals. The second we put on Danoli's covering sheet".

Tom Foley saw the sending of the medals to him from Cork as yet another indicator of the immense affection in every part of Ireland for Danoli.

Those feelings were born – and cemented – back in 1994 before Danoli and Tom Foley headed for the first time for Cheltenham. To appreciate fully the emotional outpourings of '96 it was necessary to recall how Danoli arrived on the scene and how the Irish and English public came to know Tom Foley, the "smallest of the small men" and the owner of the horse, the bonesetter, Dan O'Neill, living a stone's throw from Aughabeg in Myshall.

*   *   *

In two short years Danoli changed the life of Tom Foley. From being a traditional farmer, he has developed to the point where today he has 24 horses in training in his Aughabeg, County Carlow stables.

He is particularly proud of the fact that his owners come from all parts of Ireland – North and South in particular.

"Yes, it all came about through Danoli", said unassuming Tom, as he brought me round the spacious line of new boxes that have been built since the start of the 1995-'96 jump season.

Tom Foley recalls days when he almost despaired of making a living. He was into cattle mainly. "You get fed up scratching round and making no money", he said.

He has transformed himself now to pursue the life of a full-time trainer.

His wife, Goretti, from Aughabeg, and three girls, Sharon (20), Adrienne (18), Goretti ("we call her 'little Goretti'"), who is 13, and one boy, Pat, who is 11, are happy that being with horses all the time is their father's life. And they see to it that he is not lacking in help from his family just outside Bagenalstown.

When seeking directions to the stable, you ask at the Lord Bagenal Inn, a great haunt of racing folk before and after Gowran Park races.

Tom's is a fairytale story, one of the great romantic stories of modern-day racing.

Back in 1986, Foley diversified into training and had his first winner at Tramore on a January day. But no-one really took any notice when Rua Batric won the opening race on the card.

Tom Foley and Dan O'Neill had been friends a long time before Dan asked Tom to buy a horse for him.

Foley found that he had to utilise O'Neill's magic as a bonesetter, not on his own limbs, but on a mare of his called Motility.

Dan O'Neill was legendary as a bonesetter.

O'Neill's wife, Olive, anxious that her card-playing husband should get out and about more often, suggested racing as a suitable outlet. In Ireland the bonesetter holds a proud position and if he is good, his position is more privileged in its own peculiarly "specialist" field than that of any Harley Street specialist. As the man said "if you put it out, he will click it back in again".

So it's not surprising that Olive O'Neill should have wanted her husband to seek another form of relaxation in addition to the camaraderie of the cards in a rural setting.

Dan responded to her suggestion that he get involved in owing a horse. He turned to Tom Foley. At first Tom was rather sceptical because he had known people to say to him that they would like to see him training a horse for them – but when it came to going to the sales to buy one, nothing happened.

But Dan O'Neill pressed Tom Foley again some twelve months after the initial sounding on the subject. "Now I realised he was serious", said Tom.

No figure was mentioned. Tom Foley would just have to decide how far he was going to go.

"We went to Goffs the week of the Derby Sales in 1991 to buy a well-bred filly. The reason I had a filly in mind was that if she broke down, then at least we would have a brood mare. I marked out eight or nine in the catalogue that I felt might fill the bill – if the price was right. There was nothing that attracted me, so Dan and myself wandered round the boxes.

"Danoli stuck his head out of this box and there was something about that intelligent head of his that immediately caught my eye. I kept saying to myself: 'I like that horse'. When I returned, as often as not I found him asleep. That indicated to me that he was a very relaxed type and there would be no bother in getting him to settle."

The irony of it was Danoli was one of the horses that failed to qualify for the Derby Sale itself. He went through the ring in the pre-Derby Sale and failed to reach his reserve of IR£10,000 gns. In fact, he was only making IR£5,800 gns.

Outside the ring Tom Foley offered IR£7,000. Willie Austin, the gelding's disappointed breeder, held out for his price.

Foley pressed him hard. "Listen, Willie, the Derby Sale starts in two days time. I can go there and buy what I want and get if for seven. You have 48 hours to think about it."

Two days later the phone rang in Tom Foley's. It was Willie Austin on the line. He would take the seven grand.

✳   ✳   ✳

When Danoli won the Sun Alliance Novices' Hurdle at Cheltenham '94, creating scenes not seen since Dawn Run's triumph in the 1986 Gold Cup, it marked the culmination of a long haul by Tom Foley from the day in 1992 – October 31 to be exact – when the gelding by The Parson made a winning debut in a bumper at Naas.

Danoli went on to win a winners' bumper at Naas on January 30, 1993. He then completed a hat-trick of bumper wins when he disposed of previous winner, Diplomatic by no less than nine lengths at Punchestown on Sunday, 21 February 1993, with Hotel Minella, a winner at Limerick on his debut, third.

Wisely, Tom Foley decided not to go for the Festival bumper at Cheltenham when he heard that the going at Prestbury Park was likely to be fast. "I was afraid of jarring him up", he said.

Danoli reappeared at Fairyhouse on Tuesday, November 16, '93 for his hurdling debut. With Charlie Swan in the saddle, he led from start to finish and, jumping well, was not extended to land the odds at 4/6 as he passed the post four and a half lengths in front of Fambo Lad.

He again started at odds-on when scoring at Punchestown on December 27.

There seemed no reason why Danoli should not make it six victories on the trot when he left Aughabeg to contest the 1st Choice Novice Hurdle (2m 2f) at Leopardstown on Monday, December 27, the second day of the four-day Christmas meeting. The Paddy Predergast-trained Winter Belle had won his previous race over hurdles at Naas and Minella Lad and Cockney Lad had also both scored on their previous outings. Still Danoli started 4/5 favourite.

Danoli's normal horsebox broke down on the way. He got quite upset when he realised that he was being put into a different box. It was only after a number of attempts that Danoli finally entered the box. He had worked himself into a lather of sweat. He could finish only third in the Leopardstown race to Winter Belle.

Tom Foley's faith in Danoli remained undimmed. But he felt he had to know how good the horse really was. He took the courageous decision to throw him in at the deep end by going for the A.I.G. Champion Hurdle at Leopardstown on Sunday, January 23, 1994.

In the field was the 1993 Champion Hurdler, the Martin Pipe-trained Granville Again and also Fortune And Fame, ante-post favourite for the '94 Champion Hurdle. Danoli actually led almost to the second-last flight and, though beaten in the end one-and-a-half lengths by Fortune And Fame, it was an amazing performance by a novice.

Danoli returned to Leopardstown on February 13 and pulverised a field that included some of the country's most highly-thought-of novices.

There followed that unforgettable moment when Charlie Swan gave his arm-aloft victory wave to the heavens as he passed the winning post at Cheltenham – and the Irish contingent let rip with an explosion of cheering that made the spine tingle.

Some weeks later Danoli demolished the best in the Martell Aintree Hurdle but it was significant that the distance was 2m 4f – that is half-a-mile longer than the distance of the Champion Hurdle.

✳   ✳   ✳

At the Leopardstown '95 Christmas meeting Danoli gave a cough when he got to the track. Tom Foley found himself under a lot of pressure to run – "a lot of people had come to see him that day and I did not want to disappoint him. Anyway, I let him take his chance and he ran second to Dorans Pride", he recalled.

It was a decision that he would deeply regret and he would learn salutary lessons from it. "You learn from your mistakes", he said later when it was borne home to him forcibly how running Danoli when he was sickening on ground that he hated affected his chance in the Champion Hurdle.

The bottom line was that after that disastrous outing at the Leopardstown Christmas meeting, he didn't have another run before the Champion Hurdle.

Tom Foley would accept later that Danoli was a horse that "always had to have a couple of races" in the count-down to a major challenge. And he accepted also that it definitely had a bearing on the outcome of the Champion Hurdle.

Add the lack of an outing after Leopardstown to the mistake he made at the third last, when he was almost on the deck, and you could perhaps build a case that in other circumstances Danoli might well have triumphed in the

'95 Champion Hurdle. He recovered from his near-fall at the third last that – according to Tom Foley – left him "sore for a week" to finish third, seven lengths behind Alderbrook. But it is my belief that such was the speed Alderbrook showed from the last that he was not going to be beaten and then too one cannot forget that Danoli's victory the previous year in the Sun Alliance Novices Hurdle was over 2m 5f. Was it a fact in the final analysis he was much better at distances *beyond* two miles when it came to meeting top-class opposition at Cheltenham pace?

Danoli put the '95 Champion Hurdle defeat behind him when winning the Martell Aintree Hurdle for the second successive year, holding the 33/1 shot Boro Eight by three-parts-of-a-length in a tremendous finish.. Danoli pulled up lame and was found to have fractured his near-fore fetlock.

It seemed that the music had died forever.

A whole nation hung on tenterhooks as the 90-minutes operation was carried out at Leahurst Veterinary College in Liverpool. Chris Riggs of Liverpool University carried out the operation, pinning the cannon bone above the shattered joint with three metal screws. The people of Ireland – and his thousands of admirers in Britain – breathed a huge sigh of relief when it was confirmed that the operation had proved a success, that Danoli would not have to be put down after all, as was initially feared by many people.

He was back home in Aughabeg in June and spent two months in his box – "as bored as a schoolboy in detention", was how Graham Rock so aptly put it in *The Observer*.

Privately, Chris Riggs believed Danoli had no more than a 20 per cent chance of ever racing again, but the overwhelming optimism of Tom Foley, who never once doubted the matter, kept him going. "I suppose I'm the pessimist and Tom is the ultimate optimist", said Riggs. "He always said Danoli would be back racing again".

That confidence would ultimately be justified.

Foley mapped out a carefully-planned programme that centred around walking on the road and swimming. It went well.

But when I visited the stables early in October for a feature for the *Irish Racing Annual*, Foley, on the basis of expert advice that had come to him, decided not to train Danoli for the 1995-'96 season.

However, following consultation with Chris Riggs, that decision was reversed and Danoli was put back into training.

As we have seen, he reappeared at Leopardstown in January, then won at Gowran Park and from that moment one of the principal topics of conversation among aficionados of National Hunt racing was whether he could win the Smurfit Champion Hurdle, dethroning Alderbrook in the process.

Even his departure from Dublin Airport was news. "Danoli On A Wing And A Prayer" read the heading in the *Racing Post* over the picture of Tom Foley at the head of Danoli – a proud head looking out challengingly at the world as he departed for Cheltenham to try and make the miracle comeback complete.

Tom Foley was leaving nothing to chance. "I am bringing over Danoli's own feed – the nuts he favours – and I am bringing the water he will drink while in Cheltenham", the trainer told me.

"I will stay once again with the lads right beside Danoli's stable at the racecourse. We will be popping in and out of his box quite frequently. That will mean that he won't feel in any way left alone in strange surroundings.

"He is almost human in the way he likes familiar faces around him. He responds immediately to being handed an apple when he is in his box".

Foley admitted to never experiencing anything like the build-up to the '96 Champion Hurdle.

Danoli had his final spin on Jim Bolger's all-weather gallop at Coolcullen on the Saturday morning. "We can't be thankful enough to Jim for his co-operation in ensuring that Danoli is heading for the Festival meeting 100 per cent fit", said Tom Foley.

Danoli had already received the blessing of Fr Ned Dowling of St. Andrew's Church in Bagenalstown, who had followed his fortunes closely from the time the horse first went to Cheltenham in '94. One paper actually had a photo of Fr Dowling wearing Soutane with prayer-book in hand delivering the blessing at the Aughabeg stables. And they even produced a lady psychic who reputedly had dreamt that Foinavon would win the Aintree Grand National at 100/1 in 1967 and was now predicting that the signs were poor for Danoli.

Yes, not one single angle was being missed.

✳   ✳   ✳

When Tom Foley saw the rain falling over Cheltenham on the Monday evening, he knew that the chance of Danoli gaining revenge on Alderbrook had greatly diminished.

"There was nothing we could do about it. We had to go out the next day and give it our best shot. If I had been able to control the weather, I would have looked up at the skies and said: 'Switch off the rain and the sleet'.

"The fact of the matter is that whenever Danoli has been beaten, it has been on tacky ground. He goes best on good ground and whenever I have seen the mark of his shoe, I have known he was running on going that was ideal for him. When he's not happy with the ground, he doesn't jump well".

One of the shrewdest professionals in the business said to me in the count-down to Cheltenham '96 that, in his considered view, Danoli was not a true two-miler, that he was most effective at distances of 2m 4f and beyond. "If I was the owner of Danoli I would go for the Stayers Hurdle. A comeback victory would be a victory whether it was in the Champion or the Stayers", he said.

Tom Foley, however, was insistent that Danoli could beat more than could beat him over two miles. He pointed to the fact that in the '95 Champion Hurdle, Danoli had behind him a number of horses that were considered true two-milers including Fortune And Fame, Montelado, Absalom's Lady, Atours, Destriero and Mole Board while in fifth place was Mysilv, easy winner in a field of 28 of the Triumph Hurdle at the '94 Festival meeting.

Danoli was never going like a winner in the '96 Champion Hurdle. He made a number of minor errors early on and a bad mistake at the third last, the same flight that ruined his chance the previous year.

This time instead of being in the enclosure occupied by the winning trainer and other connections, Tom Foley found himself in a quieter corner – but still he was the centre of attraction for the media as radio men with their microphones and the television camera units moved in and the writers formed a circle around him. He was disappointed, yes, but calm and dignified. You could see that any sadness in defeat was assuaged by the thought that Danoli had survived another testing race – much more testing this time than Gowran Park – without injury. He was happy that Danoli had come again at the finish after that series of errors to take fourth place.

He praised the winner and acknowledged that others were better on the day in the prevailing going.

When I suggested that he might have been wiser to have gone for the Stayers Hurdle, he responded:"The fact is that there were twelve two-milers behind Danoli. I am convinced that he would have been much closer had the ground been in his favour".

He summed up:"I am very grateful to all the people who have stayed faithful to Danoli and who have been able to accept this defeat in true sporting fashion".

Tom Foley was thrilled that Chris Riggs was present to see Danoli run in the Champion. As far as he was concerned the wheel had come full circle. This was English-Irish co-operation of a classic kind that had made it possible for the horse, beloved by all National Hunt racing enthusiasts, to return to racing when at one point it would have been deemed a miracle if he ever saw a racecourse again.

Yes, the romance was in the return.

✳   ✳   ✳

It was the stuff of fiction how Graham Bradley came to be on Collier Bay, the winner of the 1996 Smurfit Champion Hurdle. Amazing as it may seem, he would have been on the hot favourite Alderbrook – if he had not overslept and missed riding the Kim Bailey – trained reigning champion on the gallops. And, more amazing still, he only got the ride on Collier Bay after Jamie Osborne decided that he would ride Mysilv instead. No wonder that Bradley could exclaim: "Fate has given me this win. It's typical of racing and its ups and downs".

You might say that Fate stepped in to smile on him when the previous month he went along to the Foley Lodge at Newbury for what was to turn out to be a memorable evening. "I was attending the birthday party of Dean

Gallagher (a fellow jockey) and left around 1.30 in the morning. I was pretty drunk to be honest. I would have made it for 10 o'clock on the gallops but there was a power cut in my area and the alarm clock didn't go off. I made Southern Electric send me a telegram indicating when the power cut was.

"I woke up at 10.20 and rang Mr Bailey to tell him I'd be there in ten minutes. He told me to go back to bed. It was a nightmare because I felt that Alderbrook was a good thing. I was sure I had missed a Champion Hurdle winner.

"I was lucky again when Jamie (Osborne) chose Mysilv instead of Collier Bay because it looked like being good ground. Then the rain and snow came to change the going in my favour".

Graham Bradley was 35 on the day in '96 when he brought Collier Bay back into the winner's enclosure. Thirteen years earlier he had ridden Bregawn to victory in the Gold Cup. "I was young then and a lot of water has passed under the bridge since", he said.

He had known the wilderness seasons but no one could deny the talent that was there and besides he was extremely popular with his fellow-jockeys.

There had to be unquestioned ability when Michael Dickinson saw fit to put him up as a 22-year-old on Bregawn on that unforgettable day when he had the first five home in the 1983 Gold Cup. It's a great question for a racing quiz – name in correct order the other four who came in behind Bregawn? They were:Captain John (Dave Goulding), Wayward Lad (Jonjo O'Neill), Silver Buck (Robert Earnshaw) and Ashley House (Mr Dermot Browne).

Bregawn ran in the colours of Kerry-born Jim Kennelly, a big, genial "kind of a farmer" from Timahoe, Portlaoise. I found myself in his company with some of his friends outside the Mandarin Bar as they waited to leave in a private plane that would whisk them back to Ireland.

But before they left they first sang *The Rose Of Tralee* with the kind of gusto that made that interlude one of my outstanding memories of the '83 Festival meeting.

Then one of the company broke into a spontaneous Michael O'Hehir-style commentary on Bregawn's win and as the Irish-owned runner came to the last – for the second time that day! – and took it in the style of a champion, an "Irish roar" went up from the gathering that echoed out towards Cleeve Hill and the Cotswolds beyond....

"Up the Kingdom" was the personal cry from Jim Kennelly as he held his gaberdine at a rakish angle over his left shoulder – and led us into the Mandarin Bar for "one for the road" or should I say "one-for-the-flight-home".

Some English racing enthusiasts passing on their way out to the car-parks were wondering what this belated celebration was all about but it's that very spontaneity that makes Cheltenham so different; and two uniformed policemen passing through the now long-empty Mandarin Bar, except for our group, never batted the proverbial eyelid, even when our Jim broke into the rebel song *The Boys of Kilmichael* as the champagne corks popped and dusk descended over the course.

What an evening...

Bregawn, for the record, was bred by Jimmy Fitzgerald in County Waterford and purchased from him by astute Joe Crowley from Piltown, County Kilkenny, later to become Aidan O'Brien's father-in-law. Crowley trained him to win a few point-to-points and a bumper at Punchestown before selling him to Jim Kennelly's brother, Martin who sent him to the Cashel, County Tipperary trainer, Christy Kinane.

When trained by Kinane he finished second in the Holiday Inn Amateur Hurdle at Liverpool in 1981. Later Martin Kennelly passed Bregawn on to his brother, Jim who duly put him into training with Michael Dickinson.

And that's how Graham Bradley came to have his Gold Cup winner thirteen years before riding Collier Bay to victory in the Smurfit Champion Hurdle.

✳   ✳   ✳

It was the stuff of fiction also that when Wiltshire trainer, Jim Old purchased Collier Bay, Kim Bailey was the underbidder.

Collier Bay was in second place all the way behind front-running Mysilv until sweeping past her as they came to the second-last. "As I went past Jamie, he let me have a few expletives when he realised he had chosen the wrong one", said Graham Bradley. He said 'bleep, bleep, bleep'. After the last I didn't look back and I've no idea how much I won by".

In actual fact, he had two-and-a-half lengths to spare over Alderbrook and there were intense debates afterwards on whether Richard Dunwoody had the reigning champion (who lost a shoe in the race) close enough at the critical juncture to deliver a telling challenge.

Kim Bailey would not be drawn into criticising Dunwoody and commented: "It is very hard when you're watching live to see what's happening because your hands are shaking too much. I didn't give Richard any instructions. He watched the video of last year (1995) and is champion jockey. The ground was riding quite tacky but on last year's form, with Mysliv finishing way behind us, he has probably done more than when he won that race".

It is important to place on record what Richard Dunwoody himself had to say: "I wanted to be a bit closer," he stressed, "but horses kept pulling out in front of me coming down the hill and Brad was able to quicken away from me".

The fact of the matter was that Alderbrook beat with more authority this time horses he had beaten the previous year, in particular Danoli, Absalom's Lady and Mysliv. But on the day he met his master in Collier

Bay, who had been totally under-estimated by many good judges. It stemmed from all the hype surrounding the reigning champion after the way he had cruised to a three-and-a-half lengths victory on his seasonal reappearance at Kempton on February 24th.

But, remember, Collier Bay went into the Cheltenham race unbeaten after two outings. On ground with plenty of give in it he had caused a 25/1 upset on his first outing of the season at Sandown in January, beating Atours, Mole Board, Oh So Risky and Absalom's Lady.

Again with the ground in his favour, he rallied well under pressure when beating Hotel Minella by a head in the AIG Europe Champion Hurdle at Leopardstown with 5/4 favourite Montelado fourth and Danoli, as we have already seen, third.

Jamie Osborne was impressed. He said as he departed Leopardstown that, given similar conditions at Cheltenham, Collier Bay would be very hard to beat. When the going looked like coming up fast and there was a distinct question mark over Collier Bay's participation, Osborne opted instead for Mysilv – and little wonder he let fly that string of expletives when he saw Bradley sailing by him on Collier Bay.

Jim Old had no reason this time to complain that he was being ignored. He was immersed in a sea of congratulations as he battled through the crowds to greet Collier Bay and Bradley.

"This has always been the race I have wanted to win above all others", he said. "The Gold Cup is a dream factory, the Grand National a lottery. But with this race I feel that you can buy a horse that can win it".

✳   ✳   ✳

The epilogue to Danoli's career as a hurdler on the highest plane came at Liverpool on Saturday, March 30, '96 – Grand National Day – when he finished third behind the Aidan O'Brien-trained Urubande (Charlie Swan) and Strong Promise in the Martell Aintree Hurdle, beaten a neck and six lengths.

Danoli never looked like completing the fabulous three-timer in this event, though he was staying on from the third last.

Even before Aintree, Tom Foley had announced that Danoli would go chasing in the 1996-'97 National Hunt season.

The prospect was held out that if he took to the bigger obstacles in impressive style he might even challenge for the Gold Cup at Cheltenham '97.

It made headlines naturally – even though all very premature.

One thing was certain, Danoli had created a mystique that would make him a major draw with the public while he avoided injury and was fit enough to race.

There was still another chapter - maybe more -to be written in *The Danoli Story*.

7

Norman's Double Conquest – And Then Cruel Misfortune

C ork-born Norman Williamson was able to accept philosophically the hammer-blows of Fate that prevented him riding at Cheltenham '96 when he reflected back on the breakfast morning negotiating session that resulted in his teaming up with Kim Bailey and being successful on Alderbrook (Smurfit Champion Hurdle) and Master Oats (Tote Gold Cup) at the 1995 Festival meeting.

It was the first time that a trainer-jockey combination had recorded the double since Vincent O'Brien and Aubrey Brabazon won the Champion Hurdle with Hatton's Grace and the Gold Cup with Cottage Rake in 1950 (the same trainer-jockey combination had also scored with the same two horses the previous year).

And Williamson became the first jockey since Fred Winter in 1961 (Eborneezer in the Champion Hurdle and Saffron Tartan in the Gold Cup) to ride the winners of the Champion Hurdle and Gold Cup in the same year.

Williamson was philosophical enough to realise also that he had been exceedingly fortunate in avoiding injury through the 1994-'95 National Hunt season. He finished joint second with Adrian Maguire – both on 130 winners – behind Richard Dunwoody (168) in the British Jockey's Championship. More important still, in the crucial period before Cheltenham '95 everything went right for him. A sharp contrast to the previous year when he missed the Festival meeting after picking up a four-day suspension for careless riding on Cariboo Gold at Doncaster. That meant that he was denied not only a Champion Hurdle winner on Flakey Dove but also the ride on the Sun Alliance victor, Monsieur Le Cure.

Williamson took the prestigious Ritz Club Trophy after emerging leading rider at Cheltenham '95, booting home two other winners in addition to Alderbrook and Master Oats. And two days after his Gold Cup triumph, he landed the Midlands Grand National on Lucky Lane. There was not a cloud in the sky.

But inside a month everything had begun to go wrong and the litany of misfortunes seemed cruel in the extreme, building to the point where he was due to return at Newbury on March 1st, '96 only to injure his shoulder again while schooling and that put him out for the rest of the season.

I saw a lot of Norman Williamson on crutches in late '95 and followed his progress as he discarded them in favour of a stick. He was at Leopardstown on Sunday, February 11th, '96 his shoulder strapped up as he cast a cold professional eye on Master Oats in the Hennessy Cognac Gold Cup. I talked to him at the Punchestown Festival meeting when he had to be content with being a spectator and looking back on the golden 1994-'95 season, he made the significant point that when you are on a roll, when the winners are flowing, your confidence grows with each passing day. Horses run for you and you feel you can do nothing wrong.

Much the same as it was with Nick Faldo at Muirfield in 1992 ("that was the best I felt going into a major, and we give that 10 out of 10") and the way everything he attempted at Augusta on the final day of the '96 Masters seemed to come off and he had his famous victory over Greg Norman. "The pressure comes from trying to make things happen, but if you're not at the peak of your game it is not going to happen. What I'm trying to do is to make sure I'm in the thick of things. If I can do that, the rest tends to take care of itself", he told Derek Lawrenson of the *Sunday Telegraph* in the count-down to the '96 United States Open at Oakland Hills in Detroit.

Norman Williamson didn't have to try to make things happen in that 1994-'95 season. He was on song. And Cheltenham put the seal on confirming him as a rider right at the top of his profession.

✳   ✳   ✳

The chain of events that led Williamson to becoming No. 1 jockey to Kim Bailey started with the retirement of Peter Scudamore. It was inevitable that Richard Dunwoody would take over as stable jockey to Martin Pipe for that was the time when Dunwoody saw the retention of his jockey's crown as all-important. He would suffer for his obsession before the realisation dawned that it was not the be-all and end-all of everything.

Williamson was then on the short list to become No. 1 to Nicky Henderson. "It was between me and Mick Fitzgerald", he told Geoff Lester of the *Sporting Life* in the course of an interview for the 1994-'95 edition of the *Irish Racing Annual*. "I went down one morning and Nicky indicated to me that, while I could ride most of the horses, I would not necessarily ride everything in the yard.

"To me it seemed better to have the one job to which I would be totally committed rather than bits and pieces. I left undecided".

Then followed what might be described as the crucial breakfast summit with Kim Bailey at the Upper Lambourn stables. "He offered me the post of No. 1 and I promptly accepted".

The two struck up an immediate understanding, helped greatly by the fact that Williamson was prepared to ride out every morning and his assessment of the potential of each horse he was on, proved invaluable to the Master of the Old Manor stables.

Williamson finished the 1993-'94 season on 104 winners. Such were the headlines commanded by the gripping duel between Adrian Maguire and Richard Dunwoody for the Jockeys' crown – that went right down to the last day of the season before Dunwoody finally triumphed – that Williamson reaching a total of 104 hardly got the credit at the time that it really merited, especially when you reflect that at the start of the season he had set himself a target of 50.

Then too he lost out on all the publicity he would have enjoyed had he been on Flakey Dove and Monsieur Le Cure. Rather than go off skiing in the Alps as Richard Dunwoody did when he was suspended – duly missing Cheltenham in the process – Williamson decided to attend the Festival meeting. He was convinced that he was not guilty at Doncaster. He watched the racing from the stands over the three days.

"The first person I bumped into on the Tuesday was John Edwards, and when I asked him how Monsieur Le Cure was, he said simply: 'He'll win'.

"It was hard watching on the sidelines as my horses won, but that's racing. Who knows, I might have fallen at the first on Flakey Dove!"

*   *   *

In a way Norman Williamson's rise to the top of the ladder has been phenomenal. It's difficult to imagine now that when he first went to England to join John Edwards he was so home-sick that all he wanted was to get back home. He has reason to thank Edwards for his persistence.

Williamson was still an amateur when Edwards asked him to ride Charter Hardware in the Kim Muir Trophy Chase at the 1989 Cheltenham Festival meeting.

For the majority of those attending the meeting that year, Williamson on the card was just another name on a no-hoper starting at 50/1.

The budding Williamson talent for the big occasion emerged clearly that day. He came at the last fence to collar Team Challenge and looked to have it, only to be run out of it in the battle up the hill by Cool Ground – yes, the very horse that would give Adrian Màguire his first Gold Cup victory over the French challenger, The Fellow in 1992 at odds of 25/1.

John Edwards had seen enough to be very much taken by the ability and determination that Williamson had revealed on Charter Hardware and booked him to ride the same horse in the Scottish Grand National at Ayr. This time the combination again took second place, behind Roll-A-Joint and Brendan Powell.

In the last week of the 1988-'89 season Williamson had his first winner for John Edwards when scoring on Gerami at Cartmel.

During the summer he turned professional and was back in England to win again on Gerami at Newton Abbot on the opening day of the 1989-'90 season. It seemed only a matter of course that Williamson would team up with the Herefordshire trainer but he was finding it very difficult to make up his mind.

It was a horse called Cliffalda that finally did the trick. "John (Edwards) pleaded with me to ride this good staying hurdler on his debut over fences at

Kempton", he recalled. "He started favourite but was beaten by Arctic Call. I've been here since!"

Arctic Call, of course, would win the Hennessy Cognac Gold Cup Chase at Kempton in 1990 and finish second to Topsham Bay in the 1992 Whitbread Gold Cup Chase. Cliffalda had certainly run up against a good one on his chasing debut!

The big break-through for Williamson came in the 1990 Mackeson Gold Cup at Cheltenham in November. Riding the seven-year-old Multum in Parvo for John Edwards, he scored at 12/1 from Thar-an-Bharr and New Halen.

He was on his way.

John Edwards, like David 'The Duke' Nicholson and other English National Hunt trainers, has a great love of Ireland and things Irish and loves a business holiday that is combined with hunting. He looks to Ireland to buy potential champions and he has had no hesitation either in opting for Irish talent in the saddle.

Tom Morgan, whose name will always be linked with Monanore and also with Yahoo, was No. 1. to the Edwards stable until his weight started to get the better of him. Norman Williamson will never forget the debt he owes to Edwards for appointing him stable jockey on the departure of Tom Morgan.

"I was young and relatively inexperienced and he had a powerful team of horses but he didn't think twice about asking me to become his No. 1", Williamson recalled.

Their association lasted four years in all – "we had great times together. He was straight down the line and overall an outstanding Master".

✳   ✳   ✳

Norman Williamson hails from Mallow where his parents still reside today.

He took the route that so many others took – from the pony circuit to the professional's life in the saddle, having first made his mark as an amateur.

He had his first pony when he was nine. The ambition to be a jockey was already forming – as it formed for Conor O'Dwyer, Tommy Carmody and Michael Kinane.

In fact, Williamson found himself riding work with Michael Kinane when he joined the Dermot Weld stable. He spent three-and-a-half years on the Curragh but his eyes were set on being a jump jockey and basically Weld was a Flat trainer, though he did have Greasepaint and Dark Raven at the time and some of his Flat horses were dual performers.

Dermot Weld made the suggestion to Williamson that he transfer to P. P. Hogan and endeavour to make his mark first on the point-to-point circuit. It may seem the ultimate cliché to describe P. P. Hogan as a legend in his own lifetime. But if ever a man WAS he IS.

Williamson smiles today when he recalls his sojourn at the Rathcannon, Kilmallock, County Limerick establishment. It was as brief as it was 'hurtful'...

"I won on my first ride for P. P. on a horse called Give Me A Break and when someone got injured in the next, I was told I was on duty again", he recalled for Geoff Lester.

"Unfortunately, I got a fall and hurt my shoulder and P. P. told me not to bother coming back!".

"Give us a break", he might well have said at that moment but when a man like P. P. makes up his mind, you don't argue.

A hiccup really on his way up the ladder, for the following season he had his first winner under Rules when he rode Jack and Jill to victory in a novice chase at Clonmel. A double at Tramore the following week got him good notices and it didn't go unnoticed on the other side of the Irish Sea. The Hinge of Fate saw him meeting John Edwards at a point-to-point meeting that winter.

∗　　∗　　∗

Stormin' Norman, as he was quickly dubbed by the British media, arrived at Cheltenham '95 knowing that he was riding two horses with the ability to complete the Champion Hurdle-Gold Cup double but the going had to be right for Master Oats if he was to succeed in the Gold Cup. Kim Bailey knew also that unless it came up soft, even heavy, the prospects of Master Oats winning would be greatly diminished. He would have no chance on fast ground.

Later Bailey would say: "Winning the Gold Cup and the Champion Hurdle was very special but I don't believe we will ever again have a situation where everything comes right on the day to repeat the bid. Remember, it was the first year for five years that we had soft ground at Cheltenham". Prophetic?

When he was interviewed by Richard Evans of *The Times* for the 1995-'96 edition of the *Irish Racing Annual*, he couldn't have visualised that Master Oats would be side-lined for the '96 Gold Cup. His hope then was that Master Oats would get the kind of going he revelled in but the uncertainty of racing was shown once again. Even Alderbrook, who had amazed Bailey with the speed he had shown over hurdles in his first proper schooling a week before winning the Kingwell Hurdle at Wincenton on his way to that scintillating success in the '95 Champion Hurdle, failed to catch Collier Bay in the '96 renewal and lost his crown by two-and-a-half lengths.

It was one of THE outstanding training feats of modern times, Kim Bailey winning the Smurfit Champion Hurdle with Alderbrook. While with Julie Cecil, Alderbrook developed into a high-class performer on the Flat and won the Prix Dollar at Longchamp in October '94.

Just eight weeks before the 1995 Champion Hurdle he was transferred to Bailey's yard. It seemed a tall order to bring him to the required level of fitness, and furthermore, put sufficient polish on his jumping to enable him to beat Danoli, Fortune And Fame, Mysilv, Large Action and the rest.

No one really gave him a chance up to that solitary preliminary race at Wincanton. But, after what Kim Bailey saw in the first proper piece of schooling, he realised that Alderbrook was a natural over hurdles and, into the bargain, he had an extra gear.

The 50/1 that was available in the count-down to Wincanton was snapped up by the connections and other lucky insiders. After Wincanton those ante-post vouchers were like gilts.

Under a marvellous ride from Norman Williamson, Alderbrook was produced at the last flight to make the most of his speed and class and, even though Jamie Osborne on Large Action was ahead over the ultimate flight, he was passed with consummate ease up the hill. The margin of five lengths hardly reflected the annihilation of this field by the winner. Danoli was third and Fortune And Fame fourth but, even if Danoli had not made that very bad mistake three out that nearly had him on the floor, I concluded that he would not have been able to counter Alderbrook's finishing burst.

✳   ✳   ✳

Kim Bailey had turned out Mr Frisk to win the Aintree Grand National in 1990, ridden by Marcus Armytage, but it was the fifteen-lengths triumph of Master Oats in the '95 Gold Cup that meant most of all to him – even more than the Champion Hurdle victory two days earlier which had cause him to unashamedly shed tears of emotion.

"With the victory of Master Oats, I had achieved my ultimate ambition", he confessed. "There are two races to win in every jump trainer's career – the Gold Cup and the Grand National. I had won the Grand National luckily enough, but the Gold Cup is definitely the purist's race".

When Master Oats won the Rehearsal Handicap Chase on his seasonal debut at Chepstow on December 3, '94 – the conditions coming just right for him overnight – there were few professionals who would have judged him as a Gold Cup prospect.

Then he went for the Coral Welsh Grand National – "which he turned into a procession", recalled Kim Bailey. "He was cantering the whole way through and it was there and then we decided we had a Gold Cup horse".

But that 20-lengths victory over Earth Summit was achieved on heavy going and the ground was the same when he went to Cheltenham on January 28th and won the Pillar Property Investments Chase by fifteen lengths from Dubacilla with Barton Bank third.

It was obvious now that the Blue Riband of chasing was within his grasp – if it came up soft on Gold Cup Day.

It did. And Master Oats repeated exactly the form with Dubacilla – again the winning margin was fifteen lengths – with Minnehoma a further fifteen lengths back third, the Jim Dreaper-trained seven-year-old Merry Gale, who had set the pace, fading to finish fourth.

Gold Cup Day '95 marked Vincent O'Brien's first visit to Cheltenham in 35 years.

He was the guest of honour for lunch in the Royal Box with his wife Jacqueline. The legendary Irish trainer was seated on the right hand of Princess Anne, who talked to him about the time when he was "King" of the Cheltenham scene back in the late Forties and Fifties.

Later when Vincent O'Brien entered the parade ring, he was immediately surrounded by well-wishers and it was clear that he still stood in the minds of most as the greatest trainer in racing history.

He mentioned to me how much Cheltenham had changed – with its new stands, new Tote area and new winner's enclosure – from the time in 1948 when he sent over Cottage Rake to win the first of three successive Gold Cups and 1949 when Hatton's Grace recorded the first of a three-timer in the Champion Hurdle. In 1959 he won Division One of the Gloucestershire Hurdle with York Fair with T. P. Burns in the saddle. Over a decade he dominated the Cheltenham scene.

Vincent O'Brien must have viewed with a rueful smile the money earned by Kim Bailey for his patrons as he brought off the Champion Hurdle – Gold Cup double. When Vincent achieved the double in 1950, the winning owners received a combined total of £5, 363 – 15s whereas twenty-five years on, with the Smurfit Champion Hurdle worth £103, 690 and the Tote Gold Cup worth £122,540, the corresponding figure was £226,230.

Even taking into account inflation and changed money values, little wonder that Vincent O'Brien said to me when I was researching my biography on him *(Vincent O'Brien – The Master of Ballydoyle)* – "We had to gamble to survive".

And little wonder too that it was inevitable in time that he would cut his ties with National Hunt racing in favour of a total concentration on the Flat. With millionaire owners backing him, he didn't have to gamble anymore.

* * *

One memory that remains from Cheltenham '95 is of Norman Williamson giving the impression that he was walking the high wire as he expressed his delight at winning the Gold Cup on Master Oats – a leap for joy repeated by Frankie Dettori at Longchamp in October after he had ridden Lammtarra to brilliant victory in the Prix de l'Arc de Triomphe (now the authorities have clamped down on this type of exuberance in the moment of singular triumph).

Williamson was pictured with Kim Bailey being congratulated by Dr Michael Smurfit after the presentation of the Champion Hurdle trophies in the winner's enclosure... pictured again with Kim Bailey, both holding high the magnificent Smurfit Champion Hurdle trophy...Williamson again caught giving a victory salute as he acknowledged the acclaim of the crowds after his Gold Cup success and photographed all smiles with the massive Ritz Club Trophy.

Williamson had every reason to entertain high hopes of completing a fabulous treble by adding the Martell Grand National to his Champion Hurdle and Gold Cup successes. Even though the ground was officially "good to firm" Master Oats - the ideal age at 9 and fairly enough treated with 11-10 - started 5/1 favourite, with Dubacilla at 9/1 and Royal Athlete, the eventual winner at 40/1.

"The horse was cantering three from home", recalled Kim Bailey. "He had jumped immaculately the whole way round. Norman (Williamson) said he gave him a better feel that day than in any other race but he didn't quite last home and could not quicken off the fast pace. If it had been a three-and-a-half mile race or softer ground, he would have won".

                    *   *   *

The wheel turned full circle and the *Racing Post*, under the heading "The Ups and Downs of Norman Williamson", carried in the issue of March 2, 1996 a series of graphic pictures of the Cork-born jockey...the main one of him lying on the ground in pain, hand over his face, after a cruel fall...another of him in a hospital but with a brave smile on his face...still another of him walking with the aid of crutches. So he missed Cheltenham '96.

Before the start of the 1996-'97 National season, it was announced that Norman Williamson had decided to go freelance, so his association as No. 1 to the Kim Bailey stable ended. It was an amicable parting of the ways and, naturally, Norman could not forget the breakfast summit that had led him to joining the Upper Lambourn stables and stemming from that the bringing off of the Champion Hurdle-Gold Cup double. He told me at the Galway Festival meeting '96 that he planned to ride quite a deal in Ireland and, having proved himself such a polished horseman, it was clear that he would not be lacking in opportunities on both sides of the Irish Sea.

Norman Williamson hadn't looked death in the face as Limerick-born Declan Murphy did when he lay in the intensive care ward of the Walton Hospital in Liverpool after a May Bank Holiday Monday horror fall from Arcot at Haydock where he sustained a fractured skull and such massive internal head injuries that he had to undergo emergency surgery to remove a blood clot from his brain. He had been kicked on the head and all but killed by a following horse.

First indications were that the operation had not been a success and Murphy was fading fast. Family and friends waiting anxiously outside intensive care.

It seemed that a great talent was to depart the scene at the age of 28. You remembered the way he went into the last on Deep Sensation in the 1993 Queen Mother Champion Chase and in an epic battle up the hill to the winning post getting the better of Peter Scudamore on Cyphrate and later 24,000 cheering race fans had watched his lung-bursting battle with Adrian Maguire in the King George VI Chase at Kempton...the artistic Murphy on Bradbury Star right on Barton Bank's heels as Maguire launched him at the last fence with breath-taking panache...Bradbury Star's doubtful stamina ebbing away in the dying strides but Murphy, acknowledging that he had been outstayed at the death, was truly magnificent that day and you knew that victory would have been his if he had been facing any other jockey but Maguire. An epic between two supreme horsemen.

Tim Richards of the *Racing Post* had gone to Walton Hospital to pay his respects to Declan Murphy, "whose eloquence ran like a rich vein through the jockeys' room". In secret he feared that it might be a fleeting 'good-bye'.

He would write later in a magnificent contribution about the drama of those days in the *Irish Racing Annual* that it was his mind, his strong will and his character that won Declan Murphy through the crisis.

"I always had a belief that I would be okay", he told Tim Richards from his hospital bed as his girl-fiend Jo Park watched anxiously over him. "I naturally have a positive way of looking at things in life. I simply believed that I would get my sight back, I would get my balance back. An inner strength came to life in me".

Jo Park, to whom he became engaged in July '94, had given up her job for three months so she could be on hand every minute to aid Declan's recovery.

"I don't think I am any different from any other," said Declan. "Only inasmuch as I believed I would be all right and in that belief I got incredible support from not only Jo and so many professionals from within racing but also from people who had never even spoken to me. People who had simply heard of my accident and who appreciated what I had done through my riding.

"There was the four-year-old boy from near Nottingham whose mother found him in his bedroom praying for me. That inspired me as did the strength shown by Jo, her family and my family who have also been fantastic the way they have rallied round me during the worst period of my life."

Miss Park has acted as a human shield standing between Declan and the flood of visitors wanting to wish him well. "Jo has been wonderful at working out who I should see because when I first returned home there were times when I felt good and times when I felt bad."

He liked to think that he was a better person for the dreadful experience he had endured. "I have been told that when they were doing the operation on my brain they didn't know whether I would live or if I would end up blind or what.

"When you think back to that, it helps you to cope with anything and almost makes you stop to wonder what life is all about. Now I feel guilty that I used to take so much for granted.

"I realise I am in a privileged position and whatever else I may achieve I'll feel a better person doing it and I shall get more satisfaction from it."

Murphy received over 15,000 letters and cards from well-wishers. "I can now see that people have appreciated me as a jockey.

"It is sad that you go about your business and at the end of the day we all only think about ourselves – until something like this happens.

"I want to climb back into the saddle for all those people."

He did return – a fleeting return. An aberration, you might almost say.

But it was immaterial really when set against his superb riding in the High Noon of his prowess, as in the Queen Mother Champion Chase victory on Deep Sensation and going down to Adrian Maguire in the King George. A glow still remains in the sky.

Declan, the articulate one, is in television today – a key figure on the Racing Channel.

I can understand why Norman Williamson was so philosophical about missing out on Cheltenham '96.

He realises that jump jockeys live on the edge...all the time.

Adrian Maguire realises it also.

8

How Adrian Missed Out Two Years Running

They had been four very special years for Adrian Maguire at the Cheltenham Festival meeting. His achievements from the time he burst on the scene when riding Omerta as a comparative unknown to victory in the Kim Muir chase in 1991 to that epic win on Viking Flagship in the Queen Mother Champion Chase in 1994 contributed largely to the whirlwind surge to the top of the ladder and comparisons with the legendary Martin Molony.

In between he had scored a fantastic triumph on Cool Ground over The Fellow and Adam Kondrat in the 1992 Gold Cup – his first ride in the race – then he went on to win the Cathcart Chase on Second Schedule and the Grand Annual Chase on Space Fair at the '93 Festival meeting. The Triumph Hurdle was won on Mysilv at Cheltenham '94 in addition to the Queen Mother Champion Chase.

Outside of Cheltenham, you could take in the 1993 King George VI Chase success on Barton Bank to supplement the Hennessy Cognac Cup he had won on Sibton Abbey in 1992. Add to these victories the successive Digital Galway Plate wins on The Gooser in 1992 and General Idea in 1993 and you get some idea of the impact he had made on the National Hunt scene before he celebrated his 23rd birthday on April 29, 1994.

Little wonder that he should say to me at David Nicholson's Jackdaws Castle establishment in the Cotswolds on the Monday morning of Cheltenham Festival Week '94, as he mused aloud: "It's all like a dream. Sometimes I almost have to pinch myself and say: 'Can it all have happened so quickly?'".

But then he missed the 1995 and 1996 Festival meetings – the first because of the death of his mother, the second through a string of injuries. "It's a total sickener", was all Adrian could say when it was confirmed that he was out of Cheltenham '96 and the blow became all the more cruel when you considered the host of rides he had at the meeting. "I'm desperately sorry for him", said David Nicholson.

I was about to leave for Dublin Airport to take the flight to Birmingham around lunch-time on Sunday in the count-down to Cheltenham '95 when I got the phone call informing me that Adrian Maguire's mother had died suddenly.

I had come to know Phyllis quiet well when I was researching the chapters on Adrian for my book *Tigers Of The Turf*. Husband Joe and herself had received me very hospitably in the family home in Kilmessan, County Meath. She was a real character in her own right.

Over tea she recalled Adrian when he was no more than four or five sitting on the floor in front of the television set with his young brother, Vinny watching the field approaching Becher's Brook in the Aintree Grand National. Adrian would exclaim: "That will be me, Vinny and that will be you some day", as he pointed his finger towards one of the runners right in contention.

"He never wanted to be anything else in life only a jockey", said Mrs Maguire as she went on to relate how Adrian had this favourite pony named Charlie that he would bring into the house – "and jump down the step into the kitchen right before my eyes. I was supposed to get cross at that but I couldn't, Vinny and himself were having such fun doing it in turns. I just turned a blind eye to it all".

*　　*　　*

At nine Adrian first rode the family's Shetland pony, Cresta by name. He would ride bareback in those days – falling off and getting up on the pony and falling off and repeating the act. An older brother, Michael, a professional jockey for a few years until he got too heavy, instructing him in the garden at the back of the house; he had the patience to spend hours with Adrian, recognising perhaps the immense budding talent waiting to burst forth in full flower some day.

Adrian Maguire loved that little grey pony, Cresta. He graduated to hunting with her. He broke his collarbone twice in falls but, as his father Joe noted – "he came up the hard way; it was all part of the learning process".

Then one day Cresta caught his hind leg in the bull wire when jumping a fence following the hunt. The fall broke the pony's back.

"Adrian came home and went straight to bed. He cried for hours that same evening", said Mrs. Maguire. "In fact, he cried for almost a week he was so upset at the death of the pony."

It was on the pony circuit that Adrian Maguire would reveal initially the immense potential he had and he rode so many winners that he didn't keep an exact count of them all, though he told me he reckoned the total could have reached 250. At one point he joined Alan Sweeney of Moyehill in Milford, County Donegal; he kept ponies as a hobby on his 300-acre farm. Adrian's first ride for him was on a pony called Misty Dawn, one of the best in Ireland in her particular category but very temperamental and, therefore, extremely difficult to handle.

Recalled Alan Sweeney: "The prize for the winning owner was £200. All

Adrian was entitled to get for riding Misty Dawn was £1.50 but I remarked to him just before we reached the start: 'If you win this race for me, you can have half the prizemoney'.

"I didn't back the pony as it was hard to believe that she could win out of her own category. Adrian rode a truly brilliant race in winning by a short head.

"To put that victory in true perspective, you have got to remember that he had been thrown in at the deep end against bigger lads riding bigger ponies and yet such was his control in the saddle that he made light of it all. I knew then that he was something special."

Adrian spent three years in County Donegal during the summer months. He not alone rode the ponies for Alan Sweeney but trained them as well. You could say he was the 'stable jockey'.

"He rode all around the Donegal circuit, at pony races in Rathmullen, Letterkenny, Convoy, Donegal town itself and in Derry", Alan Sweeney recalled.

"He lived in the house with us. My wife Mary was exceptionally fond of him. He almost became one of the family.

"He had a very charming personality, was always well-mannered, though he did not talk a lot and could, I felt, be quick-tempered if roused.

"He would go to discos with my nephews and their friends. In that way he was like any other lad of his age. Where he differed was that he was a natural with horses – a pure natural, uncanny almost.

"I remember the day he rode Glenside for my brother Ronan in the Dingle Derby, biggest annual event of its kind on the southern circuit. Again he emerged the winner. Brilliant he was that day. Absolutely brilliant.

"I paid him a small weekly salary and also gave him £20 a ride. He was doing extremely well by the standards of other riders on the pony circuit."

*   *   *

Mrs Maguire told me how the call of the saddle saw Adrian leave school when he was fifteen and head for England to join the stable of Con Horgan who has Meath connections on his father's side. It was a terrible winter and certainly not one to be remembered by a young lad who was away from home for the first time. He was riding out for Con for about seven months. He was very well looked after but eventually he got home-sick and returned to Kilmessan.

His first big break came when he joined Michael Hourigan's stable at Lisaleen, Patrickswell, County Limerick. Soon he was making a major impact on the point-to-point circuit. He rode six winners for Hourigan one day at Dromahane – "and four for them were never heard of before or after", said Michael with a smile.

The 1990-'91 point-to-point season and his turbo-powered end-of-season blitz at Dromahane put a spotlight on Adrian Maguire's talent that catapulted him on to a new pedestal and created the sequence of events that resulted in his joining the Toby Balding stable. In a way it had elements of the romantic that made it a fairytale story in itself.

In a cliff-hanger finish to the Riders' Championship on the point-to-point circuit Maguire and John Berry dominated the last couple of week-ends. Adrian had ridden 26 winners for his mentor Michael Hourigan and then sealed the title with that incredible six-timer at Dromahane (compared to Berry's Castletown-Geoghegan treble that same day), followed by another half dozen at the two-day Kinsale meeting with Berry only able to reply with two winners.

The final score: Adrian Maguire – 38 winners; John Berry – 34 winners.

It all happened so quickly from that point that he would be able to have his first Cheltenham Festival winner at the age of 19 and followed it up by winning the Jameson Irish Grand National the same season.

How Adrian came to get the ride on Omerta for Martin Pipe in the Fulke Walwyn Kim Muir Challenge Cup at the '91 Festival meeting is an extraordinary story in itself.

Adrian had taken a fall on one of Michael Hourigan's horses – Lisnadee Miss – and spent a number of days in Limerick Regional hospital with a leg injury.

He was back in the Patrickswell stable when the fateful call came that was to change his life overnight. "Paul Hourigan, Michael's son, came looking for me in the yard and told me I was wanted on the phone", Adrian recalled, "It was Homer Scott ringing on behalf of the McMorrows, the owners of Omerta.

"Homer started by saying, would I go to Cheltenham to ride Omerta. I thought at first that he was joking. In fact, I was certain it was a bit of a leg-pull.

"But then I realised that Homer Scott meant it and that they really wanted me to go to the Festival meeting. I dashed from the Hourigans' yard and put a call through to home asking that someone meet me off the train from Limerick."

Phyllis Maguire took up the story: "I had made up my mind to buy Adrian a car. I went into Navan and got a second-hand one from Joe Norris. Adrian's leg was still hurting him after the fall he had taken at the point-to-point meeting. I remember him saying to me: 'I don't care if the leg falls off, I'm going to ride Omerta at Cheltenham'."

After getting a night's sleep at home, he met Jim McMorrow at Dublin Airport next morning and they travelled over together. Adrian had heard a lot, of course, about the Cheltenham Festival meeting. He knew that it was part of Irish racing lore. But, accustomed as he was to riding point-to-point courses, he wasn't prepared for the impact his first sight of the historic Cheltenham racecourse would make on him. He actually stood in awe momentarily as his eyes took in the sweep of the green amphitheatre, the hurdles and fences stretching towards Cleeve Hill in the background, timeless in its beauty, unmatched in the traditions it had created.

Then he walked the course. "I was immediately struck by how much bigger the fences were than the point-to-point fences I had been used to back home".

He had arrived at what was Mecca for jumping aficionados. "There are people in Ireland who will save all the year to be sure they can get to Cheltenham. People who don't have good jobs and have to make sacrifices. When you see the place for yourself you understand why. To a lot of Irish people there is no meeting in the world to compare with the Cheltenham Festival meeting.

"For jump jockeys too it is special. Every jockey wants to win during the three days. It is a very fair track but a testing one. You have every chance to ride a race on this course."

"Nowhere else do you get a roar like you get at Cheltenham. And you don't find those sort of crowds anywhere else."

He heard the roar rise as he started the run for home on Omerta. There had been men who had seen in the racecard the name "Mr. A. Maguire" as the rider of the Martin Pipe-trained contender and it meant nothing to them, if they didn't follow happenings on the point-to-point circuit. To many he was simply an unknown, one of those gangling amateurs plucked out of the backwoods, maybe a guy who would give his right hand to say that he had ridden over the Cheltenham fences, who was willing to take a tumble in the cause of savouring the praise of his friends for his courage in a social gathering that same evening in a hotel in Cheltenham town or out in the Cotswolds.

But shrewder punters, who had spotted the talent – indeed, the blossoming genius – of young Maguire as he booted home a succession of winners for Michael Hourigan and who knew that Homer Scott wouldn't contact a rookie with no ability for the McMorrows and Martin Pipe stepped in and made a "killing".

"It was only when we were heading towards the last fence that I suddenly thought to myself, 'I'm actually going to win'", Adrian recalled.

It had been like a dream, a whirlwind unfolding in the crowded hours of a few days – from the moment the fateful call came from Homer Scott to Adrian Maguire now riding Omerta back into the winner's enclosure.

March 12, 1991 was the day that Adrian Maguire made a winning debut at Cheltenham – on his very first visit to the course. And it didn't end there. He went on to win the Jameson Irish Grand National on Omerta, wearing the colours of Mrs. McMorrow and starting at 6/1 in a field of 22.

Adrian Maguire had come a long way in a very short time from riding his first point-to-point winner – Equinoctial – at Askeaton on 11 February 1990 to his first win under Rules – Gladtogetit – for Michael Hourigan in a bumper at Sligo on 23 April 1990.

* * *

It was Adrian Maguire's great friend and mentor, Tom O'Mahony, a farmer and horse-dealer from Youghal, County Cork, who was instrumental in advising the budding young star from Kilmessan to join the Toby Balding stable at the start of the 1991-'92 National Hunt season as second jockey rather than accept a more lucrative offer from Martin Pipe.

O'Mahony knew what he was doing. Balding, who was christened Gerald Barnard, was born to National Hunt racing, just like "The Duke" Nicholson. O'Mahony was only too well aware that when Vincent O'Brien was training in Churchtown, County Cork, and indeed, later when he was still training jumpers at Ballydoyle, he used always lodge his Cheltenham horses with Toby Balding's father, Gerard, when the later was based at Bishops Canning, not far from Prestbury Park.

Vincent was a great friend of the Balding family. Indeed, when Cottage Rake, winner of three successive Gold Cups (1948-'50), started to decline he spent the evening of his racing days with Balding Snr.

Toby has always enjoyed a close affinity with Ireland and the Irish. He makes no secret of the fact that when he is seeking a potential equine champion, it is in Ireland he does his shopping.

When Adrian Maguire arrived at the multimillion pound 120-box Whitcombe Manor complex in Dorset, where Balding was training at the time – before returning to his old base at Fyfield – he was joining a stable that had built an impressive Cheltenham Festival record and indeed an impressive record overall in key races in the National Hunt sphere.

Balding has no doubt that the best thing that ever happened to Maguire was "coming to Whitcombe".

"Wonder boy", as he was known in the yard, had a great advantage over "stable-mates", Richard Guest and Jimmy Frost in that he was a natural lightweight. And, as Balding noted, he was fortunate in that "he has ridden anything but 'live' horses".

He went on: "Being here at Whitcombe meant that Adrian had no time to get used to the adulation. He would ride out for me in the morning, drive to the races and by the time he got back to the yard he was knackered and would just want to climb into bed. If he were based in Lambourn the likelihood of him falling into bad habits would have been that much greater."

And Tom O'Mahony would say later: "Adrian matured a lot under the eye of Toby, who proved an outstanding asset and a tremendous back-up at all times. Not everyone would let such a young boy ride Cool Ground, would they? And look what that did for Adrian – and Toby, come to that."

*   *   *

His girl-friend Sabrina Winters, (now his wife), to whom he was to become engaged before Cheltenham '94, accompanied Adrian to England and she played a key role also in keeping his feet firmly on the ground at a crucial stage in his career.

Sabrina, who hails from Kanturk, County Cork, met Adrian when he was attached to Michael Hourigan's stable and riding the point-to-point circuit, principally in the South.

She is of similar background, coming from a large family also, who are into sport, horse racing, greyhound racing and coursing.

Sabrina maintained that jovial outlook in England, when life was a different grind during the National hunt season as Adrian travelled the length and breath of the county in search of winners.

Always Sabrina would be by his side, sharing the driving and helping him through the good times and the bad. She provided the base he needed in the evenings. Thus he was able to avoid the bright lights and the champagne flowing circuit that can so easily catch out the unwary.

Although Adrian was a natural star, he could easily have fallen victim to the many temptations of the racing world.

At first Adrian lived in a Portacabin. Then Sabrina and he acquired a flat in Whitcombe. They now live in a lovely modern house in the small town of Faringdon on the Berkshire-Oxfordshire border and it puts Adrian within striking distance of "The Duke" Nicholson's stable.

Putting on weight is not a problem with Adrian. He is small and stockily built, but because of that same build he is able to generate a power in the saddle that led naturally to comparisons being drawn between him and Martin Molony.

"I can eat anything", Adrian told me. "And I love to eat well when I come home in the evening."

Tom O'Mahony paid this tribute to Sabrina: "She is a level-headed girl who likes to stay in the background. But when it is required, she will make Adrian toe the line, not that he would want to do otherwise.

"She is very much her own person. Overall she is a great levelling influence. They work as a team and that is of immense benefit to Adrian, as success has followed success for him. You can be at your most vulnerable on the top. Yes, Sabrina is a prize asset."

Tom O'Mahony was perfectly correct when he said that Sabrina likes to stay in the background. She understands the talent – call it genius – of the man she loves.

What struck me immediately about Sabrina when first I met her was her naturalness and the way her femininity and appealing personality shine through without any effort to impress. She is herself totally. And these very characteristics have created very close bonds between Adrian and herself. They are two people very happily in love.

Sabrina keeps out of the limelight knowing that Adrian wants their relationship to be one of complete understanding and not one that is pressurised day-after-day by the antics of the British tabloids.

When you come from a big family, you learn from an early age to live with reality, to know the basics of life.

Both Adrian and Sabrina have that going for them. They have known reality from the outset.

Adrian cemented his commitment to Sabrina when he slipped a sparkling engagement ring on her finger in the count-down to Cheltenham '94.

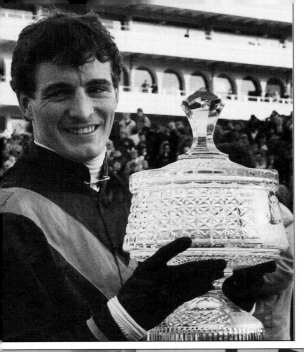

Cork-born Norman Williamson (left) proudly displays the prestigious Ritz Club Trophy after emerging as leading rider at Cheltenham '95 and (below) successful trainer, Kim Bailey and himself are congratulated by Dr Michael Smurfit at the presentation of trophies after Alderbrook's brilliant win in the 1995 Smurfit Champion Hurdle. (Pictures Bernard Parkin and Caroline Norris.)

THE SMURFIT CHAMPION HURDLE

Norman Williamson gives the impression that he is walking the high wire as he expresses his joy at winning the 1995 Gold Cup on Master Oats.

Mick Fitzgerald clears the last on Rough Quest on his way to victory in the 1996 Aintree Grand National and (inset) Fitzgerald who had an agonising wait before his victory was confirmed by the Stewards and (below) Mrs Cryss O'Reilly, wife of Dr Tony O'Reilly, presents the trophy for the Castlemartin Stud Handicap Chase at Punchestown '95 to Terry Casey after the impressive success of Rough Quest.

Adrian Maguire and Sabrina Winters after their marriage in the Church of the Immaculate Conception, Kanturk, Co. Cork, on Sunday September 3rd, 1995. (Picture: Caroline Norris)

Adrian Maguire made it a day to remember for young fan and admirer Eilis Donohue, Galway, as he stands to be photographed with her during the 1994 Galway Festival Meeting. (Picture: Peter Mooney.)

THE VICTOR'S SMILE – a delighted Adrian Maguire gives an arm-aloft salute to the heavens as he is led in after his memorable triumph on the Toby Balding-trained Cool Ground in the 1992 Gold Cup.

Adrian Maguire proudly displays the Gold Cup trophy after his epic win in 1992.

Adrian Maguire, with the loose horse Young Hustler in close contention, leads over the last in the 1994 Aintree Grand National but Richard Dunwoody looks cool and in control as he bides his time before taking command in the long run in.

CHAMPAGNE DAYS FOR CHARLIE

Champagne times for Charlie Swan at Cheltenham '93 as his victories on Shawiya (centre top) and Fissure Seal (top right) helped him win the Ritz Club Trophy and (below) he gets a congratulatory kiss from his wife, Tina. Swan won the Ritz Club Trophy again at the 1994 Cheltenham Festival meeting.

Charlie Swan receives the congratulations of an admiring Queen Mother after being seen at his brilliant best in winning the 1995 Queen Mother Champion Chase on Viking Flagship and (below left) he clears the last in forceful style and (right) acclaimed as he returns to the winner's enclosure. (Pictures Bernard Parkin and Caroline Norris.)

They were married in the Church of the Immaculate Conception in Kanturk on Sunday, September 3rd, 1995.

They had come a long way since the Autumn of '91....

❋   ❋   ❋

Toby Balding has generously acknowledged that Cool Ground would never have won the 1992 Cheltenham Gold Cup had not Adrian Maguire given him such a forceful ride – "and I am sure if the jockeys were reversed he would probably have won on The Fellow too. He made Monsieur Kondrat look very ordinary".

That Gold Cup will be remembered for the much-publicised alleged spoiling tactics adopted by the Jenny Pitman-trained Golden Freeze (Michael Bowlby) in order to enhance the victory prospects of stable-companion, Toby Tobias and at the same time disrupt the rhythm and composure of the favourite, the Martin Pipe-trained Carvill's Hill.

Brough Scott would write in *The Independent on Sunday* that Cheltenham takes no prisoners and Carvill's Hill was exposed as a "glass jaw" heavyweight, found out by the fences of the Gold Cup journey.

Personally, I have no doubt that if Carvill's Hill was in the Arkle mould – and there were those prepared to hail him as such before the 1992 Gold Cup – he would have dismissed Golden Freeze as Muhammed Ali dismissed Al Blue Lewis on a famous night in Dublin's Croke Park in the early seventies.

To all the lobbies that filled columns about "stalking" and "spoiling "tactics, one had only one word to say – just play the video of Arkle and Mill House locked in battle in that memorable 1964 Gold Cup and you will realise what it really means when two great chasers take each other on.

The Fellow could easily have gone into the record books as the winner of three Gold cups if not four-in-a-row. He had the misfortune to be beaten in a photo finish by Garrison Savannah in 1991 and again in a photo finish by Cool Ground in 1992.

"Change jockeys and we'll fight you all over again", might well have been the Gallic cry as Adam Kondrat was clearly outpointed by Adrian Maguire in the drama-laden finish to the '92 Gold Cup.

First, there was the moment when Carvill's Hill finally cracked and it looked a formality then for The Fellow. Coming to the last he was still in command but Kondrat took off in measured fashion (a few cynics remarked that it was as if he was ensuring he would have a clear round in the Aga Khan Cup at the RDS!) whereas Adrian Maguire drove Cool Ground into the fence with the fearlessness and panache of a Martin Molony.

Yet, The Fellow succumbed by only the narrowest of margins and trainer, Francois Doumen could rightly argue afterwards that if his jockey had used the whip in the same manner as Adrian Maguire then the result might well have been different. Was it a case of the French trainer not wanting his rider to incur the wrath of the English stewards while young Maguire, with glory beckoning, was willing to take the rap? And was Toby Balding going to scold him for suffering a four-day suspension for excessive use of the whip?

Not on your life!

Adrian Maguire was quite frank about it all after the four-day suspension was imposed on him by the Cheltenham stewards "There's no denying I was hard on the horse. But if I hadn't been hard on him I wouldn't have won. And it wasn't as if I was beating a 'dead' horse or anything like that; he was responding the whole time."

He added: "In a seller you'd be conscious of how many times you were after hitting a horse. But not when you land over the last in the Gold Cup and with a chance of winning it."

The suspension he incurred at Cheltenham '92 was not the last brush Adrian Maguire would have with the English stewards.

*　　　*　　　*

The retirement of Peter Scudamore in the Spring of '93 led directly to Adrian Maguire becoming No. 1 to David "The Duke" Nicholson's stable as Richard Dunwoody, who had been his No. 1, succeeded Scudamore at Martin Pipe's.

In throwing in his lot with Nicholson, Adrian Maguire was joining possibly the most powerful jump stable after Martin Pipe's – a stable in which quality mattered for everything.

It was to be a very fruitful partnership, equally beneficial to both. David Nicholson became champion National Hunt trainer in Britain for the 1994-'95 season, having been narrowly pipped the previous season by Martin Pipe, and Maguire was joint runner-up with Norman Williamson, as we have seen already, to Dunwoody at the end of the 1994-'95 season.

But what mattered most from Adrian's viewpoint was the quality of the horses he rode for David Nicholson and the successes he achieved for the stable that have passed into the annals of National Hunt racing and Cheltenham, in particular.

Nothing finer, I have always felt, than the sweeping majesty of his triumph on Viking flagship in the 1994 Queen Mother Champion Chase and one could well understand why David Nicholson should describe him as "a rare and precious talent".

It was one of those races that remain etched in the memory – the kind of spectacle that places the Cheltenham Festival meeting on a plane apart form all other meetings.

John Oaksey would write in the *Daily Telegraph* that "if ever a race was won by courage and daring, this was it". And he added: "Adrian Maguire and Viking Flagship took defeat by the throat and snatched victory from its jaws".

In Oaksey's view Viking Flagship's last two leaps were "bold to the point of foolhardiness" but then Maguire would never have won if – as "The Duke" Nicholson said to me afterwards – "he had not gone for broke and it came off".

"It was a wonderful race and we were lucky to be part of it", said

Nicholson, who watched events from the last fence and confessed that as Travado (Jamie Osborne), Deep Sensation (Declan Murphy) and Viking Flagship came to it with only a matter of inches separating them, he thought his charge would be beaten.

But even "The Duke" could hardly have foreseen what his No. 1 jockey would conjure up in that gripping climax.

"I looked at Adrian on my inside and thought I had him beaten", said Jamie Osborne but Viking Flagship, who had gone into it if anything marginally behind, produced a huge leap under the inspired driving of his rider and you felt the adrenalin course in your veins at such superb horsemanship.

Remember, Declan Murphy had come with a brilliant surge on Deep Sensation, so Maguire had not alone to contend with Jamie Osborne but with the Limerick-born jockey who had taken the crown the previous year on the Josh Gifford-trained gelding.

Maguire had raised a mighty roar at the second last also for the fearless manner in which he went into it, and those who had seen Martin Molony in his prime over this course knew that here was the man worthy to wear his mantle.

Half-way up the run-in Viking Flagship clawed his way into the lead and you knew then that Maguire was not going to be denied – even though at the post only a neck separated his mount and Travado. Deep Sensation, who looked to be going so well between the last two fences, found less than expected on the flat and in the three-way battle could not cope with his younger rivals, being a length further behind Travado in third place. But he had been magnificent in defeat.

Now at Cheltenham '95 Adrian Maguire was due to try and make it two back-to-back on Viking Flagship.

But the sudden passing of his mother caused him to remain at home and cancel taking any part in the Festival meeting.

As I phoned from my hotel in Cheltenham my story on how tragedy had hit the Maguire family on the eve of Cheltenham '95 and also my obituary tribute to Mrs Maguire, I remembered how she had enjoyed so much the launch of *Tigers Of The Turf* by the then Minister for Tourism and Trade, Charlie McCreevy – a great racing man -in the Burlington Hotel.

She got the autographs of Tom Foley and also of Aidan O'Brien. She was photographed with them and with close friends from County Meath. She met Sabrina Winters' mother who had travelled up from Kanturk. She was in her element.

Adrian was pictured head bowed in silent grief at the graveside on the day his mother was laid to rest.

Charlie Swan, deputising for him on Viking Flagship, received a thunderous reception as he came back into the winner's enclosure after the challenge of Nakir, the 1994 'Arkle' winner had been repelled in authoritative fashion and also the bid of Norman Williamson on Deep Sensation, winner, as we have seen, of the race in '93 and third in '94.

In his moment of triumph, Charlie Swan was still able to remember Adrian Maguire and the other members of the family, grieving the loss of their mother.

" I would like to think that in winning this race today I was doing it for Adrian and the other members of the family," said Swan. "I hope they feel a little better now. I am sure the whole family was hoping that the horse would win. I just wish them all my best in this week of great sadness for them."

"The Duke" Nicholson found it difficult to conceal his feelings of emotion on a day of singular success for him. "I am very upset that Adrian is not here riding for me today. I am very sorry for him at missing his moment of glory. I find it very hard to respond to any questions on this day."

In fact, Adrian Maguire missed in sharing a Nicholson treble as Putty Road won the Sun Alliance Novices' Hurdle and Kadi the Mildmay of Fleet Challenge Cup Chase. Norman Williamson was seen to outstanding advantage on Putty Road and again on Kadi.

*　　　*　　　*

After breaking his collar-bone in five places when Smiling Chief slipped up after jumping the water jump at Newbury on March 1st, '96, Adrian Maguire had to face up to the grim realisation that he would be missing the Festival meeting for the second year in succession.

The injury at Newbury that put him out of Cheltenham occurred when he was leading the field on Smiling Chief, who tripped up after landing inside the lip of the water jump, bringing down Ascot Lad and Bells Life.

Describing the fall, Maguire said: "My horse left his hind leg in the water and the loose horse didn't help. We did the splits and the loose horse hit us from behind.Another horse then cannoned into me shattering my collar-bone in five places."

Assessing the injury, the Jockey Club's medical consultant Dr Michael Turner said: "Adrian has broken the right collarbone he has broken twice before. The problem is that the collarbone is more difficult to heal when it has been broken before, so, bearing in mind his previous injuries this season, this is really bad luck on him."

Maguire was warned that another fall would break the collar-bone again and then he would face an operation. He had no option but to cry off for the rest of the season. He finished the 1995-'96 season with just 60 winners, leaving him eighth in the table – a long way behind the new champion Tony McCoy (175), David Bridgwater (132) and Richard Dunwoody (101).

You could not but reflect back to the epic battle he had with Richard Dunwoody for the Jockeys' title in 1993-'94 and, no doubt, he would have emerged with the championship crown for that season but for the spate of suspensions he suffered.

The Dunwoody/Maguire roadshow had developed into the most intense, longest-running duel in the history of National Hunt racing. And in its climactic stage it captured the imagination of the public to such an extent that bumper crowds were attracted to the venues where they were throwing down the gauntlet to one another in the last grand-stand battle for the crown.

More than 7,000 people turned up at Market Rasen on Saturday evening, June 4, to witness the final scene of the final act of the drama. Normally they would have expected 5,000 paying customers at this meeting.

At one point after Cheltenham '94 Maguire was 20 ahead. Ten more winners and he would have been certain of lifting the William Hill trophy. Ultimately, the "Pipe Factor" was to be the deciding one, for the statistics showed that in the last fortnight Martin Pipe provided Dunwoody with a non-stop flow of "ammunition" represented by 31 runners and the champion won on eight of them. "The Duke" Nicholson in contrast supplied Maguire with two runners and one of these won.

Dunwoody finally overtook Maguire on May 14 and was long odds-on to retain the championship crown when bookmakers suspended betting.

Then began Maguire's great fight-back. His remarkable treble at Uttoxeter changed the entire picture dramatically and piled on the pressure on Dunwoody. The excitement generated during the last week became white-hot. There were effectively but two winners between them as they entered the final day of the season – Saturday, June 4 – with an afternoon meeting scheduled at Stratford and an evening meeting at Market Rasen.

There was everything to play for and with Maguire exclaiming to the world "I am on a roll", it was a brave man who would have bet his house on "The Kid" not pulling it off.

On the face of it Dunwoody killed Maguire's challenge stone dead when he rode a treble at Stratford – all three provided by Martin Pipe.

So with Dunwoody five ahead Maguire knew as he left Stratford early on the forty-minute helicopter flight to Market Rasen that he would have to go through the card to become champion and win five races to share the title. An enormous task, a superhuman one.

However, hope still flickered.

The course commentator set the pitch as the horses left the parade ring for the start of the first race, noting that Maguire was setting out towards "this impossible miracle".

He won that first race on Wayward Wind and then the second on a horse aptly named It's Unbelievable. The crowd had gone wild and, as Alan Lee noted in his report for *The Times*, "the roof of the stand was almost raised by a crowd revelling in the theatre". The excitement was heightened as they saw the helicopter bearing Richard Dunwoody landing at that very moment.

Bobby Socks was the Great White Hope in the third, the Handicap Chase. Maguire looked poised for victory as they approached the last fence and 7,000 throats were willing him on in the crescendo that 7,000 people out of their skins with excitement can create. But Bobby Socks went down by two lengths in a driving finish.

Then, at 8.09 p.m. as the evening shadows lengthened over Market Rasen the curtain came down on the impossible dream as Logical Fun failed to win the Newark Storage Handicap Hurdle. That meant that Maguire was three winners behind with only two rides to come.

The young challenger was still the Young Pretender.

Ironically, Dunwoody failed to add to his total but Stratford and his afternoon treble had been the knock-out blow to Maguire's aspirations.

While Dunwoody finally emerged triumphant from this prolonged and fascinating contest, it was Adrian Maguire who in the words of his agent was the "moral victor".

He set three new records – all captured from his rival.

Firstly, as John Randall revealed in a very well-researched article in the *Racing Post*, he attained the best-ever total by a non-champion, the previous record being 137 by Dunwoody in 1991-'92.

Secondly, Maguire rode in more races than any jump jockey had ever done in one season, and with 915 mounts he beat the old record of Dunwoody the previous season.

Thirdly, he won the most prizemoney in a season in the history of National Hunt racing, his £1,193,917 sterling beating the total of £1,101,876 set by Dunwoody's mounts the previous season.

The totals achieved by Dunwoody and Maguire were respectively the second and third-highest scores by a jump jockey, surpassed only by the record of 221 by Peter Scudamore in 1988-'89.

If jockeys, like trainers, had their championship decided on prizemoney, Adrian Maguire would have emerged, like his Guv'nor David Nicholson, as the title-winner for 1993-'94.

✳   ✳   ✳

Facing into the 1996-'97 National Hunt season, Adrian Maguire was being quoted 11/2 for the title by Coral, behind 4/7 favourite, David Bridgwater and reigning champion Tony McCoy on 2/1.

His agent Dave Roberts went on record to state that he had a "burning ambition" to guide Maguire to the title. "having achieved it with Tony (McCoy), my second wish is to make Adrian champion."

But Roberts added significantly: "I've always said the most important thing is to remain free from injury. Anyone who can do that will have a chance".

In saying that he touched the heart of the matter. In Adrian's case, he had now reached a watershed. His future career was going to be bound up very much with whether he could avoid injuries and his recovery rate from them.

He simply couldn't put the winning of the title before his health and his well-being. He recognised this when he said to me at Galway '96 that while, naturally, he would like very much to be crowned champion he didn't see it as the be-all and end-all of everything. "I see the riding of quality horses and winning prestigious races as every bit as important as taking the title".

In the public mind – whether it was regulars who had seen him in his great moments at the meetings that mattered or watched him on television displaying his brilliance and unquestioned courage in the saddle – he was always going to be seen as a rider for the big-time. Granted he would do the circuit like the others but the Cheltenham Festival was poorer without the buzz he could create when going into the penultimate fence and the last fence in the Queen Mother Champion Chase or the Gold Cup. The same in the case of Aintree over the three days of the Grand National meeting.

David Nicholson had the ammunition in his stable that guaranteed Maguire, as the No. 1. rider for 'The Duke', that he would be on top-notch horses. But Maguire out of action for weeks on end, especially over the Cheltenham and Liverpool meetings, would have to suffer the sight of watching other leading jockeys taking the mounts that would have been his automatically. And it would become worse if doubles or trebles were recorded.

The feel-good factor was terribly important for Adrian when he got going again at the start of the 1996-'97 season. It didn't matter all that much that he had to be content with just a 60-winner tally for the curtailed 1995-'96 season. He was back. That was the bottom line.

As he reflected on his period on the sideline, he had to admit that in one way it was a blessing in disguise.

For two seasons, indeed longer and almost from the time he arrived in England, he had been going at an awesome pace and, apart from the constant driving during the jumping season in Britain itself, there were frequent trips to Ireland and often it was a case of rushing away before the end of a meeting to catch a plane so that he would be back, ready to ride out the next morning. You would need to be made of iron to stick the pace and , even though he had youth on his side, Adrian found that it was getting to him.

✳   ✳   ✳

It was only when the broken collar-bone brought a summary halt after the ill-fated ride on Smiling Chief at Newbury that it was really borne home to him that he badly needed a break from racing. The process of getting back to race fitness was exacting enough in itself – the physiotherapy sessions, working with the weights to strengthen his damaged shoulder and working out in the gym. Then he reached the point where he could ride out again but that didn't mean that he was ready to ride in an actual race.

He was in the hands of the medical advisers as to when he could resume.

Privately, they had to be concerned with how much his body could take. They knew only too well that to leave him back too soon could be very unwise. What he wanted was time – time to give himself a proper chance, so that it wouldn't be the same as it was during the 1995-'96 season, when he was always conscious of an arm injury that didn't seem to have fully cleared up, and was always niggling him.

"I spent a lot of time in Ireland, travelling around to friends and relations., trying to stay away from racing", he told Brian O'Connor of Ireland's sports newspaper, *The Title*. "I had to try and stop thinking about it because if you do that, it can do your head in, thinking about who is riding your horses and winning races on them. I tried to totally switch off. I never stuck my head in a paper. I'd hear the chat and see races on TV but that was it. I got totally away from it".

But in a horse-loving country like Ireland, where racing means so much to so many and racing over the jumps most of all, it would be well-nigh impossible for Adrian Maguire to completely avoid any contact with the game that is his life. He would have to go into a Cistercian Monastery for that – and, believe me, I'm sure he'd find a monk who had said farewell to the outside world but still retained a love of racing. Immediately he was recognised – and that face has become very familiar – the conversation would naturally turn to racing, especially when it was a case of strangers coming up to pay their respects. In the inner circle of relations and friends, however, if was different. They realised and understood what he wanted and they were willing to help him in switching off.

The end result was that when he returned to England and rode Sonic Star to victory in the Round Machinery Novice Chase at Stratford and then appeared at the Galway Festival meeting he was a man refreshed in mind and spirit. Dave Roberts noticed that the old hunger to ride winners was as strong as ever.

He was sensible enough to realise that there was no way he could have returned sooner than he did, because as he acknowledged to Brian O'Connor – "race fitness is so different from ordinary fitness. You can say to yourself 'I feel fine, I feel great', but once you're on a horse you're using completely different muscles. You can get yourself so fit but the rest has to be done on the racecourse".

✳   ✳   ✳

Sabrina presented him with a daughter, Shannon before the 1996–'97 jumping season got under way. They were happy to celebrate at the Kinsale Point-to-Point Festival, which will always have such warm memories for Adrian from the time that he rode six winners there before his move to England.

Now a family man, his priorities would necessarily change – but nothing would ever dim the Martin Molony-like courage that was an essential part of his greatness in the saddle. I have got to admit that in the times that he was sidelined the spectre of the manner in which Martin Molony's career was summarily cut short has haunted me as no doubt it has haunted others.

Those of us who have got to know Adrian and admired him wanted only that we would continue to enjoy his genius as a National Hunt rider, remembering the spontaneous tribute of "The Duke' Nicholson: "Adrian Maguire is a rare and precious talent".

9

Swan 'Lords' It At Sandown

After Cheltenham, there is little doubt that Sandown is the English racecourse that holds a special appeal for Irish champion jump jockey, Charlie Swan.

It was here on Saturday, April 27, 1996 that he won the prestigious Whitbread Gold Cup Chase for the second time when lording it over the opposition on the Aidan O'Brien-trained Life Of A Lord to win in tremendous style from Proud Son, winner of the Timeform Golden Miller Handicap Chase at Cheltenham in April and Amtrack Express, triumphant in the AGFA Diamond Limited Handicap Chase over the course in February.

It was rated one of the highest-quality Whitbreads of recent years with fourth place being take by Jodami, the 1993 Gold Cup winner and three-times winner (1993, '94 and '95) of the Hennessy Cognac Gold Cup Chase.

Charlie Swan had scored on the 25/1 outsider, Ushers Island in 1994, while in 1991 he won a titanic battle with Docklands Express by three-quarters-of-a-lengths on the 'Mouse' Morris-trained Cahervillahow, only to be disqualified and placed second, though it must be noted for the record that the Stewards found the interference by Cahervillahow "accidental" as he carried 'Docklands' over to the far rail in the run to the line.

Life Of A Lord's triumph was all the sweeter as it came at the end of a very frustrating week for Charlie Swan that had seen him ride five seconds at the Punchestown Festival meeting and collect a ten-day ban from the Stewards.

At Cheltenham, where he gave Aidan O'Brien his first Festival winner on Urubande in the Sun Alliance Novices' Hurdle on the Wednesday, he was in trouble with the Stewards on the Thursday, being suspended for six days for alleged "irresponsible" riding on the Aidan O'Brien-trained Magical Lady in the Daily Express Triumph Hurdle, as Embellished finished on the floor and Mistinguett also looked cramped for room.

But Swan was adamant when I discussed the incident with him at Galway

'96 that no way did he intend to take the ground of any of the other runners. In fact, he wasn't aware until after the race was over that Embellished had actually fallen. With a field of 30 runners and a number in close contention coming to the last, it was inevitable that there would be crowding on the inside.

✳   ✳   ✳

Life Of A Lord gave Charlie Swan another day to remember when this imposing gelding defied top weight in winning the Digital Galway Plate for the second successive year at Galway '96.

Swan did an Olympic-style victory leap from Life Of A Lord in the winner's enclosure and he was acclaimed by the crowd for the brilliance of his riding in getting the better of a memorable duel in the straight with Richard Dunwoody, who was in the lead on Bishop's Hall going to the last.

The honours of the day were shared by Aidan O'Brien, who pulled off a really great training feat in turning out Life Of A Lord in the peak of condition to carry 12st to victory without having had a race since the Whitbread.

In 1995 Charlie Swan opted to ride Loshian in the race and Trevor Horgan had the honour of scoring on Life Of A Lord.

King Wah Glory, in the colours of J.P. McManus, was all the rage with the punters, starting at the very short odds for a competitive handicap chase of this type of 9/4. He could only finish third. Life Of A Lord was easy to back at 5/1 before starting at 9/2.

The ten-year-old's victory sparked off spontaneous celebrations locally as he carried the colours of Michael J. Clancy of the Bridge House Hotel in Spiddal.

✳   ✳   ✳

Frank Berry, who trains today at Kilcullen, County Kildare, was ten time Irish jumps jockey champion in the period 1975-'87 which set a post World War Two record. Of course, prior to the War the title "champion jump jockey" wasn't in vogue.

The 1995-'96 season saw Charlie Swan become Irish champion jump jockey for the seventh successive time. As long as he avoids serious injury, it seems inevitable that he will equal and surpass Frank Berry's record and, indeed, reach a tally of titles that may never be surpassed. Attached as he is to the powerful Aidan O'Brien stable, he will continue to have the backing to easily reach a century and more of winners in any given season.

In 1992-'93 it seemed a considerable achievement on his part to ride 104 winners (with Kevin O'Brien next with 52 winners). In 1994-'95 he hit a total of 118 and Francis Woods was runner-up with 67.

However, by the end of the 1995-'96 National Hunt season he reached a grand total of 150 winners and Conor O'Dwyer, as we have seen in an earlier chapter, had to settle for half of that total – and that after his most successful season ever.

But an even more significant statistic, as revealed to me by the expert in these matters, Tony Sweeney, shows that Swan with 148 winners (jumps and Flat) for the calendar year 1995 set an all-time Irish record. This broke his own record of 123 winners for a calendar year set in 1994.

*   *   *

After Cheltenham '93 the world was at Charlie's feet. He had returned to his native Cloughjordan in North Tipperary with the Ritz Club Trophy after emerging as top jockey at the Festival meeting with four winners for four different Irish trainers. Then followed victory in the Jameson Irish Grand National on Ebony Jane for the Francis Flood Grangcon stable and on Camden Buzz for Paddy Mullins in the Guinness Galway Hurdle. To crown it all, he had become the first Irish-based jockey to ride 100 winners over the jumps in a calendar year and in the process had broken the record of the incomparable Martin Molony that had stood the test for 42 years.

Cheltenham '94 would see Swan win the Ritz Club Trophy for the second year running as he recorded a treble on the Wednesday, winning on Time For A Run and Mucklemeg for the Edward O'Grady-J.P. McManus partnership and taking the Sun Alliance Novice's Hurdle on Danoli to an unforgettable "Irish roar".

It's Galway race week and I am sitting in the lounge of the Corrib Great Southern Hotel chatting to Swan over coffee and bringing him back to the moment when Irish racing circles were aflame with reports that he had been sounded about taking the job as No. 1 jockey to the Martin Pipe stable following the retirement of Peter Scudamore in April of "93.

Credence had been lent to the reports when 'The Duke' Nicholson issued what was to all intents and purposes an ultimatum to Richard Dunwoody demanding of him that he make up his mind one way or the other on whether he was going to stay with him or leave. It was not proving an easy decision for Dunwoody to make.

Yes, there had been feelers, Swan told me, and he had responded that he would be "interested" – but that, of course, was different from having to give a definite "yes" or "no". The final irrevocable question had not been put.

Martin Pipe did not come back with an offer – the kind of offer it would have been difficult to refuse. Obviously, he had put more than one top rider in the sights of his gun but when it came to "bagging" one, the ultimate choice was Richard Dunwoody.

"I do not know what I would have done if I had been asked to take over the mantle of Peter Scudamore", said Charlie Swan quite simply and very frankly.

You see the Irish National Hunt champion jockey had only recently completed building work on a lovely new bungalow-style home – "The Cobs" – about a mile from the training establishment of his father, Capt.

Donald Swan at Modreeny, Cloughjordan.

* * *

Tranquillity reigns in this corner of North Tipperary and when Charlie gets home, for example, from Cheltenham, the hurly-burly of the Festival meeting seems light years away.

Cloughjordan is steeped in the lore of hurling, the game that is to Ireland what cricket on the village green is to England and baseball is to America. Love of hurling and racing go hand in hand when you assess what are the passions of the people in the sporting sense in the Modreeny area.

Charlie is not a "hurling man" in the way that the aficionados of the game are classified in Tipperary. But he understands its place and its over-riding importance in the psyche of the people.

He is "one of our own" at the same time to the residents of Cloughjordan and the surrounding area. They are proud of the way he has made its name known among lovers of the jumping game in Ireland and Britain and around the globe.

A man would not easily leave such an ideal setting. And for Swan and his wife, Tina, it's very much at home – "the place where I belong", as Charlie put it.

Swan loves his life in Ireland too much to want to depart for pastures new. "Yes, I could earn a lot more money. But I don't think I'd be happy – and that's what counts."

When, for example, I interviewed him for a *Sunday Independent* feature prior to the Leopardstown '93 Christmas meeting, he told me that he would ride out at his father's place on Christmas morning – "and then I'll probably have two Christmas dinners, one in Cloughjordan and the other with Tina's family in Kildare. Or it may be half a Christmas dinner in each place", he laughed.

"I have no desire to leave Cloughjordan at all. In fact when I have finished riding, I want to train here at my father's stables", he added significantly.

While it does appear on the face of it that it is almost inevitable that he will assume Donald Swan's mantle, it must be stressed that Charlie is not one who entertains any illusions when he contemplates a future as a trainer.

Indeed, he is quite pragmatic and clear-headed when it comes to discussing the pitfalls of the training profession. "It's essential that you get the right owners from the outset and, every bit as important, that you are training good horses. I believe there is no point in becoming a trainer just for the sake of being a trainer, simply because people assumed that was the natural progression your career would take after you retired from the saddle.

"It can be a nightmare breaking your back with bad horses that are going nowhere. They will put the same demands on you – even more – than good horses and potential champions. I wouldn't like to end up enduring that kind of nightmare."

Like fellow-country man, Michael Kinane, Charlie Swan is a man for whom quality of life has a deep significance and he would not be willing to exchange it unless he got the kind of offer which he could not refuse.

Like Kinane he is able to enjoy the best of both worlds at the present time – retain the National Hunt Jockeys crown in Ireland while booting home 100 winners in the season and at the same time pick up plum rides for English trainers.

Nicky Henderson has come to deeply appreciate Charlie's talent and is quite willing to engage him whenever the occasion demands. He gave him the ride on Thumbs Up in the Arkle Chase at the '94 Cheltenham Festival meeting and Swan had this one close up and waiting to pounce at the third last when he was brought down in most unlucky circumstances.

✳   ✳   ✳

Swan could have joined Henderson if he wished back in 1989 but turned down the offer as he would not have been No. 1 to the stable.

For a period he was No. 1 jockey to the "Mouse" Morris stable. When he vacated it, he lost the ride on Cahervillahow but the greatest tribute of all to him was that "Mouse" eventually asked him to team up again with the Deep Run gelding, who wore blinkers when finishing third in the National Handicap Chase at Punchestown in February under 12st. Having made no impression in the Gold Cup, he gave Swan an exhilarating ride when he figured in "the race that never was" – the '93 Aintree Grand National, Wexford-born John White having the distinction, if one might call it thus, of being "first" past the post in that 154th renewal in a close four-horse finish with Cahervillahow, Romany King (Adrian Maguire)and The Committee (Norman Williamson).

At least Cahervillahow had shown that he had the ability to jump the Aintree fences and Swan likewise had proved that he had the horsemanship to win a National one day.

Many people would probably think in terms of Swan being "a lucky jockey" in the avoidance of serious injury. Yet it's an indication in itself of the fearlessness of our National Hunt jockeys that Charlie reels off to me the fact that he has broken his right arm twice and his left arm once, a leg, a hand and his nose – not to mention collar bone fractures – as if such injuries happened to be an every day occurrence. He has also cracked his skull and he still has the scar on his forehead.

Now that he is champion, Swan has the right to choose. "I will ride a bad lepper if I know he has a chance of winning. But I won't ride one who has no hope."

To put it bluntly, he is a "little bit more choosy" nowadays – and can afford to be.

When you ride horses that have no hope, all you are doing is giving yourself the chance of a fall. I know you are doing yourself out of IR£71, but a bad fall could cost you an awful lot more."

He sums up the philosophy of the risk-takers of the National Hunt game thus: "You learn to take it day by day."

Survival is more important in the final analysis than the breaking of records.

✽   ✽   ✽

Charlie Swan has come a long way from the time he started pony racing at the age of ten. While a boarder at school in Headford he played cricket and one might speculate how Charlie may have progressed to the point where he was chosen to represent his country – even against the touring West Indies.

But, of course, he knew in his heart that the only profession he wanted to pursue in life was to be a full-time jockey. His father encouraged him in every way possible.

He was 15, going on 16, and still a schoolboy weighing six-and-a-half stone when he had his first ride in public at Naas in March, 1983 on Final Assault, a debutante in a two-year-old event. "I broke him at home, my father trained him and my granny owned him", he recalled. "I was thrilled that my father had enough faith in me to let me ride him"

He was hooked on riding from that moment. He had arrived – though with his cherubic countenance he looked almost too young bringing Final Assault back into the winner's enclosure.

His father was mostly into jumpers, so it was inevitable that in order to further his racing education he should become attached to a regular Flat stable. He joined the Curragh establishment of Kevin Prendergast, son of "Darkie". He quickly won recognition as an apprentice of outstanding promise and was constantly in demand by "outside" stables. He would end up with the impressive record of riding 56 winners on the Flat. Not surprisingly, his experience as a Flat jockey would stand him in excellent stead when it came to riding a finish in the National Hunt sphere.

There came a stage when Swan realised that if he wanted to remain a Flat Jockey he would have to resign himself to the rigid regime of wasting and he had a fierce aversion to this.

When he suffered a broken leg one day schooling, the result was that in the period of recuperation his weight shot up to 9 stone. "I was still growing at the time and it's work, believe me, to get weight off when you're in a situation like that. So I decided that the time had come to switch to the jumps."

"I informed Kevin Prendergast who immediately understood the problem", he added.

Prendergast rang Dessie Hughes and in a way it was the Hinge of Destiny that put Swan on the road to becoming Irish Champion National Hunt rider and to lifting the Ritz Club Trophy at the 1993 and '94 Cheltenham Festival meetings.

Jumping was his first love. He hunted with the Ormonds and Golden Vale and was quite accustomed to the point-to-point circuit.

100

In teaming up with Dessie Hughes, he was joining a man who had distinguished himself as one of the outstanding Cheltenham riders of the modern era – the man who had won the Gold Cup on Davy Lad in 1977 and the Champion Hurdle on Monksfield in 1979 after an epic battle with Sea Pigeon and Jonjo O'Neill from the last.

Swan is the first to acknowledge the benefit he gained from the time he spent with Dessie Hughes and it is significant that Tom Morgan was also a pupil of the same Academy – Morgan who rode Miller Hill to victory for Hughes in the 1982 Supreme Novices Hurdle and who was only thwarted from winning the 1989 Gold Cup on Yahoo by the "people's champion", the great Desert Orchid.

✻   ✻   ✻

Charlie Swan rides easily at 9st 12lbs and "with a sweat" can get down to 9st 7lb.

In common with most champions, he has a distinct preference for racing on the inside but not simply because it's the shortest way round.

He explained: "Horses tend to settle better when they have a rail alongside them, particularly in hurdle races. They will often run too freely when they are between other horses.

"Also if you are in the middle, you have to contend with the horses in front backing off at each hurdle, those on your left jumping across you and those on your inner jumping out.

"For the same reason I also like to be on the inside in steeplechases. But I find that on a good jumper you are better off out in front because it means you have a chance of making ground at the fences.

"If your horse is jumping well in behind, you have to keep pulling him back. This means that he loses what he has gained at his fences".

Swan's actual style is neat and effective. But coming into the last he will often ride like a demon and he is convinced that this do-or-die approach makes a big difference to the number of winners he rides.

"You can gain a length before you even get to the jump and probably another one as you take it. Whereas if you sit still, the horse will tend to back off and lose ground in the process."

✻   ✻   ✻

He will always remember 1993 as the year that lifted him on to an entirely new plane and brought his name to the notice of a vast public in Britain who up to the time of the Cheltenham Festival meeting may have thought of him as just another Irish rider of blossoming talent.

Swan's outstanding feat in recording a four-timer at the Festival meeting on Montelado, Fissure Seal, Shawiya and Shuil Ar Aghaidh – put him right in line to battle it out with Michael Kinane for the Personality of the Year Award in Irish Racing.

The Awards scheme was held that same year by the *Irish Racing Annual* in conjunction with Tipperary Crystal, who put up magnificent inscribed trophies for the winners.

Making the awards all the more prestigious and meaningful was the fact that the winners were chosen as a result of the Irish Racing Correspondents and Writers expressing their opinions through a ballot.

In the final analysis the singular triumph of Vintage Crop in the Melbourne Cup made it inevitable that the main Award would be shared by Dermot Weld and Michael Kinane.

But Swan qualified for a Special Award as did also Waterford trainer, Pat Flynn, for whom Charlie rode Montelado to that memorable triumph in the Supreme Novices Hurdle.

Donald Swan and his wife were on hand at Leopardstown to see their son receive his trophy – and Donald, reflecting back a decade to that day in Naas when he legged Charlie up on Final Assault, had every reason to be a proud man.

The Tipperary Crystal trophy would take its place beside the other crystal trophies and inscribed silverware in "The Cobs" in Cloughjordan, all testifying to Swan's brilliance as a rider over the sticks and especially to the impact he had made at Cheltenham.

Ironically, on his first visit to Cheltenham in 1987 he broke his arm when Irish Dream came a cropper. It didn't end there. The ambulance taking him from the racecourse to the medical room was involved in an accident - "a car pulled right in front of us", Charlie recalled. "I was in enough pain at the time without wanting additional shocks", he added ruefully. So much for dreams of glory on a "dream" horse that wasn't up to delivering on the day....

But four of Swan's rides at the '93 Festival meeting certainly delivered in style and the beauty of it was that all four were for stables – three of them based in County Waterford – that wouldn't rate in the big-guns category of Martin Pipe's or 'The Duke' Nicholson's in Britain.

First there was Montelado storming up the hill to put twelve lengths between him and Lemon's Hill in the Supreme Novices' Hurdle, conjuring up memories of ill-fated Golden Cygnet pulverising his rivals in similar fashion in this race in 1978.

"This horse is something else again", was the tribute paid by Tony Mullins to Montelado.

✳   ✳   ✳

It was a great training feat by Pat Flynn of Rathgormack, County Waterford, to bring Montelado to winning peak on the day that mattered.

For, as the trainer himself told me, the horse had been very sick after Christmas. However, the patience shown by Flynn in avoiding giving Montelado any recent race was fully vindicated. Nowadays Pat Flynn has forty-five horses in training in the yard which he built, mostly himself, beside his bungalow, and his wife, Catherine, does all the paper work.

One of his proudest possessions is a huge wall plaque given him by his owners to mark his hundredth success. And he won the National Hunt Stallion Owners Award for the 1991/1992 season as top trainer of mares and fillies. In all he won fifteen races with eight mares during that season.

As Charlie Swan brought Montelado, who started at 5/1, back into the winner's enclosure to a mighty "Irish roar", I heard one Irishman exclaim to the heavens: "The bumper in '92, the Supreme Novices in '93 and the Champion in '94."

The connections went wild with excitement – and who could blame them.

Montelado was owned by a County Roscommon quartet headed by Ollie Hannon, who owns a poultry factory, Brian Nolan, a State solicitor and brother-in-law of former EU Commissioner, Ray MacSharry (who was present for the occasion), Donal O'Rourke, a veterinary surgeon and his son, John, who is Products Manager of Sligo Dairies, (the O'Rourkes actually bred the horse).

I liked the comment of Ollie Hannon, pinpointing the burning desire of the Irish for success at the Festival meeting: "We feel it and we accept it, and we're pleased to have this winner not for ourselves but for the people who wanted to see it."

Tiananmen Square had gone to Cheltenham '92 hailed as the Irish banker but he was beaten by Montelado in the Festival Bumper and this was the prelude to the gelding's sweeping triumph at the '93 Festival meeting, leading to the conclusion that he would complete a historic three-timer by winning the Champion Hurdle in '94. However, he had to be bar-fired on his off-fore and that killed the high ambitions entertained for him in the 1993-'94 season.

Pat Flynn was confident that he would be back.....

He was back all right to contest the 1995 Smurfit Champion Hurdle and, despite the fact that he had been off the track so long, he still had his supporters as he started at 10/1. It would have been asking a lot of him to get into the frame in the circumstances. As it was, he finished ninth behind Alderbrook.

He reappeared at the Listowel Festival meeting in September and was the medium of an inspired gamble from 10/1 to 4/1 before going off at 5/1 as he easily won the Listowel Racecourse Bookmakers Q.R. Handicap, a Flat race over two miles, beating two previous winners, Steel Mirror and Avoid The Rush.

It was a brilliant training performance by Pat Flynn to deliver him to win such a competitive event and at the same time amply repay the confidence reposed in him when he hadn't a run since the Cheltenham Festival meeting.

Montelado went on to win the Irish Cesarewitch under top weight at the Curragh in the hands of Michael Kinane, justifying even-money favouritism after opening at 6/4.

Now he was backed by "insiders" to win the 1996 Smurfit Champion Hurdle and the ante-post odds of 14/1 to 10/1 looked very attractive – if he could arrive fighting fit on the BIG DAY. There was a big "IF" about it.

But the memory of the way he pulverised his field at Cheltenham in '93 still lingered. He started at 5/4 favourite for the A.I.G. Europe Champion Hurdle at Leopardstown on Sunday, January 21st, '96 but, having been there with every chance three out, he had to be content with fourth place behind Collier Bay, Hotel Minella and Danoli.

The dream died, and those ante-post dockets with it, when a setback caused him to miss the Champion Hurdle. In fact, he had no other run during the 1995-'96 National Hunt season after the A.I.G. Europe Champion Hurdle.

✳   ✳   ✳

Charlie Swan's victory in the Gold Card Handicap Hurdle on the Wednesday of the '93 Festival meeting provided more grist for the mill for those who like a touch of the romantic to their Cheltenham yarns.

I was thinking that day that if you had an abscess in a tooth down Waterford way, you might have had to resign yourself to the fact that your favourite dentist was away "on business".

And the "business" in this instance meant one thing and one thing only – that he was over in Cheltenham having a flutter on Fissure Seal. At least that was the jocose way that friends of Waterford trainer, Harry de Bromhead were telling it as they arrived in Cheltenham.

In the Form Book the Syndicate that owned the horse was listed simply as the "Delton Syndicate".

It comprised four dentists, Richard O'Hara, Waterford, Sheila Keneally, Cork, Con O'Keeffe, Waterford and Sean McCarthy, Enniscorthy, who went to college together and had kept in touch all through their careers.

All four had a deep interest in racing and decided to pool their resources to purchase a horse to carry their colours.

It was most appropriate that a horse owned by four dentists should have been named Fissure Seal. A seal in this instance is what a dentist performs when tackling a child's cracked tooth.

The victory of Charlie Swan on Shuil Ar Aghaidh in the Bonusprint Stayers' Hurdle created a sense of euphoria in the town of Dungarvan that could never be equalled. And it represented the highlight of Paddy Kiely's career as a trainer.

The mare's win spanned almost half a century of the Kiely family history. It was back in the Forties that his father bought Chain Gang from local man Milo Walshe as a foundation mare from which to breed. She bred such as Shee Gaoithe and Sgeal Shee – and Shuil Ar Aghaidh became the fourth generation of the line.

Shuil Ar Aghaidh was trained by Paddy Kiely for his wife, Marie, and was bred by the trainer's brother, Matthew.

The mare was completing a Thursday double for Charlie Swan, who had earlier used forcing tactics to telling advantage on Shawiya, the first filly to win the Daily Express Triumph Hurdle, and trained in County Kildare by Michael J.P. O'Brien, who did a really brilliant job in bringing her to her best on the day.

O'Brien had learned the ropes under the late Tom Taaffe at Rathcoole and had been a champion jockey in America until breaking his back in a horrible fall in 1974, which resulted in his being confined to a wheelchair. He never has what one might describe as a big string but still ranks among the best of his profession and he has achieved a remarkable strike rate in the bigger races. Bright Moments and King Spruce put him on the map in the eighties. And in 1982 he also won his first Irish Grand National with King Spruce, ridden by Gerry Newman.

His second success came in 1992 with another eight-year-old, Vanton, who was the mount of Jason Titley.

Racing in the colours of Gervaise Maher, Shawiya went on from Cheltenham to win again in the hands of Charlie Swan in the Murphy's Irish Stout Champion 4-y-o Hurdle at the Punchestown Festival meeting, beating Titled Dance by no less than nine lengths and with the favourite, the English challenger, Lemon's Mill, unplaced. Shawiya was beaten only once in six races over hurdles that season.

*　　*　　*

With the Ritz Club trophy on his sideboard for his four-timer at the 1993 Cheltenham Festival meeting, Charlie Swan also had a four-timer over the three days of the Fairyhouse Irish Grand National meeting.

"Charlie was superb", was the spontaneous tribute of Grangecon, County Wicklow trainer, Francis Flood to him after he had ridden Ebony Jane to victory in the Jameson Irish Grand National. Flood was winning this race for the second time after an interval of 23 years. In 1970 he sent out Garoupe, ridden by the late Cathal Finnegan, to beat a better-backed stable-companion, Glencarrig Lady ridden by Tom Carberry.

Francis Flood has been established as a first-class trainer for close on thirty years now.

A native of Wicklow with a National Hunt background he was associated previously with another famous Grangecon establishment, the racing stables of the late Paddy Sleator. During that period of his life Francis Flood was a leading amateur rider, with a formidable record on the point-to-point circuit, and was no less than seven times champion amateur jockey under Rules.

*　　*　　*

Swan followed up his four-timer in 1993 with a three-timer at the 1994 Festival meeting on Danoli (Sun Alliance Novices' Hurdle), Time For A Run (Coral Cup Handicap Hurdle) and Mucklemeg (Bromsgrove Industries Festival Bumper) - all three on the Wednesday afternoon.

And he came very close to making it another four-timer when he finished second on Buckboard Bounce in the Cathcart Challenge Cup Chase – beaten three-quarters-of-a-length by Raymlette (Mick Fitzgerald).

At the time of writing this chapter in the summer of '96, Charlie Swan's great ambitions centre around winning the Gold Cup and Champion Hurdle and he would also like to go into the records as the rider of an Aintree Grand National winner.

But that three-timer in 1994, following up his four-timer at the '93 Festival meeting and the winning again of the Ritz Club Trophy had already assured Swan of immortality as a National Hunt rider irrespective of whether he realised his ambition of winning the Champion Hurdle, the Gold Cup and the Aintree Grand National.

No one was going to dislodge Swan as champion while he remained fighting fit.

The Hall of Fame is today one of the special features at Cheltenham – a magnet for all lovers of the National Hunt game.

It includes a fitting tribute to the late Pat Taaffe, whose 25 winners, including four Gold Cups, over the famous course put him well ahead of all comers as the leading jockey at Prestbury Park.

Pat Taaffe's career was unusual in many respects, not least that he was in the top flight as a professional from 1950 to 1970, and for all of that period was first jockey to the late Tom Dreaper, a man unsurpassed as a trainer of chasers.

Clearly Pat's Cheltenham record will be very hard to beat. If it is to be beaten in our time – or even approached – then Charlie Swan and Adrian Maguire are probably the two men with the ability to do so, if they can match Taaffe's durability in the saddle.

10

O'Grady Celebrates His 22nd In Style

Cheltenham '96 marked Edward O'Grady's 22nd Festival anniversary – it was back in 1974 that Mr Midland won the National Hunt Chase for the stable in the hands of 'Mouse' Morris. O'Grady certainly celebrated the 22nd in style, taking the National Hunt Chase again with Loving Around (Phillip Fenton), having earlier won the Arkle Challenge Trophy with Ventana Canyon, who had twenty lengths to spare over Arctic Kinsman at the finish. Thus he brought his total of Festival winners to fifteen.

And this becomes all the more impressive when one takes into account the fact that for ten years from 1984 to 1994 he did not add anything to his Cheltenham roll of honour. He was back challenging at the 1990 meeting after spending a number of years when his concentration was mainly on the Flat. Overall that period could be termed a disappointment compared with the peaks he had known when he was identified as one of the brightest and best of the young National Hunt trainers. The family tradition created by his late father, Willie O'Grady was over the jumps. And it was as a National Hunt trainer that the public had come to see Edward from the moment he took out a licence. It was inevitable that he would return to his first love.

Back in August, 1979 when I visited his establishment at Ballynonty, seven miles from Thurles he was describing Cheltenham to me as the Mecca. It is still Mecca to him today. "I put the three days of the Festival meeting in my diary ahead of anything else", he will tell you. "At the start of every season, I pick out what I think are the best horses and these I will aim at the target that matters for me above everything else – Cheltenham in March.

"There are twenty races now over the three days and everybody wants to have a winner. It's even an honour to have a horse good enough to run there. Cheltenham is world-wide in its reputation. Everybody in the racing world takes notice. It's almost like being a Flat trainer and wanting to win at Royal Ascot. The standards are the same – the highest that you can reach for".

The very fact that O'Grady's record is so impressive means that the pressure is on him to deliver winners – just as it was on Vincent O'Brien in the era in the late Forties and Fifties when he was "King" of the scene. "Cheltenhamitis" was the word that Vincent' s brothers, Dermot and Phonsie used to describe the disease that hit the stable at the turn of the New Year.

"A terrible disease", said Phonsie to me with an amused gleam in his eye. "Not alone was Vincent affected by it himself but everybody working for him was hit by it also. No stone was left unturned in the count-down to Cheltenham to ensure that failure could not be laid at the door of human error. Vincent was totally analytical in his approach to every facet of getting the horses ready for their particular races. He knew, of course, that the money would be going on them – big money – and in his mind, there was no place for excuses once he knew he had the material for the job. The pressure was intense, terribly so".

And Edward O'Grady confessed to me during a quiet moment at Galway '96 that he feels the pressure also in the count-down to Cheltenham each year. "I am conscious of what people are expecting. The public, indeed the entire nation creates the pressure. And when you are training one that gets to be classed an 'Irish banker', then the pressure becomes greater still".

∗   ∗   ∗

O'Grady numbers among his owners J.P. McManus, whose punting exploits in the ring have become part of the very lore of the Cheltenham Festival meeting. McManus prefers to wait for the day of a particular race to go for the jugular rather than invest ante-post. He wants to know that everything is spot-on and he wants above all else to know the state of the ground.

Edward O'Grady realises that with a man like J.P. you cannot fool around. You cannot cloud the situation in vague generalities. You cannot deal in "ifs" and "buts". You must lay it clearly on the line with no equivocation – as you see it.

It's then up to J.P. to decide whether he will "go to war" or keep his ammunition for another day.

"What they do with the assessment I give them is up to them", is how O'Grady puts it. In a word, it's like the presentation of *all* the options to the key man in a multi-national concern who is about to make a major investment. His final decision will be based on the scenario presented to him.

O'Grady turned out Time For A Run (Coral Cup Handicap Hurdle) and Mucklemeg (Bromsgrove Industries Festival Bumper) to win for J.P. McManus at the 1994 Festival meeting. It is history now how 'The Sundance Kid' would have taken £1 million, maybe more, out of the ring had he got the price on Time For A Run that he sought from the rails bookmaker who earlier felt the brunt of the action when McManus set out to recoup on Danoli the losses suffered on his Gimme Five on the opening afternoon.

O'Grady stresses that someone like J.P. would never discuss with him details of his betting investments.

"It's my task to produce the horse at its peak on the day. Months of planning and preparation may have gone into aiming at a particular target. Everything can be right a week beforehand, even forty-eight hours beforehand and then you know when the day itself arrives, something may not be just right and you may have a slight problem on your hands. It can colour everything.

"It's marvellous though when all you have put into it is rewarded and you hit the target. For at the end of the day it's all about winning.

"There is no greater amphitheatre than the winner's enclosure at Cheltenham during the Festival meeting", he went on. "Invariably, I want to kiss the ground when I walk into it.

"You wouldn't be human if you didn't feel a shiver run down your spine when the cheering starts as you come in beside a winner you have trained. There are times when you get the impression that the whole of Ireland has gathered around the amphitheatre such is the sustained manner in which the roar rises. It's so special. There is nothing else to compare with it in victory.

"Of course, you get a different kind of shiver, a cold one, if at the end of the week you haven't made it into that enclosure", he said.

Summing up for the *Gloucestershire Echo* before Cheltenham '96 what the National Hunt Festival meeting means to him, O'Grady said: "Cheltenham means many things to me – memories and expectations. Three hectic days that revolve around business, the sport, the competition and, of course, the craic!"

Elaborating further, he noted that "the camaraderie in National Hunt racing is marvellous".

"We go there as part of an Irish team and if we don't win, we want to see other Irish people win. Although we are obviously highly-competitive, it's akin to a rugby international – opposing teams always drink after the match.

"The social craic is part of the Festival. You need to be in serious training to go there and probably want to be fitter than your horse!

"The horses generally only run once, but I feel personally as though I have run four times!"

*   *   *

Always it gets back to Golden Cygnet when you find yourself interviewing Edward O'Grady. The memory dominates in a strange compelling way. Vincent O'Brien had described him as the best hurdler he had ever seen. That was high praise, indeed, coming from the man who trained the three-times Champion Hurdle winner, Hatton's Grace (1949-'51).

O'Grady was only 28 when Golden Cygnet left an indelible imprint by the way he won the 1978 Waterford Crystal Supreme Novice Hurdle at

Cheltenham, pulverising the opposition with such authority in a fifteen-lengths triumph that O'Grady would say to me later: "He would have been a certainty for the 1979 Champion Hurdle".

On the way to Cheltenham he had set up a sequence of five hurdle wins on the trot. Just when it seemed that he had the world at his feet he fell on his neck when he clipped the last flight in the Scottish Champion Hurdle at Ayr on April 15, 1978.

The clearest memory that remains to this day for the trainer is of the moment – a very private one– in the stables at Ayr racecourse.

He was standing there alone with Golden Cygnet and suddenly a strange thing happened. The horse – the great swelling on his neck clearly visible – walked over to him and rubbed him with his head. It was repeated not just once, but a number of times and Edward O'Grady realised that he was getting a silent message that "Cygnet" wanted him to do something for him.

"I didn't hesitate after that to get on to Edinburgh University..."

Uncanny – quite uncanny.

Golden Cygnet was taken straight in ... the trainer flies back to Tipperary and gets a call later that evening that the horse is okay...he's ecstatic with relief and joy...but then on the Monday night another call, this time with the shattering news that they did not think he would pull through the night...vertebrae fractured, the spinal cord affected...there was no need to hear anymore...

A third call from Edinburgh...the condition of Golden Cygnet has deteriorated further...now he has lost co-ordination because of the way the spinal cord has been affected...he is in great pain...the trainer knows the awful decision he is being asked to face...it's a blur at that moment...there was a phone dispute on and he couldn't get through to Galway to inform Ray Rooney of the position. It didn't matter anyway...he knows that now. Soon Golden Cygnet was dead.

Then the letters and the messages of sympathy began pouring in from all parts of Ireland and from Britain too...to the trainer and to Ray Rooney. It seemed that the racing world had stopped at the magnitude of what had happened. Everyone who was a lover of National Hunt racing at heart sensed that a great champion-in-the-making had died with the best that he could give still to come.

❋　　　❋　　　❋

Edward O'Grady could so easily have sat – like the character in the Dostoevsky story recalling the white nights of his youth – viewing again and again the video tape of Golden Cygnet's breath-taking win that caused the great Fred Rimell to remark: "Never have I seen a horse win at the Festival meeting so easily".

But, no, he did not allow the cruel stroke of misfortune that robbed Irish National Hunt racing of its greatest potential champion since Arkle to shatter his self-confidence or cause him to flinch from the challenge of getting on with the job.

"It happens all the time in racing", he said, his 29th birthday looming before him that September. He reeled off the names of outstanding horses – like Lanzarote at Cheltenham in 1977 – which had to be put down when ill-luck struck. Later Buck House, winner of the 1986 Queen Mother Champion Chase for 'Mouse' Morris and with Tommy Carmody in the saddle, would die of the colic.

You could not wrap them in cotton-wool, hoping thus that you could off-set the quirks of fate. "A freak, a total freak", was how he described the accident that gave Golden Cygnet his fatal injury.

In August of '78 Edward O'Grady had seen his Shining Flame put down after breaking a leg at the finish of the Smithwicks Beer Handicap Chase at Tramore. He had won the Galway Plate in very impressive style and in all, the eight-year-old, bred by Nick Rackard, won a total of nine races.

"Racing is one of the greatest games of all – but at the same time the best leveller. A horse breaks a leg, a hot favourite gets beat. You are never allowed to get a step ahead of yourself", was the philosophical comment by Edward O'Grady to me at the time.

It didn't seem that you could get it worse than to lose two horses of the calibre of Golden Cygnet and Shining Flame inside a period of four short months. There are men who in such circumstances would be tempted to toss their hat at it altogether.

Not so Edward O'Grady. He had been steeled to the hammer-blows of fate long before Golden Cygnet met his tragic end.

He had not been long training when his father died at the age of 58 in January, 1972. He had put some outstanding horses through his hands and created the beacon that Edward would follow in time when he won the Cathcart Cup at Cheltenham in 1969 with Kinloch Brae (T.E. Hyde)and the Spa Hurdle in 1960 with Solfen (Bobby Beasley)and the same horse won the Broadway Novice Chase (now the Sun Alliance Chase)with Pat Taaffe in the saddle.

Now the full responsibility of managing the stables at Killeens, Ballynonty fell on Edward's shoulders. The first horse he ran as a trainer pulled up. His initial training success came when Timmy Hyde rode the five-year-old Vibrax to an eight-lengths win in the Craigue Handicap Hurdle at Gowran Park on Thursday, January 27, 1972.

"In my first twelve weeks as a trainer I had twelve winners. I was just beginning to think there there was no job in the world to equal it. Then the stable was hit by a virus. One day I had eighteen horses in training, the next day every single one of them had the virus. There was nothing I could do. It seemed my entire world had collapsed overnight.

He flew off to Rhodes on a belated honeymoon (his father had died three weeks after he had married Judy Mullins from County Meath, well known in the world of show jumping).

"When we returned, quite a lot of owners took away their horses. But three stood by me. I cannot forget their faith in me at that time. Eventually, we pulled out of it and we ended up with between 18-20 horses in the stable. I finished 1972 with fourteen winners".

At the time he was charging a fee of £10 a week for each horse he trained (compared with £140 today). The highest wage he paid was £15 a week.

His owners were mostly farmers or people with land. Some of these farmers bred the horses they sent him and in summer they could put them out to grass on their own farms. That way training fees were only payable when the horses were actually in O'Grady's stables being prepared for races. It was a mutually-acceptable arrangement.

From the outset O'Grady's was known as a "gambling stable". No trainer was more feared by the bookies when the money was down. You could have an owner putting £1,000 (quite a substantial bet then on the nose on his horse without batting an eyelid.

O'Grady himself liked to go for a good old-fashioned tilt at the ring two or three times a year. And the manner in which the gambles came off kept the connections of the winners happy and his own financial situation on the right side.

He had his first Cheltenham winner when Mr Midland won the 1974 National Hunt Chase, his second two years later when Prolan took the Kim Muir Chase and Golden Cygnet (Supreme Novice Hurdle)and Flame Gun (Stayers Hurdle) were winners in 1978.

As Cheltenham and the big Festival prizes became increasingly the primary target of the year, priorities changed somewhat, though not the wariness of the rails bookies on the domestic front. Now at the start of each National Hunt season, O'Grady would earmark a sizeable number of horses as potential Cheltenham challengers. The weeding-out process would continue to the end of the year and on into the New Year. The ones that emerged as fairly definite to be in the team for Prestbury Park in March had a different programme mapped out for them to those that were aimed at rather mundane targets.

"You absolutely must have the confidence to miss the cherries along the way that you could easily put in the bag and you must have an owner who understands why it has to be", he told Alastair Down in the course of a very perceptive piece in the *Sporting Life* on Queen Mother Champion Chase Day at the '96 Festival meeting.

"I am not a naturally patient man, but over the years I have been taught patience by the horses. Or, perhaps more truthfully, I have had to learn it", he went on.

Another thing that had to be learned, he stressed, was how to take defeat. He instanced Kilmakillogue being turned over by Bannow Rambler. "He was a very hot favourite and we are all convinced to this day that he was got at.

"I had spent the previous night in the cells at Ulverston after being arrested over the Gay Future Affair. Looking back, I think I'd have preferred to spend the next day in the cells as well:", he remarked to Alastair Down rather ruefully.

✳   ✳   ✳

J.P. McManus has been one of Edward O'Grady's most faithful owners since the mid-Seventies and O'Grady is quick to acknowledge the debt he owes him for his continued unswerving loyalty.

The association between the two began when J.P. rang O'Grady one day and asked him to buy Jack Of Trumps for him. Jack Of Trumps had won his novice chase over three miles by 20 lengths as a four-year-old "and won it with his mouth open", as the Tipperary trainer put it.

He appeared a gilt-edged prospect to win the National Hunt Chase as a five-year-old at Cheltenham '78.

No one knows the pitfalls of this lottery of a race better than Ted Walsh, the eleven-time Irish amateur champion jockey, now a trainer in his own right and a very popular and knowledgeable RTE personality in the racing sphere. "It is nearly 4/1 against a clear round – without even thinking of winning", he said.

Why then do the big gamblers plough in on this race with their heads down when the odds are so stacked against them?

"Racing men believe that if you get a good horse for this race, then you are on the proverbial good thing despite the obvious hazards. Quare Times, ridden to victory in 1954 by 'Bunny' Cox for Vincent O'Brien, was a case in point and you recall that this one went on to win the Aintree Grand National the following year. In 1986 Omerta was just right for the job and all he needed was ordinary luck in running as he won for Homer Scott", said Ted.

At the same time, however, some tremendous Irish gambles on this event became unstuck. In 1977 Mount Prague, which Ted Walsh himself rode for Mick O'Toole, was the medium of one of the biggest ever Irish gambles at the Festival meeting. He started 11/8 favourite in a field of 21 and was in mid-division on the inside when he fell at the 18th fence.

J.P. McManus came back sun-tanned from his honeymoon in Miami to the 1978 Festival meeting. He quickly ended all speculation on the vital question as to which race had been chosen for Jack Of Trumps. When he announced that it had been decided in consultation with Edward O'Grady to run the gelding in the National Hunt Chase he thought to himself "Jack Of Trumps should win barring accidents".

Considering what he was to accomplish subsequently, Jack Of Trumps certainly looked tailor-made to outclass the opposition.

Indeed, some observers were talking in terms of an "Arkle-type potential" so impressive did he look when giving 18lbs and a six-lengths beating to Shining Flame in the John Jameson Cup; then in the Embassy Premier Qualifier he beat Chinrullah by ten lengths without even being extended and he produced one of the finest performance of his career when defeating Night Nurse by six lengths in the Hermitage Chase at Newbury.

All that lay in the future as Jack Or Trumps was backed down to 8/11 favourite to triumph at Cheltenham '78. To this day many people believe that J.P. could have had as much as £40,000 on the horse. But he told me that he didn't bet on him – "as I felt the odds were too short".

Jack Of Trumps fell at the 17th and that same year the victor was the 10/1 shot, Gay Tie ridden by John Fowler for Mick O'Toole.

"While I can live with a defeat like that, it is the cheer that goes up, mainly from the bookies that I cannot stomach", said Edward O'Grady. The bookies certainly had reason to cheer that day as they counted their winnings.

They had reason to cheer again in 1979 when J.P. McManus had Deep Gale in the race, trained by Edward O'Grady and ridden my Niall Madden. "I had backed Master Smudge earlier in the day when he won the Sun Alliance Chase at 20/1. I put all I had intended putting on Deep Gale plus the winnings from Master Smudge", J.P. himself told me and it was unquestionably one of his biggest gambles of the Seventies on one race at Cheltenham.

Deep Gale went off at 11/10 favourite in a field of 25. It was a tremendous betting race as Pillar Brae, ridden by Ted Walsh, was the medium of a spectacular gamble from 10/1 to 9/2. Deep Gale fell at the 19th when closing on the leaders while Pillar Brae went at the 8th. Niall Madden told me afterwards that he was motoring like a winner when he fell. In fact, he believed that he was so superior to the opposition that if he could have caught Deep Gale and remounted, he would have won.

Edward O'Grady wiped the smiles from the faces of the bookies through the successful gambles on Staplestown in the 1981 County Handicap Hurdle and Mr Donovan in the 1982 Sun Alliance Novices Hurdle.

I recall quite vividly being outside the Weighroom when word was whispered in my ear by an insider to "get on" Staplestown, who was to be the "get-out" bet for many an Irish punter at the meeting.

When I reached the ring I spotted 12/1 on one board and was stepping in to take it when all hell broke loose. I counted myself lucky to get 10/1, then 8/1 and 7/1 and finally 6/1 before his price dropped to 9/2 in one of the most spectacular gambles I have ever witnessed at Cheltenham. Eventually he went off at 11/2 favourite and, in the hands of Tommy Ryan, fully justified O'Grady's confidence in him.

J.P. McManus had put the hammer-blows of the defeats of Jack Of Trumps and Deep Gale behind him and was ready to "go to war" with a vengeance on Mr. Donovan in '82.

"I did not have a very good first day but did not mind too much, as I felt I would get it all back and more on the first race on the Wednesday", recalled J.P. "I expected we might get 12/1 to 14/1 to our money but word got out about Mister Donovan's ability and I had to take far less than those odds".

Suffice it to say that Mister Donovan (Tommy Ryan)started at 9/2. Gaining a definite advantage on the bit three out, he held off the challenge of Spider's Web with Bob Champion in the saddle to win by one and a half lengths.

Mr Donovan represented J.P. McManus's first Festival win as an owner.

He saw his colours carried to victory again the following year in the National Hunt Chase by Bit Of A Skite, trained by Edward O'Grady and ridden by Frank Codd. J.P. didn't back Bit Of A Skite as he had an infected foot in the count-down to Cheltenham and most of his work had been done in an equine pool.

Bit Of A Skite incurred a 14lbs penalty for the Jameson Irish Grand National that same year. McManus knew that he was still thrown in with only 9st 7lbs and represented something to bet on. However, his big worry and that of Edward O'Grady was that the foot that had given so much trouble before Cheltenham was still not right. The swimming programme which had led to the Festival triumph was now repeated and, indeed, the horse's only appearance on the gallops was "a ten furlongs spin to clear his wind", as Edward O'Grady put it.

J.P., despite the risks he was taking on the gammy leg, hit the ring in a fashion that the big English bookies had escaped at Cheltenham. Starting at 7/1, Bit Of A Skite, after a copybook ride by Tommy Ryan, won by six lengths from Beech King with the English challenger, Royal Judgement, the 4/1 favourite, only ninth.

Half an hour after the race, Bit Of A Skite was found to be lame. It represented a tremendous feat of training by Edward O'Grady to get him to the start and capable of winning such a test of stamina following his exertions at the Festival meeting.

Thus in his twelfth year as a trainer Edward O'Grady won the Irish Grand National for the first time – a race his father won twice with Hamstar (1948) and Icy Calm (1951)

＊　　　＊　　　＊

It was in the early Eighties that Edward O'Grady took the fateful decision to concentrate his training efforts mainly on the Flat.

The accepted theory for his departure from the jumping scene was his desire to make it to the big-time as a Flat trainer – try, in effect, to emulate Vincent O'Brien. His many admirers were surprised.

But O'Grady revealed to me that the decision was forced on him by the recession in farming at the time. While he still maintained a good strike rate over the jumps, it wasn't reflected in his bank balance.

"Look, the farming community are the real life-blood of the National Hunt game. In the late Seventies farming was going through a very bad time and quite a number of people who would have horses with me as a matter of course just could not afford to do so. I did not change by choice. I had to change with the times", he explained.

I suggested to him that overall his days training on the Flat left no lasting impact on the racing public's mind and I reminded him what Lester Piggott had said to me of his days as a trainer – it didn't matter if he had a treble at Brighton or Salisbury, the public expected him to turn out Classic winners and when he failed to do so, they didn't deem him a success? Likewise the public had come to link his (Edward O'Grady's) name with Cheltenham Festival winners and they found it difficult to accept him as training solely on the Flat?

"I never had more than 25 Flat horses", he responded. "You cannot, I believe, hope to achieve anything of note with that number of horses, either on the Flat or over the jumps. Originally, when I was concentrating mainly on the jumps, I had a stable of 80 horses".

He doesn't regret the years he spent concentrating on the Flat. He came out of it okay financially but, more important, he discovered facets of racing he had not known before. In a word, he grew up in the commercial sense.

But he missed the adrenalin-pumping excitement that Cheltenham alone can generate. He missed also the special flavour of the other big National Hunt occasions – Leopardstown at Christmas, the Fairyhouse Easter meeting and the big Punchestown Spring meeting. The winter game had burned into his soul from the time he first became a trainer. It was in his blood from being with his father and his days as an amateur rider. It was only when he returned that he realised what it really meant to him.

He knew he wasn't going to set the National Hunt scene alight immediately he came back. It was almost like starting again from scratch.

But he still had J.P. McManus as one of his owners and how fitting it was that exactly a decade on from when Northern Game (Tommy Ryan) triumphed at the '84 Cheltenham Festival meeting Time For A Run, carrying the colours of J.P. and ridden by Charlie Swan, should win the Coral Golden Handicap Hurdle.

O'Grady was only too well aware of the old boxing dictum "they never come back" and he realised that it could be applied just as easily to racing.

Therefore, Time For A Run's success gave him a sense of satisfaction beyond words and what was an unforgettable day for him was capped when Mucklemeg, again carrying the colours of J.P. McManus, landed the Festival Bumper.

Back in the Seventies when he was in his twenties he made the Queen's Hotel his base in Cheltenham. So also did J.P. McManus. I would see them at breakfast after they had come back from watching the horses at morning exercise on the course. Mick O'Toole, Jack Doyle and others were also an integral part of the scene. The buzz was special.

At 46, as I write this chapter in the summer of '96, he is maturer, more street-wise and prefers with Judy to take a house outside Cheltenham. And this gives him moments when he can find the kind of relaxation he knows he would never find in a hotel.

He certainly needed to escape the pressure during Cheltenham '96 when his team included a number of horses that were looked upon by the betting public and the bookies as capable of putting the Tipperary trainer in line for a treble if not a four-timer.

Racing is a strange old game.On the face of it Sound Man and Time For A Run would have been taken as bankers by many ahead of Ventana Canyon and Loving Around, yet Ventana Canyon won the Guinness Arkle Challenge Trophy Chase at 7/1 while Loving Around scored in the National Hunt Chase at 10/1.

Charlie Swan had been riding under a special arrangement for J.P. McManus and rode both Time For A Run and Mucklemeg to victory for him at the '94

Festival meeting. Then the Irish champion jump jockey decided to go as first jockey to Aidan O'Brien and Richard Dunwoody became associated with the O'Grady stable and with horses like Sound Man and Ventana Canyon.

Sound Man recorded a four-timer on his way to Cheltenham '96, winning the Fortria EBF Chase at Navan on November 4th, '95 in the hands of Dunwoody on his way to a sparkling triumph in the First National Bank Gold Cup Chase at Ascot the same month. He followed this up with another authoritative victory in the Mitsubishi Shogun Tingle Creek Trophy Chase at Sandown in December and had fourteen lengths to spare over Easy Buck when taking the Comet Chase at Ascot in February.

It wasn't surprising that he should start 11/8 favourite for the Queen Mother Champion Chase but Klairon Davis, who had beaten him in the 'Arkle' the previous year, confirmed his superiority when relegating Sound Man to third place with Viking Flagship second. At Aintree Sound Man started 6/4 favourite for the Mumm Melling Chase but this time was beaten by Viking Flagship with Klairon Davis fourth.

∗   ∗   ∗

It was a superb training performance by Edward O'Grady to turn out Ventana Canyon to win the 'Arkle' at the '96 Festival meeting by 20 lengths from Arctic Kinsman, especially when you reflect on the fact that he had to restore the gelding's confidence after he had fallen two out when in a challenging position in the Baileys Arkle Challenge Cup Novice Chase at the Leopardstown Christmas meeting.

He made a blunder four out in the I.A.W.S. Novices' Chase at Punchestown when runner-up to King Wah Glory in his final race before Cheltenham – but what was important was that he stayed on his feet and he was staying on well at the finish in the heavy going that prevailed that day.

Edward O'Grady knew just how testing the Cheltenham fences were and he broke new ground the morning of the 'Arkle'.

"I did something I had never done before and schooled the horse early in the morning over one fence – I just thought it might sharpen him up", he told me in the winner's enclosure.

Richard Dunwoody, who rode a typically confident race, was away from the near-gale that hit the course and shedding weight in the sauna but he knew that O'Grady, the man with the key to Cheltenham success, would have his mount in perfect trim.

"The horse was in great form and the only mistake he made was at the ditch. He's always been a good horse – remember, he was second in the Supreme Novices' in '95", said Richard.

Ventana Canyon's task was made easier by the early exit of Manhattan Castle and the tragedy that befell the 7/2 favourite, the Martin Pipe-trained Draborgie. Manhattan Castle, who started 6/1 second favourite, veered sharply right as the tapes went up and unseated Francis Woods. Draborgie shattered a hind leg crossing the road after the second and had to be put down. Trying Again was pulled up after the fourth and Cumbrian Challenge fell when prominent at the fifth. Double Symphony crashed through the ninth and fell, firing Charlie Swan out of the saddle.

The hope of the North of England, Ask Tom, previously unbeaten over fences, was in trouble with his fencing from halfway and was struggling while King Wah Glory was eventually pulled up before two out.

Arctic Kinsman touched down in front three out and looked set momentarily to come right away but he missed out at the next. Ventana Canyon took a narrow lead and it was obvious that 'Kinsman' was leg-weary as they faced up to the hill. Ventana Canyon strode home unchallenged by 20 lengths and Carl Llewellyn, rider of the runner-up, was making no excuses when he said:"I thought I'd win going down the hill, but the winner was just too good for me".

Ventana Canyon ran in the colours of Vincent O'Brien's son-in-law, Philip Myerscough but joint-owner, Peter Curling, one of the finest equine artists of the modern era, who lives at Gooldcross, County Tipperary also shared in the celebrations in the winner's enclosure. Edward O'Grady playfully 'crowned' Peter Curling with the magnificent crystal trophy as the cameras clicked.

Jane Myerscough, wife of the boss of Goffs, had reason to be ecstatic for Ventana Canyon was bred at the Myerscoughs' own Ballysheehan Stud, Cashel, County Tipperary. Jane noted that her father had watched the race on television. Of course, he had turned out Cheltenham winners with a regularity that amazed the racing world. Cottage Rake had won three successive Gold Cups before the mighty Arkle appeared on the scene and Haltons Grace three successive Champion Hurdlers (1949-'51).

How fitting that Anne, Duchess of Westminster, owner of Arkle should present the trophies.

Nowadays Edward O'Grady is always on the look-out on behalf of his owners for horses that have the stamp of potential Cheltenham winners. He admits that on this particular plane one can be rather "fussy" and "choosy" for at the end of the day quality is at the basis of the winning of the major prizes at the Festival meeting.

In his case if it is known that he is in the market, the seller can presume that J.P.'s resources are behind O'Grady as he seeks to buy a particular horse. "Naturally the seller will want to get the highest-possible price while I have the duty to my owners not to think in terms of the sky being the limit. There has to be an air of realism in all this. There has got to be a limit to what you are willing to pay. Every deal is done differently".

As I parted with him at Galway '96, he told me that he had about 40 horses and the bulk of them were jumpers "I have only six horses over the age of six. So you might say that our hopes are pinned on the 'Busby Babes', or should it be the 'O'Grady Babes', hitting the honours trail and justifying the outlay on each one of them".

Whatever the remaining seasons of this century hold, it will be cause for surprise if by the time the new Millennium arrives Edward O'Grady has not added to his overall Cheltenham total and maybe hit double figures by reaching, if not passing, the 20-winner mark. As it is, he has achieved enough to give him a special place in the Cheltenham Hall of Fame.

He will be remembered always as the man who trained Golden Cygnet.

11

Hats Off To Moore And Woods

I t was a moment of nostalgia, a throw-back to the days of L'Escargot, which his father, Dan trained to win successive Gold Cups (1970-'71) and an Aintree Grand National (1975), when Arthur Moore placed his trilby between Klairon Davis's ears in the winner's enclosure after the Rose Laurel gelding's triumph in a titanic battle for the 1996 Queen Mother Champion Chase.

And Moore did it again after Feathered Gale had won for him his first Jameson Irish Grand National at Fairyhouse on Monday, April 8, 1996.

Jockey Francis Woods shared in both these outstanding successes and, of course, he had been on board Klairon Davis at the '95 Cheltenham Festival meeting when he overcame Sound Man in a dramatic contest for the 'Arkle' – form that would be confirmed in no uncertain fashion at Cheltenham '96.

Arthur Moore is not a man normally given to displays of emotion, either in victory or defeat. But all the barriers of reserve were unconsciously swept aside for once as he watched Klairon Davis come back to form in resounding fashion to beat Viking Flagship, bidding to become the first horse since Badsworth Boy to win this race three years running, while Sound Man, the 11/8 favourite could only finish third. Travado was fourth and Strong Man fifth.

But the bare outlining of the result can give no indication of the adrenalin-pumping excitement of the climax of a race, which provided one of the finest chasing spectacles at the '96 Festival meeting. Sound Man, despite his many jumping errors, and Viking Flagship, forced into error also by what his owner Graham Roach described as "the pressure out there", seemed to have it between them four out. In a way they cut each others throats in a fierce battle that looked to have gone Sound Man's way at the top of the hill. Notions of Klairon Davis becoming the first horse since Remittance Man in 1992 to complete the Arkle Trophy – Queen Mother Champion Chase seemed remote at this last ditch, where he made a bad mistake and was left three lengths behind the two leaders. "I thought the best we could hope for at that point was third place but Klairon Davis is as tough as they come",

Francis Woods recounted. "I decided he needed a breather. I hunted him along and did not ask him to go after Sound Man and Viking Flagship until we reached the second last. I could see the others were having a real tussle and I was hoping I could peg them back on the hill".

As the crescendo of cheering rose from the stands and enclosures, it seemed then that Sound Man was heading for victory and supporters of Viking Flagship were still hoping that he might complete the three-timer.

"My horse is so brave and has so much class that he went from looking set for third to having a real chance before we got to the final fence", Woods went on. "Only then did I believe we would win barring an accident".

Klairon Davis had gained ground so rapidly that he rose to the last in line with Sound Man and Viking Flagship. Once he had cleared the fence, however, it was all over in a couple of strides and he powered clear to put five lengths between himself and Viking Flagship at the winning post to delight owner, Chris Jones, uncle of Arthur Moore's wife, Mary.

One can understand why Arthur Moore exclaimed to the heavens:"What a horse, what a horse" and why his daughter, Anna was in tears with the sheer joy of it all.

One can understand even more why emotion was very evident in his voice as he was interviewed by Brough Scott for Channel 4 and then by the general body of racing writers and why he should describe it as "the greatest thrill of my racing life".

✻   ✻   ✻

At one stage in the 1995-'96 season Klairon Davis had been virtually written off by the pundits as a real live Irish candidate for the Queen Mother Champion Chase.

A surface reading of the Form Book would have explained why, Klairon Davis, after beating Merry Gale at Tipperary in November '95, sank into a slump which saw him fall at the fifth at Punchestown, then unseat Francis Woods when blundering badly at Leopardstown in January in the McCain Chase won by Imperial Call and in his final outing before Cheltenham later that same month, he was beaten a neck by Brockley Court at Punchestown. It emerged that in hitting a fence that day he had pulled shoulder muscles so painfully that he was barely able to walk from his horse-box on returning to Moore's yard near Naas, County Kildare. "He was on three legs and I thought that was it for Cheltenham", he recalled. Some days of inactivity followed.

It represented a tremendous feat of training then by Arthur Moore to restore the seven-year-old to full fitness and bring him to the point where he could take on Sound Man and Viking Flagship and beat them with such authority that he had to be rated unquestionably the best two-mile chaser in Ireland and Britain. And to think that he went off at 9/1!

Klairon Davis went on to add the £50,000 BMW Handicap Chase at the

Punchestown Festival meeting to his epic Cheltenham triumph.

"A fantastic horse", Arthur Moore enthused in the winner's enclosure. "He proved himself in carrying top weight to victory in testing ground. He jumped well all the way around and put in a great leap at the third last. That was the decisive moment".

Sound Man, which was getting 4lbs from the winner, went off joint-favourite with Klairon Davis but once again had to concede the advantage.

Moore noted that Klairon Davis needed time to recover from his exertions at Liverpool where he had finished fourth to Viking Flagship. "He really came into his own in the past week and I knew that he had a very good chance of success. He's a beautiful horse to train. And he's so brave".

✳　　✳　　✳

It was a memorable season overall for Arthur Moore and for stable jockey Francis Woods, who not alone was associated with the outstanding victories that Klairon Davis scored at Cheltenham and Punchestown but also steered Feathered Gale to victory in the '96 Jameson Irish Grand National.

Cheering Woods home in the Queen Mother Champion Chase was his father, Paddy Woods who suffered a couple of narrow defeats in his time riding for the Tom Dreaper stable. "I never won around here and I missed the '95 Festival meeting when Francis won the Arkle on Klairon Davis. It's a proud moment for me to see him up there being presented to the Queen Mother who really loves the jumping game", said Paddy.

Incidentally, while Paddy Woods never rode in the Aintree Grand National, he won two Irish Grand Nationals and rode Arkle to win over hurdles.

At 5ft 2ins, 28-years-old Francis Woods is one of the smallest jump jockeys in the business and he can do 9st 7lbs without the slightest problem. "With a bit of wasting I could get down to 9st and ride on the Flat, but I see no point when I have such good jumpers to ride".

It was when Tom Taaffe hung up his boots and turned to training that Woods became No. 1. stable jockey to Arthur Moore. Success came slowly to him. He had been in racing for three years – the first two with Con Collins – before he rode his first winner and, as he put it to Michael Clower of the *Sporting Life*, he was initially a "go anywhere, ride anything" jockey and really it was that way until the Moore job became his.

His hobbies include watching Formula One motor racing and rugby – "I no longer play the game" – and golf, which he does play.

"But it's riding that takes up almost all my time", he added.

A record 24,000 racegoers – easily topping the previous best of around 18,000 – saw Feathered Gale take the Jameson Irish Grand National and give Francis Woods his second win in the race. He had been successful on the Peter McCreery-trained Son Of War in 1994.

Arthur Moore was emulating his father who rode Revelry to win the race in 1947 and trained Tied Cottage to score in 1979.

The going came good to fast just at the right time for Feathered Gale, described by Moore as a summer-type horse. In fact, Feathered Gale had won the Digital Galway Plate two years previously in similar conditions and was third in the Irish National in '95.

The 1993 Gold Cup winner, Jodami was backed from 8/1 to 5/1 favouritism. As he loomed up to challenge in the hands of Mark Dwyer, it appeared that his class would tell. But the concession of 26lbs to 8/1 chance Feathered Gale proved too much for Peter Beaumont's gallant chase and he was beaten by eight lengths.

Feathered Gale is owned in partnership by Dungarvan, Co Waterford, businessman Michael O'Connor and Eamon King, a solicitor from the same town.

The Dungarvan connection was completed by breeder Nicky Connors, from whom O'Connor also bought Ballyhane, who went on to be a smart chaser in Britain.

It remains now for 46-years-old Arthur Moore to win the Gold Cup, the Champion Hurdle and the Aintree Grand National and he will have scaled the final peaks that all leading National Hunt trainers aim to try and win before they retire – granted, of course, they are lucky enough to acquire the type of horse capable of mounting a meaningful challenge for these three events. He would love, of course, to follow in his father's footsteps by winning the Gold Cup and Aintree Grand National.

※　　　※　　　※

When Arthur Moore emerged as Ireland's National Hunt champion trainer for the 1991-'92 season, he could be said to have attained a position he was destined from birth to achieve.

Like Dermot Weld, Edward O'Grady and Jim Dreaper, it seemed the natural progression for him to maintain the family tradition by becoming a trainer. Arthur's mother, Joan was a distinguished horsewoman in her own right, proved her worth as a trainer before and after Dan's death and in more recent times made history by becoming the first woman Steward of the Irish National Hunt Steeplechase Committee and the first woman to manage Punchestown racecourse. Although the latter position has now been taken over by Charles Murless, Joan Moore is still a familiar figure on race days at the track and particularly during the big Spring Festival meeting. She is a member of the Irish Horseracing Authority.

Arthur Moore had gained considerable experience as assistant to his father for six years before he took out a licence in 1975. He was also a successful amateur rider, being joint champion with Dermot Weld in 1969 and in all he rode more than 60 winners. His big-race successes, apart from the Irish Grand National win on King's Sprite, included a Troytown Chase win and a Thyestes Chase victory.

Moore did not take long to make his mark as a trainer. In 1979 he sent out his first winner of the Sweeps Hurdle (now the Ladbroke Handicap

Hurdle)when Irian scored at 25/1, ridden, quite sensationally at the time, by Mrs Ann Ferris. Moore produced Fredcoteri to take this race in successive years, 1983 and '84 and won it twice more with Bonalma in 1986 and Roark in 1988. No other trainer has as yet come near that tally of five wins.

Fredcoteri also won the Wessel Cable Champion Hurdle (now the A.I.G. European Champion Hurdle) in 1985 and in 1982 another old favourite, Royal Bond won the Harold Clarke Leopardstown Chase. He campaigned over a long period in Britain and Ireland, mostly carrying big weights with great distinction and paying his handler the ultimate compliment by continuing to race until the age of 15 when he won on his final appearance in the Murphy's Irish Stout Chase at Killarney in 1988.

※　　　※　　　※

Arthur Moore's sister, Pamela is married to Tommy Carberry, one of the finest jump jockeys that Ireland produced, his mastery as a horseman being displayed on Tied Cottage in the 1980 Gold Cup (the latter was subsequently disqualified on technical grounds); also on L'Escargot in the Aintree Grand National (1975), on Inkslinger, (1973) in the Queen Mother Champion Chase and on Anaglog's Daughter (1980) and The Brockshee (1981) in the Arkle Challenge Trophy Chase and there were those successive Irish Grand National triumphs on Brown Lad (1975 and '76).

Carberry's transition from the saddle to training may not have been marked by any singular successes but he has reason to be proud of the manner in which his son, Paul has kept the family flag flying high since moving to Britain at the outset of the 1995-'96 jumping season to take up a retainer with owner Robert Ogden who has horses with Ferdie Murphy, Andy Turnell and Gordon Richards.

He was not arriving at Middleham in Yorkshire as a young greenhorn but as the finished article and former British champion, Peter Scudamore went on record to say how impressed he was by him, adding: "He rides exceptionally well. I very much like the commitment he shows through his races. The fences at a place like Haydock are bigger and stiffer than he would have been used to at some of the smaller Irish tracks, so he has to alter a bit there. But that will be no problem to him because he is a superb horseman. I can see him going right to the top".

Scudamore was right in his prediction.

Even before he moved to Britain, Paul Carberry had already made his mark at the Cheltenham Festival meeting when he won the Festival Bumper in 1993 on the Homer Scott-trained Rhythm Section, beating Charlie Swan on the favourite, Heist in the process. That was a very significant day for Carberry. Another day of great significance for him was his victory over the Aintree fences on Joe White in the John Hughes Memorial Chase on Thursday, March 28, 1996. Tommy Carberry had won the Topham, as this race was then known, on Our Greenwood in 1975. And now twenty-one years on, his 22-year-old son earned the plaundits of all the racing writers present for a very polished performance that achieved a last-gasp victory on the 33/1 shot, who had been bought by owner-trainer Howard Johnson from his father at the Doncaster Sales as "a fun horse".

The 1995-'96 season was Paul Carberry's first full season in Britain and he finished with a total of winners.

He had accepted the offer from Robert Ogden because he was assured of far greater opportunities than he would have in Ireland and, as he put it himself, he was promised "a proper living". He had the ambition too to win big races. "There's more chance of riding a good horse here than at home", he said.

The move turned out to be a very wise one in his case but then horsemanship was in his blood as in the case of Dessie Hughes's son, Richard who established himself just as quickly on the Flat when he decided to switch from Ireland to England.

A week after Paul Carberry had been offered – and turned down – the plum job of No. 1. stable jockey to the Kim Bailey stable (in favour of staying loyal to Robert Ogden) he had the misfortune to fracture his left arm in a fall from Ballinaboola Grove in the Lockes Whiskey Handicap Chase at Kilbeggan on Friday evening, September 6, '96 . "My arm is fractured in two places and my surgeon has told me I will be out for a long time , two-and-a-half to three months", revealed the 22-year-old.

Carberry, who had been riding in Ireland on a regular basis during the summer of '96, was not due back in Britain until early the following week.

The misfortune that had struck Adrian Maguire and Norman Williamson during the 1995-'96 National Hunt season had now hit Carberry just as the 1996-'97 season was about to get into full swing in Britain.

✳   ✳   ✳

Jim Dreaper is another trainer carrying on the proud traditions set by his father, the late Tom Dreaper.

He tasted Gold Cup success with Ten Up in 1975 and there is no doubt in my mind that he would have won a second in 1978 had the race not been postponed because of snow to April 12 (the Cheltenham Stewards erred badly by not putting off for just twenty-four hours the third day of the '78 Festival meeting and Peter O'Sullevan went so far as to describe it as "a massive blunder").

If the race had been run in the soft going that Brown Lad needed to show his real talent, then he would have fully justified the Irish singing "Brown Lad in the rain...". But on April 12 it was "good" and, not surprisingly, in the circumstances Brown Lad drifted to 8/1. The Fred Winter-trained seven-years-old Midnight Court, still a novice, won deservedly in the hands of John Francome from Brown Lad, who stayed on up the hill to gain runner-up position – but the Irish were left to ponder the might-have-beens.

Brown Lad went on to make racing history at Fairyhouse on Easter Monday, 27 March 1978, when he became the first horse in the 108 years of the Irish Distillers (now Jameson) Grand National to win the event three times (he had won it previously in 1975 and '76).

It was a tremendous training feat by Jim Dreaper to produce the 12-year-old chaser to win the event under 12-2, after the setbacks in training the horse had experienced. But Brown Lad got the soft going he needed. Dreaper was enjoying his fourth Irish Grand National triumph, as aside from the three successes of Brown Lad, Colebridge, also owned by Mrs Burrell, had won the race in 1974.

But the horse that will always be linked with the name of Jim Dreaper is Carvill's Hill. In a way, the period when this exciting but so exasperating chaser was with Martin Pipe was something of an anti-climax for he failed in the ultimate challenge – in his bid for the Gold Cup.

He really caught the imagination of the public while he was with Jim Dreaper, for then the horizons were tinged with the glow of high hopes. We all entertained the dream that, as Tom Dreaper produced Arkle to lower the colours of Mill House on a red-letter day at Cheltenham in 1964 and went on to become the greatest chaser in National Hunt history, so Carvill's Hill might produce for Jim Dreaper an "Irish roar" on Gold Cup day that would bring pride to every Irish heart.

The greatest moment that Carvill's Hill gave Jim Dreaper was when he won the 1989 renewal of the Hennessy Cognac Gold Cup (first run as the Vincent O'Brien Gold Cup in 1987)at Leopardstown in breath-taking style. Dreaper had adopted the patient approach of his father, preferring not to send Carvill's Hill to contest a hurdle race at the '88 Cheltenham Festival meeting following his wins in the Paddy Power Hurdle at Leopardstown and the Sean Graham Hurdle at Punchestown.

Carvill's Hill had a terrible fall when schooling later in '88 and then back problems set in.

After the controversial Gold Cup showing in 1992, he never recovered properly. Martin Pipe announced that Paul Green's chaser would not appear during the 1992-'93 season. He never did appear again on a racecourse and was retired.

✳   ✳   ✳

When Wither Or Which won a bumper at Leopardstown on Sunday, December 31, 1995 by twenty lengths in the hands of his trainer, Willie Mullins, it created such an impact on experienced judges present that Ted Walsh described him as "one of the best bumper horses I have seen in twenty years".

It was his first time racing in public and on that particular day he carried the colours of Willie's wife, Jackie.

It was inevitable that prospective buyers would come with waving cheque-books. Mullins sold a half-share in the horse to Robert Sinclair, the well-known Belfast solicitor and racehorse owner and a quarter share to Noel Callaghan, proprietor of the Davenport Hotel in Dublin. He kept a quarter share himself.

While it was not revealed publicly what the actual selling price of the shares was, I think it can be accepted that his value heading for Cheltenham '96 was in the region of £200,000. The most significant point of all was that such was Willie Mullin's faith in the gelding that he decided to keep a stake in the horse. The last thing he wanted was that Wither Or Which should win the Festival Bumper and he would not be part of the celebrations – as a part owner.

In cold retrospect, Wither Or Which should have been THE banker for the Irish contingent heading for Cheltenham but he went off at 11/4 as Andanito, the pride of England and the mount of Jamie Osborne, was considered unbeatable by some and it was not surprising that he started 9/4 favourite.

As it was, the 25/1 outsider, the Jimmy Fitzgerald-trained Alzulu provided the only real test on the day and was actually ahead as the race reached its climax. Willie Mullins said he thought he might be beaten coming around the last bend but, taking the inside position, he rode a powerful finish. As they hit the rising ground, Wither Or Which ran on like the top-notcher he had shown he was on his Leopardstown debut and a great "Irish roar" echoed from the stands and enclosures as he passed the winning post. It was renewed as he came back into the winner's enclosure.

A massive Irish gamble had been landed and one ante-post bet of £10,000 was reported on the horse. I met a prominent racing enthusiast from the West of Ireland who told me that he stepped into the ring before the off and had £5,000 on at 2/1.

Some of those in the winner's enclosure, who could not conceal their joy at the success of Wither Or Which, were displaying ante-post dockets struck some weeks earlier that would reward them with substantial winnings.

It was inevitable, I suppose, that Willie and Tony Mullins would follow in the footsteps of their father and became trainers in their own right. But Willie, the eldest of the boys, did not actually make up his mind to commit himself to a career in racing until he was 18 when the question came up as to whether or not he wanted to go to university. "I realised then what I really wanted to do", he recalled – and as he learned the business of training while assisting his father, he also made his mark in no uncertain fashion as an amateur rider, winning the amateur's title five times.

Indeed, it was only when he succeeded John Oxx as Chairman of the Irish Trainers Association in '96 and the demands of training became heavier on him that he finally hung up his boots. It was fitting that he should have steered Wither Or Which to that famous Cheltenham victory before he stepped down.

Willie Mullins and Tony could have had no better tutor than Paddy Mullins. The Master of Doninga has seen it all and done it all. But, while many good horses have passed through his hands, it is as the man who trained Dawn Run to win the Champion Hurdle in 1984 and the Gold Cup in 1986 that he will always be remembered.

※　　※　　※

Willie Mullins at 39 is established today as one of the leading jump trainers in Ireland, with a string of 40 horses in his care at his Muine Beag establishment. He has an ideal partner in his personable wife, Jackie, who has been a champion amateur rider herself. The Mullins strike rate in bumper races has been particularly impressive.

Willie Mullins has come a long way since he started training on his own in 1989. Marked improvements at his stables and the expansion work that has been carried out provide ample evidence of the growing success enjoyed by Mullins.

He's shrewd and sharp and perhaps less gregarious than Tony who has an all-things, to-all-men demeanour on the racecourse. No better tribute has been paid to his qualities, however, than the way John Oxx readily acknowledged to me how happy he was to hand over the reins of the Chairmanship of the Irish Trainers Association to Willie Mullins. Mullins is articulate, knows his own mind and will certainly fight the trainers' corner in a way that will see them happy to march under his banner.

His ability to buy horses that have the quality and the potential to make winners has helped him advance right to the forefront of leading trainers. For example, he purchased Wither Or Which for 8,000 guineas in 1994 and it was when Mullins himself rode the gelding in a gallop at Navan in the count-down to that amazing Leopardstown win that he knew that this one was "very special".

Mullins was actually turning out his second Cheltenham winner when Wither Or Which won the '96 Festival Bumper.

The success of 25/1 chance Tourist Attraction in the Supreme Novice Hurdle on the first day of the 1995 Festival meeting showed there will always be a place for the small man at Cheltenham. Willie Mullins made a fairytale story come true for the horse's owners, the 16-man strong North Kildare Racing Club.

The Syndicate evolved out of the North Kildare Rugby Club and among them were men who had made their mark in their prime both for Lansdowne and Trinity College, though the North Kildare club itself is a junior club.

Each member of the Syndicate had been putting £5 a week into a special bank account in Kilcock to pay for the horse's upkeep.

And this investment paid handsome dividends when Tourist Attraction, in the hands of English-based Mark Dwyer from Ashbourne, County Meath powered home to a win worth £27,118 in front of a record first-day attendance of 42,875.

"We paid the training bills and all the other fees, and, frankly, this big win means that we're well ahead of the game," said one delighted member of the Syndicate.

One wit said in the winner's enclosure that the Syndicate also had God on their side – membership included Fr Dinny Cogin from Maynooth.

Another member introduced to me happened to be David Bruton, a cousin of the Taoiseach (Ireland's Prime Minister), John Bruton.

"This victory at Cheltenham crowned everything," said delighted Syndicate member, John Young from Maynooth. He revealed that Tourist Attraction was on lease from Michael O'Keeffe, a County Cork breeder.

The Cheltenham success meant that the Kildare Syndicate had won five races with Tourist Attraction and, in all, over £42,000 in prize-money. Previously with Smokey Lad they had won over £43,000.

∗   ∗   ∗

Another fairytale story from the 1995 Festival meeting was the victory of Chance Coffey on the Wednesday in the Coral Cup Handicap Hurdle.

Chance Coffey was ridden to victory by Gerry O'Neill who was given his big chance at the Festival meeting by the O'Donnell family. He rewarded their faith in him in truly convincing style as he came with a great burst from the last flight to win going away.

They landed a very nice gamble as they backed him at odds of 33/1. And they backed him again on the course at higher odds than the 11/1 at which he was returned.

It was a victory right out of the field of dreams. I will always remember the moment when trainer Pat O'Donnell and his father P.J. placed the winning trophy on top of Gerry O'Neill's flaming ginger head – a fitting coronation.

Thursday was another unforgettable day for every Limerick racing enthusiast present.

Popular Patrickswell trainer, Michael Hourigan was enjoying his first Festival success when Dorans Pride stormed to a magnificent victory in the Bonusprint Stayers Hurdle and Shane Broderick had his initial Cheltenham winner also.

"He was never off the bridle. He was fantastic really," said a delighted Michael Hourigan, who was mobbed by well-wishers in the winner's enclosure.

The West was truly awake as London-based owner T.J. Doran from Bangor-Erris, County Mayo celebrated in style with other family members and friends.

Tom Doran, who is one of 14 children – nine boys and five girls – left the small family farm for England in 1979 and became wealthy through the construction business. Today he lives in Blackheath in London.

He described Dorans Pride's victory as "the greatest moment of my life".

"If our dreams were shattered in '94, I was convinced that they would not be shattered a second time. I am glad Dorans Pride was an Irish banker."

The celebrations started on the track itself. When Tom Doran was handed a bottle of champagne as part of his prize, he insisted it be opened there and then and sprayed Michael Hourigan and Shane Broderick with the bubbly.

One prominent English scribe thought it was a terrible waste of good champagne but that thought never struck the joyous – indeed delirious –

Irish punters who had been saved from veritable extinction by Dorans Pride's sweeping victory.

The Irish contingent had been sickened by the hammer-blows of the previous two days including Danoli's failure in the Smurfit Champion Hurdle and Harcon's defeat in the Sun Alliance Chase.

The craic was good in Cricklewood on Thursday night, March 15, '96 after 10/1 chance Paddy's Return, carrying the colours of Paddy O'Donnell, landlord of the famous hostelry, The Crown won the Daily Express Triumph Hurdle and in the process gave Middleham-based Ferdie Murphy his second success at the Festival meeting.

A jubilant Paddy O'Donnell, who had backed the horse at 33/1 ante-post, said:"This is great. Drinks all round tonight, tomorrow night, Saturday and Sunday, which is St. Patrick's Day."

Ferdie Murphy was making a tremendous success of his move from Somerset to Middleham. Stop The Waller in taking the Kim Muir on the Tuesday gave him his first Festival winner.

Murphy paid tribute to Richard Dunwoody, riding his second Triumph Hurdle winner (Krisbensis had won for him in 1988).

"Richard is the boss", he said. "He decided to go wide because he thought there might be a bit of carnage. And it was also his idea to put on the blinkers."

✳   ✳   ✳

The unforgettable thrill that the members of the North Kildare Racing Club Synidicate had derived from the victory of Tourist Attraction at Cheltenham '95 and likewise the scenes of joy in the winner's enclosure at Galway '96 after Mystical City had won the Guinness Galway Hurdle for the members of the Phantom Syndicate were a vindication in themselves of the drive by Matt Mitchell of Irish Thoroughbred Marketing to attract more into ownership. His policy was designed specifically to capture new owners from as broad a spectrum as possible and, of course, groups of enthusiasts forming themselves into syndicates to own either National Hunt or Flat horses was an integral part of the policy. Indeed, he saw this as allowing people who might never be able to own a horse on their own to still enjoy the thrill of ownership – and of winning – for an individual outlay they could afford.

Mystical City, for example, followed up her victory in the Guinness Galway Hurdle by scoring on the Flat on the Thursday at the Tramore August meeting and was pulled out again by Willie Mullins the following Sunday to take the Richard Power Handicap Hurdle in runaway style. Versatility was certainly her middle name.

Space taken by I.T.M in trade and specialised papers had particularly targetted the expatriate population in Britain and the United States.

The success of this policy has to be judged over a period. The research carried out by Irish Thoroughbred Marketing has been most encouraging.

The first year of operations in this field generated a healthy 300 enquiries and the follow-up exercise revealed that 40 per cent had actually put a horse in training. "I.T.M. stimulates ownership by generally promoting ownership and by acting as a source of information for prospective owners". said Matt Mitchell.

Irish Thoroughbred Marketing advertises special offers for new owners and in one particular initiative presented a framed print of the relevant racing colours to all new registered owners. I.T.M. conducts an ongoing campaign from its Head Office, housed in the Irish Horse Racing Authority's headquarters at Leopardstown racecourse.

On another plane Matt Mitchell has travelled widely in a global bid to open up new markets for the Irish horse. His labours began to bear fruit during 1995 when 100 horses were exported to fresh Far Eastern locations, China and Korea. This was a market previously supplied almost exclusively from Australia.

The trade is extremely valuable to Ireland, mostly for young horses coming out of training, off the Flat, and some way removed from top class. Jumping has been a traditional outlet for this type of animal but there are only so many that can be taken up for the winter game.

Commercially the China trade is a valuable money earner and with Hong Kong's enormous racing and gambling industry due to be absorbed into China's jurisdiction before the turn of the century, it is obvious that racing on the mainland will come on by leaps and bounds. Officially gambling is frowned upon but the racing authorities have come up with a Chinese solution to the problem by adopting the approach that punters are exercising their judgement to solve a puzzle so to speak – the puzzle of which horse will be first past the post!

Incidentally, the Peking Derby was revived in 1996 and American and Australian expertise is now being employed in the development of a marketing strategy to increase prize-money and attendances. The signs for the future look good – Irish Thoroughbred Marketing understands fully the benefits that can accrue for the Irish horse as the Chinese economy opens still further to the world outside.

Matt Mitchell...
global bid to open new
markets for the Irish horse.

12

The Unbearable Agony In The Aintree Waiting

The unbearable agony for Mick Fitzgerald was in the waiting. And it was the same for Terry Casey. Waiting fifteen minutes for the Aintree Stewards to give their verdict on whether 7/1 favourite, Rough Quest had crossed Encore Un Peu on the run-in and merited having the race taken from him.

The ecstasy was in hearing the announcement that any interference was deemed to have been accidental and thus the celebrations that had been on hold got under way, Mick Fitzgerald heading for Franco's in Faringdon where he was wont to dine regularly with Weigh-Room colleagues, Johnny Kavanagh and Adrian Maguire. They were there, of course, as the champagne corks popped and joining in the craic that was mighty were Brendan Powell, Richard Dunwoody, Rodney Farrant, Simon McNeill, Carl Llewellyn, Michael Hourigan, Martin Bosley and Gerry Hogan but Jason Titley, who lives three doors down the same road from Franco's and had his victory party there after Royal Athlete's Grand National triumph in '95, had to miss out as he was in hospital nursing four broken ribs following his fall from Bavard Dieu.

Terry Casey stayed in the Adelphi Hotel where the champagne flowed freely. And as he left for his Beare Green stables in Dorking, Surrey at 6 a.m. with the dawn coming up over Liverpool, he could see fellow-Irishmen in the bar still keeping the party spirit going.

The celebrations continued as Rough Quest returned home to Surrey to a hero's welcome at lunch-time on the Sunday. The villagers in this affluent, stock-broker belt didn't turn it into a rollicking, roisterous affair as might have happened elsewhere. "This was as excited as rural Surrey gets, which is not very", reported the *Sporting Life*.

Mick Fitzgerald for one didn't mind the opportunity to catch his breath momentarily, for he was heading for another mind-blowing evening at The Lesters, the jockeys' awards ceremony in London on the Sunday night. He was looking forward to taking the Monday off and watching the replay of the Grand National for the umpteenth time – "I've almost worn out the tape

131

already and the inquiry seems to go on longer every time", he joked.

✳   ✳   ✳

Fate, it seemed, had conspired to give all the principals of Grand National Day '96 the reward at last for never wavering in their search to hit the jackpot in the racing arena. Everyone was thrilled that one of the most coveted prizes of all in chasing should fall to a real gentleman in Terry Casey, who had known the shattering experience twenty-one years earlier of popping out for ten minutes after Sunday lunch and when he returned he found that Elizabeth, his wife of six months, who was still studying at University to become a teacher, had choked and died at the luncheon table ("you read about these freak accidents and never dream it could happen to you. It took me a very long time to get over it", he recalled in that quiet-spoken way of his).

Henfold House, the home of the 55-year-old owner Andrew Wates, director of the family's construction business, the Wates Building Group, based in Croydon and employing more than 1,500, stands on 700 acres in Dorking – a picturesque dream of an estate. No finer setting for modern National Hunt stables.

How 50-year-old Terry Casey became trainer to Andrew Wates (he trains also for about a dozen other owners – "and the arrangement works fine") and now stood on Sunday, March 31, 1996 almost blinking with disbelief in the Spring sunshine as his Travelling Head Lad, Geoff Cox, who had celebrated his 29th birthday the previous day, arrived with Rough Quest after a five-hour journey from Liverpool, is a story in itself – a story of how a passion for horses and a resilience and admirable courage and fortitude in face of life's shattering reversals overcame everything in the end.

It's a fairytale story of how a lad from a Gaeltacht area in North Donegal was prepared to mitch from school in order to satisfy his obsession with the racing game. Terry's family own the Rosapenna Golf Hotel and the views from the peninsulas round Mulroy and Sheephaven Bays take your breath away for sheer beauty. The hope was that he would make good in school and graduate to a position in life that would leave him in time with no worries about facing his bank manager. And so he arrived at Colaiste Mhuire in Dublin and digs were found for him in Glasnevin. But soon it was obvious that his mind was elsewhere. One morning he took a bus to the Naas Road and hitched a lift to the Curragh and during that long day that culminated in Terry spending a night in a guesthouse in Kildare, he admitted to being in his element – his soul singing with the joy and freedom of it all.

He was brought back to Dublin by the Gardai and resumed his studies in Colaiste Mhuire but had spent only a year there when he started his apprenticeship with the legendary Aubrey Brabazon, who was training within a stone's throw of the Curragh racecourse. In a way it was rather surprising that a lad from an Irish-speaking district in Donegal should be so committed to a career in racing, especially when there was no history of family involvement in horses. "None whatsoever, but even though Donegal isn't a

132

horsey county, I was always horse mad", he told Brian O'Connor (now with *The Title* Sunday sports paper) for a feature in the *Sunday Tribune* in the count-down to Cheltenham '96.

While with Aubrey Brabazon, he became a good journeyman jump jockey, riding also for Bunny Cox and George Dunwoody, father of Richard (in fact, he had ten winners for the Dunwoody stable in 1967). His career in the saddle lasted from 1961 to 1982. "I was only a middle of the road rider", he said modestly.

But while he wasn't hitting the headlines like a Charlie Swan, a Richard Dunwoody, an Adrian Maguire or a Norman Williamson, he was acquiring knowledge – knowledge of the art of training.

He spent six years with Monaghan permit-holder and fromer Turf Club Steward, Bobby Patton, being involved in everything from the feeding to riding out and bringing the horses to the races.

The education process continued and, indeed, you might say the final polish was put on it when he spent three years as Head Man to Paddy Mullins. He had the honour of riding out on Dawn Run.

Terry Casey is lavish in his praise of Paddy Mullins and Paddy and Maureen Mullins in turn have nothing but the highest respect for Terry Casey.

"Paddy was quiet and allowed me to get on with my job and I liked it that way. But he had such a fantastic understanding of his horses and I learned so much from him", recalled Terry Casey when talking to Geoff Lester of the *Sporting Life* .

For a couple of seasons Terry Casey worked as Head Lad to Frank Gilman of Grittar fame. He rode Grittar in all his hurdle races and was successful on him twice, at Market Rasen and Warwick before the horse injured both tendons. Casey had left Gilman by the time the horse gained that memorable Grand National triumph under amateur rider, Dick Saunders. But he always felt that Grittar was destined for stardom when put over fences.

He added:"Saunders made Grittar and he was the most marvellous rider. He was not only the best amateur of his time but as good as any professional around in those days".

✳   ✳   ✳

It was in 1984 that Terry Casey decided to go out on his own and took out his first licence to train. For a brief period he had his base in New Ross, County Wexford, then moved to the Curragh. "I had a small, leased yard and we turned out 25 winners over an eighteen-month period".

In 1986, on the recommendation of Tom Costello, he signed a two-year contract to train for businessman John Upson, who had established a new operation in Northhamptonshire. He remained the two years and then with two partners purchased Derek Ancil's yard in Lambourn.

Terry Casey knew plenty of success at Lambourn as he had done in Northants and his notable victories included the Topham Trophy at Aintree with Glenrue, the National Hunt Chase at Cheltenham with Over The Road and the Signey Banks Hurdle at Huntingdon with Nick The Breef.

Casey's two partners in the Lambourn operation were what he described himself as "sleeping partners". The responsibility of the training fell on him and he was subsidising the day-to-day running costs out of his own pocket. It was costing him a fortune. The final season of the four years he spent there turned out to be a disaster. "The horses picked up a bug and nothing seemed to go right. My brother advised me to walk away from it all and cut my losses. I took his advice and recommended to my partners that we get out. We sold out eventually to Brian Meehan".

That was how in 1994 Terry Casey was technically "unemployed". In his disillusionment at the Lambourn setback he even contemplated getting out of the game. Then he spotted an advertisement in the *Sporting Life* looking for someone to succeed Tim Etherington, who was heading back north to take over his father's stable. Andrew Wates was the man who placed that advertisement. "I replied to the advert and got the job", said Terry Casey simply.

The two men hit it off immediately.

After that dark final season at Lambourn Terry Casey basked in the glory of success in the winner's enclosure at the Cheltenham Festival meeting of 1995 after Rough Quest, with Mick Fitzgerald in the saddle, had won the Ritz Club National Hunt Handicap Chase by an impressive nine lengths from the 1994 winner, Antonin with Cache Fleur, the subsequent Whitbread Gold Cup winner taking third place.

Then six weeks later, Rough Quest, despite going up 16lbs in the handicap, triumphed in the Castelmartin Stud Handicap Chase, again with Mick Fitzgerald in the saddle, at the Punchestown Festival meeting, scoring in impressive style from Feathered Gale, the 1994 Digital Galway Plate winner. Terry Casey was pictured receiving the trophy from Mrs Cryss O'Reilly, wife of Dr Tony O'Reilly, the sponsor.

Returning to his homeland and winning at Punchestown was a day of particular significance for Terry Casey, made all the more memorable as he was showered with congratulations by well-wishers in the winner's enclosure.

The wheel in a way had come full circle... he could contemplate at that moment leaving Donegal as a teenager for Dublin... mitching from school to satisfy his racing bug... and all the ups and downs before he stood now on the podium, a professional in his own right, a man who had been touched by tragedy but who had come through to an understanding of life that came across in his demeanour and in his dealings with his fellow-beings.

A man unspoilt by fame because he realised how effervescent it could be.

✳   ✳   ✳

Terry Casey found in Mick Fitzgerald a jockey after his own heart – a rider for the big time who, as he put it to me himself at Punchestown '96, believed that good horses made jockeys in the sense that they won the races that mattered and kept you constantly in the limelight.

So, more important than killing himself chasing all over the country and becoming obsessed with landing the British N.H. Jockey's crown, the goal for Fitzgerald was "riding as many good horses as I can ride and naturally as many winners".

And he added: "You know quality in the end is everything". So he has no hesitation in saying that it is one of his ambitions to win the Queen Mother Champion Chase because in this race you get the ultimate in quality as three chasers, maybe, rise to the last together and, as a wall of sound echoes from the stands and enclosures, the rider lucky enough to come out on top in the pulsating battle up the hill to the winning post knows that he has achieved something of deep and lasting significance.

Fitzgerald's ambitions lie in the realms of the High Sierras and the flatlands may be Cartmel and Hexham and Stratford-On-Avon in the final dying days of a season and he will not eschew them if the rides comes his way. But basically he is stirred by what a writer of ambition is stirred by in his own sphere of operation and that is why it is so easy to understand why Fitzgerald rose to the challenge on Grand National Day '96.

Mick Fitzgerald believes in treating every horse as an individual case. Each ride in a way is different. The tactics too you employ will be different.

He emphasises that you cannot go out thinking what might happen. You cannot afford to dwell on the risks. You are a professional. It's your job. It's your life. You like, however, to reach the position with success that you can avoid horses that you might have had to ride in your struggling days, at the outset of your career. In a word, horses that represented such a risk factor that you could be out of action for the big meetings like Cheltenham and Aintree – the meetings at which the trainers and owners you rode for on a regular basis wanted very much to have your services.

But he recognised that there was a lot of luck involved in a jump jockey's life, especially when it came to avoiding injury. Things can happen that no one can foresee. The element of chance is always there.

Mick Fitzgerald took a long time to get going as a recognised jockey and even longer to command a regular flow of winners. For that reason it wasn't surprising that when he lost his right to an apprentice's weight allowance at Fontwell in 1992 he was openly expressing the fear that he would be "just another rider who does well as a conditional jockey and then drops out".

But, ultimately, his talent was such that he didn't have to entertain that fear for too long and by the end of the 1992-'93 National Hunt season in Britain he was on his way to the top of the ladder.

He was born in Cork City where his father served as a mechanic in the Army. When his father left the Army in 1972, he moved with his parents to Killarney where the family lived for seven years until 1979. Mick talks with deep affection for his parents, John and Alice "for never doubting me and always being there to support me".

From County Kerry the Fitzgeralds switched to Camolin, near Gorey town and the final move was to Kilfinane in County Limerick, where John Fitzgerald turned publican and with his wife ran The Jockeys Rest.

But many of Mick Fitzgerald's happiest memories are of his school days and youthful times in County Wexford and that is why he insists that he is from Wexford and wants to be known as a Wexford man.

Indeed, it was when John Fitzgerald was prompted originally to live in County Wexford that Fate conspired to ensure that his son would take the first tentative steps towards a career as a jump jockey rather than end up in a nine to five job.

Amazingly enough, Mick Fitzgerald did so well at school (he got eight honours in his Intermediate Certificate examination, the Irish equivalent of Britain's O-levels) that he could well have aspired to a career in banking, teaching or the Civil Service.

But well before he reached that point in his education, his father bought a pony for Mick to share with his brother John and sister Elizabeth. From that moment Mick wanted nothing else only to be a jockey. Daisy was jet black and stood 13.2 hands and Mick rode her in all the shows around the East coast area.

Initially, he didn't have a saddle. "We weren't well off and couldn't afford one", he recalled. "So we rode Daisy bareback and that thought us how to be adept at staying on board. Daisy was to me the best thing since the sliced pan".

＊　　　＊　　　＊

The moment of destiny came when he got the word that there was a job going in Richard Lister's yard near Arklow. "It didn't amount to much but it was the break I wanted. Soon I was riding out for Richard Lister at 14 and it was a happy time, a very happy time for me", he recalled.

After a year he joined John Hayden on the Curragh and spent two years with him. "When I started, I was only seven stone and thought I would be a Flat jockey. I suppose in that time I had about 80 rides, but a few seconds was the best I managed".

"Then when I shot up from seven stone to ten stone, I decided I had no choice but to go jumping. And I didn't think I would be any good in Ireland because I couldn't do nine stone, so I decided to go to England".

The result was a job with John Jenkins. He got a few rides but again without success. When the rides dried up after six months, he moved on again.

Next stop was a job with Richard Tucker, a small-time trainer in Devon. On December 19, 1988 Mick Fitzgerald reached the first important milestone in his career when he rode Lover's Secret to a six-lengths victory for the stable in a selling hurdle at Ludlow. The owner may have got only £730.80 – a far, far cry from what Andrew Wates would get for Rough Quest's victory in the 1996 Aintree Grand National – but for Fitzgerald it was like a lover's first kiss. He was off the mark.

His next two rides brought him a second and a win. Complacency set in for a time before he was brought rudely back to earth. "I thought it was going to be easy and I wondered why I hadn't gone jumping much earlier. But then everything stopped again and it was 18 months before I rode another winner", he told Alan Byrne, now Editor of the *Racing Post,* for an article for the 1992-

'93 edition of the *Irish Racing Annual.*

He was thinking of emigrating to New Zealand when his third winner came in April, 1990. Just two years and three jobs later (with Ron Hodges, Gerald Ham and then Jackie Retter), Fitzgerald had ridden out his claim with a career total to that point of 54 winners.

He became stable jockey to Mrs Retter and that to an extent ended his nomadic days. But there was one more move and that was the crucial one that saw him become No. 1. to the powerful Nicky Henderson stable. The greatest tribute that Henderson could have paid Fitzgerald was telling Norman Williamson when he visited the Lambourn stables with an eye to landing the job of stable jockey that he would not necessarily ride everything in the yard. In a word, Henderson was keeping faith with Fitzgerald and indicating that he would retain a key role.

I saw for myself at Punchestown '96 the easy partnership there is between Henderson and Fitzgerald, the trainer obviously respecting the judgement of his jockey and his tactical knowledge while Fitzgerald in turn did not hide his pride in having as his Guv'nor one of the most successful of Britain's post-World War Two National Hunt trainers and a man with an outstanding strike rate at the Cheltenham Festival meeting.

Incidentally, Nicky Henderson and his wife, Diana were among the guests at Mick Fitzgerald's wedding to Jane Brakenbury at St. Mary's Church in the picturesque Devon village of Diptford in the summer of 1996. Mick met 24-year-old Jane (assistant trainer to Henrietta Knight)four years ago when he rode a winner for her mother at Chepstow.

Mick Fitzgerald's first Cheltenham Festival winner was on the Nicky Henderson-trained Raymylette in the 1994 Cathcart Challenge Cup Chase. "A dream come true", he said recalling his three-quarters-of-a-lengths victory over Charlie Swan on Buckboard Bounce with Commercial Artist a further half-a-length away third.

"The previous day I had fallen on Remittance Man and was beginning to think that my chance of having a big winner at Cheltenham was gone", he added.

One of the worst moments in Fitzgerald's career was when he got the news that Raymylette had died of an internal complaint. He was only seven at the time and Fitzgerald was convinced that there was a lot more to come – "as he was still on the way up".

The hero of his young days when he was dreaming of riding in a Gold Cup, a Champion Hurdle and an Aintree Grand National was Johnny Francome. "He made riding over jumps look easy", was how he put it to Fleetwood Jones for a Lifestyles contribution in the *Sporting Life*. "I watched him a lot. He was the first person to put some artistry into jump racing. If he could gain a length at an obstacle, it all added up at the end of a race".

Francome retired without ever winning the Grand National but then other great jump jockeys like Martin Molony, Aubrey Brabazon, Pepter Scudamore Jonjo O'Neill, Dessie Hughes and Frank Berry didn't have that honour either. Francome, of course, won the Gold Cup on Midnight Court (1978) and the

Champion Hurdle on Sea Pigeon (1981)but more than what he won was the imprint he left on racing's sands of times of the kind of unparalelled greatness that Lester Piggott left on the Flat.

$$* \qquad * \qquad *$$

"One of the greatest thrills of my life", was how Mick Fitzgerald described for me the moment when he won the '96 Grand National.

After finishing runner-up on Rough Quest in the Gold Cup, Fitzgerald knew that the gelding had the class to triumph at Aintree. Furthermore, he was in the right age-group at ten and was in with a weight that gave him every chance of victory – granted he jumped the course.

Indeed, Fitzgerald told the world in the *Racing Post* on the morning of the race: "If Rough Quest takes the whole occasion as I expect him to, and relaxes properly and jumps well, I should be coming to the line with a double handful. I'll get a good leap over the last... and then go by somewhere after the Elbow".

He confided to me that he had a secret fear that he might be jocked off because of his poor Aintree record. The previous year on Tinryland he had come down at the first and his record in other races over those daunting fences was not much better.

Richard Dunwoody, who already had two Grand National victories to his credit on West Tip (1986) and Miinnehoma (1994), was searching for a mount and one didn't have to be a soothsayer to know that feelers were going out to indicate that he was available.

No wonder Mick Fitzgerald was opening his mail rather anxiously in the expectation that there might be a letter from Andrew Wates couched in most diplomatic terms but the message would be clear all the same – he was going to be replaced by 'Woody'.

"Richard is an outstanding jockey but there was never any question of Mick not riding Rough Quest", the owner told Paul Hayward of the *Daily Telegraph*.

What really swung it in the end with Andrew Wates was the fact that Fitzgerald had come to know the horse so well. And he certainly took some knowing!

There was never any question either that Terry Casey would doubt the ability of Fitzgerald to rise to the occasion at Aintree.

Fitzgerald carried out Casey's instructions to the letter and saved the power he knew Rough Quest could unleash at the finish, though subsequently – "with hindsight I maybe ought to have waited even longer".

Praise was heaped afterwards on Fitzgerald for the brilliance of the ride he gave the favourite. Brough Scott in the *Sunday Telegraph* commended him for his coolness in the paddock and best of all for the manner in which he remained so cool during the race itself.

"There was barely a moment in the entire race when I thought Rough Quest wouldn't win", said Mick Fitzgerald in a special contribution to the *Racing*

Post on the Monday. "He took all the excitement of the preliminaries completely in his stride, just as I hoped he would, and when we jumped off I knew exactly what I had to do.

"It was a huge relief to get over the first, having fallen there in '95 and again on the Thursday on Tudor Fable. But what made it all the better was that he was so foot-sure over it that I knew he'd got the hang of it straight away, and that if I could stay out of trouble I ought to win.

"With Rough Quest jumping brilliantly and getting more and more confident, the first circuit passed without incident. But you could almost say that he took the Chair, the water, and the first fence on the second circuit too well, because I felt him grabbing his bit and I had to say to myself "steady, we're way too handy".

"The only semblance of a mistake he might have made was when he got a little too close to the one before Becher's and rubbed through the top of it. But that was just what was needed to steady him and I thought "brilliant that's done the job perfectly".

"It was only when we'd jumped Valentine's that I started to take note of what was around me, and how the likes of Encore Un Peu and Superior Finish were travelling.

"There was just a twinge of doubt in my mind where we'd landed over the third-last and got to the Melling Road, as I saw 'Bridgy' look round on Encore Un Peu and that meant he still had petrol in the tank and I couldn't afford to let him get away.

"But it wasn't just a case of not letting Encore Un Peu get away from me. I didn't want to get too close either, as I had to leave Rough Quest enough to do and something to race at from the last.

"Starting up the run-in I thought I'd judged it right and I was aiming to go up Bridgy's inner at the Elbow, so I'd have the rail to run up. But he saw me coming and, quite rightly, shut me off and pushed me wide.

"I couldn't take a pull, as I sensed that Rough Quest might be coming to the end of his tether and, when he started to hang as we were going past, I wanted to pull my stick through but daren't because I thought that if I took my hands off he might dive over to the left.

"I couldn't stop him edging over and so I wasn't surprised when I heard the klaxon announcing a Stewards' inquiry. Equally I was sure I was clear at the time, or at least I was sure enough until I saw Terry's face".

✳   ✳   ✳

Hugh McIllvanney noted in the *Sunday Times* that Mick Fitzgerald never lost his verbal liveliness for a moment during the ordeal of the inquiry. "He began by assuring us that his nine minutes of shared action with Rough Quest had left him feeling that 'sex is an anti-climax after that'. Then he continued the up-beat patter by suggesting cheekily that the man on Encore Un Peu's back, David Bridgwater, had done so much to make the most out of the incident that he should be regarded as the Jürgen Klinsman of the jumping game. It was, of course, a reference to the German footballer's alleged talent for conning awards out of referees".

Fitzgerald remembered being in a Steward's inquiry with Bridgwater three or four years earlier. "I can tell you he's improved a lot since then! He had a job to do in there and he went in and did the best he could for himself and for Encore Un Peu's connections".

The thunderous cheers that had greeted Rough Quest as he passed the post – the first favourite since Grittar in 1982 to win the race – had died away when Terry Casey heard the words delivered over the public address system that meant most of all to him on the day: "The placings remain unaltered, weighed-in, weighed-in".

"There could hardly be a neutral anywhere on the old Liverpool premises who regretted the decision the Stewards had made", summed up Hugh McIllvanney. "Both Casey and Andrew Wates are sufficiently popular to ensure that there was a wave of relief when victory was confirmed".

"It would have been a grave injustice had Rough Quest not retained the honour, glory and first prize", wrote Jim McGrath (Hotspur) in the *Daily Telegraph.*

Rough Quest might never have run in the Grand National but for a phone call from Royal trainer, Ian Balding to Andrew Wates. Balding had read that Wates was contemplating not tilting for the Aintree prize. The two had been at Cambridge together 35 years previously when they shared a point-to-pointer, named Carellie and had remained friends ever since.

" You will never get a better chance to win the National", said Balding to Wates in the 7 a.m. call he made to him one morning.

It had the desired effect.

And Rough Quest would never have won but for Terry Casey managing to finally overcome the muscle enzyme problem that had afflicted the gelding for so long – even before he had come under his wing. It caused him to tie up in his races, often with quite devastating effect.

"It is a very similar condition to a human getting cramp," Casey explained in the immediate aftermath of the Grand National victory.

"It is to do with not enough oxygen being released, and it can be treated through diet. It has taken me a long time to figure it out, and it has only really been in the last two months that we have made progress."

※　　　※　　　※

Mick Fitzgerald shared a room with his father on the eve of the 1996 Grand National – just as he had done in '95 (jokingly he didn't blame the fall at the first on Tinryland on the fact that his father's snoring kept him awake for much of the night!).

His proud parents, his brother John and sister Elizabeth were among the happiest guests at his wedding – probably the first of a National Hunt jockey to get a four-page spread in *Hello* magazine.

But then Fitzgerald had become big news overnight, especially with the tabloids in Britain, ever since his famous remark that sex was an anti-climax after his National triumph and his bride-to-be, Jane Brakenbury got her own back by playfully responding that he had "never lasted twelve minutes".

Mick and Jane started off the dancing at the wedding to Mick's favourite Patsy Kline number, *Crazy*. Fitzgerald's guitar-playing uncle Jimmy led a chorus of old-time songs like *Nancy Spain, I Am Sailing* and *Whiskey And Wine*.

Johnny Kavanagh had been a good friend to Mick Fitzgerald when first he arrived in England and he was his bestman now on the day.

Mick Fitzgerald has gone on record to state that if there were two alternative careers he could choose from they would be those of professional golfer and TV racing pundit. "I am a 20 handicap golfer, so I have a long way to go to attain the first", he joked.

But he is so articulate, so laid-back, so quick-witted that I believe that he can make a good career on television when he steps down from the saddle. He can also command sizeable fees bringing guests through the card in the corporate hospitality marquees and boxes on the big-race occasions – if he should choose to go down that road. In a word, he's a born personality who has the necessary qualities to shape a new lucrative career for himself when he retires from the jumping game.

Rough Quest was pictured nuzzling Mick Fitzgerald in a front-page four-column shot by Dan Abraham in the *Sporting Life* on Monday, April 1, 1996 – the day after the Grand National hero had returned home to the Beare Green stables in Dorking. Terry Casey and Andrew Wates were also in that picture.

"This is as good as it gets, Terry", someone whispered to Casey and the man from Donegal looked up.

He smiled in silent agreement in the Spring sunshine – a private smile, his thoughts seemingly far away.

It was lunch-time over all the affluent, stockbroker belt in the Surrey country-side.

Terry Casey, once a journeyman trainer enjoying any success that came his way in comparative anonymity, was known in every corner of Britain now as the one who had trained the 1996 Grand National winner. He had reached the very pinnacle of success.

But you wondered if another lunch hour at another time in another decade fleetingly crossed his mind. And somewhere up there in the Great Beyond, Elizabeth, the University girl, who had known but brief days of happy marriage was smiling down on him, sharing this joyous day.

And Terry Casey could echo the line from Patrick Kavanagh, in the realisation that life too had happened for him:

Something was brighter a moment. Somebody sang in the distance.

13

Yes, Tony Is The Real McCoy!

When Richard Dunwoody was no longer obsessed with the race for the British Jump Jockeys' title, it opened the way for Tony McCoy to come right out of the blue and succeed him as champion in the 1995-'96 season – just two years after he had arrived in Britain, having never ridden a winner over jumps at that point in time.

McCoy capitalised on the fact also that Adrian Maguire and Norman Williamson were both sidelined for long periods with injuries – indeed, didn't finish out the season – while he himself had a relatively injury-free run. He had the title won by Cheltenham – bar injury.

However, even allowing for the fact that the ill wind that blew harshly for others gave him a full sail, it has to be acknowledged that McCoy would never have assumed the crown if he did not have ability out of the ordinary and an extraordinary appetite for winners.

"I love riding winners and I will never get fed-up with it. Days when I do not have a winner I find depressing and a lean spell is quite boring. I just can't wait to get back on good horses", he told Simon Holt in the course of a *Sporting Life* interview in the count-down to Cheltenham '96. He thrives on pressure – the pressure on him to deliver the goods when the money is down, the pressure that comes most of all when he is on board a class hurdler or chaser and the connections look to him to land a big prize. He is so confident, especially when he's on a chaser, that he is unwilling to show sympathy in a situation where he is convinced that pressure got to an inexperienced rider.

"You put a boy up, there's a few quid down, the pressure is on and he decks him", was how he put it to Alan the barman at The Shears in Collinbourne in Hampshire while David Walsh of the *Sunday Times* was doing a day-in-the-life-style feature on him in the week that he succeeded Richard Dunwoody as the title-holder.

The statisticians had a field day in the immediate aftermath of his meteoric rise to donning the mantle of champion. Ending up with 175 winners – 43 more than his nearest rival, David Bridgwater – he was at 22 the youngest champion since Josh Gifford in 1962-'63. He failed narrowly to record the fastest 50 and the fastest 100 but of far more significance than these actual figures was the fact that it had all happened for him in the space of two amazing years.

He had been the leading conditional rider with a record 74 wins in 1994-'95 – his first season in Britain. If he had rubbed his eyes and said to himself 'it's all a dream', he could have been forgiven for doing so. On St. Patrick's Day, 1994 he had his first ride over hurdles at Leopardstown. He was brought down at the last flight and still recalls ruefully getting "the most awful bollicking because I should not have been where I was!".

He laughs now when he contemplates that the winner of the particular race was Imperial Call, so his apparent "error" didn't matter all that much. "The best I could have hoped for was runner-up position".

"I think his rise has been the most dramatic of any champion in the history of jump racing", wrote John Randall, the expert on statistical matters on the *Racing Post*.

✳   ✳   ✳

Richard Dunwoody's talent had been nurtured initially in his native County Down and a grey pony called Tony guided the future champion through his formative years in the saddle.

Tony McCoy emerged from Toomebridge in County Antrim and his brother and four sisters displayed no great interest in horses. His father, Peadar – a carpenter by trade – had a bit of land and kept a few horses as a hobby. "Our horses were the only ones for miles around", recalled Tony.

Fate decreed that the stables of Cullybackey trainer, Willie Rock, a very likeable personality, were just ten miles from the McCoy homestead. Already something had stirred in McCoy's breast – a burning desire to test his courage in the saddle, an ambition to be a jockey some day. Later he would recall the lasting impression left on him watching Jonjo O'Neill win the 1986 Gold Cup on the gallant Dawn Run and sneaking out of class in school to also watch on television Richard Dunwoody take the 1990 Champion Hurdle on Kribensis – he admits to having had a "real fancy" for the Michael Stoute-trained gelding and to even having backed him, though for how much would seem the proverbial peanuts now compared with being champion jump jockey of Britain with all the perks it brings him.

Richard Dunwoody was already his idol – the idol of his boyhood days. Today, he will still tell you frankly that 'Woody' is the one "I'd always put top, because I think he's come closer to perfecting this job than anyone" and he sees Paul Carberry as having "more talent than anyone", adding: "We were apprenticed together at Jim Bolger's and he was always a natural. And although he has a reputation for knowing how to enjoy himself, I can assure you he's a lot more clued in than most jockeys and knows exactly what ran where and how it got on".

Tony McCoy bought himself a bike when he was only 12 so that he could cycle at break of day all the way from home to Willie Rock's stables.

When mornings were wet – Rock would pick up young McCoy from his home. "He was determined to ride out no matter what the weather", recalled the trainer. "He had taught himself to ride."

Willie Rock let him ride out, realising that there was something special here, encouraged him as much as he could and, frankly, put him on his way. "He was riding 14 horses a day for me when he was only 14 years old and he was even schooling jumpers. He had amazing ability and stamina", said Rock.

"I used to take him to Dundalk for the schooling hurdles and it was there that I noticed his style. He looked like a top Flat jockey in the making with his high seat", he continued.

Before they even saw him in a schooling session, the senior jockeys had known about 'Wee Authnay', Rock was enthusing so much about him. There was pride in his voice – as if McCoy was his pupil and that some day when he made it to the top, they would remember how he had first made the name known to them.

But they were sceptical to say the least of it and who could have blamed them if secretly they felt 'Wee Authnay' was but a ghost rider in the sky!

Later, of course, when McCoy arrived at Jim Bolger's and later still when he hit Britain and began to make his mark overnight, they understood the reason why Willie Rock could not hide his enthusiasm. And they respected Willie all the more for his judgement and his vision.

✳   ✳   ✳

Such was Tony McCoy's ambition to become a jockey that by the time he was 15 he wanted to be done with school altogether and take the plunge. As he saw it then as a teenager, everything else had to become secondary to the main purpose – and that was being with horses all the time. And in Ireland where the competition was so keen, where there were so many youngsters aspiring to reach the top, those who were driven and who knew deep down that they had a fire in their soul that would not be dimmed unless they left home, had to respond to the inner voice.

By now Tony's father was into the breeding of horses and actually bred Thumbs Up, who won for Willie Rock at Down Royal and took the County Handicap Hurdle for Nicky Henderson at the 1993 Cheltenham Festival meeting with Richard Dunwoody in the saddle.

The fateful moment that put Tony McCoy's foot on the ladder that would lead him to fame and the British National Hunt Jockeys' crown came when Willie Rock contacted Jim Bolger on the phone and told him: "I have a future champion jockey in my yard".

Not one to be easily impressed, Bolger questioned Rock a little deeper. "What makes you so sure?", he asked. Willie went on to tell him how much he had been impressed by the 16-year-old lad's riding in a schooling hurdle at Dundalk and ventured to make the point that McCoy had the best seat of any up-and-coming jockey that he had seen in his career.

"He's a natural", Rock stressed to Bolger and went on: "He looked every bit as good as the experienced jockeys he was riding against that day".

Bolger's reply was prompt: "Send him down to me".

The necessary forms were signed and McCoy was on his way, fortunate in the fact that he would be working under a "Master" who would suffer no nonsense but who would nurture his talent and guide him on his way.

Tony's mother, Claire was naturally still very worried as to whether he had taken the right step and David Walsh recalled in a *Sunday Times* article how she remarked to her son: "Anthony, do you understand what you have done. This is now your life? He responded: "Mum, I would like to have been a brain surgeon, but I didn't have a brain!"

While with Jim Bolger Tony McCoy learned the Flat racing game and had his first winner when Legal Steps won the Silvermines 3-Y-O Maiden (1m 4f) at Thurles on Thursday, March 26, 1992, coming home eight lengths ahead of Anthis, ridden by Warren O'Connor with Sakanda, with Richard Hughes in the saddle, third.

McCoy was to ride six winners on the Flat for Bolger and seven over hurdles. His first win over hurdles came on Riszard in the Thomastown Maiden Hurdle (2m 4f) at Gowran Park on Wednesday, April 20, 1994.

Hard to believe that two years later he would be jump jockey champion in Britain.

Tony McCoy, as well-known Northern Ireland racing journalist, Jimmy Walker noted in an article in the *Irish Racing Annual*, readily acknowledges the debt he owes to both Willie Rock and Jim Bolger. And also to Paddy Graffin, the Ballymena, County Antrim trainer who gave him his first ride over fences and advised him to accept the offer from Toby Balding. Ian Ferguson, a neighbour, also helped him on his way, giving him the ride on Luncheon Chance in a hurdle race at Down Royal in May '94. McCoy was successful there and that same year he won on the same horse on the Flat at Sligo and Bellewstown.

※　　　※　　　※

Jim Bolger's stable is basically Flat like Dermot Weld's and in time a certain boredom set in for Tony McCoy when he was on Flat horses whereas the adrenalin coursed in his veins at the very thought of winning a hurdle race or a chase.

There was no need for the volatility of Jim Bolger to clash head-on with the primary goal in life of Tony McCoy. Nature resolved it. McCoy was a growing lad, tall even then and taller today at 5ft 11ins (he grew an inch-and-a-half from the time he arrived in Britain from Ireland and he said with a certain sense of trepidation after being crowned champion jockey:"And I can't even be sure if I've stopped growing now!").

He knew at that stage in Jim Bolger's that trying to keep down his weight would be a killer if he continued to ride on the Flat. He was extremely grateful to Jim Bolger for all he learned while in the Coolcullen stables; some others who have come and gone might voice their feelings but, no word of criticism passes the lips of Tony McCoy about the Master of Glebe House.

He followed the trail that Adrian Maguire took when ultimately he decided to try his luck in Britain. There was admirable calculation in the way he decided to opt for Toby Balding's stable rather than for any other establishment. You had to admire him all the more when you reflected that Balding hadn't exactly set the jumping world alight with his strike rate that season. But it was his overall record as a National Hunt trainer that impressed McCoy. He had won races that really mattered, including the Champion Hurdle twice with Beech Road (1989) and Morley Street (1991) and the Gold Cup with Cool Ground (1992).

He had actually put Adrian Maguire on a new pedestal through the success of Cool Ground. The way Tony McCoy reasoned it then was that if he was linked with winners for the Balding Stable – even just a few to begin with – the racing writers would talk in terms of another lad from Ireland taking the same route as Maguire and they would monitor his progress very closely.

"I first heard about Anthony when a man I do business with in Northern Ireland said he had seen the best claiming jockey in Ireland", recalled Toby Balding. "I travelled to Wexford to watch him ride and was mightily impressed. Eddie Harty made the necessary introductions. "I have been asked if he is in the same mould as Maguire who also started his English career with me and I have to say•that there is a major difference in that Maguire had already been a champion point-to-point jockey in Ireland while McCoy had limited experience over fences. In fact his win on Bonus Boy at Newton Abbot was only his fourth ride over fences.

"But I knew from the outset that he had what was required to make it to the top and, as in Adrian's case, I am naturally proud that he started in Britain in my yard".

Tony McCoy doesn't hesitate to emphasise that Toby Balding will always have a primary place when it comes to his services. The association or partnership between the two is like that between Dermot Weld and Michael Kinane. Balding doesn't put his foot down and insist when he knows that Tony has a better opportunity, especially of winning a big race, on some other horse. "It's all been very amicable", as McCoy puts it himself.

So Toby Balding has created a lasting milestone in helping establish Adrian Maguire in England as one of the finest talents to arrive from Ireland and then opened the way for Tony McCoy to win the Jump Jockey's crown long before anyone could have imagined it would be possible. Some record!

✳   ✳   ✳

Tony McCoy attributes much of his success in the 1995-'96 season to the fact that he was increasing his knowledge all the time of the varied features of contrasting racecourses up and down the country. He feels that he is familiar with most of them now.

That knowledge was reflected in the way he concluded that Zabadi was caught out by the hill in the 1996 Daily Express Triumph Hurdle. But McCoy felt that the David Nicholson-trained gelding still had that extra gear and would be eminently more suited by the flat Liverpool track – and his analysis was fully vindicated.

Ascot is one of the racecourses he has a special grá for because he has hit it lucky there.

At the time of writing – the autumn of '96 – he had had only one winner to his credit at the Cheltenham Festival meeting. He won the 1996 Grand Annual Chase on Kibreet for Philip Hobbs.

But it would be unfair, I feel, to judge his Cheltenham record on just two seasons in Britain. He has time on his side and he will obviously have a book of choice rides at each Festival meeting in the years ahead. It will be surprising if he does not add appreciably to his tally.

He won the Ritz Club trophy as the leading rider at the '96 Aintree Grand National meeting. His tally was three winners – Top Spin and Viking Flagship in addition to Zabadi.

No winner gave him greater pleasure than Viking Flagship. He was the first to acknowledge that the ride on the two-times Queen Mother Champion chaser fell into his lap – like other mounts from 'The Duke' Nicholson's stable – as a result of Adrian Maguire's season being summarily cut short because of that badly-broken collar bone. As he put it to Graham Dench of the *Racing Post:*"You dream about riding horses like Viking Flagship but don't really expect to ever get the chance. I've never, ever had a better feel from a horse than I got from him that day".

On form there was no reason to think that Viking Flagship would turn the tables on Klairon Davis, who had beaten him by five lengths at Cheltenham but 'The Duke' advised that he "make it from turning in and stretch them". The result was that Viking Flagship spreadeagled the field as he came home seven lengths in front of Sound Man with Coulton third and Klairon Davis fourth.

If that was one of the most satisfying moments of all for Tony McCoy in his title-winning season, another highlight was passing the 100-winner milestone on Amber Valley at Nottingham in January. And another momentous day for him was taking the Lanzarote Hurdle some days later on Warm Spell as it was the most important race he had won up to that point in his career.

And in achieving a grand total of 175 winners (42 for the Paul Nicholls stable), he amassed £1 million in prize-money.

No matter how memorable a season, it has, of course, to have its despairing moments and Tony McCoy's joy at landing the Ritz Club trophy at Aintree '96 was tempered by his bitter disappointment when his mount Deep Bramble injured a tendon crossing the Melling Road second time round in the Grand National and had to be pulled up. McCoy believes that

Deep Bramble would have won a National one day – if not successful in beating Rough Quest in '96.

And then there were the occasions when he was in trouble with the Stewards for his use of the whip. You could argue that it stemmed from his fierce drive for winners and yet, ironically, he did not pick up his first suspension of the 1995-'96 season until he had 700 rides under his belt. Some horses are dogs and, as Ted Walsh would be the first to agree, you won't get them to show anything unless they get a crack or two and in these instances it is much more in the category of a "reminder" for one that has a mind of its own rather than "punishment". In Britain the pets-lobby and the millions who watch racing only on television and see the whip more than the overall spell-binding power of a great finish still exercise tremendous influence and more's the pity.

At Galway '96 Tony McCoy was in trouble with the Stewards also and initially there was a suggestion that he might not ride in Ireland again because of his disappointment. But he was too much of a professional to persist in that attitude and before that week was out, reality ruled.

✳   ✳   ✳

The long angular features remind one at times of Bernard Cribbins in favourite old classics like *Wrong Arm Of The Law* (starring also Peter Sellers at his zaniest and Lionel Jeffries) that can still transport us into a world of laughter. But then the English tabloids would never expect him to come up with an immortal quote like that which Mick Fitzgerald delivered in the aftermath of his 1996 Aintree Grand National triumph on Rough Quest. Yet even though he is a teetotaller among jump jockeys who don't mind letting their hair down when the pressure is off, it's said of him by colleagues that he can join in the craic and contribute to keeping the party atmosphere going with a swing on the social nights out. And you've got to admit that he has a sense of humour when he can paint a picture of well-known Northern Ireland amateur, Paddy Graffin advising him to first find a rich lady – and then fall in love!

Apparently, he's still searching around for the ideal woman like that!

And the fact that he admits that he never enjoyed the taste of an alcoholic drink and prefers a Coke, an orange juice or a mineral water didn't prevent him heading off with a bunch of the boys for Mick Fitzgerald's mind-boggling stag party in Tenerife – the boys in this instance being as many of Mick's colleagues in the Weigh Room who felt they had the stamina to endure it.

McCoy was there from the Sunday until the following Friday – so he must fit in easily enough with the rest of the lads.

He came to the crown so quickly and so easily that the deed was done before we noticed.

But now he is exposed on his "throne" and it won't be so easy for him anymore.

He's young, however – ten years younger than Richard Dunwoody. The seasons stretch out before him full of promise and high expectation. Who will deny youth its dreams?

He must come in his own time to the maturity that saw Richard Dunwoody settle for other values when a third successive title was within his grasp.

Dunwoody had been there, seen it all and wanted to see no more of the driven days, the wasting to make a riding weight of 10st, the over-expenditure on resources both mental and physical.

A man can take only so much.

✳   ✳   ✳

I had left my friends behind drinking champagne after breakfast in the Queen's Hotel in what would become a long morning's journey into late afternoon on that anti-climax of a Friday that was the fourth day of the 1995 Cheltenham meeting.

I took a taxi to the racecourse to keep an appointment for a radio interview. Somehow the subject came around to Richard Dunwoody.

What I said, in effect, was that I could not understand how such a brilliant talent as Dunwoody had allowed himself to get caught up on a treadmill, riding around the early summer circuit for the Martin Pipe stable principally, as the **real** season as such was over to all intents and purposes for the aficionados of the game once the Aintree Grand National meeting was past. His priorities, I asserted, should be pitched much higher at this point in his career. His concern in the main should be with having the pick of the best and riding the best, where this was possible. He should go freelance as Lester Piggott did when he wanted to put himself in line to ride colts of the calibre of Sir Ivor and Nijinsky, to be the dominant rider on the big-race occasions. I made no apologies for the forcefulness of the views I expressed.

I was not surprised then when Dunwoody reached a parting of the ways with the Pipe stable. I wasn't surprised when I learned that he had opted out of what had become a rat-race for him. Something had got to give after the fierce climactic moments of the 1993-'94 season and the intensity of the battle he had waged with Adrian Maguire to hold on to his title. Alan Lee quoted Dunwoody in *The Times* as stating "I don't want to go through this again", Lee himself adding: "One look at the pale, emaciated features betraying ten months of pain and strain was sufficient to understand why Dunwoody had retained his title but the single-mindedness, stamina and sacrifice demanded of him to see off Adrian Maguire had been so severe that even he hardly knew how he had done it".

In fact, Dunwoody confessed:"I have been going to bed every night worrying about the next day and whether Adrian will ride a winner. It puts a lot of pressure on those close to you – just ask my wife, Carol".

The obsession days were past and he had lost Carol after the split between them when I met him at the Galway Festival meeting '96 and saw a new side to him – a relaxed Dunwoody, obviously at peace with himself, happy that he was free of the unrelenting regime he had set himself for two years, knowing exactly where he stood now and what should be his priorities.

You could not mistake the genuine way he expressed it when he said he was delighted for Tony McCoy that he had succeeded him as champion and that he fully deserved it as he had a lot of talent. There was not a trace of envy in his voice.

But then he realised that, even though the battle for the title had not gone right down to the wire for McCoy as it had gone for him in that dramatic 1993-'94 all-out tussle with Adrian Maguire, he had still looked at the face of Tony McCoy in January '96 – as he told Hugh McIlvanney in an interview for the *Sunday Times* – "and I could see a lot of the tension I used to feel. When you are going for the championship, you have got to be obsessive, feeling that kind of intensity even four or five months before the end of the season. I'm glad I'm out of that".

He was happy too to leave behind the blind madness that spurred him to the point, in the relentless hunt for winners, that he incurred a 30-day suspension in January 1995 and back in 1994 he had been stood down for 14 days for an incident with Adrian Maguire at Nottingham. In relation to the latter, he thought he was right until he studied the video – "and then I realised I was wrong".

He added significantly that such had become the "desperate rivalry" between Adrian and himself in the surge towards the crown in 1993-'94 and they both became so obsessed with riding winners that "we were a danger to ourselves and one another. No matter how competitive sport is, there has to be some enjoyment derived from it and practically all of that had been taken away by the pressure we were putting on ourselves".

✳   ✳   ✳

Richard Dunwoody confessed that at one point after the 30-day suspension over the Luke Harvey incident at Uttoxeter and also because of the troubles in his personal life, he was so down, so depressed that he didn't even fancy going racing anymore. The thought of retiring altogether became a real possibility.

It was only when he had made what he termed the "drastic changes" in the whole approach to his life as a National Hunt jockey and adopted new priorities that he became relaxed and happy.

The scaling down didn't mean that he gave up entirely riding at small meetings – "I love the special atmosphere of these meetings, including the meetings in Ireland outside the Metropolitan circuit", he told me. It meant that he was setting the stage for himself. It was no longer being dictated as in the days when he was No.1. jockey to the Martin Pipe stable – a winner factory at its height, irrespective of the quality of all those winners. You entered the numbers game and you took them as they came, the good ones with the mediocre. And as Martin Pipe doesn't like horses carrying

150

HATS OFF TO MOORE AND WOODS . . . In a throw-back to the days of L'Escargot, Arthur Moore places his trilby on Klairon Davis after he had won the 1996 Queen Mother Champion Chase, as Chris Jones (winning owner), Arthur Moore's daughter Anna and Francis Woods share the moment of joy and (below) Moore does it again following Feathered Gale's triumph in the 1996 Jameson Irish Grand National. (Pictures Caroline Norris.)

Francis Woods gives a victory salute as he is led in after his success in the '96 Queen Mother Champion Chase and (inset top) clearing the last on Klairon Davis as he got the better of Sound Man (Charlie Swan), on inside, in an epic battle for the 1995 Guinness Arkle Chase and (below) Klairon Davis, Viking Flagship (Charlie Swan), second and Sound Man (Richard Dunwoody), third, on inside clear the last in the titanic contest for the '96 Queen Mother Champion Chase. (Pictures Caroline Norris, Peter Mooney and Bernard Parkin.)

Proud moments for Edward O'Grady as (top) Richard Dunwoody returns to a tremendous "Irish roar" after winning the 1996 Guinness Arkle Chase on Ventana Canyon and (below) he crowns joint-owner Peter Curling with one of the crystal trophies. (Inset top) Loving Around becomes O'Grady's 15th Festival winner after taking the '96 National Hunt Chase (Philip Fenton, right, shares the mood of celebration).

THE PAIN AND THE GLORY . . . The fatal fall on his neck at the last by Golden Cygnet in the Scottish Champion Hurdle at Ayr on 15 April 1978 that was to result in the death of the brilliant hurdler seen (inset) winning the Supreme Novices Hurdle at the Cheltenham Festival meeting that year by 15 lengths and (below) six years on Edward O'Grady was again a power at Cheltenham as he shared with Charlie Swan and J. P. McManus the joy of victory after Time For A Run had won the Coral Cup Handicap Hurdle. O'Grady also scored with Mucklemeg for McManus.

David Bruton, a cousin of the Taoiseach (Ireland's Prime Minister), John Bruton holds the trophy aloft after the Willie Mullins-trained Tourist Attraction had scored a 25/1 victory in the 1995 Supreme Novice Hurdle for the Kildare Syndicate and (inset) Mullins is acclaimed after winning the 1996 Festival Bumper on his charge, the brilliant Wither Or Which. Below champagne moments for successful rider, Shane Broderick and Michael Hourigan after Dorans Pride had given the Limerick trainer his first Festival winner by taking the 1995 Stayers Hurdle. (Pictures Caroline Norris.)

The O'Sullivans of Lombardstown, Mallow have their finest hour as Lovely Citizen, trained by Eugene and ridden by Willie is led in after winning the 1991 Christies Foxhunters Chase and (below) they have another day to remember as Another Excuse (Brendan Powell), seen here clearing the last in style (left) comes home unchallenged as he scores by a distance in the '96 Midland Grand National. (Uttoxeter pictures Colin Turner.)

Trainer Pat O'Donnell (left) and his father, P.J., owner of Chance Coffey playfully crown Gerry O'Neill after he had won the '95 Coral Handicap Hurdle and (below) joy for Galway-born Pat O'Donnell and family following the convincing success of the Ferdie Murphy-trained Paddy's Return in the 1996 Daily Express Triumph Hurdle.

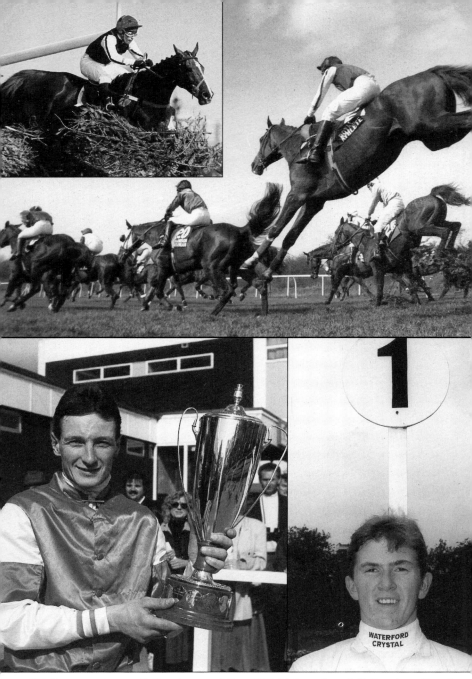

Ed Byrne captures all the drama of the 1995 Aintree Grand National as Royal Athlete (Jason Titley), nearest camera, leads Chatham over the 11th fence and (inset) Titley safely negotiates the last fence on Jenny Pitman's outsider. Below (left) Richard Dunwoody has reason to smile as he holds the British N.H. Jockeys Championship trophy and (right) Tony McCoy, who succeeded Dunwoody as champion in the 1995-'96 season.

overweight, you struggled to do a riding weight of 10st (demanding a body weight of around 9st 10lbs). The extremes of wasting brought their own depressing side-effects and you craved for the day when you would be liberated from this regime, when you would be a free spirit again.

Now he was dividing his time between Britain and Ireland and he was on board some of the best horses any jump jockey would love to have his name linked with and the winners were flowing, though his concern was no longer with statistics as such. Back at the turn of 1996 the total of winners to his name in a star-studded career was over 1,300 and he was second only to Peter Scudamore (1,678) in the all-time list. He had won two Aintree Grand Nationals (West Tip, 1986 and Miinnehoma, 1994), a Gold Cup (Charter Party, 1988), a Champion Hurdle (Kribensis, 1990), an Irish Grand National (Desert Orchid, 1990) and his "crowning glory", according to 'The Duke' Nicholson, was his victory in the 1989 Arkle Challenge Trophy Chase on Waterloo Boy and in 1990 he was involved in an epic battle on this horse with Barnbrook Again for the Queen Mother Champion Chase, losing by just half-a-length.

The 1995-'96 season saw him score a singular spreadeagling triumph on the grey One Man in the King George VI Chase at Kempton – a race he had won in successive years on another grey, Desert Orchid in 1989 and '90. One Man was to disappoint, however, in the Gold Cup when starting a warm favourite and Dunwoody had to be content with runner-up position on the 10/11 favourite, Alderbrook in the Smurfit Champion Hurdle.

But the Edward O'Grady-trained Ventana Canyon provided him with a memorable 20-length success in the Guinness Arkle Challenge Trophy Chase while he was seen at his brilliant best again on Paddy's Return for the Ferdie Murphy stable in the Daily Express Triumph Hurdle. Although Sound Man was beaten into third place behind Klairon Davis and Viking Flagship in the Queen Mother Champion Chase, Dunwoody had ridden O'Grady's charge to four outstanding victories on the way to the Festival meeting.

That he is undoubtedly one of the best riders over the Grand National fences of the modern era was shown once again at Aintree '96 when he rode Superior Finish into third place behind Rough Quest and Encore Un Peu.

The story of Richard Dunwoody's childhood in Northern Ireland in an idyllic world untouched by 'The Troubles' and of the fortuitous move by his parents to Britain that eventually set him on the road to stardom as a National Hunt jockey is fully chronicled in Jimmy Walker's authoritative and very readable biography, *Richard Dunwoody – Bred To Be Champion*. It traces also the epoch-making moments of his career to the day in 1993 when he succeeded to the mantle of Peter Scudamore

Richard Dunwoody's 33rd birthday looms on January 18, 1997.

Two years ago when he was immersed in the net of obsession, *Racing Post* writer Marcus Armytage, who rode Mr Frisk to victory in the 1990 Aintree Grand National, said of Dunwoody that he was "obsessive, professional, competitive, aggressive, intelligent... his own worst critic...

shy, sometimes distant, uncommunicative, monosyllabic and moody, yet at other times hospitable, welcoming, articulate, sometimes amusing, never boring".

Parts of that script will have to be re-written now, Marcus.

The new-style Dunwoody I met at Galway '96 has come a long way in two short years.

✳   ✳   ✳

One cannot write about the jump jockeys that have emerged from Northern Ireland in recent times without putting the spotlight also on Downpatrick-born Toby Dobbin, who while he may not have had the same meteoric rise to the top of the ladder as Tony McCoy has still established himself as a rider of real talent in Britain. The finest tribute to that talent was when he landed the plum job as stable jockey to Gordon Richards on Neil Doughty's retirement. He finished the 1993-'94 season as the leading conditional jockey with 45 wins to his credit. At the close of the following season his total was 57.

And despite being out for two months through injury in the 1995-'96 season, he still finished with a tally of 67 winners – his best to date.

He doesn't , of course, ride the horses owned by Robert Ogden that are trained by Gordon Richards as Paul Carberry is under contract to ride these. He was bitterly disappointed to lose to Richard Dunwoody the ride on One Man when it came to the King George and the Cheltenham Gold Cup but he's not the first jockey who has missed out in this way – and he won't be the last.

His early contact with horses came through his father, who was Master of the East Downs Foxhounds and was also involved with the preparation of point-to-pointers.

Young Tony's first competitive equestrian action came in local pony races, and his consuming interest in horses led to his leaving school at the age of fifteen to enter the world of racing.

His move to England was prompted by the fact that he thought "there were a lot more opportunities and a lot more racing".

Initially he was attached to the Neville Callaghan stable in Newmarket. But, as he was only 15, he soon got homesick and was back home in Downpatrick in a very short time.

A meeting with Jonjo O'Neill at Punchestown resulted in a move to the Cumbrian stable of the genial Corkman in June, 1988 and his first winner for his new boss came a year later on board Stay Awake at Hamilton Park. In all he rode some twenty-five winners whilst with Jonjo, before being offered a job at the start of the 1993-'94 season with former Grand National-winning jockey Maurice Barnes.

Dobbin lost his right to claim in November of '93 and, as well as riding for Maurice Barnes, he also teamed up with East Lothian trainer, Peter Monteith, who supplied him with his first big win with the gutsy mare

Dizzy, who landed the County Hurdle at the Cheltenham Festival meeting. Tragically, she was killed in a fall in the Scottish Champion Hurdle some weeks later.

As Tony put it: "She gave me my best day's racing ever, and my worst. She's certainly the best horse I've ridden. She was so brave, so courageous. She'd never fallen before, and it was her bravery that killed her."

Tony Dobbin was determined from the outset not to be just "one of the lads who do well for a couple of seasons and then are never heard of again".

Still in his early twenties, with drive and determination in a finish and a horseman overall, it will be interesting to watch his progress in the seasons ahead.

One thing is certain – the Northern Ireland conveyor belt of talent continues to turn them out both on the Flat and over the jumps.

14

How Jason Titley Made It Back From Near-Oblivion

At the end of 1995-'96 National Hunt season in Britain, Jason Titley was 12th in the Jockeys' Championship table with 50 winners. In Ireland he rode eleven winners, making a grand total of 61. It reflected an amazing come-back from near-oblivion.

When Titley arrived in Lambourn in August '94 it was with no fanfare of trumpets. Indeed, it could be said that he had reached the end of the line in the sense that opportunities had dried up for him at home. The knowing ones were nodding their heads and exclaiming : "Another outstanding talent that couldn't cope with fame and success has gone by the board. A pity really".

There had been that wonderful 1991-'92 season when all the world sang for him with the carefree abandon of youth and he was being described as the jockey with the Midas touch as the big-race winners fell into his lap one after the other – and for five different stables at that. The pictures that made their way into the racing publications and calendars and which were framed and displayed in hostelries around the country told of a singular success story for the Shannon-based rider-Titley leading over the final hurdle on the John Brassil-trained How's The Boss as he swept to a three-and-a-half lengths victory in the 1992 Ladbroke Handicap Hurdle; winning the Telecom Eireann Thyestes Chase on the Harry De Bromhead-trained Grand Habit by six lengths; the Coral Golden Handicap Hurdle Final on the Michael Purcell-trained My View in a field of thirty-one; the Motor Import Handicap Chase (Grade 2) at the Punchestown Festival meeting for the same stable on The Musical Priest; the Jameson Irish Grand National on the Michael O'Brien-trained Vanton by four lengths from English challenger Over The Road; the Guinness Galway Hurdle on the Patrick G. Kelly-trained Natalies Fancy.

On the Saturday after the Cheltenham '92 Festival meeting he won the Matfen Handicap Chase by a neck at Newcastle on Old Applejack for the County Durham stable of J. Howard Johnson. So that made it another small stable that was indebted to his talent and the overall total contributing to his run of significant successes had come to six.

More often than not the bookmakers joined in the applause, mindful of the fact that he was booting home winners at fancy odds: How's Boss (20/1), Grand Habit (16/1), My View (33/1) and Natalies Fancy (33/1). Only Vanton (13/2 second favourite), The Musical Priest (8/1 from 10/1) and Old Applejack (13/8 favourite) were not in the "skinner" category.

When Jason Titley scored on My View at the Cheltenham Festival meeting in the famous Buck House colours of Mrs Seamus Purcell, it was the best possible belated present he could have wished for – a mere nine days after his 21st birthday.

He was on a roller-coaster and it must have seemed to him that the good times would never end. At 21 you don't tend to think about the future.

He was setting a hectic pace both in the literal and figurative senses. "Life became one long party", he confessed to Tony O'Hehir of the *Racing Post* in a feature in the 1995-'96 *Irish Racing Annual*. "I didn't realise it at the time, but I was throwing everything away".

In a way he was lucky to come out of that dark spell unscathed and without having suffered any serious or permanent injury. Cars were written off that spoke of a reckless courting with death.

Men who don't easily suffer the wildness of youth when they see it as affecting the disciplined approach were beginning to write off a career that initially had hit the firmament like a meteor.

"I was young and foolish and I couldn't believe my luck. All those big winners meant I had plenty of money. I had a ball", he said.

He began to get careless about his weight. He began to miss schooling sessions on the gallops. He was not switched on to the cold reality that owners and trainers aiming for specific targets simply would not countenance a situation where they thought that living it up and having the proverbial ball would interfere with a jockey's dedication and total commitment to the demands of his profession.

Once the trainers, who ultimately called the shots, began to get irritated and angry with him, Jason Titley was effectively skiing downhill on a slope-face he should never have been on – and the fade-out was inevitable.

He doesn't seek to make excuses for that period in his career but does emphasise that he didn't help his cause by returning too soon from a broken collar-bone injury. This led in turn to his being run away with by How's The Boss at a televised meeting at Leopardstown. "I got plenty of stick. Everyone was talking about me and I knew I was in trouble", he recalled.

✳   ✳   ✳

The money went as the sweet music of those earlier successes died. As he slipped out of the country on his way to Lambourn in August '94 no one seemed to notice.

He had fixed up nothing definite. He just knew he had to get away and make a complete new start.

Fortunately for him, there were those who hadn't lost faith in his talent, who believed that the lad who had been so impressive in winning the Thyestes Chase and the Jameson Irish Grand National and who had also won at Cheltenham could make it back to the big-time again – given the right approach, the right attitude and the right opportunities.

"Enda Bolger encouraged me to go to England and Adrian Maguire also pressed me to give it a try. I won't forget both of them for support at a crucial stage in my life," he said.

Indeed, Enda Bolger went further and put Jason Titley in touch with Miss Henrietta Knight, who trains at West Lockinge Farm, Wantage in Oxfordshire and who in time was to become sufficiently impressed with Titley's talent that she appointed him her stable jockey.

But initially she could not promise him any rides. But he rode out for her and from the moment she gave him his break and he was back in the saddle at a racecourse, the talent of this 21-year-old blossomed anew and, little wonder, that one of his favourite horses would be Easthorpe, whom Henrietta Knight trained to win seven successive races and for the last three of these triumphs, Titley was on board. "That horse doesn't know when he is beaten", he said.

"When I came to England I knew things wouldn't be easy", he recalled. "I had to buckle down and work hard. It was a rough time and I almost chucked it in more than once.

"But I got loads of encouragement from so many people and that helped me over the difficult hurdles and helped inspire me to keep going, come what may".

Naturally high up on his list are Henrietta Knight and her partner, Terry Biddlecombe, a larger than life character who as a former top jump jockey had been through the mill, who had survived a battle with the demon drink and was certainly in a good position to give very sensible and timely advice to anyone willing to listen. "They've both been fantastic", was Jason's spontaneous tribute. "No words of mine could enumerate my gratitude for all they have done for me".

Titley got to know Graham Bradley from the Brad's frequent visits to Ireland. Now Bradley acted with a generosity that Jason could only describe as "unbelievable", especially when he reflected back on the Yorkshire-born rider putting him in for rides when he was unavailable and also suggesting that he link up with his own agent, Graham James.

Another Irish-born jockey based in England, Johnny Kavanagh came to share a house with Titley and he was there to give cool and solid advice and backing when Jason was resurrecting his career. Now he can find himself sitting in the back of the car going racing with Johnny Kavanagh and Mick Fitzgerald and that he confesses is one of his pet hates – "as they both smoke and I don't. I hate it."

⁂　　⁂　　⁂

Enter now Mrs Jenny Pitman who became the first lady to train a Grand National winner when Corbiere scored in 1983. And the following year she became the first from the ranks of female trainers to take the Gold Cup when Burrough Hill Lad triumphed for her Weatherbrook House stables. She had a second Gold Cup success with Garrison Savannah in 1991 – the year her son, Mark could have brought off the Gold Cup – Grand National double had not Garrison Savannah been caught and beaten in the run-in at Aintree by Seagram.

Jenny Pitman had the galling experience of seeing Esha Ness and John White pass the post first in the Grand National that never was on April 3, 1993 and one could understand her distress, for after the second false start she knew that her charge was on a futile exercise and foresaw the dreadful disappointment that awaited owner and jockey.

The contrast between Jenny Pitman and the Martin Pipe of the years when the numbers game – that is winner totals – seemed to be Pipe's all-pervading purpose in life was never better illustrated than by what Mrs. Pitman said when interviewed in the summer of 1991 for the *Irish Racing Annual*. "I buy my horses to be champions. I'm not interested in winning any old race – I won't run them it they are not right on the day, because I am always gearing them to reach their pinnacle".

"When I go 'shopping' I am looking for a horse who catches my eye. If he's got a good pedigree that is a bonus, but basically I've got to like him," she told Geoff Lester.

Asked why she did most of her buying in Ireland, she responded: "Why do people fish in streams?".

In the count-down to Aintree '96 she would go on record to state: "The National is what peoples' dreams are about. Owners buy horses to be Gold Cup or Grand National horses, and if those horses qualify for Aintree, they want to go there".

She was in the happy situation that six of her horses had qualified for the Grand National that year and she was glad to run all six.

"I can tell you the level of pressure reaches its maximum to get them there ready to run for their lives", she admitted to Neil Morrice of the *Racing Post*. "It takes an awful lot of effort and you need to be like one of those Channel 4 roving cameras with little lenses everywhere to make sure that everything's in the right place at the right time".

The professionalism of this 50-year-old lady, who could present a formidable front when hitting out at the powers-that-be and when embroiled with the media, was revealed when she indicated that she wanted a "quiet" jockey with "good hands" for Royal Athlete.

✳   ✳   ✳

Titley, who had never ridden in the National before, sat on Royal Athlete just once on a visit to the Pitman yard but he impressed not alone Mrs Pitman but her son, Mark who said later: "He has a lovely pair of hands

157

which is important when you are riding Royal Athlete".

The 1986 Derby NH Sales staged by Tattersalls, Ireland had proved an inspired buying session for Jenny Pitman. For a total outlay of 31,000 guineas, she secured three unbroken three-year-olds, instantly recognisable today as Royal Athlete, Garrison Savannah and Esha Ness (their combined earnings would come to over half a million pounds but the winnings would have been considerably nearer to the million mark had Esha Ness been allowed to retain the 1993 spoils, and had not Garrison Savannah failed narrowly in 1991 to complete the Gold Cup – Grand National double).

It was some time before Jenny Pitman realised she had struck a bargain at 10,000 guineas for Royal Athlete – a Roselier gelding bred by John Brophy of Rathmore House, Kilkenny.

Royal Athlete returned from a Kempton Park bumper in February of 1987 with heat in a leg. He resumed after an interval of 22 months and over the course of the next two seasons won eight races including five novice steeplechases. He was third behind Jodami and Rushing Wild in the 1993 Gold Cup – a clear indication that he had class on his side.

But Royal Athlete's legs were to prove a constant source of worry, although careful management and a light programme prevented an actual breakdown. However, disaster overtook him contesting the Hennessy Gold Cup in 1993. A severe cut demanded close on 40 stitches and only the patient, constant attention of the trainer made it possible for him to be produced for the 1994-'95 campaign. So successful was Royal Athlete's rehabilitation that Jenny Pitman expected a bold showing in the Cheltenham Gold Cup but again misfortunate struck. He became set-fast – the muscle in his quarters becoming very stiff and he had to be withdrawn. In a way it could be said that his career was a colourful story of injuries.

Not surprisingly by the time the 1995 National came round Royal Athlete on the morning of the race was one of the longer-priced among Pitman's six runners in the big race. Jenny Pitman, however did not despair of his chance of success. She had informed the owners that she had secured an ideal jockey in Jason Titley, whose quiet style would bring the best out of the horse.

Titley in the course of the race fully justified the confidence reposed in him. Royal Athlete jumped superbly, was always in a good position, and moved right up to the leaders jumping the first fence on the second circuit. He was quickly joined by the top weight, Master Oats, favourite to emulate Golden Miller by winning the Gold Cup and Grand National in the same year, and the two horses raced in company until Master Oats began to tire after the third last.

Challenges were still being mounted however, and with Romany King, Party Politics, Over The Deel, Into The Red and Dubacilla staying on Royal Athlete still had work to do.

Titley confessed later that he was not all that confident on the run to the last fence, and Royal Athlete did remove a substantial quantity of the birch with his chest, but once safely landed he took a renewed hold of the bit and moved strongly towards the elbow and home without any hint of weakening, or any evident lack of confidence on his rider's part. It was a fitting climax to a great occasion, a triumph for skill and patience over adversity, fitting compensation for earlier disappointments.

Graham Bradley had always said to Jason Titley how important it was to ride a winner on television.

Jason Titley had picked the ultimate race to catapult him on to a new plane of television exposure when he won the Aintree Grand National.

But in his new-found maturity and wisdom he confided to friends that he did not want to be remembered only as the jockey who rode Royal Athlete to victory in the 1995 Grand National.

Adrian Maguire and Johnny Kavanagh joined with him in the celebrations in Franco's restaurant in Farringdon in the aftermath of his National triumph – and it was certainly a night to remember.

But Jason Titley could now keep his head because had had learned the hard way how fickle fame can be and that you could not afford to allow one major success to go to your head.

"Winning the National put me back on the map. It was unbelievable and for a jockey struggling for rides it was a fantastic advertisement. The best you can get.

"But experience has taught me this job is never easy. You have to keep proving yourself and you can't live on the glory of winning a National. I don't intend letting things slip again."

Vincent's Return... Vincent O'Brien, King of Cheltenham in the late Forties and Fifties made a return visit in March '95 and after a number of decades to the scene of his great triumphs. He was guest of honour at lunch on Gold Cup Day and was acclaimed by well-wishers when he entered the parade ring after the big race.

15

From Lahern Cross To The Mud Of Uttoxeter

It's a long way from the cross-roads dancing at Lahern Cross of a lovely evening in Summer to the mud of Uttoxeter on Midlands Grand National Day in March.

Not far from Eugene O'Sullivan's training establishment at Brittas, Lombardstown, near Mallow, you come across the sign pointing to Lahern Cross and there of a Sunday evening – if you are in the mood – you can dance your cares away. The verse written in stone says it all:

> *Quick, medium and slow steps*
> *Including tolerating of no steps*
> *Ceili, Modern and Old-Time*
> *Allowances made for no time*

Just down the road at the Gleeson Community Centre is displayed a plaque in memory of John Thomas Gleeson, poet, scholar and patriot, who composed the famous ballad, *The Bould Thady Quill* ("Ye maids of Duhallow who're anxious for courting...").

You may well hear it sung by Corkmen – and, indeed, others – at rousing sing-songs during Cheltenham Festival week. Incidentally, the inaugural Bould Thady Quill Bardic Festival was held in Ballinagree in August '96 and it was officially opened by Fergie Sutherland. It was a throw-back to the ancient tradition of The Bard, a highly-trained Celtic poet, composer, singer and harpist who served as oral historian, political critic, eulogizer and entertainer. The events at the Festival included singing, story-telling, set-dancing and poems from local poets.

The Boys from Lombardstown had reason to sing *The Bould Thady Quill* with gusto in the aftermath of Another Excuse's so-impressive victory in the 1996 renewal of the Midlands Grand National. And if they lifted the proverbial roof in the chorus, who could blame them:

> *For gambling and sporting, for football and courting,*
> *For drinking black porter as fast as you'd fill,*
> *In all your days roving, you'll find none so jovial*
> *As the Muskerry sportsman, the bould Thady Quill.*

The colours he carried to victory were the colours of the nine-man Kilshannig Racing Syndicate and those colours were closely linked with the local Kilshannig gaelic football club, which is steeped in tradition. One member of the Syndicate, John Linehan owns the pub known as *The Local* in Glentane, where naturally there were great celebrations following the Uttoxeter victory. Today, you see proudly displayed in this hostelry Colin Turner's fine print of Another Excuse jumping the last. This picture has taken its place beside others of Red Rum, Desert Orchid and the peerless Arkle. Your true-blue follower of the jumping game is by no means insular when it comes to pinpointing the stars of the game.

The blinkered Another Excuse, who was returned at 14/1 and had been well backed in the Glentane, Lombardstown and Dromahane areas, won officially by a distance from the Arthur Moore-trained Feathered Gale who would frank the form when on ground much more to his liking he won the 1996 Jameson Irish Grand National by eight lengths from the 1993 Gold Cup winner, Jodami. The third horse home at Uttoxeter was Moorecroft Boy, trained by David Nicholson; he would go on to win the '96 Scottish Grand National by eleven lengths from General Woulfe. Behind Another Excuse also were Minnehoma, winner of the 1994 Aintree Grand National and Killeshin, winner of the 1996 Eider Chase.

Because you don't get many marathon races in Ireland and none at a distance of 4m 2f (though the La Touche Cup Chase at Punchestown is 4m 1f), Eugene O'Sullivan wisely plotted an English programme for Another Excuse in the lead-up to the Midlands Grand National "The longer the distance the better he likes it and the more testing the conditions, the more matters become in his favour", said Eugene.

He ran him in the Eider Chase (4m 1f) at Newcastle in February with Mark Dwyer in the saddle. "He ran very badly that day and was pulled up, in fact, after a bad blunder at the 16th", recalled O'Sullivan. "Our hopes looked very much dented, as he just seemed to show no interest in racing".

However, Mark Dwyer advised that blinkers might do the job. "So we fitted him with blinkers for his next outing at Warwick in the first week of March and he did much better this time, finishing third to Full Of Oats, who was receiving 21lbs while the second was receiving 24lbs".

The going on that occasion was described officially as "good" but it was much too fast for Another Excuse, who had proved himself a good money-spinner at home in Ireland when he got the conditions exactly to his liking.

Eugene O'Sullivan had reason to look happily at the heavens as he watched the rain coming down relentlessly all afternoon at Uttoxeter on Saturday, March 16th.

Even though he was now carrying only 10 stone he was easy in the market compared to his Newcastle conqueror, Killeshin, who not surprisingly started 11/4 favourite on the strength of that Eider Cup Chase victory with Richard Dunwoody's mount Nazzar, winner of his previous two races, second favourite at 6/1. Feathered Gale was a 10/1 shot and Three Brownies at 33/1.

Brendan Powell, who grew up in Mallow, had the mount on Another Excuse and this street-wise rider brought a depth of experience to the job in hand.

The picture of 35-year-old Brendan Powell smiling happily afterwards in the winner's enclosure was that of a man who had come to know more about the ups and downs of this game than any aspiring young rider could ever hope to learn in a lifetime in the saddle.

The highest moment of all in his career was winning the Grand National on Rhyme 'N' Reason in 1988. Other highs also as represented by victories in the 1989 Scottish Grand National on Roll A Joint, the 1990 Europe Champion Hurdle on Nomadic Way and the 1995 Mackeson Gold Cup on Dublin Flyer.

The lows, not surprisingly, centred around injuries, including two broken legs in the past five years, each requiring a six-month rehabilitation period and a further period trying to get back into the limelight again and regaining the confidence of owners and trainers.

A man of lesser courage and fortitude might have called it a day. But Brendan Powell never entertained the thought of quitting. "I knew I never wanted to pack up", he told Gary Nutting of the *Sporting Life*. "But at the back of my mind, particularly after I broke my left leg for the second time, I wondered how difficult it would be to persuade people to put me up again.

"That was the most difficult part because a lot of owners and trainers won't consider you until you've proved you can still ride winners. When you're a freelance, it basically means starting all over again".

"But you learn to take the knocks on the chin – it's part of the job", he summed up.

Smaller trainers like Arthur Barrow, Gerald Ham, Chris Popham and Bryan Smart and Bob Buckler, who was only in his second season, all maintained their faith in him.

Opportunity knocked for him when Eugene O'Sullivan, who would be considered small in English eyes compared with the high-profile Irish trainers who tilted annually at the rich Cheltenham events, put his faith in him to ride Another Excuse in the Midlands Grand National.

A seasoned veteran like Powell didn't need detailed instructions. He knew he was taking the mount on a horse that wouldn't be found wanting for stamina and who would actually revel in the conditions. All that was required was that he put in a clear round.

Another Excuse jumped to the front six out and when Killeshin, who was four lengths adrift at that point, fell at the second last, all danger was removed and Brendan Powell was left to coast home.

"Absolutely brilliant", was Eugene O'Sullivan's comment to the assembled media in the winner's enclosure, as he greeted the eight-year-old gelding who had earned almost £33,000 from the success.

His wife Fiona and his sister, Anne and several members of the Syndicate and many others who had come on from Cheltenham helped create a mini-Festival atmosphere not normally experienced at Uttoxeter on Midlands

Grand National Day. But then this was the climax of a marvellous week for County Cork.

Less than twenty miles separated the two small stables that had delivered two famous victories and it was a long, long way removed from one of the oil-rich Sheikhs realising his ambition to win a Classic.

* * *

It was a day in June '96 when I came up the lovely tree-lined avenue leading to the O'Sullivan stables, to be greeted in the yard by Fiona and four-year-old Maxine playing happily in the sun. Eugene joined us almost immediately.

Inside the house Fiona served tea. Eugene revealed that the stable complement of horses would be 25 to 30 for the 1996-'97 National Hunt season.

A solid foundation stone of the O'Sullivan family operation – and it is very much an extended family operation – has for long been that of members of the local farming community being happy to send to Eugene a horse that they might have bred themselves with the primary target of winning a point-to-point and it was a bonus if something bigger evolved. That would continue to be so but he was now attracting additional owners, who were prepared to trust his judgement to procure for them horses that would be aimed at higher targets. The victory of Another Excuse, coming five years after Lovely Citizen had taken the Christies Foxhunter Chase, proved that Eugene O'Sullivan could pitch for prestigious targets outside of Ireland – and deliver.

He was a trainer to be reckoned with and there was definitely no element of luck in the way he planned the programme that culminated in Another Excuse winning the Midlands Grand National.

He doesn't mind admitting that he was inspired by the story of Vincent O'Brien starting on his own at the age of 26 – after the death of his father, Dan – from his base in Churchtown in 1943 and inexorably climbing the ladder to reach the point eventually where he was acknowledged as one of the greatest trainers, if not the greatest, in the world. You don't have to travel far from Lombardstown to reach Clasganniff House where Noel O'Brien and his wife, Margaret and family reside today. There is a close affinity and friendship between the O'Briens and the O'Sullivans and Noel has sent horses to Eugene to train.

Few trainers that I have spoken to have a better understanding of the point-to-point scene than Eugene O'Sullivan. He has seen its changing face. Once there were races that might be said to offer a soft option. Now the competition is cut-throat and he has seen horses that he thought were in with a golden chance of winning having to be content with a place – and fortunate enough maybe at times to get that reward.

The reason the competition had become so fierce was that everyone knew that there were English trainers about with cheque-books on hand. Rather than buy a store that might never make the winner's enclosure after all the investment in time and money, they could pick up a ready-made jumper in a point-to-point winner that was impressive on the day. And even if he didn't go on to make it to the top, he would in all probability come good on a lesser plane and the owner would be happy to lead in a winner at Cartmel, Warwick, Market Rasen or Huntingdon.

The love of horses is bred in the very marrow of Eugene's bones. His father always had horses and bred them too. In fact, he had Under Way before selling him on and there's no need to pinpoint his exploits as one of the most prolific winners when he was trained by P. P. Hogan.

Eugene takes a quiet pride in the photo carried in my book *Tigers Of The Turf* of his father sharing with him and his brother, Willie – the successful rider that day – the moment when the mammoth trophy was held aloft at Cheltenham '91 after Lovely Citizen had won the Christies Foxhunters Chase.

His Dad has not surprisingly, come to love the Cheltenham scene. Sharing a drink with him in *The Local,* we reminisced about the 1991 Festival meeting. He naturally reciprocates the pride Eugene has in him and has watched with quiet satisfaction the O'Sullivan name making its mark in Britain and nothing could have given him greater pleasure than the culminating triumph at Uttoxeter in the 1996 Midlands Grand National.

The O'Sullivan operation, as already indicated, is very much a family one. It has got to be so, as the farm has to be looked after in addition to the training of the horses. Eugene remarks laughingly that, where he might look to his father to take care of the supervising of the milking of the cows when there was an evening meeting that called on him being away from Lombardstown, Dad loved going racing so much that he too would want to be off. But there are enough O'Sullivans to ensure that basically nothing suffers. Anyway, as it is primarily a National Hunt stable that Eugene runs, he is free enough to give a lot of time to the farming during the busy summer months.

Fiona is a wonderful support and strength in the operation. She was brought up to racing and to love the hunting scene. Following the hounds has always been part of life for her from her childhood days in Croom.

Easy of manner, affable, yet extremely knowledgeable and shrewd in talking racing matters, she's a natural in a setting like this. And you can see the communion of thought and spirit between Eugene and herself, cemented in an ideal marriage.

On the way down to see the new all-weather circular gallop of fibre-sand, extending for four furlongs, we pass the *Gortroe Inn* and this is another hostelry where the locals have celebrated the singular triumphs of the O'Sullivan stable.

In a closely-knit community much pride stems from the 1991 triumph of Lovely Citizen at Cheltenham and the 1996 success of Another Excuse at Uttoxeter. They all feel they have shared in those triumphs – even those who only watched them on television.

Much has happened for Eugene and Fiona since Cheltenham '91 and yet in a way when you assess the growth of the stable to the position it enjoys today and see the addition of the all-weather gallop, you realise that it all goes back to Cheltenham '91. Things could never be the same after that.

✳   ✳   ✳

When Fiona O'Sullivan set off with the horse-box carrying Lovely Citizen to England for his bid for the 1991 Christies Fox hunters Chase, she was entertaining the hope that the Golden Love gelding which the O'Sullivans had bred themselves from the mare Kelenham, who they still had at home, would uphold the standard of County Cork.

But in a way she felt it was too much to contemplate that the point-to-pointer trained by Eugene, and which would be ridden by his brother, Willie, would beat what many judges were predicting was an "unbeatable" favourite in Teaplanter. The latter had a string of victories to his credit.

Fiona's destination was the stable of Richard Hannon where her brother, Brian Meehan, was assistant trainer at the time (today he has his own stables in Lambourn with around 70 horses in his care).

Hannon got into the spirit of things, knowing full well what success at the Festival meeting would mean to the O'Sullivan family. When he had visitors to the yard that same week he would suggest to them that they take a look at a horse that was going to raise a winning flag at Cheltenham.

Each morning in the countdown to the Festival meeting Fiona rode Lovely Citizen at work.

Lovely Citizen had won two hunter chases and three point-to-points but when the experts were analysing how many victories Irish-trained horses might win at the 1991 Festival meeting, the Cork-trained challenger wasn't even mentioned in the reckoning with such as Nordic Surprise, Minorettes Girl, Chirkpar and Kitchi.

Eugene confessed later that he would gladly have sold Lovely Citizen in August, 1990, if anyone had offered him £4,000 for the horse. There wasn't one offer.

When Lovely Citizen was a three-year-old he suffered a broken hock and Eugene was advised to put him down. He decided to take a second opinion. This resulted in the gentle and patient nursing of Lovely Citizen back to the point where he could race. However, the swollen remains of that hock injury meant that the leg was so big and awkward that no one would buy the horse.

He was a horse too with a mind of his own. He got to know how to open the latch to the horse-box in the O'Sullivan stable. Once he went missing for two days. Eugene was beginning to fear the worst when Lovely Citizen found his own way back. They put a special lock on his box.

He proved his ability on the point-to-point and hunter chase circuit and the O'Sullivans decided to go for the BIG ONE – the Christies Foxhunter Challenge Cup. Their friends and relations booked for the Festival meeting knowing in their hearts that they would never forgive themselves if the gelding won the massive trophy. No use looking at the race on television when you could be there in the shadow of Cleeve Hill cheering your head off as the racecourse commentator announced that Lovely Citizen had got into the firing line coming down the hill. And you would want also to be part of the celebrations if he did pull it off.

No, you might never get a chance again in a lifetime to cheer home a winner from the townland of Lombardstown.

They put on their tenners and fivers at odds of 16/1 and 14/1 and they didn't even ruffle the waters of the Cheltenham betting market – the strongest in the world besides that of Royal Ascot. The professional money was on Teaplanter, quoted at 2/1 in the offices in the morning but going off at 6/4.

I will never forget the moment when Lovely Citizen came back into the unsaddling enclosure to a special "Cork roar" inherent in the Irish cheers.

The connections, forming a half circle as they linked arms, broke spontaneously into "Ole, Ole, Ole". Then they began singing *The Banks Of My Own Lovely Lee*.

Joy was written on their countenances. Fiona O'Sullivan was being hugged and kissed by friends as she exclaimed: "I just can't believe it." It was one of the happiest scenes I have ever seen at Cheltenham.

Mary O'Sullivan, mother of trainer Eugene and jockey Willie, combed her hair and smoothed her dress before she went up for the presentation. There was a world in that gesture speaking of the rural heartlands. Her husband, a man of no airs or pretensions, was smiling a broad and happy smile as he gave a victory wave to the circle of connections.

The cameras clicked. I knew that there would be colour and black and white prints catching a moment that would never fade for the O'Sullivan family. "Hold up the Cup, Owen", one photographer shouted. He lifted the big, heavy trophy and held it aloft in triumph – and in a way it was as if Cork had completed the treble in the space of six months, the Liam McCarthy Cup and the Sam Maguire Cup having been brought back to the banks of the Lee already.

"The bonfires will be blazing still stronger again when we arrive home with the Cup."

The finish of the race itself was a heart-stopper. Half-way up the run-in Dun Gay Lass was still holding on, looking to have the race won. Then suddenly her rider Martin Claxton lurched sideways and nearly fell out of the saddle. Claxton, half-way up the horse's neck, and doing the best he could, almost recovered the advantage but Willie O'Sullivan, riding like a man inspired, got Lovely Citizen up on the post to win by a head. It transpired that Claxton had performed miracles to stay on board as his off-side iron had broken clean through.

But the ill wind that cost Martin Claxton the race was blowing on this day in favour of the O'Sullivans. It was their hour and no one was going to take it from them.

Lovely Citizen has long since retired from racing under Rules but, amazingly enough, he was still point-to-pointing during the 1995-'96 season. Old soldiers never die, they only fade away...

✳   ✳   ✳

A year before the O'Sullivans enjoyed their finest hour, Sirrell Griffiths had blazed a trail out of the Welsh Valleys.

He milked 70 Friesan cows at 5.30 a.m. on that never-to-be-forgotten Thursday morning in March '90 before driving his cattle-truck (he did not have a horse-box) to Cheltenham to take on Desert Orchid, the pride of England, in the Gold Cup.

It's history now how 100/1 outsider, Norton's Coin scored a famous victory for Wales. And that same evening in the village of Nagaredig, not far from the town of Carmarthen, which had given the legendary stand-off Barry John and flying winger Gerald Davis to Welsh rugby, they put up a banner which read: "WELCOME HOME NORTON'S COIN".

The bonfires were blazing not for rugby heroes in an area where hero worship is legendary but for a steeplechaser who had upheld the honour of Wales against the most popular chaser since the incomparable Arkle.

It was a fairytale story in itself – one that disproved for all time, in the National Hunt sphere of racing at any rate, the theory that you need to have the millions of the Arab Sheikhs at your back to win one of the major prizes at the Festival meeting.

The prophets of doom had been lifting their hands to the heavens in despair on the Tuesday when Kibensis, in the colours of Sheikh Mohammed, won the Champion Hurdle. They argued that it would be only a matter of time before the oil-rich Arab princes dominated the jumping scene and there would be no place anymore for the Willie Lomans – the small men with a dream.

After the success of Norton's Coin they knew with new certainty that such dreams could be fulfilled.

Dylan Thomas could have written a poem about 50-year-old Sirrell Griffith's return to Wales with the Gold Cup trophy – transporting it back in the same vehicle in which he had headed for Cheltenham that same morning. And Norton's Coin ran with the cows in the summer months.

Griffiths hailed originally from Herefordshire but he had lived locally in the village of Nantgaredig for seventeen years and Welsh folk had adopted him as "one of our own". A three-horse permit holder, he admitted that farming was his No. 1 source of income. He could have gone into training on a much bigger scale after the success of Norton's Coin ("I had offers to train 22 more horses") but he declined all such offers. "We are too far out of the way to start training on a big scale. You need to be in a major centre. Anyway getting a full licence would mean employing extra labour – we're just a small family concern. It's Joyce, me and the boys."

On the evening of the homecoming, Sirrell's wife, Joyce and his sons, Martin and Linley hardly knew what hit them, such was the excitement in the village.

"Unbelievable", said Sirrell, recalling it all some months later when Geoff Lester of *The Sporting Life* called to talk to him for a feature for the *Irish Racing Annual*.

"We never dreamed anybody would be waiting for us at home. Remember it was 10 o'clock at night by the time I got Norton's Coin back in the lorry from Cheltenham. Then, passing the Railway, I saw this banner across the road: 'Welcome Home Norton's Coin' and our lane was completely blocked with cars.

"There were TV crews and hundreds of well-wishers from the village and afar, and I had to send the boys out for ten bottles of Scotch. There wasn't much left by the time they all went – I can promise you."

Astonishingly, however, not one of the Griffiths family had a solitary shilling on Norton's Coin. "I've never backed him", said Sirrell. "I like a bet now and then, but I could never bring myself to have a few quid on Norton's Coin.

"We told the whole village he'd run well, though. They took a coach-load to Cheltenham and with their £2 bets and fivers they came home with £17,000. My, it was one hell of a day."

✳   ✳   ✳

It was a miracle in a way that Norton's Coin ever got to run in the 1990 Gold Cup – and having got to the start, he might not have been allowed to run if the tapes had not already gone up just as he was being kicked.

"I thought our Gold Cup hopes had gone up in smoke when Norton's Coin coughed three times in the paddock before his pre-prep race at Newbury", recalled Sirrell Griffiths. "The vet had him scooped the next day and his lungs were full of muck. He was amazed how the horse had finished the race. Time was against us for Cheltenham now as we had to restrict his preparation to walking."

Norton's Coin was put on a course of antibiotics. Six days before the Gold Cup he was boxed up and dispatched east along the M4 to Peter Cundell's Compton stables. Graham McCourt rode Norton's Coin in the crucial gallop, accompanied by Cundell's smart horse, Ryde Again.

The speed that "Norton's" displayed over a mile and six furlongs surprised even Griffiths, who had always maintained that the gelding had the pace to win over two miles on the flat.

McCourt, who had persuaded Griffiths to enter Norton's Coin for the Gold Cup in the first place, told the trainer after that full-scale workout that, provided his jumping did not let him down, the horse had a first-rate opportunity of finishing in the first three.

Fast ground diminished Griffiths' confidence somewhat – "He loves the muck and the softer the better" – and then disaster seemed to strike at the start when Toby Tobias lashed out and caught Norton's Coin on his front leg. "Graham (McCourt) called out to the starter that he had been kicked",

Griffiths recalled, "but the tapes were up and they were on their way."

Desert Orchid was never allowed dominate matters as he had done in his races at Kempton, Sandown and Ascot. Norton's Coin was always going well within himself just in behind the leaders. Under a brilliant ride from McCourt he won the battle up the hill with Toby Tobias and Desert Orchid, outstaying "Toby" to win by three-quarters-of-a-length with Desert Orchid third.

Norton's Coin was lame on pulling up, the legacy of that kick at the start. And then when Sirrell Griffiths got to the stable area, after the customary interviews, he found the nine-year-old had drunk half a bucket of water – "but at the bottom were two handfuls of green slime. If he had coughed that up before the race, no way could I have allowed him to run."

Sirrell Griffiths is still a small man today as trainers go, with about a half-a-dozen horses in his care.

The pride of the stable in the 1995-'96 National Hunt season was Forestal 4 which won three hurdle races off the reel at Hereford, Chepstow and Haydock. Sirrell planned to put him chasing, though noting that he was not bred to get three miles and he would be aimed at two-and-a-half mile events.

The trainer of Norton's Coin was invited over in the summer of '96 for the annual "bash" organised by Hilary Murphy of Hilary Murphy Travel, New Ross to coincide with the race he sponsors at the Wexford mid-June evening meeting (this year the Hilary Murphy Travel Novice Hurdle was run on Friday, June 21). Sirrel was one of some hundred guests who lunched at The Horse and Hound public house and restaurant at Ballinabula before heading for the races. "It was a memorable day", said Sirrel, who had the pleasure of meeting Fergie Sutherland, who was a special guest.

The small men certainly had their hour!

✳   ✳   ✳

From sheep country in Herefordshire emerged a success story in 1994 fit to stand beside the most romantic associated with the Cheltenham Festival meeting.

Where Sirrell Griffiths had milked his cows before setting off for Cheltenham on Gold Cup Day 1990, now on Smurfit Champion Hurdle Day '94 36-years-old Richard Price delivered 20 lambs on his 400-acre farm before travelling to the Festival meeting with Flakey Dove and saw her succeed where her grand-dam Red Dove had failed in the race 31 years previously.

And adding to the romance was the fact that Flakey Dove, the first mare to win this race since Dawn Run in 1984, shared a Herefordshire field with a flock of sheep when not being asked to do the business on a racecourse.

Richard Price on the day of his greatest triumph told the media representatives in the winner's enclosure that he had a public licence for only three years but had a permit for six years before that. And he revealed also that Flakey Dove was one of only half a dozen horses he trained.

Where was his father, Tom, we asked? A lover of the hunt, he had been out that very morning with the North Herefordshire's but at 70 he didn't like crowds and, frankly couldn't be bothered trying to elbow his way through the crush of humanity at Cheltenham. So he stayed at home and would have watched the race on television.

Tom Price saddled Red Dove to finish unplaced in the 1963 Champion Hurdle. Now thirty-one years on from that day compensation was being made by Fate to the Price family, for another member of the family, Gordon, had finished third in the Champion Hurdle on 10/1 outsider Stano Pride in 1985.

They had quite a celebration in the village of Stoke Prior near Leominster when Flakey Dove returned to a hero's welcome ... and the pride of the villagers and the community in all the surrounding countryside was all the greater when they reflected on the slur they felt was offered by one scribe that same morning when he implied that really a mare from the sheep country of Herefordshire had no place taking on the more fancied runners like Large Action and Oh So Risky. "Disgraceful", said one of the connections.

But all was forgotten when Mark Dwyer, deputising for the suspended Norman Williamson, brought all his experience and talent into play in riding a perfectly-judged race to beat the favourite , Oh So Risky by one-and-a-half lengths with Large Action a further three-quarters-of-a-lengths away third.

The two inns in the village, *The Lamb* and *The Wheelbarrow* had a whale of a night and the extended nature of the Price family ensured that there was a lot of back-slapping.

They would remember always the moment when Mark Dwyer thrust his fist into the Gloucestershire skies in a fitting victory salute as he returned in triumph to receive the acclaim that echoed out to the Cotswolds.

Sirrell Griffiths ...the O'Sullivans ... and now the Prices. From Wales to Lombardstown, near Mallow, to a sleepy village in Herefordshire. And the day after Flakey Dove had won, Tom Foley, wrote his own special chapter in the annals of the Festival meeting with Danoli.

With romance like this you understand more fully why men dream dreams at which the Festival meeting is at the centre. And those for whom the dreams are fulfilled are privileged, as nothing in racing can quite compare with experiencing the roar that swells around the amphitheatre of the unsaddling enclosure at Cheltenham.

That roar represents the challenge and the spur.

PART TWO

MEN OF THE FLAT WHO RIDE THE HIGH SIERRAS

16

Aidan O'Brien – The New Master Of Ballydoyle

R ecords, it seems, are made to be broken by Aidan O'Brien.

At the end of 1995 he stood on top of the world in the sense that he had turned out 241 winners on the Flat and over the jumps in the one calendar year – and in the process smashed all existing Irish records. Not alone that, but he eclipsed the highest winning total achieved in recent times by the current English record-holder, Martin Pipe.

O'Brien's strike rate was simply phenomenal, especially over the jumps. It had reached the point in the National Hunt sector that in the battle of the Irish Trainers' crown, he had in each of the two seasons, 1994-'95 and 1995-'96, three times as many winners as his nearest rival in the table, Arthur Moore.

On the Flat in Ireland he had become one of the "Big Four" with John Oxx, Dermot Weld and Jim Bolger. This quartet dominated the scene above all others.

When Vincent O'Brien retired at the end of the 1994 Flat season, it was obvious that the showpiece gallops and other amenities at Ballydoyle would not be left idle for long. And so it came as no great surprise when early in '95 Aidan O'Brien – no relation to The Maestro – began training a string of Flat horses from the yard while in time, Anne Marie and himself would make their new home in a house on the lands.

Quickly Aidan O'Brien was dubbed 'The New Master of Ballydoyle' by the media. And that in turn put a more intense spotlight than ever on him. Now the racing public both in Ireland and Britain were waiting to see whether this amazing young trainer, still only 27 at the time of writing in the autumn of '96, could emulate the feats of the man who from these same gallops had turned out horses that had achieved immortality like Sir Ivor, Nijinsky, The Minstrel, Alleged, El Gran Senor and Golden Fleece.

When I visited him on a lovely July day in the summer of '96, I asked him directly whether he felt the pressure stemming from the speculation that he could be the means of creating a new golden era for Ballydoyle?

He replied that he did not feel pressure and neither was he going to allow it to happen that he would live a nightmare existence because he was not turning out Classic winners fast enough to satisfy the expectations of the public. He emphasised to me that he will not suffer sleepless nights on this regard. His concern was with getting the maximum out of the horses in his care and in ensuring that failure was not due to any mistakes on his part.

I could see immediately that he was very much his own man – totally confident in his own ability and his own methods, dedicated to the work ethic to the point that he can now supervise the running of four different yards between the Ballydoyle and Piltown operations, creating their own heavy demands on travel between Counties Tipperary and Kilkenny and always only too conscious of the clock. But at the same time you come to realise that he has his priorities right. He is very much the family man and you can see that he adores his children. In fact, in order that the intense racing round, especially in the summer months, won't create a situation that allows him to have little time with the children, he no longer attends every evening meeting.

The way he views it is – he trains the horses to be at their peak to hit the targets set for them and his presence is not essential at a racecourse for a particular horse to deliver. He has full confidence in his staff. In the case of the bigger meetings, however, he will be there or when a choicely-bred debutante two-year-old of real potential, is making its appearance and he wants to study with his own eye its initial run to make assessments for the future.

The 1996 season saw Aidan O'Brien turn out Rainbow Blues to finish second to the French-trained Spinning World in the Irish 2,000 Guineas and the same colt was fifth in the Budweiser Irish Derby while O'Brien had the satisfaction of seeing His Excellence take third place, ahead of Dushyantor.

Much play has been made of his apparent shyness, of his avoidance of the social round where the cameras are liable to be clicking for the gossip columns.

Aidan O'Brien can be totally himself in the company of racing people and the racing writers. When he is being interviewed after a race by the media circle – whether it be at the Curragh, Leopardstown, Punchestown or Galway or even Cheltenham – he has no problem in handling the flow of questions put to him. He is in his own domain then – a racing domain.

But he is not one I would expect to jump at the opportunity of being interviewed live on a television chat show about subjects that may not be directly related to racing – "do you take cornflakes or bran flakes for breakfast?" "And who is your favourite film star?"

If I were his personal adviser, I would certainly be the last one to advocate that he go up front for the cameras to satisfy the producer of a television chat show. I would advise also against giving an after-dinner address to some luncheon gathering. It is not his field, not his forte.

Aidan O'Brien's feats speak for him in a way that he doesn't have to be a self-publicist. Speak in the very same way that made David O'Brien, another retiring person, someone on a plane apart for what he achieved before he reached his 30th birthday.

Vincent O'Brien was always retiring and certainly not one to court the gossip columns or appear on television chat shows. In fact, I would say that he had one thing in common with Aidan O'Brien, who would assume his mantle at Ballydoyle. Neither of them could ever be classed an interviewer's dream in the mould of a Mick O'Toole or a Mick Fitzgerald. Both were happier and far more relaxed when you were with them on the gallops, no note-book in hand, just talking horses. Then they exuded knowledge – a depth of knowledge. You knew you were in the company of genius in Vincent's case and a very special talent in Aidan's.

＊　　　＊　　　＊

On that nostalgic return visit to Ballydoyle in the summer of '96, I saw the sun rise over the Old Castle and over the magnificent spread of gallops, including the famous gallop designed as a replica of the sweep to Tattenham Corner as Vincent, with his eye to detail, set out to ensure that no colt bidding for the Blue Riband of the Flat would fail because he was unable to act down the hill.

I stood with Aidan O'Brien as he watched some of the horses in his charge catering up the grass. Tommy Murphy, who rode for Vincent and has forgotten more about the game than many can ever aspire to learn, is now an assistant trainer to the new Master of Ballydoyle. And the stable jockey is Christy Roche. No trainer could hope to have a jockey of greater experience or with a better ability to run the rule exactly over the potential of a two-year-old after exercise on the gallops.

There are gallops at Ballydoyle that can be described as secondary to the main ones that many a trainer, starting off in the business, would be only too glad to utilise as his principal one. You arrive at Mecca when you arrive here and stand in awe at the finest range of gallops in the world. They extend from all-weather ones to peat gallops, semi-peat gallops and natural grass gallops.

Aidan brings me out in the Land-Rover accompanied by Anne Marie and Tommy Murphy.

They talk about each horse individually as it goes by. Recognition is immediate and where it stands in its particular schedule, whether it has been backward or under a cloud and is now well on the way back. You marvel at the attention you know each horse is given.

But that attention extends to an animal back in Piltown, carrying the hopes of one owner or maybe a Syndicate, whose targets will be set well below those of the choicely-bred Flat campaigners. Each man to his own dreams and it is the trainer's job, if he can, to make the dreams become reality. Aidan O'Brien with his flow of winners has realised a lot of dreams.

Back in the house he defines for me his role as he now sees it. For the time being he wants to preserve a duality of approach – that is training both jumpers and Flat horses. Naturally,he was thrilled to turn out his first Cheltenham Festival winner in '96 when Urubande, in the hands of Charlie Swan, the No. 1. National Hunt rider to the stable, won the Sun Alliance Novices Hurdle at 8/1 and then went on to take the Martell Aintree Hurdle at the Grand National meeting. There was further satisfaction in Life Of A Lord's brilliant win in the Whitbread Gold Cup Chase, followed by a fine performance under top weight of 12st in winning the Digital Galway Plate for the second successive year.

In moments like that it's hard to contemplate Aidan O'Brien easily saying farewell to the jumping game.

But even though Vincent O'Brien set records in the National Hunt sphere that will never be broken, he eventually had to choose between giving his undivided attention to the Flat or continuing to mix it. He came down in favour or the Flat and had no reason to regret that decision.

As John Magnier, the boss of Coolmore, lays out the finance for still greater development at Ballydoyle and at the same time spends millions with Michael Tabor at the yearling sales seeking potential Classic winners that in time may join the Coolmore list of stallions, it's inevitable that Aidan O'Brien will get a still better class of animal to train. Indeed, at the time of writing this chapter that is already happening.

Not even Sheikh Mohammed or any of the oil-rich Sheikhs can guarantee Classic success, no matter how much they are prepared to spend. Some yearlings on which millions have been spent have never raced or else only turned out to be of mediocre standard.

However, it would be a brave man who would bet against the new Master of Ballydoyle not hitting the jackpot in time. One thing is certain, he has achieved everything there is to achieve in the "numbers game" – in the setting of records when it comes to turning out an awesome flow of winners each year.

In the eyes of informed racing men, the real challenge now lies in whether all the facilities at Ballydoyle and the acquiring of more quality Flat horses can lead to Classic winners. Aidan stands on a threshold and his many admirers will hope that it is a threshold leading to the conquering of the highest peaks in the Flat arena.

It's a cruel age in sport. Cruel for managers in the Premiership Soccer League in Britain, cruel for managers over county senior hurling and football teams in Ireland. A club has a magnificent stadium and a panel with players of international calibre and the directors will feel rewarded only when a high place is achieved in the League and maybe in time a title or Cup success on the domestic front and eventually in the European competitions. The manager can pay the penalty if he fails to deliver to the targets that are set.

The rewards for success are high and the media profile of those who are deemed winners is likewise pitched at the highest possible level. There is no place for losers as the Nineties give way to the new Millennium. That is the stark reality.

Trainers can feel the cold winds like everyone else.

Aidan O'Brien is a young man who through his education and commitment has deserved all the success that has come his way.

He may not feel pressurised in any way by the racing public but they simply cannot avoid thinking in terms of ever-higher targets in his case.

It goes with the territory when you are seen as the new Master Of Ballydoyle.

For that very reason his friends and admirers were delighted when he made the break-through to win his first Group One race in capturing the Aga Khan Studs National Stakes at the Curragh on Saturday, September 21, 1996 with Desert King, which came with a late burst under Walter Swinburn to beat the English challenger, Referendum (J. Reid) by a neck with the Jim Bolger-trained Azra (S. Craine) third. Desert King, carrying the familiar colours of Michael Tabor, started at 11/1 and O'Brien's other runner, Johan Cruyff finished fifth.

✳   ✳   ✳

He hails from County Wexford – from the same kind of country that gave Jim Bolger to the training profession.

He actually spent three-and-a-half years working with Jim Bolger and was assistant trainer to the Master of Glebe House before he left. Where others terminated their tenure at Coolcullen abruptly and departed with no love lost, O'Brien will tell you frankly:"Jim Bolger is a very good and a very fair man. He expects the best from you but if you respond as he wants you to respond, then he is good to you. I learnt pretty well all I know from him."

And Bolger, for his part, has nothing but the highest praise for Aidan O'Brien, naming him unhesitatingly as "one of the top three people to have worked for me since I became a trainer."

"He is a wonderful human being and one of the nicest young men I have ever come across', said Bolger. "If anyone was to epitomise the attributes of a gentleman and a scholar it is he. Aidan is intelligent and clever and picks things up quickly.

"Any operation with which he is associated can only prosper. His industry and dedication are tremendous. I'd have done anything to keep him working for me."

Aidan O'Brien was born in Killegney, Clonroche, near Enniscorthy and it was inevitable that like Jim Bolger he should have been involved as a youngster playing Ireland's national game of hurling and he also played Gaelic football. He played at midfield in under-16 competitions with his club Cloughbawn. He still follows the game but now such is his all-consuming passion for the horses and such are the time-consuming demands of his chosen profession that he cannot any longer be put into the category of a diehard enthusiast.

But like Jim Bolger he has no pretensions. There is not an ounce of affectation in his make-up. He presents a boyish and unassuming manner that surprises when you contemplate his achievements to date and the impact he has made in such a short space of time on the Irish racing scene.

That impact becomes all the more significant and praiseworthy when you reflect on the fact that unlike Dermot Weld, John Oxx, Jim Dreaper, Arthur Moore and Edward O'Grady, he did not spring from an established training family. However, his father Denis was a very keen point-to-pointer. "He rode many winners and there were always horses around the yard", Aidan told me.

O'Brien left secondary school midway through Fifth Year. "First of all I got a job weeding strawberries and later did shift-work as a forklift driver in Waterford Co-op", he recalled.

The call of the horses was in his blood. Long-term he saw no other life. And already deep down the ambition to become a trainer was stirring in his veins

* * *

He got the break that was to set him on the ladder that would lead eventually to making him the most exciting talent to burst on the Irish racing scene in the Nineties when a family friend, Pat Kelly, put him in contact with Curragh trainer, P.J. Finn, a son of the legendary Tipperary hurler, Jimmy Finn, who was selected at right wing back on the Hurling Team of the Century in 1984.

He was with P.J. Finn for two months before the latter opted out of the game and, fortunately for Aidan O'Brien, Pat Kelly then arranged a job for him with Jim Bolger. He was on his way.

You don't come away with a full note-book after interviewing him. Like Vincent O'Brien you must come almost unawares to touch on the points that matter and you then gain a hint as to why he has become the talk of the racing fraternity. As one insider put it to me:"The Sheikhs have already taken note of his talent."

It was on the racing circuit that Aidan and Anne Marie met and fell in love.

It happened at Galway in 1989. Aidan was riding Midsummer Fun in an amateur race for the Jim Bolger stable - it came home a winner, incidentally – and down at the start his eye was caught by the dark-haired Anne Marie, who also had a mount in the race. Although shy, he was so smitten by love at first sight that it was inevitable that he should take it from there and the rest is history.

Fate stepped in to cause his departure from Jim Bolger's stable in a rather unusual way. Six weeks before his wedding he broke his shoulder in a fall – "and I just never went back".

At that stage Anne Marie had just started training on her own and Aidan found himself completely involved in assisting her in the operation. He was the first to acknowledge that the three-and-a-half years he had spent with Jim Bolger represented "an invaluable experience" and that, having started off as a stable lad doing the most menial jobs around the yard and then being given more and more responsibility as time went on, he acquired a tremendous amount of knowledge of every facet of the training profession. "I would start work in the dark and finish in the dark. I would ride out in the morning and do just about everything", he recalled.

✳   ✳   ✳

Aidan, one might say, was carrying on where Anne Marie left off when he took over the licence from her. In the two years she was a public trainer she carved a unique niche for herself in Irish jumping history. She was Ireland's champion National Hunt trainer in the 1992-'93 season with 26 winners of 53 races earning a total of IR£206,458 in prizemoney, putting her ahead of Noel Meade, Arthur Moore and Paddy Mullins. Her father was top owner the same season.

It captured the imagination of the race writers in Britain that this girl, described by one as "the 23-year-old with the stunning looks and killer instinct" should emerge overnight as the leading trainer in that area of the racing game that has generally been viewed as the natural terrain of hard-bitten men heading for Cheltenham with their charges come March each year. It was in 1993 that she sent her first challengers to the Festival meeting. Much play was made in the British media of the fact that at 29 per cent, her strike rate in Ireland was better than Martin Pipe's in Britain.

The tabloids made hay of the fact that she had forsaken the catwalks for the life of a trainer. But in reality she only took modelling assignments in Kilkenny as a teenager "as a hobby" and from the outset she knew deep down that her life would be spent in racing. "I was brought up to believe that horses were part of life itself", was how she put it to me.

One of six sisters, it was from her father that Anne Marie took over the licence. Joe Crowley didn't just fade away into the background. No, he remained very much involved as did Anne Marie's mother, Sarah. The Crowley operation could best be described as a classic regime – and after Aidan married Anne Marie – bore comparison with other notable examples like the Dickinsons, the Rimmells and Reveleys.

Anne Marie's sisters could be found riding out for her and helping out in different ways when they were at home. Anne Marie herself was very successful in the saddle, riding 23 winners as an amateur, one of her happiest memories being the double she recorded at the 1991 Galway Festival meeting. Of course, when she held the licence, she partnered the stable's bumper horses.

Before assuming her father's mantle she furthered her racing education by spending some time at Jim Bolger's stable, so both Aidan and herself can be described as pupils of the "Bolger Academy".

Anne Marie readily acknowledges the debt she owes her father, recognised as one of the shrewdest characters in the game.

Now 66, he can claim the distinction of having bought and developed and eventually sold on a young horse named after the hill under which he worked his own string, namely the 1983 Cheltenham Gold Cup winner, Bregawn.

Back in 1985 – the year he landed the Irish Cesarewitch with 20/1 shot, Ravaro carrying 9-12 – Joe Crowley was entitled to chuckle heartily at the suggestion that he was an overnight success in the racing game. He had been involved for quite a few years in the business as a hobby before circumstances conspired to propel him into the limelight.

Rejection of some of his produce at the sales and the realisation that a few of the other home-bred fillies wouldn't make their value in the ring saw this most unassuming character start 1985 with a promising though largely unproven string consisting of seven fillies, the 800 guinea purchase Camtown being his solitary "import".

But with only the help of his family and local amateur Frank Dalton – a young man who had spent two seasons with Michael Dickinson's all-conquering jumpers – Joe Crowley managed to win as many races as some more established stables.

By the start of November '85 six of those seven fillies had captured a total of 19 races between the Flat and hurdling.

And Ravaro won four Listed Races, two under each Rules including the Cesarewitch, of course.

Ravaro's Curragh triumph in the hands of Gabriel Curran was indeed a remarkable training feat by any standards. Lacking inches if not gameness or courage, the daughter of Raga Navarro was scoring for the fifth time in '85 when defying top weight of 9 st 12 lb – her first outing for almost four months.

$$* \quad * \quad *$$

When Aidan took over the licence from Anne Marie, he combined training with riding and finished the 1993-'94 season as the top amateur in Ireland with a total of 26 winners.

But as the demands on his time increased, with intense training schedules, he had to retire from the saddle.

When I called to see him in Piltown in June '94. Anne Marie and himself were actually supervising three yards – Joe Crowley's original yard, then the one that was added when Anne Marie was training and now the latest one, a model of everything that one expects in a modern stable and with a capacity to accommodate 100 horses.

The day I talked to him he told me he was planning to build a lab to facilitate the taking of regular blood tests. A canteen was also being planned for the staff.

Aidan O'Brien doesn't see horses as just inanimate machines. "You have got to approach it as if you are looking into their minds. You have got to make sure that they come out of their races as if they hadn't had them."

He is a great believer in feeding his horses well and this is something he gets involved in himself. He has a lot of faith in electrolytes and gives all his horses these before and after they race. "I find that it enables them to recover very quickly and run frequently."

Aidan confessed to me that he thrives on hard work. It's the same in the case of Anne Marie. "We enjoy every minute of what we are doing and the days seem to just fly by."

*   *   *

Orignally when they were based in Piltown, Anne Marie acted as secretary to Aidan. But now she has her hands full with the children.

Aidan has at his disposal the members of the professional and experienced secretarial staff remaining from the days when Vincent was still training out of Ballydoyle. It means that Anne Marie and himself don't have to worry about the nitty-gritty of paper-work.

Anne Marie, as we have seen, was brought up with horses and it would be impossible for her not to continue to be involved closely with Aidan in the Ballydoyle operation. While family chores monopolise quite a deal of her time, she can still make the time to watch developments on th gallops and, if Aidan is away, she can with her own experience of training take on greater responsibilities if needs be.

Team-work has always been a hallmark from the days that Anne Marie had a licence and looked to her own family to help out and it was the same when Aidan took over the licence from her. It would have been impossible for Aidan to handle all the horses under his care and supervise a number of yards in an overall singular operation unless he had the Crowleys to row in fully behind him. Today, as he moves between Ballydoyle and Piltown he appreciates the back-up support all the more. And that includes the support of Anne Marie's parents. "We all work together – we have got to, with all the horses we have", was how he put it to me.

The respect between Christy Roche and Aidan O'Brien is a deep and mutual one. O'Brien fully appreciates the depth of experience Roche brings to the task when he arrives to ride work. The two became acquainted when Roche was No. 1. jockey to the Bolger stable and O'Brien was moving up the ranks to become assistant trainer before he left. And now Roche gets immense satisfaction from every success achieved by O'Brien. He noted that this young man had a special way with horses – an understanding of them and "an uncanny ability to keep them at their peak".

"What I like about him also is that in the ring before you go out to ride one of his horses, he doesn't beat about the bush, doesn't get involved in almost lecturing you on how to ride the race. A man of few words, he says exactly what has to be said and what you want to know. He leaves the rest to your judgement and experience".

On August 15, 1994 Aidan O'Brien joined the elite band of Irish trainers who had 100 winners to their credit in a calendar year, reaching his century at Tramore through Moorefield Girl. The only other four to do so have been J.J. Parkinson, Paddy Mullins, Dermot Weld and Jim Bolger. But what made Aidan O'Brien's achievement unique was the fact that he produced "the ton" in his first FULL season as a trainer.

The following year he would smash all existing records for the total of winners on the Flat and over the jumps produced in the one calendar year.

O'Brien had his first significant group success on the Flat when Dancing Sunset was awarded the Royal Whip (group 3) at the Curragh on August 13 '94 on the disqualification of Blue Judge. He took his first Listed two-year-old prize with Glouthaune Garden at Leopardstown on August 20, '94. And then, as we have seen, he recorded his first group one success when Desert King won the Aga Studs National stakes at the Curragh on September 21, 1996.

Dermot Weld had shown that he had the ability to turn out ten winners at a Festival meeting like Galway or Tralee (he achieved the distinction at both in '94). But Aidan O'Brien proved at Tralee '94 that he also had the ability to attain a significant total when he produced eight winners.

As we said at the outset, records it seemed were made to be broken by Aidan O'Brien. One can only ponder what the record books will show when he finally calls it a day.

No one can ever break Vincent O'Brien's unique record on the Flat and over the jumps but the new Master of Ballydoyle will leave his own footprints on racing's sands of time.

17

Weld And Kinane On A Pedestal Apart

There has been no more successful partnership in racing in modern times than that between Dermot Weld and Michael Kinane and the high point was unquestionably the stunning and epoch-making victory of Vintage Crop in the 1993 Melbourne Cup.

On the first Tuesday in November '93 – November 2nd to be exact – a race that up to then had been farmed exclusively by Australian and New Zealand horses was suddenly cracked open to the world. And the man who had revolutionised the scene by his courage and initiative was Dermot Weld.

Michael Kinane flew in from Hong Kong to ride Vintage Crop. The contract he had with Dermot Weld suited both trainer and jockey. It meant that Kinane rode as No. 1. to the Rosewell House stable during the Irish Flat season and spent the other six months in Hong Kong. More important, Kinane had a freedom that allowed him to ride horses carrying Sheikh Mohammed's colours in big races that put him in line to land Classics and other major events for the Sheikh.

He also had an agent in Britain, who ensured that he picked up other mounts apart from those he would ride for Sheikh Mohammed. Thus, for example, if he was riding at Epsom during Derby and Oaks week or at Royal Ascot, at York or Goodwood, he would be assured of an enticing book of engagements. Trainers knew that in Kinane they were booking a jockey with an ice-cool temperament and at the same time one who could be expected to make no mistakes if he had the "goods" under him.

Michael Kinane had won the Epsom Derby for the first time on Commander In Chief, owned by Prince Khalid Abdullah and trained by Henry Cecil, in 1993 and had finished second on Sheikh Mohammed's King's Theatre in the 1994 Derby when he arrived at the Royal Ascot meeting of '94. The impact of his riding that week will never fade.

The opening day saw him in absolutely brilliant form as he recorded a treble in winning the Queen Anne Stakes on Barathea, the St. James' Palace Stakes on Grand Lodge and the King Edward VII Stakes on Foyer. These three victories were for three different stables – those of Luca Cumani

(Barathea), William Jarvis (Grand Lodge) and Michael Stoute (Foyer).

On Wednesday he lifted – and lifted is the operative word – the Coronation Stakes on the Henry Cecil-trained Kissing Cousin, Geoff Lester in the *Sporting Life* reporting that "unstoppable Mick Kinane turned on another magic show as he landed his second Group One race in 24 hours".

Some of the finest judges contended that nothing matched the way he brought Barathea in an inspired ride to lead in the closing stages and win by a neck from the 15/8 favourite, Emperor Jones with Gaby a short head away third.

Others argued that he was seen to even better advantage on Grand Lodge and his power-packed finish saw him snatch the spoils in the very last couple of strides from Distant View. Praise was heaped on Kinane by the most respected members of the race-writers profession, Brough Scott writing in the *Racing Post:* "All great jockeys have their time. Michael Kinane's is now...rejoice in a jockey called Michael Kinane".

He had entered the pantheon of the immortals of his profession when you reflected on his triumph on Vintage Crop in Melbourne, There was nothing else to be proved.

And yet again in one week in early summer in '96 he lit up the scene when compiling a "Magnificent Seven" tally of winners at the three-day York May meeting. "There's simply nobody better than Kinane", was the tribute by trainer Alan Jarvis to the Irish champion Flat jockey.

His seven winners had come from just thirteen rides and he had two seconds and a third into the bargain.

Overall it had been a hectic week for Kinane. He had an 18-hour day on the Sunday (May 12) involving a return trip to Italy that yielded a Group Three success on the locally-trained Beat The Drums in Rome. After riding work for Dermot Weld on the Monday morning he took to the skies with the Curragh trainer and their helicopter trip to Killarney for the opening evening meeting of the three-day May fixture proved well worthwhile as Kinane guided the 9/10 favourite Silvian Bliss to victory in the featured Heineken Handicap. At the Chester May meeting, Kinane had won the Cheshire Oaks on Tout A Coup for the Gerry Cusack, County Kildare stable and the Ormonde Stakes on the Kevin Prendergast Oscar Schindler, who had been fourth behind Winged Love in the Budweiser Irish Derby of '95.

Michael Kinane followed up his four winners at Royal Ascot '95 (Harlestone Brook in the Ascot Stakes Handicap; Blue Duster, Queen Mary Stakes; Stelvio Queen's Vase Stakes and Realities in the Royal Hunt Cup) with a fabulous five-timer at the '96 meeting. He came in for special acclaim for his victory on Classic Cliche in the Gold Cup and on Oscar Schindler in the Hardwicke Stakes. In these two races he created the clear impression that he was bound to win on the horses that he beat, such was his tactical mastery in tight finishes.

He had opened his account on the Tuesday by taking the Queen Anne Stakes on Charnwood Forest and on the Wednesday scored on Dance

Parade in the Queen Mary Stakes and on Gordi for the Dermot Weld-Alan Paulson combination in the Queen's Vase. He had become the most brilliant Royal Ascot rider of the Nineties.

✳   ✳   ✳

Dermot Weld had sent out Go And Go in 1990 to become the first European-trained horse to win a United States Classic when the colt took the Belmont Stakes, beating both the winners of the Kentucky Derby and the Preakness Stakes and in the process he also returned the seventh fastest time ever recorded in the last of the American Triple Crown races.

But Weld knew deep down that in bidding for the Melbourne Cup he was seeking to conquer the highest mountain of all in international racing. It was as if all the seemingly unconquerable peaks had been rolled into one. It was akin to testing one's climbing skill and experience against a sheer ice face with no oxygen to fall back on. It was taking on a challenge that all the experts said was impossible and which the Australians most of all deemed beyond the scope of a horse from another hemisphere.

There was the 12,000-trans-world journey, the quarantine periods at both ends of the trip, the loss of 7 kilos that Vintage Crop suffered during the long flight and over-shadowing everything else, the fact that the gelding was jumping right into the unknown in racing in another hemisphere. It all added up to a body of evidence that seemed to support the theory that the Irish-trained challenger could not pull it off.

When Michael Kinane swept past Te Akau Nick in the final furlong to go on for a highly-impressive three-lengths win over 23 rivals, it represented what the *Racing Post* aptly described as "quite simply the greatest achievement ever in international racing".

"It never entered my head that this victory would make such an impact globally" said Dermot Weld later. "In the count-down to the race itself I was totally caught up with ensuring that the horse was right and I had put everything else out of my head. The closer we got to the Tuesday the more people were saying to me that it was not a practical proposition to bring a horse this far and hope to lift the prize", said Dermot Weld.

"When Vintage Crop did succeed, it made the post-race euphoria all the greater, especially among the big Irish community in Melbourne and Australia generally. Naturally, they saw it as a historic victory for Ireland and their joy was unbounded. I was particularly happy for giving them that day."

Weld through Vintage Crop's success in the Melbourne Cup garnered £628,000 for owner Dr Michael Smurfit and translated into Australian dollars, it was a handicap race worth in all two-and-a-half million dollars.

The weights for the 1993 Melbourne Cup were framed well before Vintage Crop won the Jefferson Smurfit Irish St. Leger. It meant that the gelding got in with a weight that ensured that he should beat a field of handicappers, granted he reproduced his Curragh form.

But if you were a betting man, you knew you could not "go to war" in the ring until you saw how Vintage Cup had recovered from the energy-sapping flight and how he adapted to his new surroundings.

The loss of those 7 kilos was the biggest worry.

On the Sunday morning – two days before the race itself – the tide began to turn. Vintage Crop goes a mile, ridden by his lad David Phillips. Dermot Weld is watching the training spin with his son Mark and Tony Smurfit, representing his father, who had business commitments in the States, and the owner's bloodstock manager, Dermot Cantillon. Weld can be seen smiling in the bright sunshine. The others are a lot happier also.

But there was another great imponderable – would Vintage Crop get the good ground on which he invariably acted best?

The rain came down over Melbourne on the eve of the race. Very heavy rain. Two of the Flemington car parks were flooded and couldn't be used. The going was declared "heavy" in the Irish sense. Tremendous relief in the Irish camp when it is learned that really it's more "yielding to soft" , as we would know it. Weld believes his charge will handle it.

Vintage Crop has come right on the day and history is there for the making. If J.P. McManus and Noel Furlong had been there they would have rocked the ring with this knowledge and so too would Terry Ramsden if he was around riding the range as he did in his betting heyday. Who could resist a Classic horse available at odds of 14/1 for a two-mile handicap with many of the Australian challengers very suspect on stamina for such a test.

Because of the weather and the gloomy forecast the attendance for the 1993 renewal was down to 75,000, where normally it would be up to the 100,000 mark.

Later Dermot Weld replayed the video of the race for me... noting that the only stage that he was really worried was when Vintage Crop, after a tardy start, had to make up ground in the first quarter of a mile, Kinane was having to work to keep contact with the leaders.

But passing the post first time Kinane had him travelling smoothly tracking Drum Taps. Vintage Crop was still ten lengths behind the leaders at the final bend but Kinane knew he had the goods under him.

Straightening for home, the Irish champion jockey, cool as a breeze when there is everything to play for and a world to lose, presses the button and Vintage Crop eats up the ground in a thrilling late run that sees the chestnut leave Te Akau Nick for dead in the last one hundred yards.

A great "Irish roar" erupted from the stands and enclosures. As a mud-bespattered but smiling Kinane came back in on Vintage Crop, Dermot Weld slipped him a mini-Tricolour and he waved this to the Irish exiles who created victory scenes that outstripped anything in the history of Melbourne Cup Day. It was most moving of all for the long-term exiles who could never have contemplated that the Weld-Kinane partnership would give them such a happy link with the old land.

✳   ✳   ✳

Now the hard-bitten representatives of the Australian media had crowded into the post-race press conference. Eyebrows were immediately raised when Dermot Weld told them that his love of Australia went back to childhood days when he received a copy of Banjo Paterson's book, *The Man From Snowy River.*

The Australians thought initially that Weld was giving them a bit of the Irish blarney but then a respectful silence descended on the assembled gathering when Dermot quoted confidently and easily from *A Bush Christening:*

> *On the outer Barcoo where the churches are few,*
> *And men of religion are scanty,*
> *On a road never cross'd 'cept by folk that are lost,*
> *One Michael Magee had a shanty.*

Three months on from that historic day in Melbourne, I sat with Dermot Weld in Rosewell House on the Curragh and he recalled for me exactly how he came to acquire his prized copy of *The Man From Snowy River*, which occupies a central place on the bookshelf in his study and he recalled also how he first learned to recite *A Bush Christening* when he was ten years old.

"My father trained a number of good horses for E.P. Douglas, who resided at South Lodge in South Tipperary where later Adrian Maxwell had his stable. One Christmas he gave me a copy of Banjo Paterson's book of verse as a present. I fell in love with his ballads right away and it wasn't long before I could recite most of them.

"You know Banjo Paterson was the best-loved Australian poet of all time, the man who also wrote *Waltzing Matilda*. He came from the outback and captured its true spirit – the real Australia – in his verse."

Dermot Weld came to appreciate the real significance of the poems in *The Man From Snowy River* when he spent a period as assistant trainer of the legendary T.J. (Tommy) Smith back in 1971.

If Australian racing had been isolated – and insulated – from global challenges up to this day in November '93, this was no longer the case. A new era had dawned.

It had taken an Irish trainer of vision to internationalise the Melbourne Cup and open it up to the world. Yes, Weld acquainted with the significance of the outback in the Australian psyche through Banjo Paterson's verses, will always be remembered as the pioneer and those who were fortunate enough to be part of the day in Melbourne when he effected the great breakthrough will always cherish the memory.

Again he noted that he never thought it would create such headlines in the world's racing press. "The consequences of one race never entered my mind. I could never have foreseen all that would evolve from that one success."

He came home to a heart-warming reception ... and to an accolade from then Taoiseach, Albert Reynolds, speaking for the Irish nation.

It didn't end there. He returned to Australia in the Spring of '94 to receive the Australian Sports Personality of the Year Award.

Now they rose to acclaim him spontaneously when he recited for them Banjo Paterson's *The Open Steeplechase* in full, catching all the nuances of a ballad that runs to twelve verses and relates the story of the contest between The Ace and Quiver and its very amusing climax.

So that you can catch something of the spirit of it, we begin with the first evocative verse – and then pass on to the last three verses:

> *I had ridden over hurdles up the country once or twice,*
> *By the side of Snowy River with a horse they called 'The Ace'.*
> *And we brought him down to Sydney, and our rider, Jimmy Rice,*
> *Got a fall and broke his shoulder, so they nabbed me in a trice-*
> *Me, that never wore the colours, for the Open Steeplechase*

It developed into a battle royal between The Ace and Quiver as they left the others standing and finally they came to the final fence, as the spectators cheered and shouted. And it happened like this:

> *Then the last jump rose before us, and they faced it game as ever-*
> *We were both at spur and whipcord, fetching blood at every bound-*
> *and above the people's cheering and the cries of 'Ace' and 'Quiver',*
> *I could hear the trainer shouting, 'One more run for Snowy River'.*
> *Then we struck the jump together and came smashing to the ground.*

> *Well, the Quiver ran to blazes, but the Ace stood still and waited,*
> *Stood and waited like a statue while I scrambled on his back.*
> *There was no one next or near me for the field was fairly slated,*
> *So I cantered home a winner with my shoulder dislocated.*
> *While the man that rode the Quiver followed limping down the track.*

> *And he shook my hand and told me that in all his days he never*
> *Met a man who rode more gamely, and our last set to was prime,*
> *And we wired them on Monaro how we chanced to beat the Quiver.*
> *And they sent us back an answer, 'Good old sort from Snowy River;*
> *Send us word each race you start in and we'll back you every time.'*

✳   ✳   ✳

Vintage Crop was back at Flemington on November 1, '95 challenging to retain his crown in the Melbourne Cup. But this time the Australian handicapper set him to carry top weight of 9-7, that is 8lbs more than the eventual winner, the 16.1 ex-English Jeune, carrying the colours of Hamden Al Maktoum and trained by D. Hayes.

It was touch and go whether Vintage Crop would run at all after he shied at a paper bag on his way out to work on the Monday before the race and sustained cuts high on his off-fore as a result of colliding with an aluminium post. The cuts required stitches.

Allowing for this setback, Vintage Crop who started 5/1 favourite did exceedingly well to finish seventh and, remember, he was only seven lengths behind the winner, despite the fact that he had been checked down the far side of the course.

The Timeform writers in *Racehorses of 1994* noted that Michael Kinane, who had been praised in victory in 1993, "saw the other side of the Australian Press afterwards when he came under fire for taking Vintage Crop wide after a slow break from a wide draw".

But the fact of the matter was that a combination of increased weight plus that injury he suffered in the count-down to the race killed his prospects of a repeat. Michael Kinane could not be blamed for Vintage Crop's failure to make it two back-to-back.

At the Curragh on Saturday, September 17, '94 Vintage Crop made history by becoming the first horse to win the Jefferson Smurfit Memorial Irish St. Leger in successive years when, in the hands of Michael Kinane, he powered home by three lengths from Rayeska with Kithanga third. Here was a seven-year-old beating seven four-year-olds and *Racehorses of 1994* described it as "one of the best staying performances of the year".

In 1995 Vintage Crop endeavoured to complete the three-timer on Saturday, September 16 but this time starting 11/10 favourite, he had to be content with fourth place behind the Paddy Cole-trained Strategic Choice.

Vintage crop was retired before racing on Jefferson Smurfit Memorial Irish St. Leger Day at the Curragh on Saturday, September 21, 1996. He led the parade for the final Irish Classic of the season, won in great style by the Kevin Prendergast-trained Oscar Schindler in the hands of Stephen Craine. Oscar Schindler, bred by his owner, Ollie Lehane, had been successful previously in '96 at Chester and Royal Ascot and fourth in the King George VI and Queen Elizabeth Diamond Stakes in which he met with interference.

Vintage Crop, a nine-year-old gelding, won more than £1 million for his owner Dr Michael Smurfit. "This is a very sad day", said Dr Smurfit. "He's been part of my life for six years now".

It was announced that the horse would take up residence at the Irish National Stud, where he would be billed as a tourist attraction. Explaining the decision to retire Vintage Crop, Dermot Weld said: "He lost his speed and his sparkle on the gallops. I want to remember him as the champion he was at his best.

*   *   *

Dermot Weld, who came into the world on 28 July 1948, was born into the racing game and bred to the training profession. But his father, Charlie Weld, a successful trainer in his own right, showed no great enthusiasm to see him following in his footsteps. Indeed, he made it abundantly clear to Dermot from the beginning that he would be happier to see him making his career in another field, as few knew better the constant pressures and pitfalls of the trainer's life.

So it was agreed that Dermot would study to be a veterinary surgeon and, on completion of his studies, they could then assess whether the ambition still burned in his soul to become a trainer. His father was happy with this compromise solution.

Before he actually graduated from University College, Dublin – becoming at 21 the youngest vet in the world – Dermot Weld spent a time working in New York with Dr. Bill Reed as an assistant at Belmont Park and Aqueduct. "I did all the menial jobs but I was learning all the time", he recalled with a laugh.

He went back to serve a second stint with Dr. Reed after he had received his degree.

He rode his first winner at the age of 15 and was already beginning to make his mark as an amateur rider at the age of 16 in bumpers (Flat races under National Hunt rules for potential hurdlers and chasers). In the very week back in 1964 that he celebrated his sixteenth birthday and received word from his school, Newbridge College, that he had passed his matriculation examination, he rode his father's charge, Ticonderoga to victory in the Player Wills Amateur handicap (2 mile) at the opening stage of the Galway Festival Meeting.

Dermot Weld won this highly-competitive event and one that was invariably a tremendous betting race four times in all. He rode Mrs. M. T. Jackson's Spanner to victory as a five-year-old in 1972 and scored again on the same horse the following year. Then in 1975 Spanner, now an eight-year old, justified 2/1 favouritism.

Weld also won the Player-Wills Amateur Hurdle at Leopardstown. He had the distinction of being champion Irish amateur rider three years running (1969, '71 and '72).

His successes in the saddle were not confined to Ireland alone. "While I was in New York as a vet, I went down to Camden in South Carolina where the Colonial Cup is run and rode the winner of a big amateur race on the programme", he recalled. He also rode winners in France and South Africa and took the Moet & Chandon Trophy at Epsom.

The stints that Dermot Weld had in the states with Dr Bill Reed gave him invaluable experience of American training methods. He gained further experience while with Tommy Smith Down Under.

By the time he returned to Ireland from Australia he was ready to get involved in the one and only career he wanted to pursue – training. By now his father had resigned himself to that fact and realised it was useless to try and discourage his son any longer.

Dermot, in fact, spent a year as assistant trainer to his father. He was fortunate that it was a stable accustomed to turning out the winners. The winning philosophy was ingrained in him from the outset.

Three years after he got his licence, Dermot Weld took the Pretty Polly Stakes with Miss Toshiba, carrying Robert Sangster's colours and ridden by

Johnny Roe. The previous year Klairvimy, carrying 9-13, had won the Royal Whip.

Weld won the Irish Lincolnshire Handicap with 25/1 shot, Shaw Park in 1978 and the Naas November Handicap (Division Two) with French Lane in 1977.

But it was in 1981 that he had his first big success outside of Ireland – Blue Wind triumphed in the English Oaks.

✳   ✳   ✳

"A true champion" was how Dermot Weld would describe Blue Wind, who gave the Curragh trainer his first Classic success when sweeping to a majestic seven-lengths victory in 1981 English Oaks in a time that was almost four seconds faster than that credited to the ill-fated Shergar in the Derby on the Wednesday.

Controversy surrounded the victory in that Lester Piggott had been engaged over Walter Swinburn, who was on Blue Wind at the Curragh on Irish 1,000 Guineas Day when she earned her ticket to Epsom by running Arctique Royale to a short-head in a photo finish.

Asked about the jockeying off of Swinburn, all Weld would say in the winner's enclosure at Epsom was: "I don't wish to comment on the switch of jockeys. I booked Lester ten days ago."

He added: "Blue Wind is my first runner in the Oaks and she has given me my first Classic success. I've had some fast fillies but this one is very good."

Ice-cool Piggott, who was winning his fifth Oaks, said: "She did it very easily." Asked if Blue Wind was the best of his Oaks winners, he replied: "No, that was Petite Etoile."

In opting for Piggott, Weld was being coldly professional in his approach by ensuring that he had in the saddle on Blue Wind on the day that was going to mean a lot to him as a trainer a man who knew the Epsom gradients like the back of his hand, and who had no peer when it came to producing an inspired ride at the death – if it came to that – as he had shown for Vincent O'Brien on Roberto and The Minstrel.

Weld was not one to indulge in sentiment when he was tilting at the major prizes.

Walter Swinburn may have been disappointed at being denied the chance of making it a unique and memorable family double at Epsom in '81 as his son Walter, of course, was the hero of Shergar's scintillating Derby triumph.

But Swinburn Snr. was back on Blue Wind when on Saturday, 18 July 1981, she became the first Irish-trained filly to complete the English-Irish Oaks double. Starting at 4/6 she won in emphatic style from Condessa and Stracomer Queen with Arctique Royale, her conqueror in the Irish 1,000 Guineas, finishing sixth.

The sky seemed the limit for Blue Wind after her brilliant English Oaks triumph followed by her success in the Irish Oaks, making her the only

Irish-trained filly to complete the Classic double.

The ultimate target of that '81 season was going to be the Prix de l'Arc de Triomphe. She finished fifteenth, seven lengths ahead of King's Lake. The race was won by the Alec Head-trained Gold River (G.W. Moore) from Bikala and April Run.

Dermot Weld said that Blue Wind had had a very busy summer campaign and the edge was gone when the ground came up very soft at Longchamp.

Dermot Weld won the Irish 1,000 Guineas with Prince's Polly (Walter Swinburn) in 1982 and when he won again in 1988 with Trusted Partner, Michael Kinane was now the No. 1 jockey to the stable.

✳　　✳　　✳

They described Dermot Weld as being in the Columbus mould when he scored a unique and historic win on a dirt surface with Go And Go in the 1990 Belmont Stakes, the third of the American Triple Crown races.

But that pioneering success – making him the first European trainer to win an American Classic – had already been presaged when the same colt scored an equally-historic triumph by landing the £100,000 Grade Two Laurel Futurity at Laurel Park in October, 1989. The son of Coolmore's Be My Guest thus became the first Irish-trained of British-trained two-year - olds to win in America. What is more, this tremendous breakthrough success was recorded on dirt and it had an extra significance in that Dermot Weld became the first Irish trainer to top £1 million in prize-money in a year.

From the time he worked as a track veterinarian at Belmont Park, Dermot Weld had always harboured a dream – to bring a colt over some day to bid for an American Classic and if it was not possible to attain the target of winning the Kentucky Derby, then the Belmont Stakes, a really true twelve-furlong test, attracted him greatly.

Dermot Weld knew after the Laurel Futurity triumph that Go And Go could go on dirt and it was now decided to lay him out for an ambitious American programme. "It was very much on my mind to make a bid for the Kentucky Derby", recalled Dermot, "but our plans in that respect were knocked on the head for two reasons. First, wet weather made it extremely difficult to have horses forward in the early part of the Spring and, second, travelling and quarantine problems virtually ruled out any possibility of making it to Churchill Downs. So we put all our concentration into the Belmont Stakes".

Go And Go wasn't rushed. He won a Listed Race over a mile at the Phoenix Park and was fourth in the Derrinstown Derby Trial at Leopardstown on his way to Belmont Park. On the Saturday before the Belmont Stakes he worked with a visor for the first time; it was revealed that he had made considerable improvement since the Derrinstown Derby Trial and that the visor helped him to keep his mind on the job.

Came the day of the Belmont Stakes. That morning, by special permission, Go And Go had a canter round the Aqueduct track with Michael Kinane in the saddle. He was so well in himself that he was bucking out of his skin.

Go And Go held a handy position in fifth place in the early stages of the race, Michael Kinane, riding superbly, saving ground from the inside draw.

The Kentucky Derby favourite, Unbridled, having been ridden with stamina limitations in mind, loomed up menacingly to the leaders turning into the home stretch but his challenge faded as quickly as it had begun. Kinane, in total command at that point, had only to press the button on Go And Go and the colt quickened away in magnificent style to win by eight-and-a-quarter lengths from Thirty Six Red with Baron de Vaux third and Unbridled fourth.

The general verdict was that Unbridled did not get the testing Belmont mile-and-a-half (the Belmont Stakes is a quarter-mile more than the Kentucky Derby).

There were those who claimed in the aftermath of Go and Go's spreadeagling Belmont Stakes triumph that it was not a vintage year on the American three-year-old scene, that there was nothing to be even mentioned in the same breath as Secretariat or Affirmed. In a word, it was a sub-standard season.

But that in no way can take from the authority with which Go And Go won this Classic or from Dermot Weld's courage in opting to take on the leading American colts rather than bid for the Irish Derby, for which he was also entered. As that most respected of American racing writers, Dan Farley, put it in his report for the *Racing Post:* "Dermot Weld was rightly elated that his daring decision to challenge for the prize had paid off so handsomely".

"Sensational" was how Farley – a man not given to easy praise – described Go And Go's runaway win and Michael Kinane summed up afterwards: "Once I saw Unbridled in trouble on my outside, I knew we could win".

In winning the Belmont Stakes in 1990 and the Melbourne Cup in 1993 the combination of Dermot Weld and Michael Kinane had conquered two of the greatest peaks in international racing.

18

Kinane Walks In Fancy Dress Parade As Lester

When Michael Kinane was ten, he walked in a fancy dress parade in Killenaule as Lester Piggott, complete with riding breeches and boots and carrying a little saddle.

No one could have foreseen that when Michael brought King's Theatre into the starting stall for the 1994 Epsom Derby he would be seeking his second successive victory in the Classic and Lester would be riding in his 37th Derby – and seeking a fabulous tenth victory on Khamaseen.

The records show that King's Theatre finished second to 7/2 favourite, Erhaab with Khamaseen failing to add to Piggott's unmatched record as he came in fifth.

Michael Kinane's mother, Frances revealed that the champion Irish Flat jockey had a talent from childhood, expressed in different ways, that was special. And he was also a born character who would have the rest of the family "in stitches" as he did his impression of Donald Duck.

His mother recalled that the very first prize he won was when he finished first in the under-12 sack race at the sports meeting in Glengoole. "He was so competitive that there was only one place for him always and that was in the No. 1 spot."

She recalled too how he entered an art competition that was linked with the Tidy Towns effort in Killenaule and the pupils of the school were asked to come up with the lettering for two posters – one for Ballingarry and one for Killenaule.

Michael's winning words were:
BIG, LITTLE AND SMALL SHOULD TIDY KILLENAULE
and
EVERY TOM, DICK AND HARRY SHOULD TIDY BALLINGARRY

His creative imagination also came into play when with his brother, Jayo he designed the crest for Killenaule Athletic Club.

He was an outstanding boxer as a youth and champion of Tipperary, Waterford and Munster in his own class for three years. He was actually training for the Irish Championships when he left home to join Liam

Browne's stable as an apprentice jockey. But for a dispute arising in the Mullinahone Club that meant that he – and others – did not participate after all, it seems certain that he would have been crowned a national title-holder.

"He boxed southpaw", his father, Tommy told me. "He was very skilful and at the same time very aggressive. One night he demolished the reigning Munster champion in two rounds. He had a vicious streak in him that made him deadly when he went after an opponent looking for a quick knock-out victory."

All the Kinane boys were champions. The love of boxing was instilled in them by their father who was wont to box in the open air in London on Sunday afternoons. Tommy coached each of the boys individually as they were growing up and then in the Mullinahone Club they came under the wing of the official coach and trainer, Stephen Waters. The Club really had an outstanding record.

It was inevitable also that Michael should follow in his father's footsteps in another sphere – the hurling arena. When the family were based in Holycross – a great stronghold of the national game – Tommy Kinane played junior for the club.

Tommy said that his son Thomas was "a skilled player" but "Michael would pull on anything".

"He'd take the ball and your ankles and all", he laughed again, adding – "put that in because it's the truth!"

Tommy Kinane bought a grey Arab-bred pony for the boys. A top-class show jumper, he carried Michael to a succession of successes and the rosettes that filled the Kinane home were evidence of his prowess.

But, whereas Adrian Maguire hit the pony circuit as the road to eventual stardom and overwhelming acclaim as a National Hunt rider, Michael Kinane only rode in one pony race that his parents can remember.

That was at a place known as Barrys of the Two Trees at Wilmount between Ballingarry and Mullinahone.

True to his determination to be in the No. 1 spot he came home the winner on the Arab-bred.

✳   ✳   ✳

The Kinane family hailed originally from the Glen of Aherlow, one of the most picturesque beauty spots in County Tipperary.

There were 14 children in the family into which Tommy Kinane was born.

The Kinanes became synonymous with riding and horsemanship. Mick was associated with a famous show jumper called Aherlow which was bought by the British Army.

Danny rode a lot of winners in his prime and later turned his hand quite successfully to training. Jim and Billy entered the winner's enclosure also.

Christy was a good jump jockey in his prime and went on to do very well as a trainer from his stables at The Green in Cashel, enjoying a few notable successes at Liverpool in the mid-Seventies.

Michael Kinane's father, Tommy started with the late Tim Hyde at Camas Park and then spent some time with Chally Chute before heading for England in the early Fifties. He got a few rides on the Flat and over hurdles but then in 1954 gave it up and went to London where he worked on the building sites with McAlpine. "Yes, I was one of his 'fusiliers'. I was adept as a scaffolder and within two years was fully qualified", he recalled.

"There was a big job in progress for the BBC and I was doing extremely well. But the call of the horses was in my blood. I used go down to Wantage to ride out and actually got the mount in the odd hurdle race. There was one very difficult horse and it was felt I was the only one who could manage him.

"My brother Danny, who is retired from training now, was doing very well at this time from his Mullinahone base. I decided to come home and team up with him. My employers offered to promote me to foreman. I was on the permanent staff at the time.

"While I saw it as a tribute to my work and a very genuine one at that, I had made up my mind to leave and nothing was going to make me change. We parted on good terms and I was happy about that.

"I often reflect back, however, on the moment I made that fateful decision and I know that if I had decided to stay so much would have been different."

He had met Frances, a girl from Knockaville in County Tipperary, in the Emerald Ballroom in Hammersmith. They danced in the Ballrooms of Romance from Hammersmith to Cricklewood, to Kilburn. They married and Michael Kinane was one of seven children, four boys -Thomas, Jayo and Paul were the other three – and three girls, Suzanne, Kathryn and Janette.

Frances Kinane can laugh now as she recalls the labour pangs as she arrived at Our Lady's Hospital, Cashel, to give birth to Michael and a good nun telling her – "offer up each contraction for your sins".

"I never got a whiff of anything and we hadn't the faintest notion what an epidural was."

*　　　*　　　*

Tommy Kinane will be remembered best as a jump jockey as the man who rode Monksfield to victory in the 1978 Champion Hurdle. Then as a trainer he first spent twenty-two years in Killenaule before moving to his present quarters at the Curragh.

His ease in conversation and his ironic wit contrasts sharply with the way Michael presents himself today as a man who knows that there is a constant media and public spotlight on him and therefore, he has to choose his words very carefully and can often only be frank and forthcoming with very close friends.

Michael's parents are naturally immensely proud for him and his achievements and Tommy has been out to Hong Kong to see Michael riding there.

A lot had happened for Michael Kinane from those happy childhood and boyhood days in County Tipperary and later the apprentice days on the Curragh.

He had started at the age of 15 as a pupil of the famous Liam Browne apprentice academy, where apprentices were assured of not alone being given outstanding tuition in the art of riding but also worked in a no-nonsense, character-building atmosphere that stood them in good stead for the rest of their lives.

Michael was only in his second season as an apprentice, aged 17, when his weight jumped to 7st 13lbs. "You might as well have a few years on the Flat while you can but you will have to go jumping eventually", Liam Browne told him.

It was then that Michael Kinane turned to Dr. Austin Darragh, father of showjumper, Paul Darragh, and a man who had helped countless jockeys with their weight problems.

"He put me through a very tough regime for a time. It wasn't so much a case of cutting down on food but the monotony of missing certain foods you liked. I was quite plump when I went to him but had slimmed down by the time I finished. Most important, I learned how to control my eating and learned what to avoid."

Fortunately also, he stopped growing at the critical time – "and I was soon okay".

Standing 5ft 4ins, he rides easily today at 8st 5lbs and it doesn't entail sweating it out in the sauna, which he confesses he doesn't like.

Breakfast consists of a cup of tea on waking up and maybe a bowl of cereal later and at lunch he will have another cup of tea and a sandwich or two.

He's the envy of many another jockey in that he can tuck into a really good dinner prepared by his wife Catherine, maybe lamb with plenty of potatoes and vegetables.

There are rivals for whom it would be a mirage during the season and who, to break the fierce monotonous regime, will let fly on occasions and then go to the men's room and do what a man has got to do in order not to put on weight.

Kinane is sorry for them, so is Christy Roche – but it is the nightmare that is hidden from the public who see only the flashing silks maybe on a sun-drenched day as they cheer home an idol on a horse that has carried their money.

After winning the Apprentices title in 1978, he became first jockey to Michael Kauntze. Then after he had ridden Dara Monarch to a 20/1 victory in the Irish 2,000 Guineas in 1982 for Liam Browne (winning the St. James's Palace Stakes also the same season), Browne had him back as his stable jockey.

In 1983 he finished runner-up to Christy Roche in the Irish Jockeys' title race and the season was highlighted by his finishing second on Carlingford Castle to Teenoso and Lester Piggot in the Epsom Derby.

Dermot Weld had seen enough of his talent to ask him to become his No. 1 stable jockey.

It was a partnership, as we have seen, that blossomed to the benefit of both.

And, from Kinane's viewpoint, the most important aspect of their understanding was the freedom he got to ride outside the Weld stable on horses that could win Classic and other major prizes.

As Michael was heading for the Phoenix Park on the Saturday of the 1989 Cartier Million with Catherine, he remarked: "I feel lucky".

Somehow, he had a premonition that he could strike gold not alone in the "Big One" at the Park but at Longchamp also.

"Why not the Lotto?", remarked Catherine laughingly – as there was over £600,000 in the kitty that same week-end to be won.

Michael didn't have time to think of filling in Lotto tickets.

He hit the jackpot, however, with his own cool riding and panache at two different venues – and didn't have to depend on luck as he went smiling all the way to meet his bank manager.

✳   ✳   ✳

He won the Cartier Million on the 7/4 favourite, The Caretaker for the Dermot Weld stable. Earlier the same day he had won the Phoenix Champion Stakes on the Michael Jarvis-trained Carroll House, a victory that ensured that he would get the ride on the same horse in the Prix de l'Arc de Triomphe. The magnificent Ciga Arc jockey's trophy that adorns the mantelpiece of his home on the Curragh in testimony to his 'Arc' triumph in '89 and how highly he was regarded by the Italian connections of Carroll House. In 1990 Kinane landed the English 2,000 Guineas on Tirol for the Horgans of Cork and Richard Hannon. But Kinane knew deep down that there was still a sizeable and influential lobby that would not accept him in the premier league of jockeys.

He expressed the view to me that the race that made a major difference to the advancement of his career to a new pinnacle was the winning of the 1991 King George VI and Queen Elizabeth Stakes on Belmez for Sheikh Mohammed.

"I was involved in a great head-to-head battle with Steve Cauthen over the last two furlongs and I had to pull out all the stops to get home by a neck as Old Vic rallied again after I had headed him at the quarter-mile marker. They could not call me lucky after that!"

Belmez with Steve Cauthen in the saddle had beaten subsequent Epsom Derby winner, Quest For Fame in the Chester Vase before finishing third – again ridden by Cauthen – in the Budweiser Irish Derby behind Salsabil and Deploy. But with Cauthen siding with Old Vic, the dual Derby winner of 1989, Kinane was booked for Belmez, who had made a sensation comeback from injury when it appeared that he would have had to be retired to stud in May.

Kinane actually wore Sheikh Mohammed's third colours as the second went to Steve Cauthen on Old Vic and the first to the Coronation Cup winner, In The Wings.

He grabbed the opportunity presented to him with both hands.

Ironically, this win resulted in Michael Kinane emerging as the clear favourite to land the plum job of first jockey to Sheikh Mohammed in January 1993 after a statement from the Sheikh's Dalham Hall headquarters near Newmarket confirmed that the three-year association with Steve Cauthen was being ended.

The split came after the 32-year-old jockey from Kentucky had rejected what was a significantly-reduced retainer for the 1993 season.

Anthony Stroud, acting for Sheikh Mohammed, became the front-line personality in the contacts with Michael Kinane, who was in Hong Kong riding under contract for the winter months for British trainer, David Oughton – an ideal arrangement as it allowed him to be back in Ireland in April.

It was generally accepted by the media that Michael Kinane would join the elite club of the super-earners if he became the first jockey to Sheikh Mohammed, wearing those famed maroon and white silks in the Classics and other major races.

But quality of life and family, which means so much to Michael Kinane, contributed greatly to his saying "No" in the final analysis to the overtures being made.

He weighed very carefully with Catherine, his attractive Kildare-born wife, the schooling of Sinead and Aisling and how this and the friendships they had locally would be affected if he signed a contract with the Sheikh that would mean moving to Newmarket and a far more punishing schedule than the one to which he had become accustomed.

His quality of life meant that it wasn't all work and no play. As a native of County Tipperary, he loves Ireland's national game of hurling and whenever he gets a chance he will not miss a big game, especially a Munster championship tie involving Tipperary and Cork.

On afternoons when there is no racing, he may go golfing. He admits to the fact that he does not practice and plays essentially for relaxation but still he is no mean performer off his handicap.

He can also indulge in "a bit of shooting and hunting" and all told, the Irish way of life offers the kind of outlets in the type of atmosphere that Kinane would be loath to leave.

However although the offer from Sheikh Mohammed was in the six-figure league, it was not of the scale that made it one he simply could not refuse.

As he sat back talking to me in the sittingroom of his home on the edge of the Curragh against the background of the paintings depicting peak moments in his career and many trophies I put the question to him that if he had been offered £500,000 a year or say a contract that would have netted £2 million or more over three years, would he have refused?

"No", came the quick and unequivocal reply. So in the final analysis it came down to a question of what was put on the table. And when Kinane balanced the figure against what he was already earning, he was not prepared to accept it when it would have meant at the same time losing out on his quality of life.

"The offer was not good enough to give up what I have at present", was how he put it.

Ironically, Kinane would end up later with a contract with Sheikh Mohammed anyway, so from purely diplomatic consideration he will never reveal what was the final figure offered to him at the outset of 1993.

When Kinane said "No", the South African Michael Roberts was signed up but after an unhappy year there came a split. No replacement was appointed as first-choice jockey for the Sheikh's entire international string. Kinane, however, became committed to the Sheikh for big races. The new arrangement suited Kinane ideally. It meant that he could continue as No. 1 to Dermot Weld, ride for six months in Hong Kong and be in line to land classics and other major races for Sheikh Mohammed. And his agent in Britain ensured that he picked up other mounts apart from those he would ride for the Sheikh.

✳   ✳   ✳

Commander In Chief was the less fancied of Khalid Abdullah and Henry Cecil's two runners, in the 1993 Epsom Derby, the mount becoming available to Kinane after Pat Eddery had opted for the same combination's Tenby.

Commander In Chief was yet another unbeaten colt. He had not, however, been raced as a two-year-old – it was 20 years since Morston had overcome that handicap in the Derby – had while he was looked upon in the yard as a very bright prospect, there was a general impression that Commander In Chief might lack that experience and maturity required for an Epsom Derby. Nonetheless, he started second favourite, marginally shorter at 15/2 than Fatherland, who represented the familiar old-time partnership of Vincent O'Brien and Lester Piggott.

Michael Kinane had gone over to Newmarket to ride Commander in Chief at work and was very impressed. "I knew he would get the trip and that he was really on the upgrade", he said.

Still the professionals rowed in behind Tenby because he had won that most revealing of Derby trials – the Dante Stakes – by three lengths and he had a pedigree that guaranteed him getting the twelve furlongs, being by Coolmore's Caerleon, who had won the French Derby and he was out of the Park Hill runner-up, Shining Water.

The grand-dam Idle Water went back to the great Mill Reef.

Pat Eddery had Tenby in close touch behind front-running Bob's Return but as Blues Traveller took it up three furlongs out, the favourite's backers knew their fate. Eddery had been niggling at him without much response and as Michael Kinane later explained: "Turning for home I looked across and spotted Pat Eddery hitting the panic button. I knew then we would win. Commander In Chief was travelling so well I decided to go on and he went away from the others."

Michael Kinane returned from Epsom to the evening meeting at the Curragh to be the recipient of a special presentation from the Curragh Committee to mark his first triumph in the English Derby. "A fantastic gesture", was how he would describe it later.

✳   ✳   ✳

The clock moves forward to May 25, 1994 and on the Newmarket gallops Henry Cecil is seeking to persuade Michael Kinane that King's Theatre is the one he's got to be on in the Derby a week hence. It didn't really take Cecil's selling pitch to convince Kinane that the Sadler's Wells colt out of Regal Beauty (by Princely Native) was the one he should partner. His mind had already been made up by the morning's work, though he admitted he had reservations about him getting the trip.

Kinane had King's Theatre placed perfectly to win the Derby and looked to have got the measure of Colonel Collins when Willie Carson, defying all the rules, managed on Erhaab to "get out of prison", to quote Tim Richards' very apt description in the *Racing Post* and produced an electric burst of acceleration to win going away by one-and-a-quarter lengths. It was Carson's fourth Derby.

"He ran a great race but he just couldn't quicken in the final furlong", said Kinane of King's Theatre.

Still overall he had reason to be happy. One win and two seconds in six rides. Not a bad Derby record. Not at all.

Even if he were to ride in ten more Derbys, he couldn't emulate Lester's amazing record and even in his wildest dreams, he could hardly hope to equal his "bag " of nine winners.

But in two years he had won international respect as a man who really knew how to ride the Epsom course in the most sought-after colts' Classic and it was a tribute in itself to him that immediately he opted to ride King's Theatre, Ladbrokes cut his price from 20/1 to 10/1, though on the big Day itself he eased to 14/1.

✳   ✳   ✳

I recall Michael Kinane saying to me in his home on the Curragh: "Every time you go out to ride in a race you know that a fall when horses are going at 40 miles an hour can mean serious injury, even death. It is something you have go to live with in our profession.

"It's worse, of course, for the jump jockeys and let me say that I would never begrudge them anything they get".

Michael Kinane has been not just once but three times extremely fortunate to escape fatal injuries on the racecourse.

"I'm the luckiest man alive", he said after he had survived a horror fall in Hong Kong during his sojourn there in the winter of 1933-'94.

He was kicked by three horses after being thrown from his mount on the rails at the Colony's Happy Valley track.

"I honestly thought this was it. It was one of the worst falls of my career. I still don't know how I wasn't killed", he said. Then allowing his sense of humour to cloak how near he could have been to suffering fatal injuries, he added with a smile: "But I suppose it's very hard to kill a bad thing!"

"We were going flat out at the turn and I was trying to come in between two horses on the inside rail. But my fellow chickened out and clipped another horse. The next thing I knew he went down and I went flying over his head.

"The three other horses behind kicked me all over the place. It probably looked a spectacular fall but unfortunately I felt every bit of it."

Kinane was removed to hospital with two broken ribs and extensive bruising. "It's a miracle the injuries weren't worse. I'm in a hell of a lot of pain but I don't care, the main thing is I'm alive", he told a local newspaper at the time. "There is very little they can do to stop the pain. The only thing the doctors recommend is two weeks solid rest."

Later Kinane would realise just how lucky he was when 26-years-old Steve Wood was killed in a fall at Lingfield on Friday, 7 May 1994, and again it would be borne home to him very forcibly when he saw the brush with death that Declan Murphy had in the aftermath of a terrible fall at Haydock that same month.

Kinane himself had another amazing escape when a young man from Berkshire climbed over the perimeter rail as the Ribblesdale Stakes was reaching its climax at the Royal Ascot meeting and ran right into the path of his mount, the Sheikh Mohammed-owned Papago.

The filly was disputing last place with Frankie Dettori's mount, Little Sister. Dettori, who was just behind Kinane, managed to take some kind of evasive action as Papago went down, noting: "The guy shot out from the rails and ran across the track. Mick saw him at the last minute and shouted at him but it was too late.

"Mick's horse hit him very hard and knocked him to the ground. I think I managed to avoid hitting him, although my horse collided with Mick's.

"We were so far behind the others that the guy must have thought the race was over. It's lucky we were only hacking at the time, otherwise the impact would have been much worse."

The young man was removed to Wexham Park Hospital in nearby Slough.

Kinane, visibly shaken by the incident , said: "For a while I was trapped with one leg in the iron under the filly. Luckily, she was winded and lay on the ground and did not attempt to run off."

Michael Kinane came out of it unhurt – the second time inside the one year that he had come out alive from two horrific falls.

And he was extremely lucky for a third time in '94 when winning the

King George VI and Queen Elizabeth Stakes in dramatic style on King's Theatre. Ezzoud, winner of the Eclipse Stakes, unseated Walter Swinburn at the start and then caused havoc as he proceeded to run loose, harassing the other runners all the way, Erhaab, the Epsom Derby winner, being one of those who suffered from his unwanted attentions.

Kinane first thought of coming outside the riderless Ezzoud, then went inside to tackle front-runner Bob's Return and drove King's Theatre clear to win by one-and-a-quarter lengths from White Muzzle, the mount of four-times Japanese champion jockey, Yukata Take. "The loose horse was going everywhere", said Michael Kinane. "Some got caught up with him as he weaved about. I had to react quickly but I think a couple of horses were unlucky.

"When Ezzoud went right, I had to go left. And then he would go left, so I had to go right. Because he had a hood he couldn't see the other runners and my biggest fear was that he might go right across us and bring one of us down. That could have caused a real tragedy.

"But it was all right in the end, thank goodness", he added.

※　　　※　　　※

Incidentally, Michael Kinane rang his father in the immediate aftermath of the Hong Kong fall. He was seeking his advice on what way he should approach matters after his fortuitous escape, knowing that his father had seen it all during his career as a jump jockey.

Tommy Kinane told me that it was terrible to see jump jockeys who had lost their nerve completely after bad falls. "In some cases a situation could be reached where you could see terror in a man's eye as he left the weighroom to ride in a chase, more so if he knew he was on a dodgy jumper. His only purpose then would be to get round and try and avoid another crippling tumble.

"Those who lost their nerve like this could hide it for a while but shrewd trainers, knowing the game inside out, would spot that a man was stalling and pulling back instead of riding fearlessly into a fence and then the mounts would get fewer and fewer until eventually the one whose courage was gone had to accept the inevitable and call it a day."

Tommy Kinane said that he was lucky himself in that while he suffered the "normal injuries" – broken collar bones and cracked ribs and severe bruising – he was never out with a broken leg or arm. Therefore, he never had the kind of fall that would have rally tested the undoubted courage he brought to the saddle.

"I didn't know fear", he admitted – and that was transmitted to his son Michael, who came out of the Hong Kong experience without any permanent mark as far as his own courage was concerned and he continued to ride at a level of excellence that won him the plaudits of racing enthusiasts far and wide.

19

Weld Completes Classic Double in the Same Season

Dermot Weld became the first Irish trainer since the late Paddy 'Darkie' Prendergast in 1952 to complete the Derby-Oaks double in the same season when Zagreb took the Budweiser Irish Derby at 20/1 on Sunday, June 30, 1966 with a stunning performance.

In the process Weld completed a Full House of Irish Classic victories, having won the 1,000 Guineas with Trusted Partner in 1988, the 2,000 Guineas with Flash Of Steel in 1986, the Oaks with Blue Wind in 1981 and the St. Leger with Vintage Crop in 1993 and again with the same horse in 1994. Of course, Dance Design would give him his second Oaks triumph in '96.

'Darkie' Prendergast's duo were Thirteen Of Diamonds and Five Spots, both ridden by Jimmy (Corky) Mullane, a born stylist in the saddle.

But for once Michael Kinane, who had never chosen wrongly in a situation like this before, made an uncharacteristic error when he opted to ride Dr Massini in the 'Budweiser' instead of Zagreb.

Kinane could only watch in frustration from seventh position as Pat Shanahan, described as a "Super Sub" by Dermot Weld, powered home to a magnificent six-lengths victory from French Derby runner-up, Polaris Flight with the Aidan O'Brien-trained 50/1 shot, His Excellence a further six lengths away third.

Michael Kinane, who had won virtually every major race around the globe from Melbourne to New York, from Hong Kong to Epsom via Longchamp, was clearly disappointed at missing out on his first Budweiser Irish Derby win. He shrugged his shoulders as he said: "I guess I made the wrong call. What can I say? I'm delighted for the connections and for Pat (Shanahan), who's been a pal for a long time".

Pat Shanahan said: "Michael is allowed one mistake and he's made it. I saw him afterwards and he said 'well done'. He's taken it well".

And he added significantly: "If I was faced with the same decision as Mick, I would have made the same choice. It's tough on him as he would dearly love to win an Irish Derby. But I'm sure he'll do it within the next few years".

Irish-trained colts took two of the first three places home as the challenge of the hot favourite, the Henry Cecil-trained Dushyantor was repelled. He had to be content with fourth place but later he was to win in courageous style at the York August meeting.

Pat Shanahan had only been told on the Friday that he had the ride and he described his success as "the greatest day in my life".

Pat Eddery had Dushyantor poised behind pacemaker Private Song as they entered the home straight but when Shanahan eased Zagreb to the front over two furlongs out, the contest was virtually over and while the winning margin was only half that achieved by St. Jovite – the last Irish winner in 1992 – the impact was no less dramatic.

Indeed, Eddery was prompted to say: "I was never really travelling, but when Zagreb came alongside he was not pulling a cart, but a tractor! Where have they been hiding him?"

"This means so much to me", said Dermot Weld who could have been forgiven if he concluded that the Irish Derby was going to elude him eternally. He had seen Definite Article beaten a short head by Winged Love in 1995 and Theatrical had been second in 1985 to the Vincent O'Brien-trained Law Society.

In fact, as his 48th birthday loomed – just four weeks away – Weld described the victory of Zagreb as the fulfilment of a lifetime's ambition and an even bigger thrill than winning the Melbourne Cup with Vintage Crop. He even put it ahead of winning the Epsom Derby.

Theatrical had carried the colours of Alan Paulson and it was fitting that he should now go into the record books as the sire of Zagreb. Paulson, who watched the race from his home in California, held a 50 per cent share in the colt with the other shares being split between Mike Watt, Dr Michael Smurfit and Dermot Weld himself. Michael Smurfit said cheerily: "I can afford to pay a few bills tonight!"

Zagreb, who had not run as a two-year-old because he was so backward, had looked a Derby winner in the making when winning from 26 others on his racecourse debut over ten furlongs at the Curragh on April 13. But then he was beaten by a short head by Damancher in a twelve-furlong event at Leopardstown on Wednesday evening, June 12 (Damancher, incidentally, could only finish third in the Curragh Cup on Budweiser Derby Day). To many observers it appeared that the bubble had burst and Zagreb was dismissed as a real live Classic contender.

Dermot Weld explained, however, that he had been a very sick horse before he recovered to run in the Leopardstown race. He had been on antibiotics for a flu which he contracted during the very cold weather on the Curragh. He was off the gallops for several weeks.

He missed a Listed race and he also missed the Gallinule Stakes.

Weld was beginning to fear that he might not get a preliminary run into him before the 'Budweiser' – so he really had to let him take his chance at Leopardstown, despite the fact that he was not completely back to himself.

When Mick Kinane rode him about eight days before the Curragh Classic, the colt was not sparking. Kinane rode him again on the Tuesday and this time he performed much better. It was then that Weld decided "we'll have a go". The rain on the Friday was very welcome and confirmed Weld in his view that Zagreb would make them all go.

Kinane concluded, however, that as it was only Zagreb's third run in public, he might not be mature enough for a race like this.

Weld, who has a wonderful rapport with Kinane, said: "We have an unique relationship. Nothing would have given me greater pleasure than for Mick to have shared in this victory. But he was keen to ride Dr Massini, so we agreed to release him".

One could understand Kinane's eagerness to take the mount on Dr Massini, who had been favourite for the Epsom Derby until he had to be pulled out at the eleventh hour because of a foot injury. Having touched 5/2 in the betting, he went off a very firm 9/4 second favourite behind Dushyantor, who started at 5/4.

∗　　　∗　　　∗

"If I had been asked to choose between Dr Massini and Zagreb, I too would have plumped for the Doctor. After all, Zagreb had only won a maiden and then been beaten next time out at 4/7", said Pat Shanahan.

It was the biggest win of 33-year-old Shanahan's career. He hails from County Tipperary like Michael Kinane and they both have been friends – and golfing companions too – for many years now.

Pat Shanahan's career had largely been based around two trainers, Con Collins – to whom he was apprenticed – and Dermot Weld.

It was Collins who provided him with his most important success before the 'Budweiser' triumph of '96. And that was an Irish Oaks win on Princess Pati in 1984.

Shanahan, who comes from Nenagh, is a graduate of the Ormond Hunt Pony Club in North Tipperary where Walter Swinburn and Charlie Swan, among others, also learned the basics of riding.

Champion apprentice on three occasions in the early Eighties, he also rode regularly for Michael Kauntze, who announced in the summer of '96 that he was retiring from training at the end of the season.

Pat Shanahan had every reason to celebrate on the evening of Sunday, June 30 and one could understand his sentiments when he said: "This victory has more than made up for all the travelling to the smaller meetings around the country".

On the Tuesday, he was back to earth as he headed for Bellewstown, far removed from the thronging thousands at the Curragh on Derby Day and the popping champagne corks of the social whirl – but with a tradition and unique atmosphere all its own.

Shanahan rode the appropriately named Forsake Me Not to a length victory for the Con Collins stable in the fifth race, worth just £2,740 to the winning owner, Mrs H.R. Norton and none of the leading English racing writers, who had been in the Press tent to interview him – along with Dermot Weld – in the aftermath of Zagreb's scintillating triumph were there to chronicle this particular success. And that is as one would expect it to be.

Shanahan was back on his travels up and down the country seeking winners wherever he could find them – a true professional. No way would his Derby win go to his head. He was too level-headed and mature for that. Mick Kinane's loss had been his gain but everyone in racing, who knew Pat Shanahan, delighted in the fact that he had enjoyed a big pay day.

As Alastair Down drove back from the Curragh to Dublin he saw the floral tributes at the set of traffic lights where Veronica Guerin, the crime correspondent of the *Sunday Independent* had been brutally murdered the previous Wednesday. An event, he noted in his column in the *Sporting Life* that had clutched the soul of the Irish nation and he added that at that moment one could see the kernel of truth at the heart of Phil Bull's remark about racing being "the great triviality".

I had gathered with colleagues from all of the Irish media at the removal of the remains of Veronica, who had been with us not very long before at the *Sunday Independent* annual party in the *La Stampa* Bistro. As I left the church with two veterans of the game, Trevor Danker and John Kearney, it did not escape us that we were leaving a husband and young son behind – with the coffin in front of the altar. Veronica had paid the ultimate price which no journalist wants to pay if he or she can avoid it. She paid it in a way for press freedom – one of the things most valued of all in any democracy which would be the greatest milestone of all to her sacrifice and to her memory.

*   *   *

Dermot Weld paid tribute to Michael Kinane for the "fantastic ride" he gave Dance Design in winning the 1996 Kildangan Stud Irish Oaks by a short head from the Aga Khan's Shamadara with the John Oxx-trained Key Change third and impressive Epsom Oaks winner, Lady Corla a bitter disappointment.

"I'm delighted Michael rode her, having missed out on the Irish Derby", said Weld adding:

"Dance Design is a lovely, honest filly to train and it's great that an Irish filly has won this race for the first time since 1984".

The form was franked when Key Change won the Yorkshire Oaks on going that did not have the cut in it that John Oxx would have liked.

It now remained for Dermot Weld to win an Epsom Derby and he would have conquered all the main peaks in the the Classics arena.

A pity in a way that Shaamit was not in the line-up for the Budweiser Irish Derby. He was found lame three days beforehand and had to be withdrawn.

The peerless Lester Piggott had finally retired from the saddle in 1995 and he was watching from the stands at Epsom as Shaamit, trained by his son-in-law William Haggas and ridden by Michael Hills, held the late thrust of Dushyantor by a length-and-a-quarter.

Piggott, winner of the Derby a record nine times, utilised all his knowledge and experience in advising William Haggas first of all to let Shaamit take his chance and then devising the battle plan itself for the assault on the Blue Riband, Piggott told Hills to take the route he had invariably favoured himself over the years – and that was on the inside. But, in truth, the blueprint had to be thrown away half-way down the descent to Tattenham Corner, where a dozen rivals raced ahead of the winner.

"He's an inexperienced colt, but was good enough to go on the outside and glide past them", said Hills." I've been waiting for this a long time – my whole life".

"I told you it would be like winning my 10th Derby, and it is", said an overjoyed Piggott. "This is marvellous. We always thought we had a good horse. I only gave some advice but had nothing else to do with the training and am very pleased for all the family".

The Vintage Crop, who was retired from racing on Jefferson Smurfit Memorial Irish St. Leger Day '96, is immortalised in bronze opposite the Weighroom at the Curragh. The bronze was presented to the Turf Club by Vintage Crop's owner, Dr Michael Smurfit, who said:"He's been part of my life for six years".

20

Trans-Atlantic Tensions Over St. Jovite

It will be twenty years come 1997 since Mrs Virginia Kraft Payson from out of the Blue Grass country of Kentucky took up horse-breeding with her second husband, financier Charles Payson. It was after his death in 1985 that she became totally involved and the Payson Stud stands today as a monument to her untiring efforts over two decades and to the knowledge she acquired.

Fate decreed that St. Jovite, a product of the Lexington stud farm, should be sent to Jim Bolger to be trained, leading in turn to the awesome twelve-lengths triumph in the 1992 Budweiser Irish Derby and subsequently to a breach in relations between owner and trainer that was irreconcilable, rocking the racing and bloodstock worlds on both sides of the Atlantic.

Jim Bolger experienced a day as a lion on that June afternoon at the Curragh – June 28th to be exact. Before I go deeper into his rift with Virginia Kraft Payson, it has to be stitched into the record that he will certainly scale many more peaks before he retires but nothing will ever surpass his achievement in turning the tables so decisively with St. Jovite on Dr Devious, his Epsom conqueror.

I could not have foreseen then – indeed, no one could – that eleven months on from that red-letter Derby Day, Virginia Kraft Payson, who had been pictured all smiles beside Jim Bolger in the winner's enclosure, would almost break down as she talked to me on the trans-Atlantic phone from Kentucky.

In that long interview, searing in the diamond-hard edge of bitterness that permeated her comments as she set down publicly for the first time her response to the headlines engendered by her decision to have Laffit Pincay Jnr. ride St. Jovite in the Breeder's Cup Classic (over $1/4$ miles on dirt) instead of Christy Roche, she admitted to being close to tears as she said: "I have been so brutalised, so crucified by sections of the Irish media over certain decisions that were made last year in relation to St. Jovite, especially the decision that Laffit Pincay Jnr. would ride him in the Breeders' Cup Classic, that I do not want to set foot inside an Irish race track for a long time."

That amazing outburst and all that surrounded it lay ahead as Jim Bolger listened to Des Scahill in the course of his racecourse commentary tell the teeming thousands thronging the stands and enclosures: "John Reid has gone for his whip on Dr. Devious."

"The roof nearly came off the stand in the roar that erupted around me. I knew then that bar a fall or that he would break a leg that St. Jovite would gallop all the way to the line," recalled Jim Bolger.

And then he added: "It was one of those days when everything went exactly according to plan. We had some very obliging owners who were prepared to supply pacemakers. We had a breakneck pace from the start and when the two pacemakers we ran had done their job, St. Jovite was brave enough to take it up and defy catching to the line."

Virginia Kraft Payson is a formidable lady by any standard. Now in her sixties, she was a prominent journalist in her younger days, writing for one of the most prestigious American and international sports magazines, *Sports Illustrated*. Her career extended over a twenty-years span. When it came to contributing features on subjects as varied as sailing to scuba diving, from tennis to pool and hot-balloon racing, she was writing from first-hand experience. She had done it all and more.

She was into wild game hunting. She shot boar and stag, riding alongside General Franco in Spain, as she revealed to Adriaane Pielou for an article in the *YOU* magazine of the *Mail On Sunday* early in '96. She hunted in Iran with the Shah and tracked tiger with the King of Nepal.

Ernest Hemingway was her hero. This was only natural when you reflect on his exploits and read his idyllic account of a big-game safari in East Africa in *Green Hills of Africa*. Journalism was her ticket to a memorable meeting with him in Cuba that turned into a long afternoon's journey to a sharing of experiences over the bottle that Hemingway produced. He had heard of her, so she was arriving as no unknown on his door-step.

"We talked about everything – people we both knew, hunting, shooting, Africa", she told Adriaane Pielou. "I was amazed – he'd read my feature about hunting with Franco and had remembered the gun I used. My only regret is that I didn't put my arms around his neck when I left and give him a kiss".

This was the same lady who was so high in praise of Jim Bolger in the immediate aftermath of Budweiser Derby Day '92. Then she told the world: "I was introduced to Jim at the Keeneland Sales. I was told he was going to be the best trainer in the world, so I got in quick".

She had been shattered after the death of her second husband and lived a solitary life for five years afterwards as she tried to come to terms with her grief. Charles Payson had predicted that he would die before her and impressed upon her more than once that, after he had passed on, the horses would keep her occupied.

He was right in that.

She became a very sound judge of horses and their pedigrees and was respected as a shrewd breeder. For example, she bought St. Jovite's dam, Northern Sunset by Northfield (a Northern Dancer sire) to inject stamina and toughness into the breed, as she believed that the emphasis on speed had been over-done.

St. Jovite's sire, Pleasant Colony, a grandson of the mighty Ribot, had been America's champion three-year-old in 1981 when he won both the Kentucky Derby and the Preakness Stakes. Incidentally, St. Jovite's great-grandam, Blath Na Greine, not alone bred two good horses in Prince of Greine and Time Greine but was a half-sister to the English 1,000 Guineas and Oaks winner, Godiva, and the immortal Irish Triple Crown winner, Windsor Slipper. So there was class on every side of St. Jovite's pedigree.

✳   ✳   ✳

There was not a cloud on the horizon on that beautiful summer's day as St. Jovite in trouncing Dr. Devious, Contested Bid (third in the Prix du Jockey-Club), Ezzoud (runner-up in the Irish Two Thousand Guineas that season and subsequently to win the 1994 Coral-Eclipse Stakes from Bob's Return and the '94 Epsom Derby winner, Erhaab) and Marignan (runner-up in the Prix de Jockey-Club) recorded the widest winning margin returned officially in the Irish Derby since it was first sponsored as a major international event by the Irish Hospitals Sweeps in 1962. Shahrastani and Assert had both won by eight lengths while Santa Claus, Troy and the ill-fated Shergar had won by four. The twelve-lengths margin actually equalled the record set by Portmarnock in 1895.

St. Jovite completed the twelve furlongs in 2 mins 25.6 secs. – three seconds faster than the record set by Princess Pati in the Irish Oaks in 1984. It was all the more remarkable because the winner came back with cut heels after being struck into during the race.

The then Taoiseach, Albert Reynolds, joined Michael J. Roarty of Anheuser-Busch Inc. in congratulating a delighted Mrs Kraft Payson as she received the magnificent Waterford Crystal trophy – a Derby Day graced by Dynasty star John Forsyth, Hart to Hart star Stephanie Powers and by film star Paul Newman among other famous personalities.

It would have been impossible to have imagined at that moment of singular triumph for the millionairess American owner that in the Spring of 1993 she would be severing her last remaining link with the Bolger stable when a "messenger" arrived at Coolcullen on the Carlow-Kilkenny border giving what was effectively one hour's notice that she was taking the remaining horses away from him.

The messenger was no mere nobody. He happened to be Dean Grim, son of Mrs Kraft Payson and President of the expanding Payson Stud where St. Jovite was to be retired to stud.

While two of the horses being removed from Bolger's stable – Charette, a half sister of St. Jovite, and St. Elias – were in Mrs Payson's name, her son had an interest in both. He had come to Ireland from Britain where he was on business and, according to Mrs Kraft Payson, it was considered convenient that he should use the opportunity to oversee the transport of the two horses back to the States.

This represented the last act in the breach of relations between Mrs Payson and the champion Irish Flat trainer.

*   *   *

It would be easy to conclude that the defeat of St. Jovite by Dr. Devious in a photo finish to the Kerry Group Champion Stakes on Sunday, September 13th, saw the beginning of Mrs Kraft Payson's disenchantment with Jim Bolger.

But Bolger himself, amazingly enough, makes it clear that there was no "perceptible cooling" in relations in the immediate wake of that defeat. The real crisis would develop over the decision to let Laffit Pincay Jnr. ride St. Jovite in the Breeder's Cup Classic and the castigating of the owner over that same decision by sections of the Irish media, who saw it literally as the "jocking off" of the man who had ridden the colt to one of the most spectacular Derby triumphs of modern times.

Disillusionment did not set in either between Mrs Kraft Payson and Jim Bolger in the wake of defeat in the Prix de l'Arc de Triomphe, as some so readily assumed. Because it had to be accepted that St. Jovite's chance was gone when rain came down in the proverbial bucket-fulls on the eve of the race itself.

The general view of the English and Irish experts in Paris for the weekend was that St. Jovite would be surmounting impossible odds to win the "Arc" in the circumstances.

Jim Bolger himself would reveal later to me: "I was not optimistic."

"However, it was his last race in Europe. We had nothing to lose. As it was, he ran fourth behind the French horse Subotica on ground that was totally unsuitable to him and again confirmed his superiority over Dr. Devious, who was sixth.

"I have no doubt that if he had got the ground conditions that suited him he would have won. I always believed that he was at least as good a horse, if not better, on ' Arc' day as he was on Irish Derby day."

It was generally assumed in Ireland that Christy Roche would ride St. Jovite at Gulfstream Park. Roche had proved his versatility and his adaptability as a big-jockey in his Derby triumphs from Chantilly to the Curragh to Epsom. And on the score of experience he did not have to answer to anyone.

Mrs Kraft Payson was to claim in her interview with me, however, that she had discussed frankly with Jim Bolger the question of Laffit Pincay Jnr. riding St. Jovite in the Breeders' Cup classic instead of Christy Roche – "because of Pincay's thorough knowledge of American tracks and his outstanding record in the Breeders' Cup series".

She asserted that Bolger had gone along with that decision. She went further and said that she had confronted Bolger on the issue when they met in Lexington in January 1993 and expressed to him in no uncertain terms her disappointment at the fact that when she was castigated by sections of the media for replacing Roche with Pincay, he had not made a statement defending her.

Jim Bolger, when I talked to him in the Berkeley Court Hotel in February 1994, had this to say on the controversial decision to replace Christy Roche by Pincay: "The way she put it to me, I had no option but to go along with it. Frankly, I did not like it but, as I have said, I was left with no option."

Responding to Mrs Kraft Payson's charge that he had not defended her in face of the criticisms in the Irish media, he said: "She did not ask me to go to her defence. I always regarded her as a woman of the world – a woman who would not be easily fazed by the media in any part of the globe, especially when she had been a media person herself for so long.

"And because of this assumption on my part, I did not see any need to jump in on her behalf. I had full confidence in her to fight her own battles. A so-called roasting from the Press does not necessarily mean the same thing to me as to other people."

Laffit Pincay Jnr. never did get to ride St. Jovite in the Breeders' Cup Classic as the colt never got to the starting stalls.

Coming up to the race, St. Jovite suffered an upper respiratory track infection which manifested itself in a discharge from both nostrils.

"Mrs Kraft Payson had been understandably very keen to have St. Jovite run in the Breeder's Cup Classic," recalled Jim Bolger, "Some days before he was due to leave Ireland, he went down with the respiratory problem. It proved somewhat debilitating. It was not possible to train him further. Consequently, he missed the Breeders' Cup. This was a big disappointment to the colt's owner and shortly afterwards she decided to take St. Jovite to the States."

Jim Bolger stressed that there was no hint at that point that St. Jovite would not be returning to Ireland to be trained as a four-year-old in 1993. "Some time in November 1992, in fact, I presented Mrs. Kraft Payson with the programme I had already mapped out for St. Jovite for the 1994 season. It envisaged another tilt at the King George and the Arc and was to be climaxed with a bid for the Japan Cup.

"I sent two of my best staff to the States with St. Jovite to remain with him as he settled into his new surroundings. He was subsequently transferred to Roger Arfield's stable. It was announced he had suffered a recurrence of an old injury and was being retired to stud. So he never raced again after the Arc of 1992."

It remains a mystery to Jim Bolger to this day that the official cause of St. Jovite's premature retirement stemmed allegedly from an "old" injury. As far as he is concerned, the colt did not suffer an injury while he was in training with him that would have affected in any way his racing future.

Yes, there had been that respiratory problem in the countdown to the Breeders' Cup Classic, an infection, as seen already, that resulted in his being scratched from the race. But Bolger, as he supervised St. Jovite's departure from his stable to the States, knew in his heart that the colt was sound of limb and wind and was looking forward to welcoming him back in 1994 and training him, hopefully, for another glittering campaign.

✳   ✳   ✳

Mrs Kraft Payson told me that her arrangement with Jim Bolger was that any of her horses in his charge that were not up to Group class would be sent back to the States. But it was generally assumed in racing circles in Ireland and Britain that Charette, as a half-sister of St. Jovite, would be trained by Bolger with top targets in mind.

Mrs Payson contended that Bolger told her Charette was not going to make top class and that was one of the reasons she decided to bring the filly back to America.

There is little doubt in my mind that, as relations between owner and trainer soured over the events leading up to the Breeders' Cup Classic, Mrs Kraft Payson sought to exercise greater control and an open conflict developed between her interpretation of what constituted a "trainer's agreement" and Bolger's.

Asked what the signing of a trainer's agreement would have meant for him, Bolger responded: "It would have tied me down and could have damaged my professional career. I refused to sign.

"You cannot have a situation where the owner wants to take decisions over and above the head of the trainer – to restrict his freedom of decision and action.

"In the States an owner-trainer relationship may be like that between a football or baseball club and the manager. A trainer may not enjoy, or expect to enjoy, the same loyalties that obtain in Europe."

Mrs Kraft Payson claimed Bolger made certain changes in the draft agreement she presented to him and claimed further that she did not get around to sending him the final draft for his signature as she was so caught up with other matters at the time. She said the signing of such agreements are normal between trainers and owners in the States.

"I did not seek to restrict Jim Bolger in the actual training of my horses but the horses were my property and I believed I had the right to bring my horses back to the States if and when I chose to do so. I would not see the autonomy a trainer might enjoy in the actual training of my horses extending to his having control over what should happen my property," she said with emphasis.

Mrs Kraft Payson contended that it was always understood that St. Jovite would return to the States when his racing programme in Europe had been completed. She said that Jim Bolger was aware of this from the outset.

✳   ✳   ✳

IN THE SHADOW OF MT. BLANC . . . J.P. McManus pictured in Geneva in the count-down to Cheltenham '96 and (below) outlining to author, Raymond Smith the guide-lines he adopts before he "goes to war" in the ring at the Festival meeting.

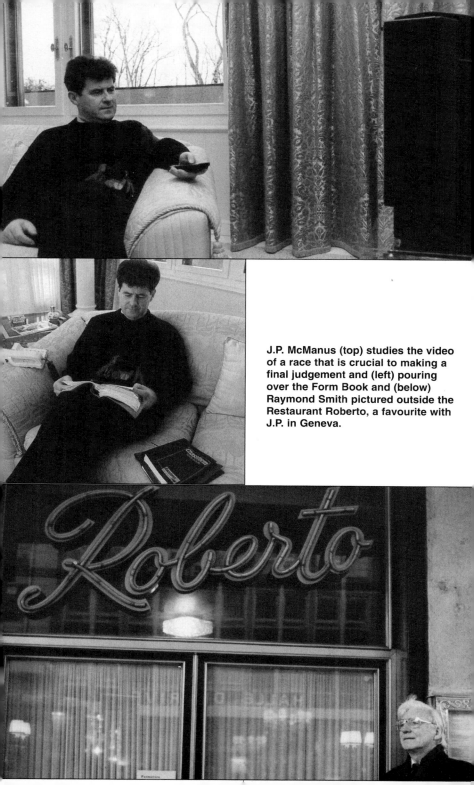

J.P. McManus (top) studies the video of a race that is crucial to making a final judgement and (left) pouring over the Form Book and (below) Raymond Smith pictured outside the Restaurant Roberto, a favourite with J.P. in Geneva.

J.P. McManus and his close friend Dermot Desmond in happy mood after the Jonjo O'Neill-trained Front Line, carrying J.P.'s colours, had won the National Hunt Chase at Cheltenham '95 and below (left) Front Line (Mr. John Berry) is led back to the winner's enclosure and (right) Dermot Desmond with Dr Tony O'Reilly and his wife Cryss at Heinz 57 Phoenix Stakes Day '95.

THE NEW MASTER OF BALLYDOYLE . . . The sun rises over the Old Castle at Ballydoyle and over the dreams of Aidan O'Brien, who is seen watching some of the horses in his charge cantering up the grass and (inset top) Aidan and Anne Marie pictured at the launching in the Burlington Hotel of Raymond Smith's book, *Tigers Of The Turf.*

ON THE GALLOPS MADE FAMOUS BY VINCENT O'BRIEN . . . Christy Roche and Tommy Murphy pulling up in front of the Castle after doing a piece of work and (below) horses walk around in a clearing in the trees before going out on the gallops and (right inset) Aidan O'Brien and Christy Roche discuss the morning's work. (Picture special by Caroline Norris.)

A delighted Dr Michael Smurfit and Dermot Weld (with trophy) share with Mike Watt (centre) the joy of Zagreb's brilliant win in the 1996 Budweiser Irish Derby as American Ambassador, Mrs Jean-Kennedy Smith joins in the celebration of a great victory for Ireland and (below left) Pat Shanahan returns in triumph and (right) Stan Cosgrove and Michael Kinane in happy mood after Dance Design had completed a Classic double for the Weld stable by winning the Kildangan Stud Irish Oaks.

The Belle Of New York

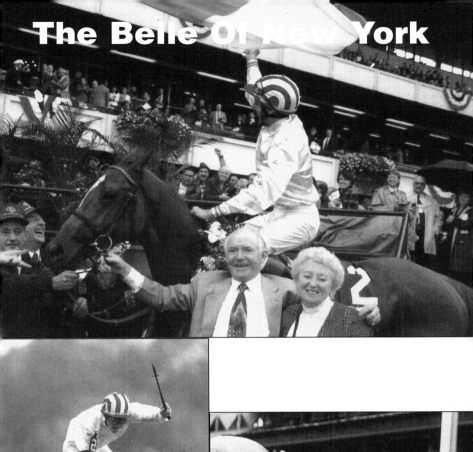

Ace racing photographer, Ed Byrne captures the moment (top) when Johnny Murtagh waved the Tricolour in triumph to the delight of the crowd at Belmont Park, New York after Ridgewood Pearl, pictured with delighted owner, Mrs Anne Coughlan and her husband, Sean, had won the 1995 Breeders Cup and (bottom left) the John Oxx trained super filly wins going away and (right) John Oxx talks tactics with Johnny Murtagh.

Jim Bolger proudly displays the trophy after St. Jovite's awesome triumph in the 1992 Budweiser Irish Derby.

Christy Roche gives an arm-aloft victory salute as he passes the winning post (left) and a smiling Mrs. Virginia Kraft-Payson with Mike Roarty of Annheuser-Bush.

The epilogue came down to one word – loyalty. And the depth of significance it has on this side of the Atlantic as against the interpretation placed on it in the racing world in the States.

And here I am thinking of the kind of loyalty that saw Robert Sangster sticking with Vincent O'Brien even when the number of horses trained at Ballydoyle had been reduced to a dozen or so – by Dr O'Brien's own choice – as he passed his 76th birthday in the Spring of 1993. Sangster would never forget what he owed to the Master of Ballydoyle – would always remember the golden triumphs they had shared together with such brilliant horses as The Minstrel, Alleged, Golden Fleece and El Gran Senor. In a word, you cannot quantify that kind of loyalty.

Jim Bolger was immensely proud of the level of consistency he had delivered with the horses he had trained in Mrs Payson's colours, apart altogether from the singular achievements of St. Jovite.

Caressed and Carrnassier both won on their debuts in 1992. In fact, four two-year-olds in the Payson colours went into the winner's enclosure first time of asking.

When Mrs Kraft Payson removed Charette and St. Elias from the stable and finally broke all ties with Jim Bolger, it was a far cry from the enduring bonds of loyalty between Robert Sangster and Vincent O'Brien.

Her argument to me was that she had so many commitments in the States that it would not be worth her while travelling over and back for "just two horses". She revealed that she had made no less than eleven two-day trips in 1992 alone.

As our long conversation on the trans-Atlantic phone came to a conclusion, I emphasised to her that no one could ever forget the job Jim Bolger had done in producing St. Jovite to overwhelm Dr. Devious in that memorable twelve-lengths victory on Derby Day 1992 at the Curragh, a performance described by *Racehorses of 1992* as "the most exhilarating exhibition of the European season."

I suggested that everyone in Ireland would have thought that she would have repaid it by continuing to provide Jim Bolger with the material to come up with a repeat. I suggested further that the Irish sense of loyalty demanded that the links between owner and trainer should not be irrevocably severed.

But I had to accept that we were on different planes. This was certainly not a case of talking to the converted.

Never again would the twain meet. It was wishful thinking to believe that there could be a reconciliation, such was the sad souring of what at one stage had been a very happy relationship for the benefit of the Irish racing and breeding industry.

In the winter of Mrs Kraft Payson's discontent there would be no going back and I wondered if I would ever again see her setting foot inside an Irish race track.

✳   ✳   ✳

Jim Bolger is his own man and always will be. Virginia Kraft Payson could not have realised that, with all her wealth Bolger's independence of spirit – who might even be described as "a rebel with a cause from the County of the Pikemen" – would never bend the knee just to retain her patronage. All right, he would suffer in the short term from her departure, for you don't get horses sent to you every day of the week of the calibre of St. Jovite. But the Bolger I have come to know and admire would plough his own furrow – a lonely furrow at times, perhaps as he rejected the rubbing of shoulders and the bonhomie of the bar – but that would not worry him.

People are taken with his integrity, his straight-from-the-shoulder talking and his tilting at the windmills of authority when he believes there is a case to answer.

He has been coloured by his roots – roots in the rural heartlands and he will not adopt a fake Oxonian or Old Etonian accent to impress people in Britain. Indeed, he expresses a certain pity for those, including members of the racing profession, who, from a basic inferiority complex, have felt the need to change their accents in order to progress in life or be at ease in the Royal enclosure in Ascot.

Jim Bolger today speaks with the same accent he had when he left his native County Wexford. And he makes no apology to anyone for being himself.

He came into the world on Christmas Day 1941. One of eight children – five boys and three girls – raised on a farm in Oylegate. It was a mixed farm, maintaining 25 cows and also cattle and horses. Jim's father, Walter, who died in 1987 aged 84, was a breeder of and dealer in half-bred horses. His mother, Katie (nee Doyle) came from the locality and at the time of typing this chapter in the summer of '96 had reached the grand old age of 89.

Incidentally, Jim Bolger's uncle, also christened James, wrote on hurling and football under the nom-de-plume *Recorder* in the *Irish Independent* for a period of years. He had started in journalism on the *Enniscorthy Echo*. He was grandfather of Booker Prize winner and best-selling author Roddy Doyle.

Ask Jim Bolger if life was hard for the family in those days of the Emergency when at first Hitler's panzers carried all before them until in the irrevocable turning of the tide, the Third Reich fell when he was still only four and he responds: "There was never any shortage as far as food was concerned. We were no different from any other farming family in the Forties and Fifties. My father as the principal bread-winner worked very hard and my mother, with eight children to look after, worked equally hard.

"They never complained. People didn't complain about their lot in that era. We had wonderful neighbours. You must remember that there was no thought then of a five-day week or a four-day week or holidays abroad in the sun. Daylight hours were for working. There was a wonderful happy family atmosphere in our home.

"I learned to milk the cows at 7 a.m. before I went to school. You took that for granted, as you took so many other tasks for granted. These were routine tasks, like helping to make the hay, like getting involved with the threshing.

"I can still recall the excitement when a pig was killed to provide bacon and all of us joining with mother in the making of the black puddings. It just seemed to be one long happy time."

He cycled seven miles each morning to secondary school in the CBS in Enniscorthy and back the same distance in the evening. He got his Intermediate Certificate and his Leaving Certificate but didn't go to university. He admits that the only time in life that he ever entertained self-doubts was when sitting exams.

He had learned to ride at an early age, the nursery being to use his father's half-breds and workhorses.

When he left for Dublin at the age of 17, he carried with him an ingrained love of horses in his veins, From as early as he can remember he loved to have a bet but he didn't acquire this from his father. "As far as I can recall, my father never had a flutter, not even on the Grand National. But it gave me immense pleasure to stake a bob each-way on my fancies and to see my judgement proved right."

Bolger, amazingly enough, dabbled in the buying and selling of cattle before he got involved in horseflesh. He actually bought his first horse at the age of 16 with £50 he got together dealing in cattle. "You might say that I cashed the bovines and bought equine," he laughed, as if talking stocks and shares.

In his teens we find him buying and selling show-jumpers and hunters. And ridding as an amateur. He did not exactly set the world alight with his riding exploits but still could boast three wins from twelve rides.

✳   ✳   ✳

On his arrival in Dublin Jim Bolger worked as a trainee accountant in an office by day and attended evening classes in the College of Commerce in Rathmines, progressing in time to a job as an accountant with a Dublin motor company. Deep down, however, he never intended to make accountancy his life. He saw it as a stop-gap career – a training ground on the way to what was going to be his chosen profession.

At one point he was four weeks behind with the rent on his flat in Dublin. It was the longest period he had endured of "severe financial restraint", extending from March right through to April 1962.

He decided that Kilmore, the mount of Fred Winter, was going to win the Aintree Grand National. "I put £1 each way on him at 33/1 and he duly obliged in a field of 32."

Jim Bolger recalled meeting Fred Winter later when both of them had become racehorse trainers. "I was seeking to sell him an ex-flat horse I favoured as a potential winner over the jumps. I told him the story of how I cleared off my rent arrears in one stroke by backing Kilmore to win the National. But he didn't buy the horse from me after all."

"Let us say that I learned to shop in the bargain basement for flats and digs," he told me with a smile. "Accommodation that would be regarded as O.K. in the summer months was not so good in winter. But it was all part of my education.

"I met some wonderful people from all walks of life and all parts of the country both in digs and in flatland.

" I went to the races and to the dogs, to hurling and football matches and athletic meetings. But somehow I never got into following soccer and rugby. Hurling has always been the game that has meant most to me."

Today it's par for the course for him to meet you for lunch or dinner in the main diningroom of Dublin's most prestigious hotel, the Berkeley Court, or in the George V off the Champs Elysees in Paris during Prix de l'Arc weekend. But he is totally at ease among rank-and-file Wexford supporters, proudly wearing the colours and favours of the Model County, on the day of a Leinster Hurling Championship, against Kilkenny or Offaly in Croke Park. He was thrilled to watch Wexford winning the 1996 All-Ireland crown.

His love of horses dominated much of his leisure time in those early career days in Dublin. He even arranged his annual holidays so that he could fit in the bloodstock sales. Again there was calculated method in this.

He was prepared to learn from the Masters – P.J. ("Darkie") Prendergast and the Master of Ballydoyle himself, Vincent O'Brien. Indeed, Vincent O'Brien had been his idol from childhood and he was a keen follower of the stable when it came to betting, supporting Nijinsky to win the Triple Crown in 1970.

"I was particularly taken by the fact that Vincent O'Brien was a self-made man, that he had climbed up the ladder to the very top from what you might describe as humble beginnings as a trainer in Churchtown, County Cork," he said.

Bolger, able to move about unobtrusively because he was unknown then to the big players, noted carefully the yearlings that Vincent O'Brien and "Darkie" Prendergast bought, assessing the conformation that attracted them and the breeding lines.

"You might say that during all this time I was a trainee trainer, getting a grounding in the real essentials of what would dominate and dictate my life from 1976 onwards," he told me.

He would reach the point where he could go to the sales and with confidence pick out a yearling that he knew had the potential to be a Group or Classic winner and, more important still, he could evaluate an animal's worth, knowing how high to bid and when to fold.

The days, so to speak, at the feet of Vincent O'Brien and "Darkie" Prendergast had paid off handsomely.

✳   ✳   ✳

In Tigers Of The Turf I related how Jim Bolger one day put his last tenner on a horse (which he judged to be a certainty on form) at the Phoenix Park – "when a tenner was worth far, far more than it is today" and he had the galling experience of watching as the one he backed "never tried an inch and wasn't even put into the race". Imagine Bolger's feelings when next time out it bolted in.

From that moment on he was determined to control his own destiny when it came to horses – in a word, that he would be certain that an animal was running on its merits when he put his money on the nose.

After he had taken out a full training licence in 1976, he made rapid progress. Operating from a base in Clonsilla, he sent out 22 winners in his second season, finishing in the top six in the Trainer Championship. By 1981 he was challenging successfully in Britain, Condessa winning the Musidora Stakes at York and later that season the Group I Yorkshire Oaks.

Then in the summer of 1982 he returned from Gowran Park races to find that a fire had ravaged his Clonsilla stable. Then came the move to Coolcullen, a short distance inside the Carlow border with County Kilkenny. He turned Glebe House, once the homestead of the Church of Ireland Bishop of Ossory, and its 240 acres into a model of what a modern training establishment should be. Jim and Jackie are proud of the fact that they have added 20,000 trees since 1982 and, now in addition to beech, the visitor can pick out chestnut, birch and walnut as well as oak. There is a rural splendour about the whole place and when first I saw it, I was reminded to an extent of the impact of Ballydoyle House.

Jim Bolger sent out his first Classic winner from Coolcullen in July 1983 when Give Thanks won the Irish Oaks in the hands of Declan Gillespie at 7/4. The filly enjoyed an outstanding season as she also won the Lingfield Oaks Trial, the Musidora Stakes and Lancashire Oaks.

Bolger was building a name for himself as a brilliant handler of fillies. Other leading ladies who helped establish his reputation even more firmly as the 1980s progressed were Park Appeal (1984 Moyglare Stud Stakes and Cheveley Park Stakes), Park Express (1986 Phoenix Champion Stakes) and Polonia (1987 Prix de l'Abbaye).

Likewise he was proving himself outstanding as a trainer of two-year-olds, especially in the way they were able to hold their form.

He arrived at the point when he had total confidence in his own ability and his own methods when he was given St. Jovite to train and he went on record in the 1991-'92 edition of the *Irish Racing Annual* to predict "I will not be surprised to hear St. Jovite described as awesome from another Continent when he moves to middle distances". And that almost seven months before the Budweiser Irish Derby of '92.

✳   ✳   ✳

In cold retrospect now, it has got to be acknowledged that Epsom came too soon for St. Jovite. He had been very difficult to train in the early part of the season. But he made remarkable progress between Epsom and the Curragh. Like a sleeping giant he was beginning to awaken. "Seven or eight days after he came back from Epsom, I rode him in a strong piece of work", recalled Christy Roche. "He was such a different animal that day, so impressive that I said to myself: "I will win the Irish Derby"".

Not alone did he win it but he destroyed the opposition including the Epsom Derby winner, Dr Devious who started at 5/4 (in fairness, it has got to be recorded that Peter Chapple-Hyam reported the next day that Dr Devious was not a well horse on his return to the Manton stables).

In the absence through suspension of Christy Roche, Stephen Craine had the mount on St. Jovite in the King George VI and Queen Elizabeth Diamond Stakes and, generously acknowledging the eve-of-the-race advice he got from Roche, he excelled as St. Jovite fully vindicated the pre-race confident claims of his trainer in pulverising a high-class field. Included in that field were Saddler's Hall, winner of the Coronation Cup and the Princess of Wales's Stakes; Opera House, the Coral-Eclipse runner-up; Sapience, the Eclipse third; and with Rock Hopper, the Coronation Cup runner-up, fifth. The winning margin of six lengths had only been surpassed by Generous who won this race by seven lengths.

I do not intend here to recount again the bruising battles that Jim Bolger had with the Turf Club. They were covered in detail in *Tigers Of The Turf*. At the time of writing in '96 six years have elapsed since "The Ashco Affair" which was to become a *cause célèbre*. Hard to believe now that so much passion and legal argument could have been generated about a filly allegedly not running on her merits in a minor race at a Dundalk evening meeting. Neither was she the medium of any gamble. Jim Bolger was fully vindicated in bringing an appeal as far as his own reputation of integrity was concerned.

Then we had all the headlines stemming from the suspension imposed on Christy Roche for "improper riding" at Naas in the count-down to St. Jovite's Budweiser Irish Derby. The duration of the 15-day sentence meant that Roche would miss the Irish Derby unless he appealed successfully to the Turf Club or the hearing was held after the Derby. The Friday *before* the Curragh meeting was named as the crucial date.

Roche sought a postponement in the High Court. At the eleventh hour there was a compromise, the Turf Club announcing that "in the interest of the sport of racing" it had responded to a personal plea from Roche's solicitor and named July 6 as the new date for the appeal. A great furore was aroused over the fact that Jim Bolger had previously intimated that "it is just possible that St. Jovite might not run in the Irish Derby if Christy is suspended". When I put it to him at an explosive, no-punches-pulled press conference at the Curragh on Derby day, he denied categoricaly the he had made any threat to the Turf Club – direct or indirect. However, in the days before the Derby a section of the racing public perceived that the authority of the Turf Club had been called into question.

The situation was compounded further when Roche lost his appeal when it was heard by the Turf Club but again went to the High Court in Dublin. He was granted an injunction temporarily lifting the 15-day ban. This enabled him to ride in the Irish Oaks. But when the full case was heard before Mr Declan Costello, an injunction against the suspension was refused. And thus Roche lost the ride on St. Jovite in the 'King George'.

Christy Roche would say to me in his home on the Curragh in the Spring of 1994 that the one mistake he regretted in his life was to bring that case before the High Court.

"I was alleged to have hit the boy with my whip. I did not hit the boy. I think people who know me will accept my word for that. But in the end I got caught up in a clash between personalities and I could do nothing at all about it.

"I am a big boy now. I made a decision at the time and I know now I made a wrong one. It was a racing matter essentially and not a matter for the courts. It still bothers me that I could have been so wrong to take the decision I did."

But it could be argued perhaps that if Roche had not gone to the High Court in the first place, the Turf Club might not have postponed the date of the hearing of the appeal on the Naas incident and he would have missed the ride on St. Jovite in the Irish Derby.

Roche's regret at having been drawn into Jim Bolger's head-on confrontation with the Turf Club was not the reason for the irrevocable break in relations that occurred between himself and the trainer of St. Jovite. Before the start of the 1994 Flat season, close friends of Roche knew there was a problem. They knew also that it had nothing whatsoever to do with the short fuse, the volatility of either party. The two had shown in the High Noon of their golden days that they could live with one another. Like a volatile couple in a volatile marriage who have come to understand one another completely. No hang-ups about the petty squabbles.

When the "divorce" came, nothing was said publicly by Christy Roche to give any insight into why he had broken with Bolger. All that appeared in the media was that he would be riding freelance in 1994.

Bolger sat down beside him at a Naas meeting and asked him if he was prepared to ride for him again. Roche replied with a firm "No!", adding, "You know full well the reason why, Jim."

They left it at that. His son-in-law, Kevin Manning (married to Una) continued at No. 1 effectively to the Bolger stable during 1994 and subsequently.

It was obvious that nothing had changed Jim Bolger's admiration of the qualities of Christy Roche as a big race specialist, a tremendously-keen competitor whose basic interest was "results". While he wasn't into style, he was certainly into "effectiveness".

And he summed up: "I think his big thing as a jockey is his finishing power. In those desperate head-to-head finishes over a furlong or two furlongs, he nearly always comes out on the right side. I'd say without doubt that he's the best finisher in the world today, due in no small measure to his physique. He's not very tall but he's very strong, built like a tank."

✳   ✳   ✳

Christy Roche was trained in the hard school of the late, great P.J. "Darkie" Prendergast, with whom he had instant success, and ended up riding first jockey to the stable and winning five Irish Classics. Later he linked up as second jockey to Vincent O'Brien at the stage in Vincent's career when "gambling was out" and the making of stallions was the priority. Then came the highly-successful partnership between Roche and David O'Brien which saw the Tipperary-born jockey win three Derbys (a French, Irish and English) through Assert and Secreto and later still he would ride successfully for Aidan O'Brien and Vincent's son, Charles.

Roche's admiration for David O'Brien as a trainer goes every bit as deep as his admiration of the qualities that made Darkie" Prendergast and Vincent O'Brien outstanding world-renowned trainers. He believes that if David had not decided to opt out of the profession so early in life, he could in time have gone on to scale even greater heights than he did, granted, of course, that the right horses came along. And to any knockers of David, he points succinctly to the fact that he bought Assert for £16,000 and made him into a dual Derby winner.

Roche is the first to acknowledge the "unbelievable amount of success" he enjoyed while attached to the Bolger stable as first jockey. And the first to acknowledge also Bolger's ability to turn out his charges fitter than anybody else could make them.

But he would put David O'Brien ahead of both Jim Bolger and Dermot Weld and all the others of the current crop and right up there as a trainer of genius like Vincent O'Brien and "Darkie" Prendergast.

"He spent so much time with the horses in his care", said Roche. "He came to know them so well. Few realise, as I do, the job he did in making Assert into a champion. He started out looking an ordinary horse. But such was David's patience, such his way with the colt that he trained him to the point that he improved 100 per cent and emerged as the leading three-year-old in Europe in the season he won at Chantilly and the Curragh."

Such has been the emphasis that Jim Bolger has always placed on discipline in his stable and on attention to detail by every member of his staff that, as Christy Roche so aptly put it, relations with the Master of Glebe House, even for experienced pros, will always be difficult. Even the best can make mistakes and even the best can have an off day.

Roche, the old pro, was too long on the road to be upset by a touch of abrasiveness, too long around to take his cards and leave if it came to a clash over some point. Bolger respected his experience as Roche in turn respected the level of success that Bolger achieved but it was always going to be a purely business arrangement.

The public perception of Jim Bolger is of a man with a short fuse but he flatly rejects this perception as he stoutly defends himself against the charge that he can be too demanding and that by not making allowance for human frailties he can create the situation where aspiring youngsters feel they have no other option but walk away.

"All right, I have never set out to be all things to all men. It's not my way, never has been and never will be. But it's not entirely true to say that I don't suffer fools gladly if by this you mean that I don't give people a chance to prove themselves. I have given every chance to a few lame ducks in my time.

"People, like horses, have degrees of ability. If you don't realise this fact, you will think that everyone is marked out to be a genius, as you will conclude that every Flat horse is a potential Classic winner. It doesn't happen that way in life and it certainly doesn't in racing.

"I can say quite truthfully that I have given people who have worked with me plenty of time. I have helped them along as much as I could. But there is one thing I can't abide and I don't mind admitting it – and that is that I find it very difficult to tolerate people who don't give of their best," he said.

Christy Roche, the Man from Bansha in Co Tipperary, in summing up his relationship with Jim Bolger had this to say: "It was always difficult and possibly unnecessarily so. Jim I found to be very, very critical of people. It appeared to me that he liked to come across as the perfect fellow, one almost incapable of making a mistake. Yet in the case of his own mistakes – and he made quite a share of them – he was never willing to accept criticism for these.

"I won the 1991 English Oaks for him on Jet Ski Lady by adopting the tactics which I knew in my heart represented the only way this 50/1 shot could have any chance of beating the opposition. I knew that if the filly was held up she would have no chance. Stamina was her strong suit and she would have to be ridden to bring this into play – right from the start. As it turned out, my judgement was fully vindicated."

✳   ✳   ✳

You might well argue that Jim Bolger would be more relaxed in his day-to-day relations, less likely to be confrontational if he could sit at a bar stool and let his hair down with friends who liked a laugh and a bit of "craic".

But he has an abhorrence of alcohol. And what the evils of drink have wrought makes him voice very strong opinions publicly on this subject.

He is only too conscious of the battle one of Wexford's greatest hurling sons, Nicky Rackard, fought with drink until he finally conquered it, working unselfishly in the years before his death to help others to conquer it also. Rackard was a trainer of horses in his own right, apart from being a veterinary surgeon and landed a few famous gambles in his time. A portrait of Nicky hangs in the front room of Glebe house.

"I have heard more waffle talked in pubs than anywhere else in Ireland or in any part of the world for that matter," said Jim Bolger very forcibly. "Over-indulgence in alcohol is one of the greatest single problems in this country – a problem that many prefer to shove under the carpet rather than face head-on."

I put it to him that after a day's writing, I liked nothing better than to have a few drinks before dinner and then share a bottle of wine over the meal itself. "You can count yourself lucky if you can control matters in that way," he responded. "Not everyone is so lucky. So few can drink in moderation that I maintain that it's almost an impossible situation to achieve. People think they are letting their hair down and then go too far and the consequences can be terribly serious, especially if someone is involved in an accident after taking too much drink.

"The wisest course to pursue is to stay clear of it altogether," he added.

I put it to him that he had upset a lot of moderate drinkers – people who like a pint or a "small one" for relaxation – when he was quoted by Paul Kimmage in the *Sunday Tribune* – (now Paul is with the *Sunday Independent*) as saying: "I can't see how shifting your butt from your fireside to the publican's fireside and getting a pint in your hand is a panacea for all ills." I put it to him that he was implying that to even mingle socially and enjoy the "craic" with friends over a few drinks was a total waste of time?

He responded that for his part a good long walk was more beneficial health-wise and provided as much relaxation as spending some hours in a pub. Some of his horses, he noted, were "head-bangers" but they seemed to want to cure the problem by walking the box. "Walk, walk, walk – they don't go to the drinking pot and drink, drink, drink."

✻   ✻   ✻

Jim Bolger then has the name of being one of the hardest task-masters in the business. He must live with the legends, some of them apocryphal, I do not doubt, that have grown around him. Some who have pulled up camp and left abruptly keep their silence in public but the scars can run deep.

Even media representatives who have put silly questions or in a moment early in the morning when they might not be sharp enough have said "she" instead of "he" when talking about some horse, have found themselves brought up short with a verbal sting.

But for myself personally – I know that if Jim Bolger says he will be at the end of a phone at lunch-time, at one o'clock on the dot, he will be there. You know the meeting of your newspaper deadline is secure. Frank and honest in his assessments, concise and articulate and no wasting of precious time on either side.

Jim Bolger is the TOTAL professional. I bow to no one in my admiration of him on this plane.

As his 55th birthday approached on Christmas Day, 1996, it had to be acknowledged that he had made a lasting imprint on the racing scene both for his big-race achievements and his battles with the Turf Club.

Even when he was not commanding the headlines, he was at the heart of speculation and rumour, something he knew he could not control but he wasn't deterred from his single-mindedness of purpose as a trainer who maintained an impressive strike rate.

I put it to him straight that he was reputed to have lost a cool £1 million when GPA ran into difficulties (the basis of this story, circulating in racing and business was that his wife, Jackie, is a sister of Maurice Foley of GPA) but he did not blink as he responded: "My financial position is the same now as it was before these rumours ever began to circulate".

I pointed out to him that it wouldn't have mattered one iota to me personally if he had lost £1 million – his reputation as the Man Who Trained St. Jovite would still remain intact. Just as Vincent O'Brien's reputation survived the collapse of Classic Thoroughbreds.

Then Jim Bolger remarked significantly: "There are those who like to argue that much of Vincent O'Brien's success as a Flat trainer was due to the money power of the millionaires he had behind him after he moved to Ballydoyle. But I maintain that he would have been a success even if he was training on the top of a mountain".

One cannot help feel that perhaps the same could hold true of Jim Bolger himself.

Mrs Jackie Bolger, wife of Jim Bolger, receives the trophy for the 1996 Heinz 57 Phoenix Stakes from Mrs Cryss O Reilly after Mantovani's 20/1 triumph.

21

Ridgewood Pearl – The Belle Of New York

Sean Coughlan, husband of owner, Mrs Anne Coughlan handed a Tricolour to Johnny Murtagh and he waved it proudly to the cheering crowds as he was led back in by the happy couple to the winner's enclosure at Belmont Park after that famous victory on Ridgewood Pearl in the 1995 Breeders Cup Mile.

The thousands of Irish thronging the New York track set up a victory roar that might not have been as over-powering as the "Irish roar" that normally greets a sure-fire winner at Cheltenham but for sheer enthusiasm it was something the American regulars here had seldom experienced.

As Ridgewood Pearl won going away by two lengths from the grey Fastness, she was hailed deservedly as the Belle of New York.

In the eyes of all Irish racing enthusiasts John Oxx was unquestionably the Man of the Year. 'Ridgewood' was completing a marvellously planned and executed campaign when saving Europe's face with her late, brave dash under an inspired Johnny Murtagh through the Belmont Park mud. Everyone acclaimed quiet, unassuming John Oxx for his outstanding feat of training.

It was a considerable feat to keep Ridgewood Pearl going from the Athasi Stakes in April until the Breeders Cup in late October, more especially when one considers the distance she was asked to travel for that final triumph.

Oxx's feat was made all the greater by the fact that he had delivered Ridgewood Pearl first to win the Airlie/Coolmore Irish 2,000 Guineas; then she equally emphatically disposed of the opposition in the Coronation Stakes at Royal Ascot (Oxx's first winner in England)and went on to slam the best France and Britain could offer in the Prix du Moulin at Longchamp in September. The crowning moment was the devastatingly courageous surge in the closing stages of the Breeders Cup Mile to collar the flattering Fastness and put no less than nine lengths between herself and that high-class mare Sayyedati.

So John Oxx had managed to win four prestigious prizes over a period from May to October and that demanded an assured hand and a depth of knowledge and experience of the training art that one could only expect from a man who was carrying on the singular traditions set by his late father, John Oxx Snr., masterly in his handling of fillies.

The only bleep on her record was the six-lengths defeat by St James's Palace Stakes winner Bahri (third in the English 2,000 Guineas and Irish 2,000 Guineas) in the Queen Elizabeth II Stakes, and everything Ridgewood Pearl accomplished before and subsequently suggested that she had an off day on the important Ascot date in September. Apart from the astonishingly successful blitz of international prizes that brought Pattern Race victories in six countries, Oxx became champion trainer in Ireland for the first time and stable rider, Johnny Murtagh beat Christy Roche and Michael Kinane for the Jockeys title.

The reception Ridgewood Pearl and Murtagh received in New York surpassed the excitement of the Vincent O'Brien-trained Royal Academy's historic victory in the same race in 1990. Her breeder, Sean Coughlan was justifiably ecstatic as was his wife, in whose colours the filly raced. When Sean arrived in the winner's enclosure bearing the Tricolour to hand Johnny Murtagh it was a moment that captured the hearts of Americans viewing the race on television, as it did all those at Belmont Park itself.

Raised initially in Kildare town and then on the Curragh, Sean Coughlan emigrated to London. "I arrived at Euston Station with, I think, tuppence in my pocket; I know my mother gave me ten cigarettes when I was leaving home. It was all she could afford, and I remember her for it".

Coughlan got involved in construction and eventually built up a highly-profitable engineering business. His venture into racing, undertaken in 1979, has been equally successful. His first horse provided David Elsworth with his first winner as a trainer. Then Indian Ridge won the Jersey Stakes at Royal Ascot in 1988 and has gone on to become a major stallion at the Irish National Stud. Mated with Ben's Pearl which won the Irish Cambridgeshire in the Coughlan colours, the union produced Ridgewood Ben and Ridgewood Pearl.

The emergence of this family is a good illustration of how unpredictable the breeding of thoroughbreds can be. Sean Coughlan recalled: "I bought Joshua's Daughter to race, but they rang me up one day to say that she had been injured on the gallops and should be put down. I got in touch with the vet to ask would it not be possible to save her to breed from. The vet told me she was not worth breeding from, but I felt that if I had hurt an ankle I would not like to be put down and decided to keep her".

Joshua's Daughter died three years ago, having produced eleven foals and eight winners of numerous races and stakes. "I often think the Man above has rewarded us for not putting down Joshua's Daughter. She did us proud and is buried here at Rathbride in the garden behind the house", said Sean Coughlan.

*   *   *

The son of a Co. Meath steel erector and sand blaster, Johnny Murtagh was, like Michael Kinane, an outstanding school-boy boxer and won an All-Ireland title when he was 15. In fact, he was an all-round sports enthusiast in his youth.

His initiation to the saddle was through riding his cousin's ponies and donkeys. It was obvious that it stirred the idea in his mind of becoming a jockey and when he became a pupil of R.A.C.E. he may not have known it then but he had taken the first step on the road to becoming Irish champion Flat jockey in time. It was fitting that on the final day of the 1995 Irish Flat season he should be honoured with a presentation at Leopardstown from Stan Cosgrove and Derek O'Sullivan, Director of the Apprentices School on the Curragh.

Murtagh served his time with John Oxx and was leading apprentice in 1989 at the age of 19. He was only 20 when he was appointed stable jockey by John Oxx. He was runner-up to Warren O'Connor in 1990 and in 1991 – his first year competing on level terms with his seniors – he divided Michael Kinane and Christy Roche in the Jockeys' table, riding 82 winners. Fame took its toll and he also lacked maturity. He hit a valley period for a time as he went on the tiles most nights. Weight and the other problems contributed to John Oxx having to adopt a firm hand. Oxx stressed that he could not continue as No.1 to the stable unless he pulled himself together and faced up to his problems. Meanwhile, Oxx, recognising that here was an exceptional talent, kept Murtagh's job open.

A brilliant treble at Galway showed that he was on the way back. But he was still fighting an unrelenting battle with the scales and he began to despair that he couldn't win it. He sought specialist help. The result was that he spent seven weeks in hospital and eventually he was back as No. 1. to the John Oxx stable, riding 44 winners in the '95 season as he finished fourth in the jockeys' table.

It was a victory for determination and courage. He acknowledges now that, having to go through the nightmare of that valley period, made him a better person and also made him grow up and realise his responsibilities.

When I talked to Johnny at the Galway Festival meeting '96, he readily acknowledged the debt he owed to John Oxx, a true gentleman. "He's the fairest man I know. He guided me through a crisis in my life and when I had put my problems behind me, he gladly welcomed me back as his No. 1. stable jockey.".

And Murtagh was quick to praise John Oxx also for keeping faith with him as the rider of Ridgewood Pearl in all her races in '95 outside of the Irish 1,000 Guineas (the reason he missed the ride that day was that he opted to partner a filly for the Aga Khan). He might easily have gone for a 'name' French jockey who knew Longchamp like the back of his hand when it came to the Prix du Moulin and an American rider for the Breeders Cup Mile.

But Oxx believes in loyalty and loyalty was the password in the partnership with Johnny Murtagh right through the memorable 1995 season.

Oxx knew that Murtagh was ice-cool on the big occasion and thrived on pressure. Murtagh admits that the only occasion when he felt real pressure was before riding Ridgewood Pearl in the Coronation Cup, as he knew people would say that he hadn't enough experience if he had got beat. "But the way I looked at it was that I was not going to get the necessary experience unless I rode these big races", he told Michael Clower of the *Sporting Life*. "In fact, I never had a moment's worry on her. I got a nice lead and, when I went on over two furlongs out, I knew it was going to take something pretty good to beat her".

Trainer and jockey walked the Belmont Park track on the morning of the race. Ridgewood Pearl had cantered on the track the previous day and that helped Murtagh to become acquainted with the course.

Oxx's principal concern, as he expressed it to Murtagh, was that the filly would be left in stalls and then have a lot of ground to make up. So Murtagh concentrated on getting her away quickly from the stalls – and it came off to perfection. He aimed to conserve that finishing burst for as long as possible and followed Fastness into the straight, and the Belmont Park straight gives every chance to a colt or filly that can come with a powerful surge.

Even though Gary Stevens on Fastness may have seemed to many of the onlookers to be heading for victory, Murtagh knew he had plenty in the tank to take the grey and when he pressed the button, 'Ridgewood' responded in a manner that certainly earned her the tag "super filly".

"It was one of the greatest days of my life as I came back in and heard the roar of the crowd", recalled Johnny Murtagh. "The many Irish who were there that day, exiles living in New York and others who had come in from various parts of the States and Canada and also those who had travelled over from Ireland, helped make the atmosphere special.

"When Sean Coughlan handed me the Tricolour in the winner's enclosure and I waved it to the crowds, a great 'Irish roar' went up. You never forget a moment like that".

Johnny's father-in-law, Michael "Babs" Keating, the famous Tipperary All-Ireland hurler and later successful manager of the County senior hurling team, had travelled over and was photographed all smiles in the enclosure, as he joined in the celebrations. He had been with Murtagh in the days leading up to the race itself and even managed to get in a round of golf.

Johnny Murtagh met Orla Keating for the first time at the Jockeys' dance in 1991. Christy Roche, a close friend of "Babs" Keating, was in the company as introductions were made and Murtagh took Orla out on the floor.

Then he went to India and on his return he met her again and it developed from there.

Today Johnny and Orla are the proud parents of a daughter, Caroline. The christening party in June '96 led Johnny to have lunch and break momentarily the strict diet regime. He had ridden at 8st 7lbs two days earlier but now found himself struggling to do the weight for the Roscommon meeting. Because he was hungry he took a cup of tea and a sandwich. He breached a rule in weighing out and got suspended for four days.

Again it proved to him that the slightest deviation from your normal dietary routine and it can tip the balance – or the scales – against you. Apart from riding out two lots six days a week, he walks a lot and also spends the inevitable time in the sauna.

Breakfast is a cup of coffee at 9a.m., lunch just fruit – a small amount – and dinner consists of fish or chicken with vegetables. He doesn't take potatoes, even though he would like to, of course,. He has to be very careful in the early part of the season before the summer round of meetings gets under way. The more activity, the more it helps him in controlling his weight.

If the Breeders Cup Mile triumph was an unforgettable moment for Johnny Murtagh, the winning of his first Jockeys' crown represented another milestone in his career. The championship had developed into a three-way contest between the reigning champion, Michael Kinane, Christy Roche and Murtagh. It had become a match when Kinane broke off early to take up his riding contract in Hong Kong. It still hung in the balance with two weeks of the season remaining but Murtagh clinched it by riding a treble for Oxx at the Curragh on November 7.

Roche, a veteran by Murtagh's standard, had won his sixth title in 1990 with 113 winners. He paid a glowing tribute to the new champion: "He has become a great rider. He has battled with his weight for a long time and to become champion riding at 8st 8lbs or over is a great achievement".

✳   ✳   ✳

The Aga Khan's Timarida had an even longer campaign than Ridgewood Pearl, starting in the Castrol Stakes on St. Patrick's Day '95 and culminating in the E.P. Taylor Stakes on October 15 at Canada's Woodbine track, only two weeks after the same filly had won the Prix de l'Opera at Longchamp. Timarida lost only one of her eight races in '95 and was unlucky not to remain undefeated.

Sheikh Mohammed's Russian Snow had initiated a Group Two meeting double for John Oxx and Johnny Murtagh at Longchamp by winning the Prix de Royallieu.

In her opening race of the 1996 season Timarida was second, beaten a length by Definite Article in the Tattersalls Gold Cup at the Curragh on May 26. There were high hopes that the filly would make amends in the Queen Anne Stakes at Royal Ascot, for which she started at 6/1. But, having run prominently until three furlongs out, she was eventually tailed off and was found to have burst a blood vessel. The race was won by the 10/11 favourite, Charnwood Forest ridden by Michael Kinane for Godolphin.

On her next outing Timarida started 6/4 favourite for the Sea World International Stakes (Group 2) at the Curragh during Budweiser Irish Derby week-end.

Carrying 9st 7lbs, she failed by a length to the English challenger, Gothenberg, who had won the Tetrarch by six lengths over the course in April.

She finally came good, revealing again the class she had shown in '95, when she won a Group 1 ten furlongs event in Germany on Sunday August 1st.

As John Oxx would note later: "That was a pretty good run against a pretty good field. It set her up perfectly for the Beverly D Stakes (Grade 1) at Arlington International, Chicago on Saturday August 24."

In her final gallop at home on the Curragh she worked better than at any time during the season and Oxx knew she was spot-on for the American Challenge. Then too, as he pointed out, she was a filly that travelled very well, indeed, she seemed to thrive on travelling. Timarida came home two-and-a-half lengths in front of the local contender, Perfect Arc in the Chicago race.

Johnny Murtagh was always travelling well on Timarida who started the 8/5 favourite in the nine-and-a-half-furlong event and now she had recorded victories in Ireland, France, Germany, Canada and North America.

First prize-money was £193,548 and with this victory Timarida kept her slate clean in five starts against her own sex.

This success crowned a memorable week for John Oxx, who had won the Group One Yorkshire Oaks with Key Change on the previous Wednesday.

Timarida stamped her class on the 1996 Irish Champion Stakes at Leopardstown on Saturday, September 14 when coming from last to first to sprint clear for her third successive Group 1 success.

The Aga Khan, who received the winning trophy from Michelle Smith, Ireland's golden heroine of the Atlanta Olympics, described Timarida as "an exceptional filly" while John Oxx, not hiding his admiration for the winner, said: "She's a fantastic filly" and John Murtagh summed up: "She is something special. She has unbelieveable speed".

Timarida had a length-and-a-half to spare over Irish Oaks winner, Dance Design. The big disappointment of the race was Epsom Derby winner, Shaamit, who found little when asked and finished fourth.

✳   ✳   ✳

Several times in the past the Trainers' Championship has given rise to controversy – whether it should be decided by total prize-money won, win prize-money only, or by the number of winners a trainer saddles during the season. However, in the case of the 1995 Flat season in Ireland, John Oxx left no room for argument. He led the table on all three counts and also, for good measure, attained a higher percentage of winners to runners than any other home-based trainer – almost 30 per cent.

John Oxx, who succeeded his late father as the licence-holder at Currabeg on the Curragh in 1979, built a high reputation on the home front, a reputation recognised by the patronage of owners such as the Aga Khan and

Sheikh Mohammed and by appointments as Chairman of the Irish National Stud and Chairman of the Irish Racehorse Trainers' Association (he handed over the reins of the latter to Willie Mullins in 1996).

Oxx, for all that, was less well-known outside Ireland than several of his compatriots – but how dramatically that situation altered through the achievements of Ridgewood Pearl and Timarida in '95 and again through the victories of Timarida in '96.

John Oxx was born into a racing stable and it never occurred to him that his destiny would lie anywhere else. His father, who trained the winners of eight Irish Classics, took the same view and made sure that his only son devoted his school holidays to acting as his assistant.

When John Oxx Jnr. left school, he went to University College Dublin to spend five years qualifying as a vet – "but even then everyone looked upon me as my father's official assistant and, for my part, I never had any intention of practising".

Oxx's knowledge of training came solely from his father. "I did have a brief look at the scene in Australia but that was really only a holiday and I never went to any other stable".

When John Oxx Snr. retired at the end of 1978 just days before his 69th birthday he did things in reverse by promptly becoming assistant to his son. It worked well. "He was an easy man to get on with – and he was always willing to stand in for me if I couldn't go to a particular meeting", recalled the current Master of Currabeg.

Oxx's second year saw his total of winners shoot up to 40. Success brought new owners and more horses. But there were problems also. In 1981 he had too many two-year-olds, putting himself in a high risk situation, on his own admission, and the net result was that he had his worst ever season with 15 winners.

Pat Eddery had joined Vincent O'Brien and in his second year at Ballydoyle he came to an agreement with John Oxx. The association prospered.

"Vincent had a very quiet 1986 season and so Pat and I had a great run together", he recalled. "He was still coming over most Saturdays and, as he didn't have many rides for Ballydoyle, I was able to make plenty use of him and I had a lot of smart three-year-olds. I was so sad to see him go. He was a superb jockey to be associated with."

Enter Cash Asmussen. Whereas he came in for a lot of criticism as No. 1. stable jockey to Vincent O'Brien, he was strongly defended against his critics by John Oxx. "Horses run just as fast for him as they do for Pat Eddery", was a comment of his at the time that added fuel to the debate.

Oxx's faith in Asmussen was rewarded as the 1987 season progressed. Cash crowned a great year for the stable by winning the Jefferson Smurfit Memorial Irish St. Leger on Eurobird – Oxx's first Classic and coincidentally his 50th winner of the season.

John Oxx Snr. had passed on by then. He would have been very proud of his son if he had been at the Curragh on Sunday, October 11, 1987. In 1978

Sorbus, trained by Oxx Snr. had finished first in the Irish Oaks only to be disqualified in very controversial circumstances and placed third.

The Oxx Snr. tradition of integrity was carried on by his son. Indeed, John Oxx personifies training on a plane that makes him very much admired by the racing public. You expect his horses to run on their merits and you find it impossible to imagine him being hauled in before the Stewards for actions that would be entirely foreign to his character. As Chairman of the Irish Racehorse Trainers' Association he set standards as an individual that made him an ideal man to carry the flag on behalf of his colleagues, especially when it came to dealing with the ruling bodies.

✳   ✳   ✳

There was a time when John Oxx was insisting that 75 horses was a sufficient number for any trainer to train. In 1991 the stable was accommodating no less than 140, at the time the Aga Khan withdrew his horses from training in Britain and dispersed them to Ireland and France after the English Jockey Club disqualified Aliysa, his 1989 Oaks winner for having traces of a prohibited substance in her system).

Oxx admitted at the time that if he were moving from 50 to 100 he would find it a fairly sudden and steep jump. But really he didn't find the adjustment from 75 to 140 all that difficult.

Sheikh Mohammed had about 30 horses with him – so the Sheikh and the Aga Khan between them were paying for the upkeep of 100 horses in the Oxx stable.

The result of having such a power-packed stable saw John Oxx turn out 68 winners of 99 races in the 1995 Flat season for prize-money totalling £IR 649,337. It put him ahead of three of the other "Big Four", Dermot Weld, Aidan O'Brien and Jim Bolger.

The debate arose in recent seasons about maidens belonging to the Aga Khan being run at meetings outside the Metropolitan circuit.

"The Aga Khan wants to see his horses reach their full potential," Oxx explained. "He is interested in all levels of achievement and his broodmares are constantly under review. Breeding is related to racing. The racecourse tells him how a broodmare is doing. If the progeny of certain broodmares fail to make it, then these will be weeded out and replaced by others.

"I know that nearly all the fillies I train for the Aga Khan will be given a chance at stud in due course. If I can win a race with each of them, no matter how moderate – whatever the level of a particular individual – then it adds to the value of the filly in question for breeding purposes. The scenario is different from aiming to win races simply for the stake money."

Oxx makes the point that there are not enough maiden races on the Metropolitan circuit, so a trainer has to run them whether he likes it or not on the Provincial circuit.

Personally, I contend that the Aga Khan's family, going back many decades, have been outstanding beneficiaries to Irish racing and breeding and John Oxx is merely doing what he has to do and to say otherwise would indicate that one was not prepared to face reality.

Another aspect that must not be overlooked is that nearly every horse that carries the Aga Khan's colours is choicely-bred. Sometimes when they do not make the hoped-for mark on the Flat, they are sold on to other trainers who put them to the jumping game. And they can then enjoy success, even notable success, that was never going to be their lot as Flat performers.

Thus there is a cyclical benefit to Irish racing as a whole.

While there are trainers today who have to struggle to make ends meet, John Oxx does not have to worry on that score. Outside of Sheikh Mohammed and the Aga Khan, he has long-established owners who had horses with his late father. These owners deeply respected John Oxx Snr. for his integrity. Likewise John. He can be the embodiment of patience where he feels that infinite patience in required.

The magnificent victories of Timarida in the Aga Khan's colours (she was bred by her owner and described by Tony Morris in the *Racing Post* in August '96 as "another gem for the Aga") in 1995 and '96 were further proof that few could match John Oxx when it came to handling fillies.

And when Ridgewood Pearl emerged as the Belle of New York in the Breeders Cup Mile at Belmont Park in October '95, carrying the Coughlan colours, John Oxx joined his neighbour Dermot Weld in smashing the Atlantic barrier. Vincent O'Brien had earlier blazed a trail when he won the Washington DCInternational Stakes with Sir Ivor and, as we have seen, he would win the Breeders Cup Mile (Turf) in 1990 with Royal Academy.

The Aga Khan receives the magnificent owner's trophy from Michelle Smith, Ireland's golden heroine of the Atlanta Olympics after Timarida had won the 1996 Irish Champion Stakes. Also pictured Johnny Murtagh and John Oxx (Picture: Carolin Norris).

PART THREE

THE HIGH ROLLERS WHO NEVER LIVED LIKE LAMBS

22

How J.P. Put The Wheels Back On The Bike

One evening, over dinner in the Restaurant Roberto in Geneva, I suggested to J.P. McManus that he struck me as the kind of man who might like to have his ashes spread near the winning post at Cheltenham, where he has already seen seven horses carrying his colours win at the great March Festival meeting. "I only hope my ashes have not vanished into thin air before that point is reached!" he laughed.

He was talking, of course, in the betting sense, as the punter most respected for his steely courage by the big bookmakers in Britain. His awesome tilts at the ring have made him a legendary figure wherever men gather to talk about spectacular betting coups.

Staying alive in the battle with the bookies has been McManus's vital concern since he first hit Cheltenham around 1976, earning the sobriquet "The Sundance Kid" from the renowned English sports writer, Hugh McIlvanney. He admits to having been reckless then. Now in the maturity of his 40s, he is a far wilier customer, having acquired the discipline that he asserts is essential to success as a punter. And nowhere is discipline more necessary than at Cheltenham during Festival week.

"I don't want to have bad memories at one Cheltenham or even two," he remarks as the Chateau Margaux is poured. "I can walk away from having a bet, something I couldn't do in my youth when I knew what it was like to be skint not just once but a number of times."

He acknowledges that Cheltenham can become a graveyard for the unwary and the headstrong.

"It's different from any other race meeting in the world in that the Festival generates an atmosphere all its own. You can get mentally worn out over the three days. What amazes me always is that you get normally very cool characters doing everything right the first day and halfway through the second. But then they can blow everything from that point on, either through a failure of stamina or breaking their own ground rules on betting. Yes, discipline is the key to survival as a punter at Cheltenham."

He admitted he had a "terrible" Cheltenham '95.

"I had taken a firm decision to quit betting by the time Dorans Pride won the Stayers Hurdle on the Thursday. Going to the meeting, I had marked him down as one of my prime fancies and he duly obliged by five lengths at returned odds of 11/4. But when I make a decision like that, I don't change. Liverpool however, was kind to us, Royal Ascot also."

$$* \qquad * \qquad *$$

At Cheltenham '94 he had gone for a "killing" the first day on his own horse, Gimme Five, who could only finish 20th. The following afternoon he bombarded the rails bookies with bets of £155,000 to £80,000 and £60,000 to £30,000 on Danoli. It was reckoned that he cleared at least £250,000 on one race. "That put the wheels back on the bike," was his immortal comment.

He sought 10/1 or better on Time For A Run in the Coral Cup. The rails bookies with whom he had accounts were still reeling from the body blows he had inflicted on them and would only offer 7/1 at best. He decided not to have a bet. Time For A Run won at 11/1.

And then Mucklemeg, also carrying his famous Green and Gold colours, won the Festival Bumper at 7/2. I do not doubt that if J.P. had got the 10/1 he sought on Time For A Run and followed up by going for a major "touch" on Mucklemeg, he would have taken a cool £1m out of the ring.

But you don't find him dwelling on the might-have-beens. On a glorious sunny morning, I join him in his magnificent suite of offices in the prestigious Rue du Rhone, looking out from the sixth floor on the Rhone River with timeless, snow-capped Mont Blanc dominating everything. On one table is a bronze of two hurlers clashing overhead on a dropping ball – a gift from Pat Hartigan and his wife Kate. "We are never far from home," he says quietly almost to himself.

Home means summer afternoons watching key inter-county championship matches. He has never lost his love of the national game, but where once he cycled to matches, he may now go by helicopter.

$$* \qquad * \qquad *$$

On his working desk are two computers, one linked to Reuters, giving the changes in the money markets, the other showing the latest ante-post prices on the Cheltenham races. J.P. McManus is now a player in the financial markets. "It's a different form of gambling, a different form of risk," he tells me.

"Let me confess that in this game the stakes are far, far higher than I ever operated at when it came to backing horses" he said. "We are talking about the world of high finance – of dealing in currencies, in bonds and to put it in the simplest possible terms for the ordinary man in the street, in money as a commodity to gamble on".

"Skill is transportable, as is knowledge and expertise," says his close friend and golfing and racing companion, financier Dermot Desmond. "What J.P.has done is display the mobility to bring to the financial world all that he acquired as a punter in the racing sphere. And, having gathered all the available facts and data about a currency, he will exercise his judgement in playing the market. He brings to this sphere also the discipline he shows nowadays in his betting on the horses."

But even though his main theatre of operations is now in the financial world. J.P. McManus has not lost his fundamental love of the Cheltenham scene and neither has his appetite diminished to "go to war" with the bookies. The man who is accepted as an international businessman today in Geneva knows that in the eyes of the Irish people, he is one of the key wearer's of Ireland's colours at the Festival meeting. He wears those colours as an owner and he wears them as a punter and he revels in the traditional friendly Ireland v England rivalry that is an integral part of the meeting.

"People – the bookies most of all – want to take him on because they know he is good", says Dermot Desmond. "But he, for his part, will not respond to the challenge of begin sucked in where he is at a disadvantage. He will want the balance with him".

It strikes me forcibly from my own conversations with J.P. that his head will never be turned by the headlines he has commanded as a result of his mind-boggling tilts at the ring. He is not egotistical. He strongly resists the temptation to become a victim of the legends that have grown around his name.

"I want to go to Cheltenham until I die," says J.P. "I hope that I will always have the appetite to play the ring. I can only do that by observing the ground rules, to walk away when I think it is time to do so. I have learned that there is always another day."

Far from the quiet world of computer screens telling in a twinkling whether your gamble on the movement of a currency in the money markets has come off or not, you find in sharp contrast a frenetic pace over the three days of the Cheltenham Festival meeting, the fierce bustle in the ring, the tic-tac men signalling frantically and the fever that is generated when the cry goes up: "The Kid is having a go".

In that office in the Rue du Rhone you don't even feel your feet touching the soft thick pile of the rich carpets. More spacious offices are being prepared beside those already furnished and completed. J.P. was able to give an hour at this interview session. There was an appointment he had to meet at 11.20 a.m. and a Board meeting then, followed by a business lunch. He resumed our interview at 2.30 p.m.

Is he happy in his new life?

"I could not be happier," he says . "I am very pleased I chose Geneva as my new base. I have quite a number of friends here. I had certain key contacts before I came. These were very important to me in getting started and ensuring that everything was operating properly from the outset. Now it's up and running and we have no major headaches".

I get to understand and appreciate why he has settled in so well in Geneva.

The city is not too big and neither is it too small. You couldn't look for better communications anywhere in the world.

It's so easily accessible by air also. J.P. spends most week-ends at home with Noreen and the family, that is when Noreen and himself are not at the Cheltenham Festival meeting or at any of the other big meetings in the racing calendar. He wants their three children to be brought up in an Irish atmosphere, open to Irish values, which mean so much to him and, in a word, to be instilled with an outlook on life and with principles that will never desert them, no matter what part of the globe they might end up in later on.

✳   ✳   ✳

On my first trip he revealed to me how the "Money Wheel" had now become an integral part of his daily life. We were talking over the bacon and eggs cooked Irish style with the glorious sunshine outside making the snow gleam white on the peak of majestic Mont Blanc.

We were in his "pad" in the exclusive Cologny suburb overlooking Lake Geneva. Before breakfast he had been on the phone, checking the present position of sterling against the dollar and the mark – getting the very latest on its fluctuating position. In one day – in the time span between breakfast and dinner – he can make a "killing". But then, of course, he can lose also. You have to know what is happening in the markets; you have to have all the information at your disposal before you make the decisions on which so much can hinge.

Stripped of all its mystique – and it holds mystique for the ordinary person – the world of finance and operating in the markets demands the same ground rules, the same dedication that marks out the successful student of form in racing. Dermot Desmond whispered to me over dinner in the Restaurant Roberto that J.P. had made a "killing" that day in the financial markets.

The television set in the corner of the living room is not alone for relaxation – watching soccer matches in the evenings, for example – but is a weapon in the eternal war against the bookies. In the count-down to Cheltenham, J.P. will put on the videos of key races, whether they have been run at Leopardstown, Navan, Fairyhouse, Punchestown, Ascot, Sandown, Haydock, and he will study again and again horses that he believes will come strongly into the reckoning over the three days of the Festival meeting.

At hand too are the Form Books – the Irish Form Book and the English Form Book – and naturally he gets the *Racing Post* and *Sporting Life*.

He has to know everything that matters about a horse before he will wager on it. Above all, he has to know what kind of going favours it and one of the reasons he avoids ante-post betting is that he realises that if a particular horse goes best on good ground and the going comes up heavy on the day, then you might as well tear up your ante-post docket as his chance will have gone out the window. Better back at shorter odds when you have the knowledge than at long odds when you cannot control what happens in the lead-up to the moment when a race gets under way.

J.P. McManus has come a long way – a very long way – from the time when as a boy attending the Christian Brothers School in Limerick, he had a few bob on Merryman II when he won the Aintree Grand National in 1960 at 13/2. "I was only nine then", he recalled. Already he had been bitten by the betting bug and it would never leave him.

He laughed as he reminded me of the philosophy propounded by an old Christian Brother: "You guys who think you are clever, be nice to the guys you see as no-hopers, because they could be employing you one day!"

In all the time that I have known J.P. – from our first meeting in Tralee in 1976, as a Jazz band played *When The Saints Go Marching In* outside the Mount Brandon Hotel, to dinner in Geneva in the count-down to Cheltenham '96 – I have been very much taken by the way he has never forgotten his roots. Impressed by the way he has never in the middle of a high-powered existence failed to keep in touch with close friends from the days when at the age of 21 he was Chairman of the South Liberties GAA Club in Limerick (his distinctive colours of Green and Gold are the colours of the Club).

At Galway '96 Joe McKenna was in the winner's enclosure as Charlie Swan came back in on the Aidan O'Brien-trained Vicar Street after the gelding by The Parson had taken the maiden hurdle, the opening event on the card on the Monday evening (this one started at 9/10 after being a "morning board prices" gamble of 3/1 in the offices and it was backed down from 7/4 on the course).

Later we met J.P. in the company of Pat Hartigan, heroic full-back on the 1973 Limerick All-Ireland winning team and, of course, Eamonn Grimes, who had the honour as captain of lifting the Liam McCarthy Cup high in triumph at Croke Park has been a good friend of J.P.'s ever since that memorable season for Limerick hurling.

And "The Sundance Kid" was in Croke Park for the 1996 All-Ireland Hurling Final as Limerick failed to Wexford.

✳   ✳   ✳

J.P. McManus confesses that he has known no greater satisfaction than seeing his colours carried to victory at Cheltenham. "I have been lucky to have had seven winners there already, Mister Donovan (1982), Bit Of A Skite (1983), Danny Connors (1991), Time For A Run (1994), Mucklemeg (1994), Front Line(1995)and Elegant Lord (1996). There are owners who have given a life-time hoping to win one race while others simply want to have a horse good enough to run there."

His great ambition now is to win a Champion Hurdle and a Gold Cup – at least one of the two principal races at the Festival meeting. He knows that in Thats My Man he had his best chance to date to realise the dream of winning a Champion Hurdle (this hurdler of outstanding potential was killed in a freak accident on the gallops at Aidan O'Brien's).

In the case of the Gold Cup he would love to see a chaser of his jumping the last safely and storming up the hill to victory – preferably beating a favoured English challenger in the process.

The dream will not die because of any setbacks – even the tragedy that befell Thats My Man. J.P. will always be prepared to step in and acquire the talent that he thinks may help him to realise his Festival target. His love of horses runs deep, as deep as his knowledge. He accepts that for him ownership is "luxury".

Amazing to think that twenty years have elapsed since he went into a bookie's office in Cheltenham on Gold Cup Day with a bag of readies and put it all "on the nose" on an Irish-trained apparent certainty that lost. The wheel has come full circle. He doesn't have to carry cash to the track anymore. His credit is good with every rails bookie with whom he choose to bet. He is seen as the "King of the ring" during Festival week.

The mobile phone means that he need not leave his box high up in the Stand when he wants to cause a flurry in the ring. Or he can chooses to send one of his lieutenants down to "do the business" for him – granted the odds are right. Because you don't see J.P. nowadays going down the line of rails bookies doesn't mean for one moment that his presence is not felt. It is always felt during the three days of Festival week – as awesome when he is unseen.

Back in the mid-Seventies when the legend was being born, he used to stay in the Queen's Hotel at the top of The Promenade in Cheltenham itself. He now prefers the quieter life in the Cotswolds where he moved in the early Eighties.

Close friends will join him there. The councils of war over breakfast and over dinner are part of the very essence of what makes Festival week what it is.

As we shall see in the next chapter J.P. McManus is what world poker champion, Johnny Chan would describe as an "action guy" – in fact, an action guy to the last drop in his veins.

I get to thinking that if he was a poker players competing at the highest level in Binion's card-room in Las Vegas, Chan would love to take him on in a head-to-head- duel and in the no-limit game at that.

23

'Yes, We're Dancin', Man!'

The action moves with the seasons whether on the racecourse or the golf course or following sports of different kinds – from soccer to rugby and Ireland's national game of hurling.

Operating to the rule that allows one to spend 140 nights in a given year in one's native country, J.P. McManus can still fit in all the major race meetings in Ireland that he wishes to attend and other big occasions in the sporting calendar.

Outside of the Irish racing dates, you will find invariably ringed in red in his diary the Cheltenham Festival meeting, Liverpool's Grand National meeting, Royal Ascot and the Prix de l'Arc de Triomphe week-end in Paris. These days too he may even take in the big Breeders Cup meeting in the States.

J.P. McManus is the total professional when it comes to "going to war" in the ring. Money is like chips for the world poker champion. You move them wrongly at your peril. But you move them with ice water in your veins instead of blood.

J.P. McManus makes no secret of the fact that the adrenalin flows in his veins when he is taking on the bookies head-on or playing the financial markets. Away from the betting ring, away from the office in Geneva that has now become the engine-room so to speak of his operations in the financial markets, J.P. McManus loves the cut-and-thrust of action on the golf course.

The more intense the pressure, the more he likes it. The satisfaction of winning, when a game may go right down to the wire, transcends the stakes themselves.

He has been involved with Coolmore boss John Magnier and his other close friend, Dermot Desmond in team events, a Pro-Am or a Classic for charity. They have formed a formidable trio.

J.P. McManus flew to the States with some pals of his for the last Ryder Cup and delighted in cheering the European team to a famous victory and, or course, Philip Walton for the thrilling role he played.

They took the opportunity to get involved in games in the early morning at different courses. Knowledge of their prowess had by now reached high rollers of the golfing scene on the other side of the Atlantic. There were plenty of "bandits" wearing mythical outsize sombreros ready to ride into town to take them on in a High Noon shoot-out.

Once David Leadbetter, guru to Nick Faldo and a host of others, was engaged for a private session. J.P. made it clear that he didn't want a complete reconstruction job done on his swing. It was serving him well enough. What he would like was a hint or two that would give him an edge over the opposition when he was in a high-stakes match!

✳   ✳   ✳

Down in the Caribbean in January you find the high rollers congregating in Barbados, arriving like migratory birds, for the big four-day Robert Sangster Pro-Am Golf Tournament over the Sandy Lane course.

Robert Sangster and his wife, Susan stay at their beachfront holiday home, "Jane Harbour" right next to the Sandy Lane Hotel and across the road from the golf course.

It's an invitation-only charity tournament – a time of high-powered action on The Golden Coast or Platinum Coast, of awesome side bets, a time for wearing T-Shirts and shorts in the Caribbean sunshine where at Royal Ascot the high rollers sport topper and tails. But then it can reach 86 degrees out on the course and if you can't lay your hand on a cooling drink half-way round, you feel you will literally die of dehydration.

John Magnier is a regular each year along with J.P. McManus, John Horgan of Cork also and Phonsie O'Brien. The last time I was there in 1994 Curragh trainers, Mick O'Toole and Kevin Prendergast participated as did Northern Ireland-born Billy McDonald, the legendary agent who picked out Alleged as a yearling for Robert Sangster, who purchased him for the giveaway sum of 120,000 dollars. Trained by Vincent O'Brien and carrying Sangster's colours, Alleged won the Prix de l'Arc de Triomphe two years running (1977 and '78) in the hands of Lester Piggot and was syndicated as a stallion in Kentucky for 13 million dollars. Sangster never forgot McDonald for that coup.

That year the professionals included Christy O'Connor, Jnr., John O'Leary, Eamonn Darcy and David Jones.

Dr Michael Smurfit was accustomed to anchoring his yacht on the coastline off the Sandy Lane Hotel and to slip on to the island when he chose to do so. But that year he picked Antiguae as the yacht's Caribbean base. His brother, Dermot took part in the Pro-Am Tournament.

It's not all monied people who are invited to play in Robert Sangster's Pro-Am. Billy McDonald is no millionaire. Neither is Mick O'Toole. But they are both the kind of characters who are liked by Sangster for themselves. As one friend put it to me: "Robert likes around him when he is holidaying in Barbados characters who can raise a laugh, men of wit and repartee, who love to have a gamble, guys who live by the motto: 'Better one day as a lion than 100 years as a lamb'".

Ever since the golden era he enjoyed on the Flat with Vincent O'Brien, he has had a particular regard for Phonsie and his special brand of humour (Phonsie has been a winner of the tournament in recent years).

✳   ✳   ✳

The one unforgivable sin in the eyes of the management of the Sandy Lane Hotel is to be loud and flaunt your wealth.

But then the wealthy, multi-millionaires and millionairesses among them, who book suites in this Palladian-style hotel year after year, don't have to worry about breaching the cardinal, unwritten rule. They come here because they know they will escape the herd and they won't be gaped at or pestered constantly by autograph hunters.

The Sandy Lane will send one of its two Rolls Royces to pick you up at the airport if you are a VIP, or what they term "a valuable previous guest". It's par for the course and taken for granted by the regulars who generally arrive by Concorde, if Irish or English, or in their own private jets if they are super-rich Americans or Arab Princes.

The way to achieve exclusivity in travelling to and from Barbados – if you are Irish or British – is to go by Concorde which cuts the journey from Heathrow to three hours (as against eight hours normal flying time).

I remember this little old English lady was reading the *Sunday Times* near me on the beach around midday one Sunday morning. I couldn't refrain from asking her for the sports section to see the football and racing results. She easily obliged. When I was handing it back to her we got chatting for a moment. She told me that when her millionaire husband was dying, he said to her that they had always lived to a special style, travelling first-class by air – by Concorde when possible – and she had to promise him that she would continue in the grand manner and avoid any hassle. Of course, she would have the chauffeur-driven car.

That morning she had just arrived from London. The pilot apologised to the passengers for saying it would take three hours when they landed five minutes ahead of time. And apologised also for offering only a Chateau Talbot 1978 by way of a claret from Concorde's cellars!

I envied her the ease of it all.

One Arab prince keeps his yacht off the coast for a month. At the same time he books a suite in the Sandy Lane Hotel for the duration of his holiday. He may use it only a handful of times over the four to six weeks – but he can't be bothered to book in and book out again. He simply ensures that he has it when he wants it.

I heard that Pavarotti was so impressed by the service he received from one Bajan waiter at the Sandy Lane that he asked him to join his staff as a butler.

A big furore was caused when Michael Winer in the *Sunday Times* took the Sandy Lane to task principally over the fact that John ('Fawlty Towers') Cleese wasn't allowed into the dining room wearing jeans. But it hadn't caused the alarm bells to sound. Super-rich Americans, as they check out one year, automatically book their suite for the next. I was told on good authority of one English patron who has been holidaying in the hotel for nine years (spending £16,000 sterling for a fortnight) and he hadn't yet managed to get his "dream" suite overlooking the Caribbean. There's such a demand for the most exclusive sea views through the New Year's Eve holiday!

But the Sandy Lane is not the only exclusive hotel patronised by the wealthy. There are members of "the glitterati" who prefer the luxurious Royal Pavilion Hotel – and its wonderful garden, ringed by royal palms that can rise as high as 120 feet over tiger grass lawns; the flamboyant shrubs and flowering cherry trees, with humming birds hovering over them and bougainvillaea gracing the edge of the sandy beach and blue sea. As someone put it aptly: "Who needs the beach when you can sit under a mahogany tree with a book or laze over a rum punch?"

The Royal Pavilion has a sister – Glitter Bay – right next door, but hardly in the same class as the Pavilion. Yet, I met two English people of the racing set who attended the New Year's Eve dinner and show and (taking in their champagne and wine bill) the total came to £600 sterling. This same couple drank two bottles of Dom Perignon one afternoon by the pool – at £100 sterling a bottle! If you think of eight ordering a grand cru at £100 a bottle in the Royal Pavilion soon notched up a wine bill of nearly £2,000 sterling. As my Bajan caddy put it when I sank a long putt on the last:"Yes, we're dancin', man!"

I will retain nostalgic feelings always for the Discovery Bay Hotel for it was here that I stayed with some English racing writers when I was covering the Cockspur Gold Cup, the Island's biggest race of the year.

✶   ✶   ✶

"Life is about timing", said Robert Sangster to me once. He went on to emphasise that the timing was "just right" when he became involved with Vincent O'Brien and John Magnier as the main partners in 'The Syndicate' – established to buy yearlings, mainly American-breds, at sales such as Keeneland – and in the creation of the Coolmore Stud complex.

"We decided we would make our own stallions", recalled Sangster. The dynamic trio were Sangster, Magnier and Vincent O'Brien, though initially Stavros Niarchos, the Greek shipping tycoon was involved.

A three-year plan was devised. The inspired move was the decision to make the best of American blood – Northern Dancer blood especially – available to European breeders through Coolmore. The year 1975 saw the first major assault by The Syndicate on the Keeneland Sales.

The package brought back to Ballydoyle included The Minstrel, Alleged, Artaius and Be My Guest. There were a few outstanding purchases at sales in Europe also. But really the epoch-making event was the successful invasion of Keeneland.

Everything the Sangster-Magnier-O'Brien team touched over a decade from 1975 to 1984 turned to gold. Godswalk, Golden Fleece, El Gran Senor, Sadler's Wells, who was to become one of the most dominant sires in the world.

It's history now how The Minstrel, bought at Keeneland for 200,000 dollars, was syndicated for 9 million dollars... how too the Northern Dancer colt, Storm Bird was sold for 24 million dollars – that is 24 times the original purchase price – the deal being clinched in the suite of American bloodstock agent, George Harris in the Hyatt Regency Hotel in Lexington in the summer of '81 by Vincent O'Brien, John Magnier and Robert Sangster.

By the dawn of the Nineties the heady days for The Syndicate were past and they had to give way to the financial muscle of the Sheikhs. But as the new Millennium approached John Magnier had teamed up with Michael Tabor, the former bookie,now based in Monaco and inspired purchases were made, with the horses being put into training with D. Wayne Lukas in the States and Aidan O'Brien at Ballydoyle. You could never under-estimate the genius of John Magnier when it came to the business he knows best – the making of stallions.

✻   ✻   ✻

If you are a Barbados regular and still fear that you won't find exclusivity in the most sumptuous hotel, you can always rent a plantation-style private villa. The facilities will include a swimming pool, plunge pool/Jacuzzi, private access to the beach, tennis court and staff comprising butler, cook, maid, laundress and security guard.

But remember, it will set you back IR£1,650 a day (yes, a day) if you book a seven-bedroom villa; a three-bedroom villa will cost you IR£620 a day. That's before food and entertainment and, if you're a high roller, you won't escape without holding a dinner party or two for friends and acquaintances.

And if you aren't a member of the Sandy Lane Club, golf isn't cheap at £100 a day. A three-week holiday in the Caribbean sun in high season could easily cost £50,000.

Keen racing enthusiast and owner, Chris De Burgh, I discovered on my 1994 trip, was accustomed to stay in a rented villa when he hit the island. Like Bono he patronised a restaurant with French cuisine (La Maison as it was then) right beside the seashore where he knew he would not be bothered by over-enthusiastic fans.

One evening he was so delighted with the service he received that he sat down and played *Lady in Red* at the piano when everyone had departed except the proprietor and staff.

Bono found his own quiet table in a corner here with the Caribbean waters lapping right up to it and he has returned more than once.

✻   ✻   ✻

The members of "the glitterati" and the high rollers have created their own legends about the high jinks that have taken place in their private parties. Then, as Scott Fitzgerald put it in his immortal phrase, the rich are different.

R.D. Hubbard, the American sporting tycoon – "call me Dee" – who owned the Hollywood race track in California had become renowned for throwing the biggest bash of the week in his magnificent villa. The effects were noticeable the next day on those who graced it as they tried to cure their sore heads!

Dee Hubbard's party back in January '94 was a lead-up to one of the great society weddings of the racing world – that of Billy McDonald to Susan Park in Las Vegas (they would part in '96).

McDonald, now domiciled in California, but a man who makes the world his oyster as he hits the yearling sales, appeared briefly in that classic so-amusing film on the racing and gambling theme, *Let It Ride* (starring Richard Dreyfuss). He won the Amateurs Event in the 1994 in Robert Sangster Pro-Am edging out J.P. McManus, leader for three days, by one shot in the final round. The champagne flowed in style that evening. A number of the high rollers accepted the invitation to fly in Dee Hubbard's private jet to Las Vegas for the wedding.

Hubbard himself made sure, however, that he was going to enjoy the action right up to the eleventh hour and still not miss the meeting of the Dallas Cowboys – he's Texan – and the Buffalo Bills in the Super Bowl '94 at Atlanta. That's where the benefit of having one's own private jet comes in. You can have it waiting on the tarmac to take off at a moment's notice.

＊　　　＊　　　＊

J.P. McManus was not born with the proverbial silver spoon. He made it to the top because he knew how to grasp an opportunity, and showed courage and resilience in face of setbacks. And he had the vital edge also which is required to survive in the jungle, whether it be in the punting or financial sphere.

In my book *The High Rollers Of The Turf* I chronicled how J.P. caught the gambling bug as far back as his primary school days in Roxboro National School in Limerick and how his education as a punter continued outside of school hours when he went to Sexton Street Christian Brothers in Limerick. He was only 20 when he acquired a bookmaker's licence. He was "skint" not just once but twice after he started as a bookie. His mother lent him a few hundred pounds and, as he has recalled, "I suppose I had more respect for it than for any money I ever had before or since in my pocket".

He was never skint again. "Granted, I was often very, very short of money but there is a world of difference between having just a little in your pocket and being flat broke with nowhere to turn".

He combined his role as a bookie with punting. Jimmy Hayes of Fethard was the brilliant student of the Form Book and was "Butch" to J.P.'s

"Sundance" – an inseparable pair in the Seventies who liked nothing better than to go gunning after the bookies but they did not aim to go down in a blaze of glory, in the betting sense, as Newman And Redford did in the classic Western.

J.P. graduated in time to becoming a leading rails' bookie but sold his pitches to his brother when he moved to Geneva. Today, he hardly gambles at all in Ireland. His main punting operations are confined to Cheltenham, Liverpool and Royal Ascot.

$$* \quad * \quad *$$

Time is of the essence to J.P. McManus. Because time can mean money.

That is why communications are vital in his life and he has them as he wants them in the working day in Geneva.

That is why too it's essential that he has easy access by air to any destination he wants to reach.

If needs be he will incur the cost of hiring a private jet to make travel easier and cut out the hassle involved in making too many connections. Thus he knows he will arrive for the key discussions more relaxed and in a better frame of mind. If a deal is concluded successfully, it can make the outlay look quite meagre. In a word, the cost factor must be balanced against the level of the negotiations one is involved in – and in J.P.'s case they can be at a very high level, especially in the financial sphere.

As far as he is concerned, it's all a question of convenience.

Life is action for J.P. McManus. It's nothing if he is not involved in the action – all the time. And in the High Sierras.

When he makes a call on the mobile phone while you are having breakfast with him in Geneva or takes one at dinner in the evening, it can mean that money has been made or lost.

He will never flinch when there's a world to win and lose in a fourball on the golf course.

An action guy – right down the line. And when the long putt goes in that nets the pot, I'm reminded again of my Bajan caddy:"Yes, we're dancin', man!"

24

'Mincemeat Joe' To 'The Coal' And The Moss Bank Gamble

'**M**incemeat Joe' Griffin was one of the biggest gamblers of his day – in the early Fifties - but a classic case of a mug punter.

Like Terry Ramsden, who came after him and who spurned all the dictums on betting that the professionals would regard as sacrosanct he was picked clean by the bookmakers as the vultures pick clean the bones of a dead body under the hot desert sun. One year after Jack Swift had framed the cheque he sent to 'Mincemeat Joe', the same bookmaker was in the position that Griffin had liabilities extending to £65,000 to him. That in itself gives an idea of the extraordinary level of 'Mincemeat Joe's' gambling.

When Vincent O'Brien told 'Mincemeat Joe' that Early Mist would win the 1953 Aintree Grand National, the intrepid Dubliner backed the horse to win £100,000 – an absolute fortune in those days – in just two bets with English bookmakers, Wilf Sherman and Jack Swift. The latter had the cheque framed in his office.

In the period 1950 to 1953 the man to whom they gave the tag of "Lucky' achieved what members of the aristocracy and money barons had spent their lives trying to achieve and yet failed to realise. He won the Grand National not just once but twice in succession and could have made it three-in-a-row had he taken the advice of Vincent O'Brien and purchased Quare Times when it was offered to him of £2,5000 – and if his fortunes had not taken a plunge in the meantime.

In three short years he won £65,000 in stake money and winning bets brought that figure well beyond the £100,000 mark. Multiply it by ten and you can quickly calculate that he was in the millionaire class as a successful owner.

He was born in Dublin's Montague Street – the kind of area immortalised in Sean O'Casey's *Juno and the Paycock* and *The Plough and the Stars*. He was christened Joseph Harold Griffin but from the time he was nine years old, he was known as nothing else but "Lucky" Joe. The "Mincemeat" tag would come later. On the strength of a borrowed £16 he built an export empire that would make him the envy of men who knew more about business and figures than Joe had even begun to learn.

He remembered always what his mother had said to him when be bought two tickets at a Christmas raffle at the age of 9 and won the hamper: "Joe, it's better to be born lucky than rich".

Subsequently, he never forgot belief in his own star and the feeling that his luck would always hold became almost pathological.

At one stage he had 500 workers employed in the Tallaght factory of his Redbreast Preserving Company.

The tragic climax culminated on Black Friday in July, 1954 when he was adjudged as bankrupt and he closed the door for the last time on his magnificent Georgian residence, Knocklyon House, standing on 24 acres with orchards, paddocks and gardens, which he has bought for £8,000 and on which he had lavished £60,000 in decorating and renovating it to palatial standards (its accommodation included four reception rooms, eight family bedrooms, a ballroom and a billiard room).

Two bailiffs, on the Sheriff's instructions, had gone to Vincent O'Brien's Ballydoyle stables and impounded all Joe's horses, including Grand National winner, Royal Tan. Joe looked on helplessly as all his other possessions – even down to his racing binoculars – passed into the hands of the bankruptcy court's official assignee. Subsequently his two Grand National Gold Cup trophies – gold cups each weighing 50 ozs – were auctioned in Dublin.

At the sale of the Griffin horses, Royal Tan was knocked down to the representative of Prince Aly Khan for 3,900 guineas and Early Mist was sold for 2,000 guineas to Vincent O'Brien, who also bought Galatian. "I like to keep old friends", said the trainer.

It was undoubtedly his blackest hour.

But there had been a time when it seemed that the days of wine and roses would last forever.

*   *   *

Joe was small and stocky with twinkling eyes – the direct opposite of the archetype business tycoon. But he had a sharp brain and that native Dublin cunning that made him see a good business opportunity.

In the food shortages that still persisted after the Second World War, the English hankered for 'goodies' that were taken for granted in Ireland. "Joe, we haven't seen mince pies for years", an English friend remarked to him. His mind immediately began to tick over.

He bought on 'tick' from the Greek Government a £100,000 shipload of dried fruit, a cancelled order from a British grocery chain. He used the fruit in mince pies and sold the product in jars to the same British grocers for £20,000. It was easy to pay the Greek Government on the resultant profit. Joe was on his way with the tag of "Mincemeat" that he never subsequently lost.

The Redbreast Preserving Company was on the crest of a wave for a time, turning over, according to Joe Griffin; "£1/2 million to £2 million a year in exports for three years and that at the time was a lot of money coming into the country for a single exporter".

After the fall, however, Joe would admit: "I had no background training for big business. I had nobody to help me – it was a one-man show. I brought in an accountant whom I hoped would have been able to keep everything on a proper legal and financial footing. I had the brains to do things and to sell but I lacked the experience to control the finance."

During the bankruptcy hearing Joe had to spend a month in jail for contempt, having, in the opinion of Mr Justice Budd, failed to answer the court's questions satisfactorily.

Men and women who had cheered him the night he came home to a hero's welcome to his native city, heading Early Mist in the great victory parade through Dublin's O'Connell Street, now watched in silence as 'Mincemeat' Joe was led away to prison between two Gardai after saying goodbye to his weeping wife. All he carried with him were his pyjamas and shaving kit in a small bag.

Many friends deserted the ship. The hangers-on had long since gone.

$$* \qquad * \qquad *$$

Even jail for contempt did not end the torture and torment. He was to find himself behind bars again after purging his contempt. At one point he received a six months' suspended sentence for a forged £20 cheque and then went to prison for fraud.

During his twelve months in Mountjoy Prison, his spirit never broke. He managed to survive.

Again far from the adulation and back-slapping he had enjoyed at Aintree on the days that Early Mist and Royal Tan triumphed, he had to listen to one Grand National on a transistor radio in the recreation yard in Mountjoy.

"I know I gave everyone the winner of that race. All the prison warders had backed it and there was great cheering when it came in. Naturally, I was treated with the height of respect in Mountjoy. I was the Lord of the Manor."

He even claimed that he had been put in charge of the kitchen and the cooking in Mountjoy. When he was leaving the officer in charge said to him: 'Joe, I hope you won't come back but if you do, you'll come straight down here to the kitchen because you're the best cook we ever had'!'

In Mountjoy jail he had ample time to remember the Camelot days...the fabulous victory parties in the Adelphi Hotel in Liverpool (the bash after Early Mist had triumphed in 1953 costing £1,500)...the success his Redbreast Preserving Company was enjoying with profits running in the region of £1,000 a day with the result that money had lost its value for him and, as he put it, "you just spend and spend". There was never a cloud in the sky.

On the morning of the 1953 Grand National, Peggy Griffin handed Bryan Marshal a St. Christopher medal and said to him – "Well, if you don't win, at least don't break your neck".

Bryan won by 20 lengths and received a present of £5,000 as Joe Griffin netted a six-figure sum in winning bets.

Joe and Peggy gave a diamond bracelet in platinum, worth £1,000 then, to Joe's secretary, Rose O'Duffy and later it would emerge in the bankruptcy court that Rose pledged the bracelet for £600 and gave a loan from this money to Mrs. Griffin.

The parties in the Adelphi were followed by Joe taking over the bar on the boat home and it was free drinks for everyone.

There were homecoming parties too in the Gresham Hotel and in the Kilcoran Lodge Hotel in Cahir, County Tipperary with bonfires blazing and bands out to lead the victory parades.

Yes, 'Mincemeat Joe' had a lot to remember during the hours he spent in his cell in Mountjoy Prison...

He left Ireland in the early Sixties after – as he put it himself – "the life and soul had been squeezed out of me by the lawyers and the creditors".

"I am on the way back," said Joe about fifteen years later, no doubt convincing himself that his mother's original words would somehow come true again for him.

He even dreamed of winning a third Aintree Grand National – "to beat 'Teasy Weasy' Raymond and the other owners who had won the race twice. Yes, I am going to win it for the third time."

He never did make it back to the big-time. Like Willie Loman he continued to live a dream that was never to be realised.

He died quietly in London in January, 1992 at the age of 75.

✻   ✻   ✻

Tommy O'Brien, known as 'Tommy Coal', 'The Coalminer' or simply 'The Coal' blazed a trail as one of the biggest gamblers to hit the Irish ring in the Sixties. By today's money values, some of his most spectacular wins and losses were absolutely astounding.

He returned from Cheltenham in 1960 with winnings totalling £30,000. I checked with the Economics Department of the Central Bank to ascertain what that would represent when I was writing my book *The High Rollers Of The Turf* in 1992 and the answer came back £385,240".

He waded in on Irish winners like Albergo (7/4), Fortria(15/8) and Solfen (5/4) when winning the Broadway Novices Chase and again when taking the Spa Hurdle the following day at 5/2. He rang up his private trainer, Willie Treacy in Clonmel to tell him with glee: "I've won so much that I can't lose now, as the bookies won't take any more bets from me".

But there were other Cheltenhams, other racing days that were disastrous. He was another classic mug punter in the sense that he didn't know when to fold when he was ahead. Compulsion was his middle name. Nothing illustrates this better than a day at the Curragh in April, 1960 when his own horse, Miss MacDonald won the April Scurry Handicap.

O'Brien took £22,000 out of the ring and in the flush of winning that amount he was hell bent on aiming for the moon. He ended up owing the bookies £30,000. (At the time I was editing Tommy's own paper, the *Munster Tribune* from its Clonmel office for around £10,000 a year and here was the proprietor losing in one afternoon more than I could earn in three years).

No wonder that Willie Treacy should say to me with a tinge of regret in his voice when we met for a long morning's conversation in Clonmel in the summer of '92: "If Tommy O'Brien could have confined himself to backing his own when we had them fit and ready to win, he would have stayed ahead of the bookies. But he was an inveterate gambler and was never prepared to shut up shop when in front."

Tommy O'Brien, who was born in County Mayo, had come back in the Fifties from England, where he had gained ample experience in mining, to re-open the Ballingarry mines in South Tipperary. A Clonmel man who knew him well told me that Tommy made a lot of money in Britain by getting the contract to demolish after the Second World War buildings that had been left in a dangerous condition after the blitz. He actually hit Clonmel with a case-full of readies.

By dint of hard work and a real go-go attitude, he proved that a local area in County Tipperary could be resuscitated in an era of depressing emigration. He had soon turned the Ballingarry mines into a going concern, giving good employment in the locality.

Giving him the appelation "Tommy Coal" distinguished him from the other Tommy O'Brien of Clonmel, who was a national institution from his popular radio programme, which gave so much pleasure and helped to popularise Opera throughout Ireland. Once a visitor to Clonmel stopped his car in the centre of the town to seek directions to Tommy O'Brien's house and a wit standing at the street corner, asked him:"Do you mean 'Tommy Coal' or "Tommy Ceoil'?"

Tommy O'Brien, that is Tommy of the Ballingarry mines and the *Munster Tribune*, lived with his wife Mary – they had no family – in Woodruff House about five miles outside Clonmel. The house and magnificent estate going with it had belonged to a Mrs. Masters. Tommy O'Brien set out to create on the land the finest gallops imaginable and stabling for fifteen horses. Willie Treacy, who had been riding over the jumps for fifteen years, both in England and Ireland, became his private trainer and they would enjoy a very rewarding partnership together, landing some outstanding coups. "He was a genius in many ways, a man with a great brain who was well ahead of his time in the way he could see things," said Willie Treacy. "He would buy into a share when you couldn't give it away and in that way, I know, he cleaned up. Despite what he lost in the end through gambling, he was always comfortable and he left so much to

Mary that she didn't have to worry."

Tommy O'Brien was a man brusque of manner, with no airs or graces. But there was a spontaneous and very generous side to his nature – seen in his kindness to renowned racecourse characters of his day like "Buckets", "Big Andy" and "The Toucher".

✳   ✳   ✳

There are few episodes in the history of great racing gambles to compare with Tommy O'Brien's bid to clear £100,000 on the 1961 Champion Hurdle on his own horse Moss Bank – and, remember, that by today's values that would have been equivalent to taking £1 million out of the ring, if he had succeeded.

So certain was he of bringing it off that he had booked a luxury cruise for his wife Mary and himself in the immediate aftermath of the Cheltenham meeting.

All through the winter he had been taking all available ante-post odds on Moss Bank, which had been bred by Frank Tuthill, then the Senior Irish Racing Judge, who sold him as a foal at Ballsbridge for 635 guineas. There was no doubting the fact that he was a horse with a touch of class. His half-brother, Gustav won the 1961 Middle Park Stakes At Newmarket.

O'Brien's confidence increased when Moss Bank, ridden by Doug Page, won the Dolphin Hurdle at the Leopardstown meeting at 4/6. Now more than ever he was going for the jugular and he laughed inwardly at the thought of the bookies going pale at the gills as Moss Bank stormed up the hill to a great "Irish roar" come Champion Hurdle Day at Cheltenham.

With Doug Page committed to ride Albergo in the 'Champion', Johnny Rafferty had the mount on Moss Bank, wearing the familiar O'Brien Cross of Lorraine colours. Rafferty in his day had been a wonderful horseman with a wonderful pair of hands but he would die at a tragically young age. His symmetry of style in the saddle was a joy to watch as he brought one to the last hurdle for a thrilling victory. Sadly, he would become a victim of the demon drink like others in this game.

However, there is no denying that he would have won on Moss Bank had Tommy O'Brien not insisted that he hold the horse up for a late run. Rafferty should have been allowed ride a tactical race, changing course as the race evolved if needs be.

As Rafferty came to a challenging position approaching the second last, Albergo fell at this flight. Moss Bank had to swerve to avoid him. It meant that Rafferty had to start his run all over again. Moss Bank was eating up the ground at the finish but had too much to do and was beaten three lengths.

Victory went to the 4/1 shot Eborneezer, trained by Ryan Price and ridden by Fred Winter.

Tommy O'Brien went ahead with the luxury cruise. When Willie Treacy conveyed to him, before they parted at Cheltenham, that the losses on Moss Bank could be recouped on Antirrhinum "tried a certainty" to win the

251

Portmarnock Handicap at Balydoyle on St. Patrick's Day, O'Brien told him:"Tell Michael O'Hehir to do the commission for me and that I want £10,000 on".

Michael O'Hehir managed to get £7,000 on at 7/1 and £49,000 was an immense amount of money to take out of the ring on one race in 1961. Antirrhinum, with Peadar Matthews in the saddle, started at 6/1 and won easily by three lengths from the Charlie Weld-trained favourite, Flower-De-Luce in a field of fifteen. Unplaced, incidentally, was Le Levanstell who later the same year in the Queen Elizabeth II Stakes at Ascot beat the 2/9 favourite Petite Etoile (Lester Piggott).

Bill Quinlan was the rails bookie with whom he was always doing battle and nothing gave him greater pleasure than to see Quinlan moan when he pulled off a good gamble though in the end Bill got the better of the argument.

However, Tommy O'Brien did so well out of shares and other investments that there was no debt to any bookmaker that wasn't fully cleared.

One of his closest friends, incidentally, was Dan Breen, a legendary figure in Ireland's War for Independence.

Tommy moved to Kinsale but because of his nature wasn't satisfied just enjoying the company of "the boating set". He was too down-to-earth. He needed a challenge always. Soon he was back running an earth-moving business.

He loved Clonmel. One day he was heading there for the vintage car rally – the one they knew as the stone thrower's rally. But first there was a job to be done. Tommy wanted to see it completed and took the wheel of a tractor himself when there was no need for him to do so. Again his impetuous nature had got the better of him. He drove it down a sharp incline into a pit. It turned over and he was crushed under it.

He had been a High Roller in the true sense...long before J.P. (The Sundance Kid) McManus, Noel Furlong and Barney Curley became household names.

When I was researching *The High Rollers Of The Turf* I met his widow Mary O'Brien, a gracious lady, living quietly with her memories in a lovely bungalow-style home on Ireland's south coast. Talking to her, you form the immediate impression that Tommy is still very much alive for her.

But then could it be otherwise?"The Coalminer" was larger than life, one who left an indelible imprint as one of the most fearless – if compulsive – gamblers of his era.

Whenever the cards are cut in the Donoughmore Club in Clonmel, they talk affectionately of one Tommy O'Brien...and memories come flooding back of great poker "schools" in which he was involved on long winter evenings.

Yes, the legend of "The Coalminer" still lives on.

✳   ✳   ✳

Tim O'Toole was a gambler from Ireland's Midlands area who was not content just to aim at the moon but wanted to conquer the Galaxy. In the end this proved his undoing.

In any book on mug punters he would figure very prominently but the irony of it was that he had knowledge – tremendous knowledge of horses but he could not apply limits and neither was he satisfied with winning a set amount. Laying off to reduce the risk wasn't part of his vocabulary.

The O'Toole tragedy – with a capital "T" – lay in the fact that while he lived for nothing else only the continuing "war" with the bookies, he eschewed the basic dictums by which the true professionals operate and he never knew when to shut up shop.

Thus, for example, if he won at the horses at Leopardstown or the Curragh, he would head straight for the dogs at Shelbourne Park to play up his winnings and from there it was nothing for him to take a flight to London to play Punto Banco in some private club.

On one occasion when both the horses and the dogs had gone badly for him, he decided that he would try and get it all back in London. He arrived at his favourite club late. He thought he could bet at the Punto Banco table until 4 o'clock in the morning but he was told politely:"Tonight, Mr O'Toole the law states that we must end at 2 o'clock and no later".

His protests went unheeded. To placate him they laid on the Rolls-Royce to bring him to his hotel. They understood, of course, from the level of his betting, that he would probably be staying in the Dorchester, the Savour or the Cumberland. In actual fact, not being unduly fussy where he slept, he had booked into a place in Soho that never made it to any of the "good hotel guides".

The driver of the Rolls-Royce left him at a taxi rank near Piccadilly with the immortal comment: "They'll know, Sir, where your hotel is!"

Alex Bird, as we have seen, always asserted that doubles, trebles and accumulators were "for the mugs". But that dictum of one of the most successful of all post-War professional gamblers didn't deter Tim O'Toole from investing in crazy trebles that spanned not only racing but soccer and tennis. And, contrary to all set principles, he netted £48,000 through one of them in the Seventies.

He had successfully picked Night Nurse to win the 1976 Champion Hurdle, Wollow the English 2000 Guineas that same year, and Liverpool the English Division 1 title. He admitted to really 'sweating it out' the night Liverpool met Wolves in the very last game at Molineaux to decide the Championship (Liverpool. incidentally, won 3-1 and Wolves were relegated in the process). "I didn't take any chances but laid off to ensure a profit anyway even if Wolves won," he said.

He had gone for a win of £70,000 (he showed me the docket) on another treble, and two legs came up – Flying Water winning the 1976 English 1000 Guineas, Wollow the 2000 Guineas and Malinowski, his choice to win the Epsom Derby did not run.

The Dewhurst Stakes, he told me, was the race each October that had opened the way for some of his biggest and most successful ante-post gambles. "The Dewhurst has thrown up more than one 2000 Guineas and Derby winner," he said.

Wollow's win over Malinowski in the 1975 Dewhurst convinced him that he had seen the 1976 English 2000 Guineas winner – and also the potential Epsom Derby winner in Malinowski.

The trip to Newmarket certainly paid off, as we have seen, in Wollow providing the basis for a £48,000 treble – and we can only wonder would the £70,000 treble have come off, if Malinowski had taken part in the Derby.

There was tragedy in Tim O'Toole's inability to control his gambling and tragedy in his passing – but wherever racing men gather in Ireland to reminisce about fearless punters and born characters, his name invariably arises.

He was likeable, always good company and really only lived for one thing in life – tilting at the ring and at the tables in the clubs which true professionals of the racing game avoid because they know the edge is not with them.

25

Curley and Furlong And "The Flyer" Begley

Barney Curley derives no greater joy from life than in taking on the bookies and making them squirm. It causes the adrenalin to flow in a manner that he could never experience if he spent his life chasing wealth for wealth's sake and accumulating all its trappings

It could be a Buddhist monk talking as he looks at you intently from those deep-set eyes under the shaven domed head and elaborates on his beliefs: "I don't believe in gathering a whole lot of earthly possessions that I know I can't bring with me to the after-life.

"Answer me this – have you ever seen anyone cross the Divide carrying antiques, oil paintings, line drawings and share certificates and anything else you care to name that is associated with having money in the bank? No bookmaker will quote you a price on that happening!"

It wouldn't cost him a thought if he cleaned out a particular bookmaker and sent him to the poorhouse. And I suspect that nothing would give him greater pleasure than if he overwhelmed Ladbrokes – if that were possible – in one glorious strike as Stormin' Norman so swiftly won the Gulf War.

But the same man would be spontaneous in his generosity to a broken bookmaker and his family. You see, just as belief in an after-life is an integral part of his make-up, so is helping charitable causes and lame-duck individuals.

Terry Ramsden was down on his luck, broken by the financial markets and the bookmakers, when Barney Curley bought his Stetchworth home at the outskirts of Newmarket from him. He purchased it before it went to public auction and he admits he got it for "a reasonable price".

"No, I wouldn't have had the money to buy if I had to bid the price it would have gone at an auction".

As he brought me on a tour through the house and the adjoining stables and showed me the spot in a back lot where Ramsden once had his helicopter pad, he turned suddenly and remarked: "The name of the game is SURVIVAL. I have managed to survive – so far".

"When I used to meet Terry Ramsden at race meetings and see the way he was gambling, observing none of the rules that true professionals observe. I told him again and again that he was a madman and that the bookies would get him without fail. He wouldn't listen. They cleaned him out."

Terry Ramsden, the flamboyant cockney who was dubbed "Little Tel" and "Our Tel" by the British tabloids was big as an owner at one stage – and awesome in the level of his gambling. In three short years before the money ran out in 1987, it was estimated that he lost a staggering £57 million to the bookmakers. It was nothing for Ramsden at his peak to have £100,000 on one of his horses. Once he netted £1.5 million on winning bets on one horse and little wonder that the Racing post described him as "the biggest punter in the history of the Turf".

The final irony was that, having gambled away between £57 million and £80 million during his career as a racehorse owner and big-time punter, he was warned off by the Stewards of the Jockey Club for a "mere" £2 million – a sum he would have views as "small change" in the heady days of his glittering performance in securities trading. Ladbrokes pulled the plug on him in the racing sense when they took him to Tattersall's Committee, the Jockey Club's watch-dog Committee to which the bookies turn when someone defaults on betting liabilities. When he had the cash all the big bookies wanted his business because they knew he was a mug punter and no one was ready to try and stop him plunging over the precipice. In a word, he had unlimited credit while he could meet his commitments.

At his peak Ramsden had 75 horses in training and was listed in Money magazine as Britain's 57th richest individual, with a fortune estimated at £87 to £100 million.

Ramsden generated an estimated £3 billion turnover in Japanese warrants in the period 1979-'85. The awesome scale of his operations on the international stock market can best be gauged from the fact that when Glen International crashed on "Black Monday" October, '87, there were accumulated losses of £142.2 million and Ramsden faced personal liabilities of some £98 million on deals worth £343 million.

He was only 36 at the time of the fall.

Barney Curley felt for Terry Ramsden in the same way as he felt for his own father when he was 'skint' at the dogs.

Engraved indelibly in Barney's mind is the memory of the evening in Belfast's Celtic Park when his father lost everything on one make-or-break tilt on a dog he owned himself.

"He had £300 on at 7/1. Sheer disaster befell him when the dog broke his neck at the first bend. I can still see my father carrying the dead dog up the track and inside I knew he was weeping for his shattered hopes".

Barney Curley was home on holiday from boarding school when that happened. Being the eldest of six children (his parents ran a local grocery store in Irvinstown, County Fermanagh), he was taken out of the school and crossed to Manchester with his father to raise the money to clear the gambling debts.

"We lived in one room together, working double shifts in a plastics factory for fifteen months until we had raised enough money to allow my father to come home with the knowledge that he could hold his head high again in the local community because he owed no one anything. But it had affected him so deeply, it had caused such an inner wound that he wouldn't return to Irvinstown until he had bought himself a new suit. And even then he couldn't face the challenge of walking through the town. He got a friend to pick him up in his car and drop him home".

Barney Curley swore he would never be broken by the bookies. In a way every time he has hit them for six with spectacular coups, he has been settling that old score for the way his father was made suffer, especially in those grinding days of work in Manchester – the days that Barney had shared and which proved a university of life that was incomparable in its own way.

✳   ✳   ✳

I chronicled in my book, *The High Rollers Of The Turf* how he went to Mungret College in Limerick to study to become a Jesuit...was well on his way to becoming a priest when he contracted T.B....was sent to a special hospital in Northern Ireland and was lucky that they'd just discovered a cure...it took him another eighteen months to get back to health...he returned to the Seminary briefly but wasn't strong enough to finish the gruelling studies to become a Jesuit priest...he packed it in at 24 and became manager of a band on the road, touring the Ballrooms of Romance...and recalls proudly how Frankie McBride, under his management, became the first Irish showband singer to get a record into the British Top Ten.

Barney Curley met and married Maureen who was from Cheshire of Irish parentage and the daughter of a bookmaker.

Barney was still gambling even when on the road.

He hit a lucky streak. It saw him take a cool £100,000 from the bookies. He was able to buy three pubs with the money. But that didn't satisfy him. Neither did the life of running a betting shop.

One night Maureen and himself were lying in bed and Barney asked her if it would affect her attitude towards him if he became a full-time professional gambler? Her reaction was that whatever he decided was best, she would go along with it. She had faith in him. She trusted him.

So Barney Curley became a professional gambler and has been one now for almost a quarter of a century.

He won between £200,000 and £250,000 at the 1992 Cheltenham Festival meeting, principally through substantial wagers on Royal Gait and Keep Talking.

But he lost £250,000 by backing against Golden Fleece winning the 1982 Epsom Derby and the same week gave a further £100,000 to the bookies in losing wagers.

Rather than being tempted to take an overdose, he flew with his wife and family to California for a holiday and came back refreshed in mind and spirit and "rarin' to go".

Curley took £200,000 out of the ring when he trained Assultan to win the Snow Hill Handicap Hurdle at Ascot on November 19, 1988. The four-year-old carried 10st 1lb in a field of 13 and was backed down from 4/1 to 5/2 favourite. It was one of Curley's most fearless gambles.

But when he has passed on, he will be remembered as the man who masterminded the "Yellow Sam Coup" at Bellewstown.

Curley's Yellow Sam hadn't shown any form in his nine previous outings. It wasn't surprising that he should be unconsidered in the betting for an ordinary handicap hurdle event at one of Ireland's smaller tracks.

Curley had his trusted "troops" lay bets on the nose in the S.P. offices – bets of £30 £40 and £50 mostly. In all, the bookies were cleaned to the tune of between £250,000 and £300,000.

By 1975 levels it was an awful lot of bread.

The S.P. bookies who at the point hadn't their own blower system (that is their own lines into the track) were thwarted from getting any money back to the ring to reduce the starting odds. If the "blower" had been operating, Yellow Sam would have started at odds-on.

"You see there was only one phone line to the Bellewstown track", Curley himself explained to me. "There was this heavily-built man, a tough sort of guy, who suddenly discovered that a close relation of his was seriously ill and he had to keep in constant touch with the hospital. Once he had the phone in his hand he was not going to let go. He was broad enough in the beam not to permit anyone past him into the box. You could trust him with your life in a situation like that!".

Curley flatly rejects all insinuations that there was anything morally wrong with what he claims was a beautifully-executed "stroke".

"Look, if the bookies had got even the slightest hint that money was being laid in the offices, they would have been forewarned and it would have been a case of 'no show' Yellow Sam.

"Because we thwarted them in getting a whiff of gunsmoke in the air as we went for the kill, they moaned afterwards. Naturally, they'd moan. They always do when you go for the jugular and leave them gasping.

"They know as well as I do that the Yellow Sam Coup could not be brought off today with the more sophisticated blower system for getting money from the offices back to the tracks. It was because of that very coup that they had to learn to update the system and that when there is only one phone into a racetrack, some guy is going to discover that his dear old granny is dying and he just has to hog it for the duration!"

✳   ✳   ✳

With the money from "The Yellow Sam Coup" and other successful gambles, Curley was able to move from Ashford, County Wicklow and buy Midleton Park, a 30-room stately Georgian mansion set in almost 380 acres of County Westmeath countryside, 50 miles from Dublin. It was once owned by the Boyd Rochfort family, trainers of the Queen of England's horses and it had family connections also with Lawrence of Arabia. The house came complete with 50 horse boxes and sheds for 300 cattle.

Nothing has ever matched the headlines commanded by Barney Curley when he decided to raffle Midleton Park – and ran foul of the law in the process, bringing Michael O'Hehir, who performed the act of drawing the winning tickets, into Ballinarcargy court with him for a case that seemed to have a global spotlight on it.

He sold 9,000 tickets. It was estimated that the raffle netted a gross £2 million. After allowing for costs, Curley was reported by the media to have cleared £1 million and, taking into account what he originally paid for Midleton Park, he would have banked £500,000 at least.

Curley contended that it would not be a lottery if an element of skill was introduced. So, everyone who bought a ticket was asked a number of questions, like:"Name the winner of last year's Derby?"

Barney Curley walked out of the courthouse at Ballinarcargy on July 5, 1984 with a three months jail sentence hanging over his head. He appealed and it was November by the time the appeal was heard. Barney had to face up to the thought that he might be spending Christmas '84 in prison.

With the application of the Probation Act by Judge O'Malley, Curley left Mullingar Court breathing a big sigh of relief.

He moved to England to start training – not horses of Premiership class, on his own admission, but Third Division status (and they would have been of Fourth Division calibre before the Premiership was inaugurated!). Only by landing clever-executed coups was he able to survive and through his operations as a professional gambler generally.

"Life would be meaningless if I didn't believe in a God and there was no after-life", he said to me when I talked to him in his seven-bedroom mansion with its indoor swimming pool and snooker table at Stetchworth on a lovely sunny morning during the July '91 Newmarket meeting.

What kind of God did he believe in? "For me he's a merciful God. At the same time, let me make it clear that I am not the sort of chap who thinks that you will go straight to heaven if you spend half-an-hour every Sunday inside the door of a church. As far as I am concerned belief is a very searching and personal business".

Now I asked him about his concept of Heaven? "I visualise it as a place that you can count yourself very lucky – if you get there. I like to think of it as a great peaceful garden where you never have to worry about anything anymore".

"And Hell, Barney?" I asked tentatively.

"I think it must be very, very hard to get into hell," came his reply. "I mean you would have to be an intrinsically evil person – I mean very evil – and unconcerned about doing the most terrible things against your fellow-man before you would be consigned by what I view as a merciful God to eternal darkness.

"Most people have the best of intentions. The just man falls not just seven times but seven times seven, we are told. So I can only conclude that about one in a million – the ratio might even be higher – end up in hell".

The depth of his belief was to be greatly tested later when his only son, Charles (20) was killed when the car skidded on ice. I had met Charles on that visit and realised how much he meant to Barney and Maureen (they have two other children Katherine and Marie-Louise). I sat down and wrote a personal letter, one which I hoped would help in very sad and traumatic days.

Tommy Stack and his son James ("Fozzie") along with Billy Dowling of Thurles had travelled over to be with Barney Curley as his son was interred. So also had Barneys great punter friend "The Flyer" Begley.

Barney Curley came over to Dundalk for the funeral of "The Flyer" when he passed away suddenly in the Spring of 1996. It was extremely difficult, coming not all that long after the funeral of his own son. But he did it and the Begley family will never forget him for it.

✳   ✳   ✳

"The Flyer" Begley, who had had a heart by-pass operation some years back, had been at the Leopardstown meeting on the Sunday, March 3rd. He wasn't feeling very well afterwards and booked himself into a Dublin hospital for an angeogram the next morning.

His daughter, a student in Dublin, called to see him and he instructed her to make sure that friends of his saw to it that he was "on" the Barney Curley "good thing" which he knew had been laid out for an up-coming race in England. She promised her father that this and all other instructions would be carried out. He gave her the money to take a taxi home.

That night he took a bad turn and did not survive.

Curley's "good thing", running in his wife's colours, was named appropriately All Talk And No Action – only that this one first of all set the ring alight as it was backed from 10/1 down to 4/1 and then cruised into action in the race itself, moving to the front approaching the final flight and leaving his rivals for dead as he won going away by ten lengths. On his form in three outings in '93, he hardly inspired confidence as a betting medium and he had not been seen on a racecourse since.

For the record the race was a selling handicap hurdle at Folkestone and "The Flyer" had reason to rub his hands in delight somewhere up there in the Great Beyond at how Barney could deliver when he went to the well.

"The Flyer's" sudden passing spread like wild-fire among his wide circle of friends. They came from all parts of Ireland for the funeral. He was in the cattle business but you felt that it was almost incidental to his first love – having a cut on horses he fancied. It gave him immense pleasure to have a successful tilt at the ring or bring off an S.P. job but he could take on the chin the hammer-blows of the game as well.

He would have enjoyed being there as his friends swapped yarns about the poker games he was involved in – he loved nothing better than a game of cards with associates – and his love of gaelic football.

No better yarn was spun than the one about the time he gave the referee such verbal "stick" from the sideline that the man with the whistle couldn't endure it any longer. He not alone ordered "The Flyer" from the ground but banned him from attending the next match. It resulted in "The Flyer" handing his mobile phone to his daughter and telling her to give him a running commentary on the game as he sat at home on tenterhooks for the duration...

"He loved the racing scene and the action in the ring", recalled his friend, Sean Shields of Cootehill. "He was a fearless gambler and was prepared to put it down when he believed there was one to bet on. The bookies respected him when he went into action as he had plenty of inside information. He never missed the Cheltenham Festival meeting or the Aintree Grand National meeting and Royal Ascot was another big favourite of his.

"It was a tribute to him that a bunch of the boys – bookies included – went to the Management of Navan racecourse after his death and suggested that a minute's silence be observed as a mark of respect to his memory at an evening meeting. It wasn't taken up. Naturally they were surprised and disappointed.

"But he will be remembered with great affection by all who knew him. He was a larger than life character – one who saw racing and having a punt as an integral part of life, indeed one who saw life as nothing really without the risk element is involved in betting in having a keen interest in football and having a game of cards with friends. Guys like 'The Flyer' leave their own storehouse of memories and legends".

✳   ✳   ✳

Noel Furlong is a BIG man. He is big and swarthy physically. They knew him simply as "Big Noel" in the days when he was deeply involved in dog racing in Belfast. "It was natural, I suppose, when there seemed to be so many small guys frequenting the tracks", said a friend who added with a smile: "No, you could never describe him as a *wee mon*".

Noel Furlong in time would get out of the dogs because "he couldn't get on", to quote one of his friends. "Immediately a Furlong dog went up on the boards, it would almost invariably open at 4/6, if not less".

Another friend told us: "If Noel was £10,000 down going into the last and wanted to have £15,000 to £10,000 on a 6/4 shot or even £30,000 to £20,000 on a 4/6 shot to get out, there was no way he could get that kind of money on. Really, it was hopeless".

So he came south and today he is big in the world of carpets. You have only to visit his giant warehouse on the industrial estate off the Naas road to realise how big he is. He even has carpets made to his own specifications as far away as Pakistan. All the time big trucks come and go, either supplementing supplies or heading off to meet orders that come in from various parts.

Noel Furlong will always be remembered for "The Illiad Gamble". To this day he laughs heartily at the way he had the bookies literally shaking to the soles of their feet at the prospect of facing the biggest pay-out in racing history – globally – had The Illiad won the 1991 Smurfit Champion Hurdle at the Cheltenham Festival meeting.

First of all, Furlong caught the bookies with their pants down when he won £1 million in a "morning board prices" coup on The Illiad in the 1991 Ladbroke Handicap Hurdle at Leopardstown.

With these winnings at his back, he took a reputed £1 million out of the ring when backing Destriero at odds of 6/1 and better to win the Supreme Novices' Hurdle at Cheltenham '91.

He had separately coupled Destriero in doubles with The Illiad to win a further £4 million.

"You may only get one chance in life of a real killing – catching the bookies for the kind of gamble from which they will not easily recover", he told me. "I went for that kind of touch in doubling Destriero with The Illiad. I knew that Destriero was as near a good thing as there can be in racing as he had come out level with The Illiad in his final gallop on the Curragh and if a novice hurdler could do that with the Ladbroke Handicap Hurdle winner, then he represented some bet. I had won enough on The Illiad in the Ladbroke to make it so that I was playing with the bookies' money in going for the jugular and the kill.

"If they had never prayed before, there were certainly praying that Tuesday at Cheltenham and it would have been their 'unlucky 13th of March' with a vengeance. Who was it – Ladbroke's man, I think – who said afterwards: 'It was a wonderful advertisement for the power of prayer".

For the record The Illiad hit the fourth hurdle and the bookies cheered when they saw it kill whatever chance he had of winning the Champion Hurdle.

I quoted to Noel Furlong the maxim of the professionals that the only good bet is one where the element of risk can be all but eliminated. "I am not a professional punter", he replied.

"I know that a professional punter or one adopting the approach of a professional would have laid off in the circumstances in which I found myself. It might seem crazy not to do so. But with what I had won on The Illiad and on Destriero in the Supreme Novices' Hurdle, I was actually £2 million in front of the bookmakers before the Champion Hurdle got under way. The double bets would have been a bonus if they had come off", he said.

Noel Furlong wasn't crying over the lost opportunity. It wasn't his way. From the outset, there was a streak in him that saw him cut out to take risks – and go for the jugular.

✳   ✳   ✳

A gambler all his life, he knew you had to be able to take the heat in the kitchen.

The gambler's life is not one for wimps.

The career of this most colourful of characters could fill a book in itself, as it involves chapters of history from Northern Ireland to South Africa, Britain to the gambling halls of Las Vegas and back to the private roulette tables and poker games in Dublin. And awesome tilts at the ring.

Friends talk to this day of how, after he had become Irish poker champion at the Texas Hold 'Em game, he took on Stu (The Kid) Ungar and Doyle (Texas Dolly) Brunson, both dual world champions, and a host of others and actually reached the final table in the 1989 World Championship with over one million dollars in prize-money, of which the winner would receive 755,000 dollars.

As it came down to the final crucial hand, Furlong drew two fours and facing him was Johnny Chan. Furlong reckoned he had an Ace/Jack or Ace/Queen at best. As it was, Chan had a pair of Queens. There was a half million dollars in the pot at that point and they both went all in. If Furlong could have drawn a four, he would have taken the pot and probably gone on to be crowned world. As it was Chan's pair of Queens sufficed.

Furlong ended up being effectively placed sixth in the world, winning 52,850 dollars. That was peanuts to him as he went for the jugular.

"If I had drawn a four, I would have been credited with out – drawing the reigning world champion and I would have been a hero. It has happened of Fifth Street before but it didn't happen for me in this instance", he said.

He can meet his commitments to the bookies when he loses and that is why he could get a bet of £10,000 each-way on The Illiad with Ladbrokes and why he was able to get such big money on Destriero at Cheltenham.

Up in Belfast the small men who frequent the dogs and who knew him from his days as a fearless layer talk with new respect these days of "Big Noel".

No, he was never a *wee mon.*

THE STATE OF PLAY

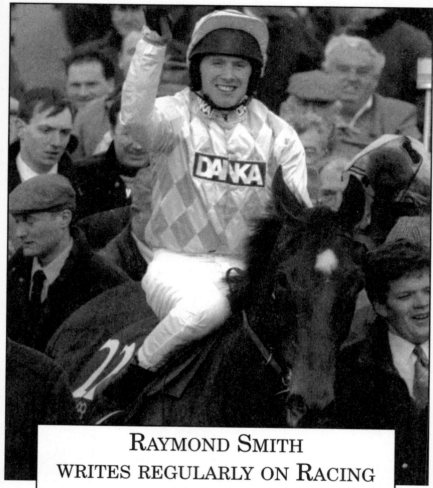

Noel Furlong talking to the racing writers (top) and (below) Pat Mc Williams acknowledges the "Irish Roar" as he comes in on Destriero after landing a massive gamble for Noel Furlong in winning the Supreme Novices Hurdle at Cheltenham '91.

Dr Michael Smurfit leads in Vintage Crop (Michael Kinane) after his victory in the 1993 Jefferson Smurfit Memorial Irish St. Leger. Vintage Crop was retired in the autumn of '96.

Paddy Sleator (top), one of Ireland's greatest National Hunt trainers, who passed away in 1996 and (below) Caroline Norris captures the exciting moment as the field sweeps over the double bank at Punchstown, scene of memorable Sleator triumphs.

The Man They Knew As 'The Brab'

Aubrey Brabazon, who passed away in the autumn of 1996 at the age of 76, was one of the greatest jump jockeys that this country produced in the golden era of Irish steeplechasing, the era when Vincent O'Brien (below left) was King of the Cheltenham scene and combined with Brabazon in winning three successive Gold Cups with Cottage Rake (1948-'50) and three Champion Hurdles with Hatton's Grace (Aubrey was successful in 1949-'50).

The man they knew affectionately as "The Brab" was involved in this era in some tremendous duels with the incomparable Martin Molony (below right). It was fitting that Martin Molony should speak the words of tribute at his graveside, noting that he would have won more than one Gold Cup were it not

for the fact that he had to give second best to Aubrey in awesome battles that have passed into racing history.

Our picture above shows Aubrey Brabazon (right) in conversation with Martin Pipe and 'Mouse' Morris on Gold Cup Day on one of his last visits to the Cheltenham Festival scene.

Frankie's Magnificent Seven

Frankie Dettori seems to be walking on air with joy as he dismounts from Lammtarra following the colt's brilliant victory in the 1995 Prix de L'Arc de Triomphe and Dettori is also seen (inset) punching the air in triumph as he passes the winning post.

In an astonishing and unprecedented lion-king display on Saturday, September 28' 1996,Italian-born Frankie Dettori won all seven races on an Ascot card whose overall quality ensured an intensity of competition which made the 25-year-old jockey's historic achievement all the more remarkable.

His seven-winner 25,095-1 accumulator thrilled the punters who backed him, creating three half-millionaires and stung the bookies for an estimated £18 million on the blackest day in their history.

However, Dettori in the following days failed to beat the record set in August, 1938 by Sir Gordon Richards who rode 12 winners in succession, spread over three days. Incidentally, Dettori's father, Gianfranco was himself a jockey of the highest calibre, a domestic champion in Italy and a classic winner in Britain.

Pictures: Ed Byrne

Dettori celebrates as he wins the 1994 Prix De L'Abbaye De Longchamp on Lochsong.

Dettori in joyful mood as he sweeps to victory on Classic Cliche in the 1995 English St.Leger at Doncaster.

Select Index